Psychotherapeutic Strategies in the Latency Years

Psychotherapeutic Strategies in the Latency Years

Charles A. Sarnoff, M.D.

𝒜

Jason Aronson Inc.
Northvale, New Jersey
London

The author gratefully acknowledges permission to reprint the following material:

Chapter 3: "Normal and Pathological Development During the Latency Age Period" from *Child Development in Normality and Psychopathology*, edited by J. Bemporad. Reprinted with permission of Brunner/Mazel, 1980.

Chapter 5: "Latency-Age Children" from *Emotional Disorders in Children and Adolescents*, edited by G. P. Sholevar, R. M. Benson, and B. J. Blinder, pp. 283–302. Reprinted with permission of Pergamon Press, 1980.

Chapter 13: "The Father's Role in Latency" from *Father and Child*, edited by S. H. Cath, A. R. Gurwitt, and J. M. Ross, pp. 253–264. Reprinted with permission of Little Brown & Co., 1982.

Chapter 15: "Psychoanalysis and Personality Change" from *The Academy Forum*, edited by A. Turkel, Volume 25, Number 4, Winter 1981. Reprinted with permission of *The Academy Forum*.

Library of Congress Cataloging-in-Publication Data

Sarnoff, Charles A.
    Psychotherapeutic strategies in the latency years.

    Bibliography: p.
    Includes index.
    1. Child psychotherapy. 2. Child psychology.
I. Title. [DNLM: 1. Psychosexual Development—in infancy & childhood. 2. Psychotherapy—in infancy & childhood. WS 350.2 S47p]
RJ504.S273 1987   618.92'8914   87-24194
ISBN 0-87668-936-5

To Carole

Contents

Acknowledgments

I would like to thank the organizations and educational institutions that have been helpful in the advancement of the present work, parts of which have been in preparation since 1964. For providing dialogues and forums through which issues could be presented and details challenged, I am grateful to the Staten Island Mental Health Society, Brookdale Hospital, Long Island Jewish/Hillside Hospital, the Detroit Psychoanalytic Association, the American Psychoanalytic Association Interdisciplinary Colloquia on Anthropological Fieldwork and on Symbols, the New Jersey Psychiatric Association, and the Psychoanalytic Center for Training and Research of the College of Physicians and Surgeons of Columbia University. I wish also to thank those educational institutions that, by their invitations, kind attention, and the questions of their members, aided in the preparation of this book. Among these are Princeton University, the University of Texas at Dallas, Columbia University, Dartmouth College, the University of Colorado at Boulder, Emory University, Tufts University, Adelphi University, Harvard University, the Long Island Psychoanalytic Society, the American Psychoanalytic Association, and the Association for Child Psychoanalysis.

Great Neck, New York, 1986

Introduction

A description of a psychodynamic developmental approach to the psychological problems of the latency-age child was introduced in 1976 in my book *Latency*. This was a first step. It awakened a need for additional developmental information and background in depth about latency-age children. Such data could provide therapists with an ability to adjust psychotherapeutic techniques to the swiftly changing nature of the growing child's personality.

Latency described a personality style and a set of cognitive structures that typify the internal response of those healthy children, aged 6 to 12 years, who can produce states of latency (e.g., periods of pliability, calm, and educability) on command. An interest was roused in the inner and outer life of these children from the standpoint of their total experience, including children with aberrant or alternative styles of adjustment.

Expanding knowledge of techniques for the psychotherapeutic approach to these children was sought. This could come about only if there were available clearly defined lines of normal development for latency-age cognition, symbols, and fantasy, against which the child therapist could compare in judging the results of therapy. Normality needs definition to serve as a background for psychotherapeutic activity.

A timetable of child development is of importance to parents. They must change to keep pace with the shifting sands of cognitive maturation in childhood. They must be alert to changes in their child's personality skills as the child shifts from a self-centered and inexperienced being to a culture-centered person with refined social skills. In concert with this, parents must traverse a course that takes them from the role of absolute caretaker to behavioral guide for an increasingly independent personality.

The same developmental shifts that concern the parent demand no less than a parallel virtuoso performance on the part of a child psychotherapist. The technique and therapeutic strategy of the therapist must often change in midtreatment to keep pace with the changing nature of the growing and changing child. The therapist must adjust his perceptions of the child and the child's behavior to accord with the youngster's maturing cognitive and emotional scene.

The therapist who treats children requires a specialized body of background knowledge if he is to work with the unique and shifting cognition of the growing child. Whereas the therapist who treats adults must know one cognition, one culture, and one set of relationships between the patient and authorities or close ones in the patient's life, the therapist of latency-age and early-adolescent children must be tuned in to an ever changing kaleidoscope of ordered developmental changes in the child's cognition, culture, and close ties.

Internal changes interact with two sets of environmental fellow protagonists. These protagonists are social demands and expectations and parental demands and expectations. A book on latency-age psychotherapy is required to contain not only therapeutic approaches for dealing with the internal structure of the child's mind, but should also give information on cultural and parental influences that provide the background against which the unfolding of the internal cognitive events of latency-age period takes place. These requirements are covered in the four parts of this book.

Part I explains the nature of latency and the internal ego structure that makes latency possible.

Chapter 1 contains an overview of the latency period. As the child approaches 6 years of age, the growing strength of body, drives, and mind place him on a collision course with a reality that he has not the experience or power to handle. His loves and hates are directed toward his parents. Yet he is totally dependent on them for food, clothing, and shelter—the stuff of life itself. The expression of drives with the available objects is fraught with peril. He can actively pursue knowledge and exercise his strengths in dealing with the reality of facts and measurements in school. He dare not seek revenge with people other than his peers, or love in circumstance removed from fantasy. His defense is to regress away from the oedipal involvement with his parents to the safety of urges he can readily master. Anger and cruelty mark this new orientation, which for the most part is only seen during his interaction with his peers. When he must maintain decorum in the presence of teachers and parents, he blocks these urges with controlling mechanisms of defense. When there is danger that these defenses will be overwhelmed, he turns to a modification of the symbolizing function, which permits him to discharge his tensions through the distorting lens of fantasy.

The ability to use fantasy as an organ for the discharge of drives is the product of the ego structure of latency. Immediate discharge of drives through symbol and fantasy is but one of its functions. Early on, through fantasy formation, it weds drives, affects, and memories of early experiences to words. This is achieved through the use of fairy tales and myths to express, in masked form, affect-laden memories from the prelatency years. The fantasies so used serve two purposes: (1) they attract the attention of consciousness at the expense of the affects and experiences of the prelatency years, producing infantile amnesia; and (2) they link drives to the ethical demands contained in the hallowed myths of a culture. Thus, the structure of latency serves as a conduit for drawing the child into a socially dominated object world of rules, ethics, and cultural conventions. At latency's end, the structure of latency loses the power to channel drives into fantasy. The very symbols it has used have shifted from fantastic to real. This change is the product of cognitive maturation. It still possesses the power to diminish uncomfortable affects. Humiliation can still be neutralized by fantasies that reassure and promise hope, through the use of symbols drawn from elements in the real world. As a result, the structure of latency passes into adolescence as a mechanism for solving problems of adaptation through planning that could change future reality. The structure of latency becomes an important part of future planning.

Chapter 2 defines latency as a period (dominated by) dynamic defenses (during which) the child experiences a complex reorganization of the defensive structure of the ego. A state of good behavior, pliability, and educability is maintained only as a result of an equilibrium between the defenses and drives. This state is possible because of the evolution and ontogenesis of mechanisms of defense that can produce it. However, it is not obligatory and is facultatively present at the discretion of the culture in which the individual lives. The ego structure that contributes to the formation, the potentials, and the dynamics of the latency-age child are dealt with in depth.

Chapter 3 introduces latency-age aspects of depression, phobia, cognitive development, and the development of the organizations of memory. Of special importance to the psychotherapist is an understanding of the child's ability to remember the therapist's interpretations. In the prelatency years, the child is capable of the recall of experiences and affects without verbal encoding of memory. This is

the affectomotor memory organization. Verbal-conceptual recall begins to take over in the second year of life. It hits the peak of its
dominance at about 5 years of age, when affectomotor memory is
pushed aside and memory becomes more verbal and more inexact.
This provides a form of repression. Verbal fantasy using masked discharge-oriented symbols becomes the dominant pathway for drive
discharge with the onset of latency. Verbal-conceptual memory using
verbal symbols becomes the primary system of memory. At the age of 8,
a more efficient system of memory enters the picture. In place of
fantastic masking of verbal symbols, with low valence for attracting
affect, memories begin to be carried by affect-isolating reductions of
experience to abstractions. These carry the intrinsic characteristics of
an event or experience into memory shorn of valence for attracting
affect. With the dominance of concepts reduced to abstractions, the
need for fantastic fantasy diminishes. Symbolic interpretations of
events that bind and defend against uncomfortable affects are replaced
by representations of reality that recall the real while being less than
real in the totality of the experience recalled.

Part II is devoted to the basic data for assessing the child and for
creating psychotherapeutic strategies during the initial clinical contact. This includes chapters on principles of evaluation and psychotherapy techniques.

Chapter 4 emphasizes the importance of assuming a perspective
from which to judge childhood psychopathology. Symptoms such as
transient phobia can interfere with the life and plans of the family.
Although such conditions have little in the way of negative prognostic
value, the immediate disruption they cause will force the child and
family to seek consultation and treatment. On the other hand, extreme
shyness and friendlessness, with its serious implications for future
psychopathology, may be ignored because it creates no problems for
the moment. The special requirements of a diagnostic interview with a
child whose background is outside the cultural mainstream are presented. A poorly developed structure of latency is not necessarily a sign
of pathology in a society in which academic potentials are not stressed
nor calm and pliability rewarded. The culturally relative position of
the structure of latency is emphasized with principles derived from the
nature of the latency years in primitive societies. Development that
does not include an abstract conceptual memory organization is aberrant and disruptive in social groups organizing their world around
magical thinking, rituals, slogans, and mythological explanations for
phenomena. Techniques of interviewing and a table of differential
diagnoses are included in this chapter.

Chapter 5 focuses on psychotherapeutic problem cases. These include parents whose understanding of therapy is counterproductive, children who break up the playroom, youngsters whose cognition is insufficiently developed for them to comprehend logic or remember abstractions, and verbally nonproductive children. Special emphasis is placed on youngsters whose mental life is devoured in an immolation by symbol that is so intense that charged and traumatic events are held in repression by a persistence of fantasy. The meaning of these fantasies can only be unlocked by the interpretation of play activities. Such interpretation is demonstrated. In addition, there is a list and a description of the therapeutically effective activities that take place in child therapy sessions. These include the encouragement of fantasy play, the introduction of coping skills, the encouragement of obsessional defenses and identification, and help toward achieving cognitive maturation. Developmental considerations in the formulation of interpretations is introduced here and is further developed in Chapter 10. The requirements of the therapist, the way to set up a playroom, and termination in child therapy are dealt with extensively.

Part III is devoted to phenomenological and theoretical information required as background for carrying out the work of the child therapist. Examples of psychotherapeutic techniques and strategies to be considered during treatment in specific normal and pathological developmental contexts are presented.

Chapter 6 deals with phobias. Projection is the predominant mechanism at work here. The presence of a transient true phobia during the latency-age period is usually prognostically a benign event, no matter how disruptive and painful the condition may be to child and parent alike. The bedtime phobias of early latency children are evidences of health. The presence of projection is the element to which one should relate when phobia appears. Intense or persistent use of projection foreshadows serious problems with reality testing, ego boundaries, and omnipotent hypercathexis of fantasy during adolescence and adult life. Clinical entities such as *pavor diurnus*, prepubescent schizophrenia, and adult schizophrenia of early onset must be considered in the differential diagnosis of childhood phobia.

Chapter 7 deals with clinical depression. Depression as it is understood in adolescents and adults is rarely seen in latency-age children. Depressive affects are rare. The clinical manifestations of the latency years include listlessness with a decrease in school performance, moodiness, general unhappiness, being hard to please, rapid changes of mood, a tendency towards crying, clinging behavior, a return of thumb sucking, diarrhea and vomiting, generalized and often intractable pruritis, sleep disturbances, accident proneness, and other forms of aggression directed toward the self such as suicide attempts and hallucinations with negative content. The relative exclusion of depressive affects from the manifest symptoms of depression ceases with the decline of the power of the symbol and the structure of latency to mask or defend against uncomfortable affects through the creation or mobilization of comforting defensive grandiose fantasies. Depressed mood begins to manifest at about 12½ years of age, when the defenses of the latency age no longer oppose and vanquish affects with the countercathectic powers of symbols and fantasy.

Chapter 8 details the development of the ego structure of latency as it rechannels aggression into fantasy. This produces the impression that a child's anger is fleeting anger, easily turned aside by a gift, distraction, or the passage of time. The changing nature of defenses as the latency period progresses through the years produces a kaleidoscope of manifestations of aggression whose passing parade adds to the impression of transiency. This draws observers of the latency scene to conclude that, in speaking of the hostile child, "He'll outgrow it." Actually nothing could be farther from the true circumstance. The age period in which the structure of latency is set is provided with a complex set of mechanisms and structures for adjustment. Although symptoms that discharge latency-age aggression may be transient, the juggernaut of unresolved earlier conflicts, neurotic underpinnings, personality weaknesses, and newly acquired developmental aberrations that produced the symptoms rolls inexorably toward the precipitation of adult psychopathology. There is a complex psychological organization to latency that only produces the calm appearance of anger outgrown.

Chapter 9 traces the derivatives of sexual-drive discharge as they grow and pass from one manifestation to another with each unfolding developmental stage. The maturation of the drive–discharge apparatus precedes and forecasts the form that object relations (libidinal drive discharge) can take at a given age. During the latency years, the symbolizing function serves as an organ for discharge. As the manifest symbols that make acceptable representations progress toward the more realistic, sexual-drive discharge becomes more involved with objects in reality. With the development of primary organs for sexual-drive discharge, the development of a cognition that permits the inclusion of another person in one's consideration and planning is forced. This produces the ability to fall in love and enables one to establish a lasting sexual partnership.

Chapter 10 explores the problems produced by the fact that the adult therapist and the child patient are miles apart cognitively. They have difficulty understanding each other from the start. Furthermore, cognitive skills (ability to comprehend, organize, and recall events, perceptions, and experiences) of the child undergoes continuous changes. As a result, the therapist must do two things: (1) he must constantly change his approach to interpretation to match maturation in the cognition of the child; and (2) he must, at times, encourage early maturation of cognition to facilitate the therapeutic process. Essentially, the task of the therapist in this context is to help the child develop verbal and abstract representations through which his experiences and nonverbal thought processes can be removed from expression through toys, symbols, affects, and play. These thought processes can then be brought into the area of consensually validated verbalizations and abstractions, through which the cognition of the child and of the therapist can be used for communication with effectively conducted psychotherapy (confrontations, interpretations, clarifications, reality testing, and so forth). When the therapist helps to develop the capacity to store abstractions in memory, he has taken a first step in enabling the child to acquire a context of abstractions against which to judge and interpret his own behavior. The abstract conceptual memory organization is the *sine qua non* of verbally based psychotherapy. Only when it is in place can interpretations that are understood at the moment they are said be made available for use in the moments that are yet to come. In essence, the abstract conceptual memory organization is the carrier of the capacity to step back from oneself and take the role of the observing ego (e.g., self-reflecting awareness, see also Chapters 14 and 15). Strengthening of this skill enhances the results of the work of child therapy. In this chapter, the ontogenesis of memory modes and cognition is presented along with the theory of their development and the clinical application of this theoretical material to the psychotherapy of children.

Chapter 11 looks at fantasy play as an identifying characteristic of the latency time period. Through such play, the discharge of drives and the resolution of conflicts is attempted with varying success. Such play is the latency equivalent of adult free associations and of dreams. The treatment of latency-age children revolves primarily around the experiencing by the patient and interpretation by the therapist of fantasies that are derivatives of drives that, although stirred, could not be discharged. For each age there is a typical conflict around which fantasies are spun. These are the universal fantasies of latency. For

early latency, the conflicts emphasize the Oedipus complex and regressive anal-sadistic material. Middle latency is dominated by sibling
rivalry and concerns with loneliness and separation. Late middle
latency struggles with passivity. Late latency emphasizes ethical individuation. Late latency–early adolescence is preoccupied with sexual
identity crises. These fantasies are universal and typical. They are
evoked by universal situations and experiences that could not be resolved at their inception and are carried as extra baggage in memory.
They are brought out on every possible occasion in an attempt to
master and resolve them. One such occasion is the child therapy
session. In such sessions there are two uses of fantasy. One can either
help the child by encouraging him to play out his fantasy (evocative
play; see Chapter 12), or one can lead the child to talk about his
problem at its traumatic root. Both techniques are illustrated clinically in this chapter.

Chapter 12 deals with repetition compulsion and reparative mastery. There are two ways in which repetitive fantasies are used during
the latency-age period. Both are manifestations of a need to fantasize in
order to master emotional stress. Repetition compulsion fails to
achieve mastery of conflict or memory-haunting trauma. As a result,
repetition goes on ceaselessly, and its associated behavior is un-
staunched. Like the Flying Dutchman who must sail on endlessly
without hope of reaching port, children whose fantasies express repetition compulsion go on fantasizing without end, with the need to evoke
moods and express feelings in an objectless context. Their symbols are
used in terms of their evocative pole of meaning. Self-centered, objectless, uncommunicative, the children who use fantasies in this way
manifest heightened narcissism, which primes them for omnipotently
tinged defensive behavior in adolescence and adult life. Reparative
mastery achieves discharge and mastery. As a result, the latent conflicts
and aberrant behavior pendent to the fantasy cease. Safe harbor is
swiftly to be found. These children use fantasy as a means to communicate moods and express feelings in an object in the context of
psychotherapy. Their symbols are used in terms of their communicative pole of meaning. Outgoing, sharing, object seeking, communicative—the children who use fantasies in this way are on their way to
good object relations, positive results from therapy, and the testing of
reality in adolescence and adult life.

The techniques for converting symbol use from evocative to communicative modes are explored in this chapter. The influence of the
evocative-communicative pole in symbol and fantasy formation is
relatively limited in latency. With the development of early adoles-

cence, this polarity takes center stage as the ability to express drives communicatively becomes the criterion for good adjustment and the prerequisite for establishing object relations and for falling in love.

Part IV deals with the prognostic significance of environmental influences and the various developmental vicissitudes that occur during the latency-age period.

Chapter 13 describes the latency period as a time devoted to the acquisition of culture in areas that are parentally approved, although outside the home. In prelatency, culture elements within the home are emphasized. In adolescence, the door is opened for influences beyond the boundaries of the home and the inclinations and wishes of the parents. Self-esteem, superego contents, and sexual identity are all contributed to by the parents. Parents have a special influence during the latency years on the areas of personality that dominate development in that phase. Thus, cognitive styles of perception and understanding and the preferred organization of memory are influenced by parental preferences, precepts, and examples.

Chapter 14 emphasizes, for one doing psychotherapy on a long-term basis, the usefulness of acquiring an awareness of the expected character transformations that accompany transitions from one stage of life to the other. In this way one does not run the risk of explaining characterological improvements on one's psychotherapeutic techniques alone. There are character profiles for a given age that are so sharp that often it is possible to identify the age of a person from a description of her character traits. Such a series of descriptions, with emphasis on superego, is presented in this chapter. Reflective self-awareness is discussed extensively.

Chapter 15 reviews the development of cognition, conscience, memory systems, and self-reflective awareness, all part of a progression that occurs during the latency years. Forward movement through these zones of development shapes important aspects of adult personality. As such, a healthy latency presages a positive adult adjustment. The role of psychotherapy during the latency years in guiding development through freeing the child of neurotic conflict and mastering internalized psychopathogenic fantasies is illustrated. Also discussed is psychotherapeutic strengthening of personality and ego functions, which form the roots of adult cognition, superego contents, memory organization, and character.

The process involved in the transition from latency to adolescence involves the dissolution of the personality structures that had produced latency. *Psychotherapeutic Strategies in the Latency Years* presents a grounding in the aspects of latency that provides the platform from which adolescence springs. The reader interested in exploring the transition from latency to adolescence as well as psychotherapeutic strategies and pathological digressions pertinent to this period of transition may wish to refer to my book *Psychotherapeutic Strategies in Late Latency through Early Adolescence.*

Part I
Understanding Latency

Chapter 1

The Developmental Period

One of the primary thrusts in psychiatry in recent years has been the investigation of the developmental phases from birth to maturity. Initially, workers pursued an understanding of the phases of childhood through reconstruction based upon observations of adults in states of regression that approximated earlier phases. Though accuracy was achieved for the most part, a certain amount of inexactitude was bound to slip in. For this reason, direct observation of developing children was undertaken. Workers such as Mahler (1969) and Piaget (1945) have pursued this work in research settings, while those who work with children in therapy contributed insights based on clinical observations. Vast amounts of data began to accumulate in regard to the child from birth to 5 years of age, and much attention was paid to the adolescent.

Although the latency-age child contributes the lion's share to the case rolls of clinics and private practitioners of child therapy, little in the way of observation or investigation into the finer points of the development of children of the latency age was undertaken or published. In psychiatric educational programs scant time was assigned to lectures on latency. Honor went to those who, though devoting themselves to the care of the child in his latency years, could recount the details of the latest theories about the first years of life. Worse yet, when it came to explaining the events of latency, the technique of reconstruction was invoked and the latency child's behavior was explained on the basis of theories derived from observations from other ages and circumstances. The events of latency more often that not were approached with preconceived ideas based on experience with other ages.

Latency, a period that direct observation has shown to be a seething caldron of developmental events, was viewed as a wasteland, its features no more than patterns of shadows cast from other zones of development.

The devaluation of the latency period as an area of study has been an intermittent phenomenon. During the last decades of the nineteenth century, when Freud first called attention to the importance of understanding the child as a basis for comprehending the adult, the differentiation of the latency period from early childhood was established. Freud (1950) observed that the time period we associate with latency is one "during which repression usually takes place" (p. 163). He noted a paucity of material in adult analyses related to sexuality from this period. Thus he reconstructed the latency period as a time of aversion to sexuality. During this time Freud (1905) reconstructed that "the influx of sexuality does not stop even in this latency period, but its energy is deflected either wholly or partially from sexual utilization and conducted to other aims" (p. 178). Reconstructions of mental life in the latency period became a matter of concern. Emphasis ran to the development of morality and defense mechanisms (ego).

Then in 1926, Freud declared that latency occurred when "the sexual drives diminish in strength" (1926c, p. 210). This shift was followed by a deemphasis of the latency years in reconstructions and observational studies: where drives are diminished, there is little reason to search for their derivatives or for ego functions that defend against them. Latency underwent a latency period of its own that endured for forty years. Latency, a time of waiting and of few beginnings in the development of the person, had little to call attention to itself. Yet given the cognitive growth and sexual maturation that occurs between the end of early childhood and the onset of adolescence, these were clearly not six empty years. Explanations were called for. In addition, more children from cultural backgrounds with fractured or nonexistent latency states came to the attention of psychotherapists. Freud's early observation—that latency was a time of much defensive psychological activity—was seen to conform more closely to the actual state of affairs.

Psychiatric training programs, child psychiatry, and child analytic programs began to include more material on the events of latency. In essence, sexuality in masked form was now recognized, cognitive maturation was depicted, and the role of a successful latency in preparing for a successful adolescence and a successful adult life was stressed. With the introduction of latency as a developmental period with characteristics of its own, a whole new area of study has been opened on the psychiatric horizon.

There are two definitions for latency that are both useful and commonly used. These are:

1. *Latency as an age period.* Latency is used as a term to represent the time period from 6 to 12 years of age.
2. *Latency as a psychological state.* Latency is here used to describe a period of dynamic defenses during which the child experiences a complex reorganization of the defensive structure of the ego. A *state* of good behavior, pliability, and educability is maintained as a result of an equilibrium between defenses and drives. This state is possible because of the evolution and ontogenesis of mechanisms of defense that can produce it. It is not obligatory, however, and is facultatively present at the discretion of the culture in which the individual lives.

The main clinical characteristic of the *state* of latency is a manifest behavior pattern of calm, pliability, and educability. This apparent quiescence encouraged the use of the term latency in describing the entire time period, and seems to give credence to the concept of diminished drive energies as the biological factor in its onset. Actually, the state of latency (calm, pliability, and educability) is the result of an active process of organization of ego functions in the service of social demands. As Bornstein (1951) has pointed out, there is, as a response to the dangers inherent in oedipal fantasy (castration fears), a defensive regression from phallic to anal-sadistic levels of drive organization and associated fantasy structures. This regressive shift is a characteristic of the latency-age ego, dominating the typical latent fantasies and drive activities of latency-age children. Yet the child's behavior is not dominated by overt anal sadism because of the modifying influence of the special ego organizations of latency.

These special ego organizations of latency provide an adaptive alternative to the undifferentiated massive drive discharge patterns typical of anal-sadistic regressions in early childhood. The range of control typical of late childhood, which makes learning possible in the classroom, is achieved through the following steps. When a child has made the defensive regression he is confronted by a situation different from that found in the original anal stage. There are newer and more mature ego mechanisms of defense to use in dealing with anal-sadistic drive energies. These provide for the interposition of modifications of aggression. Among the defenses available are sublimation, obsessive-compulsive activities, doing and undoing, reaction formation, and repression. Their activities produce the psychological state of calm, pliability, and educability that characterizes the latency state. They help the child to adapt to a world requiring social compliance and the ability to acquire knowledge.

In the latency-age child capable of entering into the state of latency, the defenses of reaction formation, obsessional activities (collecting coins, stamps, and shells), cleanliness, symbolization, and sublimation are available to keep in check otherwise disruptive id derivatives. The latency-age child is physically too small to express his aggressive drive effectively in his relationships with adult caretakers. Latency-age children are, with few exceptions, maturationally incapable of achieving orgasm or ejaculation and are therefore physically incapable of expressing sexual drives effectively through the direct use of a primary organ and physiological apparatus for discharge. There is no way out, in reality, for this biologically celibate soldier–dwarf. Regression and the defenses described above serve as the primary techniques for coping with the sexual drives during the latency period. Fantasy, reaction formations, and carefully monitored socially accepted behavior patterns (i.e., school recess and athletics) become the primary outlets for aggression. The child is expected to surrender and to attempt to please his masters by learning well what there is to be learned.

The patterns of defense learned from a template acquired in latency will influence the permissible expression of the drives during puberty. Thus there develops, as a byproduct of the formation of this part of the latency ego, a deformation of possible derivatives and expressions of the drives during adolescence and adult life.

The defenses that help to produce the state of latency may be overwhelmed if the child's drives are strongly stimulated by seductive behavior, either in direct form or in a form that stimulates sympathetic activation of the drives. In order that these defenses may maintain the state of latency undisturbed, a safeguard is provided to preserve their function in the face of these seductions and traumas. A child with a normal symbolizing function and capacity for symbolization organizes a "structure of latency." The child quells the humiliation of trauma and the excitement of drive activation through seduction, by dismantling the memories of the traumatic event or seduction and the latent fantasies they arouse and actively reorganizing and synthesizing them into highly symbolized and displaced stories (manifest fantasies). By living through these stories in the form of latency play, the child finds a safety valve for his heightened drives, and maintains the state of latency. Thus he gains comfort or revenge without threatening the situation (such as school) in which he hopes to function well or interfering with his emotional equilibrium or adjustment.

Mechanisms similar to those involved in actively producing discharge fantasies and symbols, in which the hero can be covertly identified with the child's own self, can be utilized for passive identification with the myths and legends provided by the child's social group. These ego organizations, similar to the structure of latency, persist beyond latency. Through them the individual acquires, and will continue to acquire, the imagoes for cultural patterns of behavior, ritual, and belief that will guide his life, his mores, his opinions, and his social reactions for as long as a lifetime.

The manifest behavior observed in latency-age children is an amalgam of the drives, the defenses of latency, and the manifestations of ongoing maturational processes. Maturation influences the achievement of states of latency from as early as the first year of life. Disorders in latency and interferences with entrance into the state of latency can often be traced to pathological interferences in development during very early developmental stages. The developmental lines most related to the latency state are those involved in cognitive and sexual development. The state of latency is in itself a developmental stage whose proper negotiation is necessary for the establishment of socially oriented aspects of the superego and such group phenomena as participation in culture.

Cognitive Development

Of all the precursor cognitive capacities that lead to the development of the state of latency, the capacity to form symbols of a special sort is the most important. There is a regular march of symbolic forms from early childhood on. With each step, the symbol is marked by greater complexity. Prior to the years of latency, the symbols in primary use are ordinary metaphorical symbols. These flourish from 18 to 26 months. They consist of "thought" elements and "thing" elements in the child's field of knowledge and experience that can be used to represent something else. Here the use of a single item in achieving a dual representation is conscious. Such play symbols are the precursors of masking symbols. Masking symbols, sometimes called psychoanalytic symbols, are characterized by their masking of meaning. They first appear at about 26 months of age. They are essential for the development of the latency state. In essence, in their formation, the conscious link between the signifier (symbol) and what is signified (latent content) has been repressed. Through the use of such symbols, latent fantasies can be expressed in the form of distorted manifest fantasies. Treasured loved ones can thus be spared the role of targets of forbidden drives.

The work of the structure of latency during the age period 6 to 12 in developing manifest fantasies, which distort the latent fantasy to the point that is unrecognizable, depends heavily on the capacity to form masking symbols and, in turn, upon the acquisition of abstract thinking, delay, and repression. As early as 26 months of age there are evidences of the development of fantasy distortions for conflict resolution and drive discharge. This is a precursor of the structure of latency.

It is not uncommon for a young child, as a neophyte symbolizer, to utilize concrete objects found in the environment as symbols around which to build distortion fantasies. The use of concrete objects as symbols thus precedes the use of spontaneous verbal symbols in the creation of distortion fantasy. As a parallel to this, the early latency child uses found symbols encountered in stories for the discharge of his own drives. Because he has not actively created the symbol, this is called passive symbolization. Symbols and tales passively acquired become the prototypes and precursors of the spontaneously produced masking symbols and fantasies of the state of latency.

An important step in the first year of life is the development of the capacity for memory, especially recall memory, which consists of recognition of that which has been previously experienced in the absence of any concrete representation or reminder of it. Eventually this skill reaches the point at which a child is able to evoke an image of a mother who is separated from him in the absence of reminding stimuli. Recall memory contributes to what is called object constancy, providing the ability to comfort oneself with a psychic representation of a departed object. It is based on the ability to retain images and concepts for spontaneous recall at moments when it is required.

This phenomenon becomes fully effective by the third year of life. A related phenomenon, also occurring during the early years of the latency age is basic to its development: an improvement in the syn-thetic function in relation to the ability to integrate the self in society. Differential patterns of behavior in specific situations, such as school or recess, are acquired, retained, and recalled in appropriate situations in response to concrete cues as well as spontaneously. This occurs in the period between 4 and 7 years of age. Consistent behavioral responses ensue, resulting in behavioral constancy. This facilitates the ability of the child to function in the classroom.

Through this he can acquire and retain admonitions based on the precepts of the parents and other important adults and examples acquired from tales and myths. Information about expected patterns of behavior is gathered, integrated, and retained by the child, becoming part of the ego ideal. The ego ideal calls for pliability, calm, and educability. Control over the latent sadomasochistic drive organization of latency becomes mandatory in order to conform with this ego ideal. In conformance with these demands, the group of defenses consisting of obsessional responses and reaction formation produce the calm of the latency state. Its maintenance is effectuated and supported by activation of the structure of latency, whose product, play, is itself governed by patterns acquired through the mechanisms of behavioral constancy. Channeling of energies and recognition of permissible locations for the more direct discharge of drives, such as school recess, is thus maintained.

Patterns of social behavior guiding the discharge of drive, which have been learned in this way during latency, dominate the development of patterns for discharge of drives in adolescence and adulthood. This mechanism aids in the acquisition of superego elements during the latency time period and is part of the work of latency. These superego acquisitions are epigenetic products of the development of the state of latency. Other contributions to the superego that occur during the early latency time period include the internalization of parental imagoes of the oedipal phase, which accompanies the passing into repression of the Oedipus complex. This is, in part, a concomitant of the regression to anal-sadistic drive organization.

A third contributor to the superego is a shift in the style of memory, in about the fifth and sixth years of life, from the predominance of affectomotor to verbal concepts in memory. In this shift, memory elements that relate primarily to recall of things, feelings, and experiences in a primarily visual and sensory context are superseded in part by a memory style that is primarily conceptual and verbal. Drives that formerly had found expression through topographic regressions (i.e., sensory recall of prior experiences organized into fantasy content or in organized motor syntaxes appearing in play) are forced to find conceptual verbal expressions. Fortunately, myths, tales, and concrete symbols are provided by the environment (society) and can be used for the expression of these drives.

As elements of the verbal fantasy have become familiar enough to the child for him to form identifications with the content, subtle messages related to expected patterns of behavior are conveyed to the child. These undergo internalization and incorporation into that portion of the superego governing social behavior and ethical relationships between people. The contents and identification thus acquired are retained through the mechanisms that produce behavioral constancy. The fact that these retained identifications can be represented and recalled verbally, indeed that they can be expressed, codified, checked, reinforced, and validated in words, forms the basis of social intercourse and makes it possible for the individual to participate in moral philosophy and to comprehend law.

During latency many verbal concepts are remembered in association with high charges of affect. Defensively, they are excluded from consciousness. These concepts are the ones that find their way into the masking manifest fantasies of the state of latency. Through a process utilizing symbols that have other meanings, their latent import is hidden to such a degree that the painful affects are lost to consciousness. Also lost in the bargain is the possibility of working through, recognizing, and modifying distortions through the correcting and validating effects of verbal communication. As a result, latency play, though quite informative in psychotherapeutic situations, becomes counterproductive once its living through and discharge functions have been served. Technically, it is necessary to work back from the fantasy to the words of the original conflict and then to work it through psychotherapeutically. The more a child has matured into adolescence, the greater will be his tendency to spend longer periods of time in verbal, conceptual discussions rather than in the defensive and therapeutically diluted world of latency state play.

Once a socially approved doctrine of behavior or heroic attribute has been internalized, it is cathected with narcissistic energies and becomes identified with the individual. Thus is established the social identity that will cause the child to reject new inputs as foreign. Rejection of foreign inputs persists until early adolescence, when an upsurge of exploratory projections occurs. Such adolescent explorations are aimed at the acquisition of culture elements not approved of by the parents and result in the establishment of superego elements in conflict with parental views.

A modification in creativity occurs during the transition from prelatency to latency. The prelatency child is considered more creative in that he is freer in his concepts, while the latency child seems more bound to societally dominated, directed, and indicated themes. Yet from another viewpoint the latency child could be considered more creative, for he is richer in representations and symbolizations used in the creation of stories and works of art. During the latency years, cognitive shifts have occurred such that the child expresses the resolution of conflict through fantasy on a culturally dominated, verbal level; the child is locked into verbal representation of verbal memory. For him, the rich tendency to use verbal symbols from a preestablished vocabulary informs the quality of creativity. In contrast, the prelatency child deals more with an awareness in memory dominated by affective, sensate, affectomotor elements. Ideas of things are communicated in affect-laden words and in play, less dominated by cultural patterns than the expressions of latency-age children. They are far less influenced and modified by repressions and as a result their symbols are less rich. The concepts of the prelatency child are more free; the stories are transparently about himself and his experiences, while the latency-age child tends more to tell stories based upon tales he has heard. The prelatency child lives close to his feelings and to his memories of feeling, whereas latency-age children—especially those in a state of latency—are usually far from their feelings and live in terms of verbal memories whose patterns are dominated by the expectations of others. An intensification of this shift affecting the symbolic forms used is characteristic of the cognitive changes accompanying the transition from latency into adolescence. The role of the structure of latency in modifying and hiding affects produces a latency-age child who appears hardly to mourn or to experience depression.

Within the latency time period there is a turning point with the development of concrete operational thinking. This Piagetian term describes a step in the improvement of reality testing which begins at 7½ years of age. Simple and concretely conceived scientific principles (abstractions) can now be appreciated and applied to concrete situations. The importance of this development to the state of latency is that fantasies, which are under the impact of improved reality testing, become less useful for discharge of drives. A substitute object satisfies less when love for a real object becomes possible. Magical fulfillment through fantasy succumbs to reality. With the development and strengthening of concrete operational thinking, the use of fantasy created by the structure of latency as a means of discharge thus becomes less satisfactory. Fortunately, with adolescence there is a concurrent shift in object to nonincestuous peers, as well as maturation of the primary organs for sexual gratification. As a result, after fantasy declines as a means of drive gratification (for all but neurotics and the creative), the world of reality can be met with physiological capacities for the articulation of drives.

The normal latency-age child shifts, at about 9 years of age, from a cathexis of the parent as a primary arbiter of social behavior to an appreciation of the environment and the social situation in which he lives. The acquisition of self-concepts and identifications through internalization of experiences with objects in the environment are pertinent to the future role of the child in society.

In late latency, modification of identifications occurs when there is comparison of fantasy contents with reality. It is not uncommon for a child, during periods of guilt, to project punishing parental imagoes into the shadows of dusk. Comparisons can be made between the realities of the world and the contents of these projections. In those with appropriately modulated narcissism, a reassuringly benign reality may result in modification of the original fantasy and of the internalized self-punitive concepts upon which it was based.

Sexual Development

Most drives, such as the hunger drive, have, from birth, an organ and object for discharge (i.e., mouth and food). For the sexual drive, the maturation of this apparatus awaits puberty. Latency-age sexual experiences are attempts on the part of the organism to express drives in the absence of a mature physiological organization for discharge, namely an exclusive effector organ and an object. In early childhood the sexual drive found outlet through a sort of parasitic arrangement whereby other organ functions, such as sucking with the mouth to obtain food, were also used as a pathway for sexual discharge. Such a parasitic arrangement is called autoerotic. Subsequently, excretion and manipulation of parts of the body, including the genitals, served in a similar capacity vis á vis the sexual drive. With the development of conceptual thought during the period of 18 months to 3 years, concepts (both affectomotor and verbal) become an erotic pathway, in the form of fantasies.

By the time the child reaches latency age, although he may occasionally discharge through genital stimulation with rare climax or even with an object in reality, he expresses sexuality mostly through distorted manifest fantasies by means of movement of the whole body in play activities. All early latency children have some erotic sensory response to stimulation of the genitals. A small percentage even have the capacity for orgastic-like responses. Because of parental pressures, reactions to the content of fantasies, and the strength of sensations experienced, there is a tendency for early latency-age children (6 to 8 years old) to limit direct genital stimulation and to deal with intensifications of drive through the creation of fantasies and action for discharge according to the patterns described above under the structure of latency. Direct stimulation, though still available, becomes less and less common.

In late latency (9 to 12), with the advent of heightened sexual sensations from the genitals and the acceptance by the superego of more realistic objects in fantasy, an increase in genital masturbation occurs. The advent of ejaculation and orgastic competence signals the maturation of the organ for the discharge of the sexual drives. Concurrently there is a shift in the thought representations of the acceptable objects. In early childhood these were the parents. In early latency the symbolizing function produces amorphous fantasy figures, often in the role of attackers or historical figures. In late latency, realistic figures appear. In late latency and early adolescence, thinly masked representations of parents appear in fantasies that accompany masturbation, soon to be replaced by mature objects in the form of nonincestuous peers who appear first in fantasy and then as partners in sexual play and related activities. When this step has been firmly established, all vestiges of latency have passed.

Conclusion

In spite of neglect in recent years, the concept of latency as a developmental stage in child development has persisted. The term and concept describe a discrete clinical phenomenon that must be taken into account if the nature of childhood is to be comprehended in its entirety.

The latency state has always intruded itself into the awareness of mental health scientists in the form of unexpected behavior that called for an explanation. The explanations have resulted in the various theories of latency. At first it was noticed that adults in analysis do not bring to their sessions associations that reflect sexuality during the latency time period. This caused the pioneers of psychoanalysis to observe children of this age and to attempt reconstructions of the factors that make the difference. At first explanations of latency emphasized ego function. In time, observations of children revealed periods of quiet, calm, pliability, and educability to which the term *latency*, derived from the fact that sexual memories from this period remained latent in adult analyses, was then transferred. Calm was then equated with latency. Recently (Sarnoff 1976) I have described a disparity between the memory organizations of the latency child and the adult. In the analyses of adults, this disparity has resulted in difficulty in recalling the affectomotor (memory in action) and symbolically distorted (fantasy) memory organizations to which the latency child resorts in time of trouble. Through the creation of fantasies embodying symbols and whole-body activity (memory in action in latency-age fantasy play), the child is able to maintain latency calm, quiet, and educability in the face of stress. There is thus an intrinsic link between the paucity of verbal memories for sexuality during the latency period as reflected in adult analyses and the quiet of the latency state. The tendency to maintain calm by turning uncomfortable memories into symbols and play activity later creates problems in associative retrieval of memories for this period.

That there is, in the latency years, a process with consistent intrinsic characteristics defined in terms of ego functions (the mechanisms of restraint and the structure of latency) can no longer be denied or ignored. This process of ongoing development during the latency years may be defined in terms of normal and pathological aspects of both functional and maturational elements. Clinically normal and pathological characteristics may be delineated and may be of use to the therapist in evaluating the underpinnings of aberrant behavior.

Chapter 2

Ego Structure

Since its introduction in 1905, the term latency has been used ambiguously. Understanding of the concept is obscured by confusion surrounding use of the word. There are a number of definitions of latency, the most common of which follow:

1. The time period from 6 to 12 years of age. Here age is taken as the sole criterion.
2. A psychic phase whose time of onset and content are physiologically determined. Clinically this phase is characterized by a well-behaved, pliable, and educable child. A change in the defensive organization of the ego is not implicated by this definition; rather, modifications in the behavior of the child are attributed to a biological lessening of the drives at a preordained time.
3. A period of static defenses during which reorganization of the ego defenses results in a stable condition in which the child is well-behaved, pliable, and educable. Hereditary, historical, and phylogenetic factors are implicated.
4. A period of dynamic defenses during which the child experiences a complex reorganization of the defensive structure of the ego. The state of good behavior, pliability, and educability is maintained only as a result of an equilibrium between defenses and drives. This state is possible because of the evolution and ontogenesis of mechanisms of defense. However, it is not obligatory and is facultatively present at the discretion of the culture in which the individual lives.

Disparate as these definitions are, the word *latency* is rarely used with identifying qualifications. Yet a clear usage for latency can be achieved if modifying phrases are added that sharpen meaning. "Latency age period" and "state of latency" are examples.

Freud and Latency

In "Character and Anal Erotism," Freud (1908) fixed the timing of latency to that period of life with which we now associate it: "the period of 'sexual latency'—i.e., from the completion of the fifth year to the first manifestations of puberty (round about the eleventh year) (p. 171).*

The idea that latency is the product of a biological lessening of drive activities is mentioned directly by Freud only once, in *The Question of Lay Analysis* (1926c): "During (the period of latency) sexuality normally advances no further; on the contrary, the sexual urges diminish in strength" (p. 210). The drive diminution theory emphasizes the role of biology, heredity, and the id while lessening the role of the ego. Latency is seen as a preordained, physiologically determined, obligatory state in human development. The great influence of the drive diminution theory probably relates to the fact that it was Freud's final statement on the subject. Though some thoughts on latency later appeared in *Moses and Monotheism* (1939) and *An Outline of Psychoanalysis* (1940), there was little in these works that could be used to support a contradiction of the drive diminution theory.

The concept of latency as an organization of ego defenses, both static and dynamic, was explored in depth by Freud well before 1926. The forerunner of an idea of a unique mechanism of defense in latency is contained in a letter to Fliess dated May 30, 1896 (Freud 1954). Freud mentions two periods as "the transitional periods during which repression usually takes place. . . . Morality and aversion to sexuality . . . provide the motives of defense for obsessional neurosis and hysteria" (pp. 163, 165).

In "Three Essays on the Theory of Sexuality" (Freud 1905) the concept of defense in latency is presented. "It is during this period of total or only partial latency that are built up the mental forces which

---

*In Freud's writings, references to mechanisms of defense in latency may be found in the following works: sublimation, (1905, 1924b); reaction formation, (1905, 1923b); fantasy, (1911a); regression, (1916–17, 1926b); and repression, (1921, 1923a).

are later to impede the course of the sexual instinct" (p. 177). What are these mental forces? Freud points toward suppression as the mechanism responsible for latency. "(The) germs of sexual impulses are already present in the newborn child and . . . these continue to develop for a time, but are then overtaken by a progressive process of suppression. . . . Nothing is known for certain concerning the regularity and periodicity of this oscillating course of development" (p. 176).

What is the origin of this "oscillating course of development"? Freud (1905) tells us that the ego structure in latency develops from phylogenetic and physiological-hereditary bases. The "period of total or only partial latency . . . is organically determined and fixed by heredity" (p. 177). The strength of the drives is seen as sustained; "the activity of those [infantile sexual] impulses does not cease even during this period of latency, though their energy is diverted, wholly or in great part, from their sexual use and directed to other ends [that is, sublimation and reaction-formation]" (p. 178). "From time to time a fragmentary manifestation of sexuality which has evaded sublimation may break through; or some sexual activity may persist through the whole duration of the latency period until the sexual instinct emerges with greater intensity at puberty" (p. 179). One of the factors that can effect this breakthrough is seduction: "external influences of seduction are capable of provoking interruptions of the latency period or even its cessation, and in this connection the sexual instinct of children proves in fact to be polymorphously perverse" (p. 234). Latency was seen as a situation in which the strength of the defenses dammed up the drives. At any time the defenses might be shattered and the ever present undiminished impact of the drives revealed. Here we find the beginning of the concept of latency as dynamic defense.

Latency as dynamic defense is further developed by Freud (1908) in "Character and Anal Erotism": "During the period of life which may be called the period of 'sexual latency' . . . reaction-formations, or counter-forces, such as shame, disgust and morality, are created in the mind. They are actually formed at the expense of the excitations proceeding from the erotogenic zones" (p. 171). The question of whether latency produces defenses or vice versa is not clearly delineated at this point. A relationship to defense is seen as of primary importance, and the drives are seen as qualitatively transmuted but not quantitatively changed.

In "Formulations on the Two Principles of Mental Functioning" Freud (1911a) introduced fantasy formation as an adaptive regressive defense related to latency: "The long period of latency, which delays sexual development until puberty . . . [results in a situation in which] the sexual instinct . . . remains far longer under the dominance of the pleasure principle. . . . In consequence of these conditions, a closer connection arises . . . between the sexual instinct and fantasy" (p. 222). Satisfaction in reality is withheld, and fantasies develop for the alternative discharge of the drives. A predominance of the fantasy-forming function of the ego in the presence of immature reality testing is one of the key elements in the ego structure of latency.

In *Introductory Lectures on Psychoanalysis* (1915) Freud wrote, "From about the sixth to the eighth year of life onwards, we can observe a halt and retrogression in sexual development which, in cases where it is most propitious culturally, deserves to be called a period of latency. The latency period may also be absent: it need not bring with it any interruption of sexual activity and sexual interests along the whole line" (p. 326). Here we find the implication that latency is culturally influenced.

In "Group Psychology and the Analysis of the Ego" (1921) defenses are described as factors which produce latency. Freud writes ". . . the Oedipus complex, succumbs . . . from the beginning of the period of latency onwards to a wave of repression" (p. 138).

In "Two Encyclopoedia Articles" Freud (1923b) referred to the role of latency in the transmission of ethics. "Towards the end of the fifth year the early period of sexual life normally comes to an end. It is succeeded by a period of more or less complete *latency*, during which ethical restraints are built up, to act as defenses against the desires of the Oedipus complex" (p. 246).

Development of the concept of latency had now reached a point at which a purely psychological theory of latency as a manifestation of ego function might have been formulated. In 1923, however, Freud's writings on latency again acknowledged the hereditary, biological, and physiological factors first mentioned in "Three Essays" (1905). In "The Ego and the Id" (1923a) he speaks of the biological and historical factors in the child's lengthy dependence and "of his Oedipus complex, the repression of which we have shown to be connected with the interruption of libidinal development by the latency period and so with the diphasic onset of the man's sexual life" (p. 35).

In "A Short Account of Psycho-Analysis" (1924b), Freud again describes latency in terms of defense. He says, " . . . sexual life reaches a first climax in the third to fifth years of life, and then, after a period of inhibition, sets in again at puberty" (p. 208).

Thus in 1923 Freud's concept of latency contained two divergent points of view which might be considered contradictory. One was the sociological-psychological theory in which the defenses of the ego respond to psychological needs under the pressure of the social demands; the other, the theory that latency is produced by a phylogenetic historical-physiological hereditary complex. In the latter, latency is a state in which defenses are brought to bear on the drives as part of a developmental step whose timing is determined by heredity. In 1924 Freud's works again contained both points of view.

In "The Dissolution of the Oedipus Complex" Freud (1924a) indicates that the passing of the Oedipus complex and the onset of latency are defensive responses to the fear of castration. There is a clear statement of the role of defenses (sublimation) in the onset of latency. "The libidinal trends belonging to the Oedipus complex are in part desexualized and sublimated. . . . The whole process has, on the one hand, preserved the genital organ . . . and on the other has paralyzed it—has removed its function. This process ushers in the latency period, which now interrupts the child's sexual development" (p. 177). Elsewhere in the paper he describes the passing of the Oedipus complex with the appearance of latency as the "next preordained phase of development" (p. 174). In a single paper, then, the view of latency as a preordained phase is juxtaposed with the notion of latency as a phase ushered in by the ego mechanisms of desexualization and sublimation of libidinal trends. The two points of view seem irreconcilable. Freud, of course, recognized the dichotomy and stated that "the justice of both these views cannot be disputed" (p. 174).

Freud finally resolved this problem in "An Autobiographical Study" (1925), indicating clearly that repression initiates latency; reaction formations are produced during latency; and the ego that produces latency is, in turn, a product of phylogenesis. Freud states: "For the most remarkable feature of the sexual life of man is its diphasic onset, its onset in two waves, with an interval between them. It reaches a first climax in the fourth or fifth year of a child's life. But thereafter this early efflorescence of sexuality passes off; the sexual impulses which have shown such liveliness are overcome by repression, and a period of latency follows, which lasts until puberty and during which the reaction formations of morality, shame, and disgust are built up" (p. 37). In a footnote added in 1935 he said: "The period of latency is a physiological phenomenon. It can, however, only give rise to a complete interruption of sexual life in cultural organizations which have made the suppression of infantile sexuality a part of their system" (p. 37, n.).

At some time in the phylogenesis of man, mutation and selection provided the ego function that would permit and support latency as we know it. This much is the hereditary and physiological sine qua non of latency. In individuals who live in a society demanding a latency period, and whose parents conform to the society's demands, these ego functions produce latency.

Physiological views of latency, then, have their roots in the physiological and hereditary factors described by Freud. The concept of latency as a state characterized by social determinants also has roots in the views expressed by Freud in "An Autobiographical Study" (1925). Here he describes factors that trigger ego structures to produce predictable patterns of behavior, which may not be fixed throughout the entire period.

In "Inhibitions, Symptoms and Anxiety," Freud (1926b) gave an even more detailed picture of this role of the ego functions in the development of latency in man. The concept of retrogression mentioned in *Introductory Lectures on Psychoanalysis* (Freud 1916–1917) is elaborated into the view that regression is active in the establishment of latency. He says: "The genital organization of the libido turns out to be feeble and insufficiently resistent, so that when the ego begins its defensive efforts the first thing it succeeds in doing is to throw back the genital organization (of the phallic phase), in whole or in part, to the earlier sadistic-anal level. This fact of regression is decisive for all that follows" (1926b, p. 113). Here regression is described as one of the defenses. "We can most clearly recognize that the motive force of defense is the castration complex and that what is being fended off are the trends of the Oedipus complex. We are at present dealing with the beginning of the latency period" (p. 114).

Current Concepts of Latency

The theory of the primary diminution of drive activity in latency is mentioned by Anna Freud in *Normality and Pathology in Childhood* (1965). She speaks of "the post-oedipal lessening of drive urgency and the transference of the libido from the parental figures" (p. 66). Later she states: "Extreme castration fear, death fears and wishes, together with the defenses against them, which dominate the scene at the height of the phallic-oedipal phase, and which create the well-known inhibitions, masculine overcompensations, passive and regressive modes of the period . . . disappear as if by magic as soon as the child takes the first steps into the latency period . . . as an immediate reaction to the *biologically determined lessening of drive activity*" (p. 163; italics mine). "The drop in pressure from the drives at this time corresponds to the high level of social response during latency" (p. 179). In a panel discussion on latency at a meeting of the American Psychoanalytic Association in 1956, it was speculated that "there may be a biological diminution in the libidinal drive, in addition to repression, which then allows the aggressive energy to predominate" (Friend 1957, p. 528). In a 1951 panel discussion on child analysis Bornstein divided latency into two phases (5½ to 8, and 8 to 10), and asserted that one of the characteristics of the later period is that "sexual demands have become less exerting" (p. 281).

The theory of the origin of latency ego defenses was also put forth in the panel discussion and in Bornstein's paper. She described "surging impulses" and said that "temporary regression to pregenitality is adopted by the ego." She notes further that new defenses against the pregenital impulses must be evolved by the child, and that reaction formation is one of these (p. 280). These concepts relate to those delineated in "Inhibitions, Symptoms and Anxiety" (Freud 1926b). Throughout the recent literature, mention is made of a sustained masturbatory temptation in latency which must be continuously defended against. One can well conclude that the existence of this temptation attests to the sustained strength of the drives during the onset of latency. Nor is a diminution in the urgency of the drives reflected in any lessening of the defenses that are maintained to counteract them.

Clinical Findings

The theory of latency as defense is supported by clinical findings, as the following observations of latency age children will show.

When a child moves from prelatency into latency during a psychoanalysis, one can observe a shift from acting out of pregenital, genital, and oedipal wishes with members of the immediate family to a state in which excited feelings with the family are felt only momentarily. These are dealt with through a complex of defenses resulting in the appearance of fantasies or fantasy-oriented actions which at one time both conceal and reveal the true attitudes and reactions of the child. These fantasies require little energy, and free the rest of the child's energies for useful work.

A little girl was brought to analysis at age 6 because of failure to progress to reading readiness in the first grade, lack of spontaneity, regressed behavior, and uncontrolled masturbation. As an infant she was picked up continually; she was weaned at 28 months. She walked at 12 months and talked at 16 months. She had been toilet-trained at 3 after a stormy and scream-filled period of pressure from her mother. Bladder training had been delayed until this age because of a constriction of the urethra which required sounding. Concurrent with a separation of several months from her parents, which took place after toilet-training had been completed, there was regression in bladder control.

At the start of treatment the child would come into the playroom without her mother, but would soon want to return to her in the waiting room. After about three weeks she began to have episodes of encopresis on the way to, and during, the sessions. Because of these episodes it was necessary for the mother to clean her. Just preceding the onset of the encopresis the mother had stopped washing and cleaning the child's perineum after she had gone to the bathroom. It can be assumed the resulting diminution in stimulation was a factor in a concomitant cessation of the child's open masturbation.

I repeatedly told the patient that she wished to remain a baby and not to grow up. At times she herself said this spontaneously. I pointed out to her the role of the encopresis in helping her to remain a little baby who is taken care of by mother and that if she were successful, she wouldn't learn or get to be a mommy herself. The encopretic episodes soon gave way to periods during which she would insist upon straightening up my office. During this activity she talked about how the maid would scream if she could see how messy things were. With this change of behavior, she began to report fantasies and was able to begin the first steps in reading. She had entered the latency stage. A return to perineal cleansing and stimulation by the father after toileting evoked a resurgence of oedipal feelings. When the mother reproved the father, the child ordered the mother out of the room saying, "Go away and leave us alone. I like it." Thus the drives were available to the child in full strength in spite of the onset of latency.

This case illustrates the association between anal regression, reaction formations, and the freeing of energy for useful work that occurs with the onset of latency. It also shows the sustained availability of drive strength during the latency period.

Perhaps the most telling clinical observation to contradict the theory that in latency "sexual urges diminish in strength" (Freud 1926c, p. 210) is the fact that sexual intercourse is possible during latency. It occurs in children who have been seduced into genital sexual activity.

A 9-year-old girl, who lived in a foster home, was seen once a week in psychotherapy because of periods of excitement and forgetfulness whenever the family was preparing to visit the foster mother's aunt. At other times she was alert and calm, and did average work in school. The child had little to say about the episodes of excitement and confusion. Matters were somewhat clarified when the child's social worker received a report from the foster mother that during a visit to the aunt, the child had as usual retired with her 13-year-old foster cousin to his room to play. When the foster mother found that she had to leave earlier than expected, she went to the room to get the girl and found the two children "mating." This behavior was prohibited on subsequent visits and the child's episodes of excitement and forgetfulness stopped.

The child explained to me that she had first been introduced to sexual intercourse by her brother when she was 6 and he was 7. At the time, they lived with their mother in a two-room apartment with curtains, but no doors, between the rooms. The children, peeking through the curtains, were able to observe the mother having intercourse with a series of men. Eventually they imitated what they saw. The brother had initially been placed in a cottage setting with other boys, but frequent attempts to seduce these boys into anal intercourse led to his placement in a foster home at the age of 8. There were unsubstantiated reports from his school that he was accepting money from older boys for his passive participation in anal intercourse.

In such children urgency of the sexual drive is not diminished. Hence the changes that occur in latency cannot be explained in terms of a diminution in drive energies, but rather in terms of a shift in the way they are discharged. The drives in latency may be stirred into activity at any time by seduction or sympathetic stimulation. The regression that occurs in the face of oedipal stresses results in the replacement of phallic with anal–sadistic drives, which are then defended against by the emerging mechanisms of defense that typify the character of the latency child. These are sublimation, reaction formation, fantasy, regression, and repression.

These latency defenses permit the child to direct his energies toward cooperative behavior and learning. What happens when a situation in real life threatens to bring the sadomasochistic drives out into the open? What happens when life situations reawaken the phallic oedipal wishes? In some children, as in the second case above, there is a deterioration of the latency defenses. Normally a protective set of mechanisms within the ego structure of latency comes into action, producing fantasies that serve as a safety valve and preserve the latency. When a latency-age child has thoughts, excitements, and fantasies about an overstimulating parent and the structure of latency is not available, drives may be stimulated. These can threaten the stability of the latency adjustment. Examples of this may be seen in the case of a cruelly punishing father who provokes aggressive or murderous feelings in his son, or in the case of a seductive parent who stimulates fear of retaliation from the parent of the same sex. In the presence of the structure of latency, the content of the stimulating situation is repressed quickly and replaced with substitute mental events, including highly detailed fantasies. These may take such forms as fantasies of carefully planned robberies, fears of being attacked or kidnapped, romantic thoughts of marriage, and sexual relations that are abruptly interrupted by a punishing intruder. Needs of the moment are satisfied through the medium of fantasy. Feelings toward the primary objects or their substitutes are safely displaced onto symbols.

An 8-year-old boy was brought to analysis because he talked back to his parents, failed to learn in school, had a diminished attention span, fidgeted, stole, had few friends, was the butt of jokes and beatings by other boys, and was a clown in class. Further, his parents feared he would become a homosexual. When first seen he was unable to pay attention to any activity for more than three minutes. Although he tried to be cooperative he was repeatedly overwhelmed by his feelings, frequently teasing and attempting to provoke the interviewer by either verbal or active threats to destroy objects in the room. This behavior recurred frequently during the analytic sessions. More commonly, however, he would play out his fantasies, and invariably the stories he played out could be related to events of the day with which he could not deal directly.

When it was discovered that the patient had stolen or had failed to do his homework, his father scolded and beat him. The boy reported feelings of intense humiliation and anger. He would run from the room swearing vengeance, and in his own room his mind would be filled with fantasies of killing his father. After a few moments his mind would go blank. He could then return to his father and be friendly. This is not an uncommon reaction in children after being beaten. However, later in the day, the child would dwell on fantasies of his own greatness and schemes for robbing. He worked out the street plan near my office, and evolved a design for a bank robbery. Another scheme, a play fantasy, involved the entry of men into a house in which a great deal of money was hidden in a safe. After the owner of the house was forced to open the safe, the gang prepared to kill him. They were stopped by the police, who fought and killed the robbers. This was acted out with gusto, the patient playing all the parts. At one time, when punishments had raised his aggressive drives to new heights, he actually broke into the house of a neighbor and stole some coins. When the lights of the neighbor's car indicated that they were returning, the patient left the house, buried some of the coins, and then reentered the house and hid, waiting to be captured and punished.

During one session, while describing a particularly strong interchange with his father, he "ran out of things to say" and decided to make up a story. He went from the playroom into my office and announced that the desk was a castle. He told the story of poor peasants who were being mistreated by a king and who were arming themselves for revolt under their leader, Marshall (the patient's middle name). They stormed the castle and took the king captive. The multitude cried, "Kill him, Marshall, kill the king." Marshall went up to the king with sword drawn. He raised his arm to kill. At that moment, the patient turned to me and said, "I'm thirsty. I'll be right back after I get a drink of water." He returned but could remember nothing of the fantasy of killing the king. It had been subjected to repression. The symbol for the father, in the context of killing, had lost its mask and had acquired a valence for attracting affect. The story could not continue under these circumstances. It had failed in its function.

In reflecting on the relationship of punishment, feelings of humiliation, and the creation of these fantasies, the youngster once remarked, "I get angry. I run away and think of killing them and saying to myself, 'I hate them. I hate them.' But then I forget it and before you know it, I'm making up these stories to take out my feelings."

When he was 16, he reflected on the story of the peasant killing the king in association to the following dream fragment: "I'm in this hotel. I walk into a room. There is a woman there undressing. She has large breasts like my sister. She smiles. Then her husband comes into the room. He asks what I'm doing there. I say that I was pushed down the staircase and fell into the room. He looks like he's going to hit me. I don't know whether to fight or run." His association to this dream was, "I can't get even with my father any more by making up stories of killing the king. I've got to find another way to handle my problems." Fantasies had become ineffective as a discharge of his parricidal wishes.

From the three cases just described we can discern three separate clinical pathological states that are encountered in relation to latency: failure to enter latency, a regressive deterioration of the structure of latency, and regression to prelatency behavior.

Failure to enter latency, illustrated in the first case, resulted from a maturational defect in an ego function. The child lacked the capacity to form symbols, which impaired her capacity to form fantasies. Thus hobbled, she could not vent the drives stirred up by parental seductions, and remained in a state of constant excitation. There was no energy left to devote to learning. Parental stimulation together with the ego defect destroyed her latency in its beginnings.

The third case illustrates regressive deterioration of the structure of latency. All components of the structure of latency, especially fantasy formation, were present and operable. Latency-age fantasy formation provided for some drive discharge while preserving a degree of pliability, educability, and socially acceptable behavior. As long as this child could discharge aggression toward his father through fantasies he maintained his ability to learn and appeared to be a normal latency child. When his aggression reached large proportions, though, he became anxious and distractible. He ceased to daydream, and instead acted out his fantasy of being a thief by entering the house of a neighbor and stealing. Petty pilfering in department stores is sometimes related to similar dynamics. When fantasies are constantly being acted out, neurotic delinquency as a pattern of maladjustment results (see A. Freud 1949). Such behavior in latency presages the possibility of delinquency in adolescence.

If regressive deterioration of the structure of latency becomes chronic, the child becomes so involved in his fantasies that he has no energy for useful work. There is a regression to prelatency behavior, as illustrated in the second case. Parents often participate in the acting out of pregenital fantasies. In these situations, the latency state is no longer available. The child experiences difficulty in peer relationship, impulse control, and learning.

It should be noted that the latency phase is typically characterized by an instability manifested in shifts between normal latency and the three states mentioned above. There is no intimation of serious pathology when one of these shifts occurs unless, as mentioned in the prior paragraph, the shift becomes characteristic, chronic, and results in behavior that interferes with the progress and growth of the child. The potential stability of the state of latency in a child is defined in terms of the strength and stability of the ego structures related to the production of latency.

When a conflict or feeling which occurs during the latency period cannot be experienced consciously by a child because of strong fears and intense feelings, the conflict cannot be dealt with on a realistic level. The ideas are repressed and represented in consciousness in the form of distorted fantasy. The repression serves as a two-edged sword. In a positive sense, it holds reactions in check so that there can develop a period of calm when learning can take place. On the other hand, as a result of repression, pregenital and oedipal conflicts are not resolved. In adult life the presence of wishes and conflicts more appropriate to childhood may persist, causing emotional difficulties.

Except in those situations in which the drives are so strongly stimulated that acting out occurs, fantasies are positive influences on development. They serve to reduce tension and to help the child resolve otherwise unresolvable conflicts. The term "structure of latency" is used to denote the configuration of defenses in the latency ego that provides stabilizing discharge by way of fantasy. It is introduced for heuristic purposes, in the belief that naming helps students to focus on a concept so that its limits, form, and phenomena will be more effectively delineated.

Freud (1911a) first pointed out that in latency "a closer connection arises . . . between . . . instinct and fantasy" (p. 222). Here we expand on this concept. In latency, more than in any other period of psychological development, fantasy is linked to the drives as a derivative and a sole outlet. In adolescence and beyond, fantasy detracts from relationship with the real world and object seeking as the means of solving emotional problems. Only in the creative artist is fantasy seen as a form of sublimation.

In latency, however, fantasy gives vent to the drives and permits the child to live in peace with the parental figures. This can be illustrated by further material from the first case above.

The child, as a result of analytic work, had developed reaction formations and some capacity to learn. She was then confronted by a frustration which stirred murderous feelings toward her mother with accompanying oedipal feelings toward her father. A description of a fantasy in statu nascendi of this 6-year-old girl follows.

A friend had spent the afternoon with her. In the evening the mother took the friend home. When the mother returned she found her child in a rage. She pulled at her hair, wrenched the cloth of her dress, and said, "I want someone to sleep with at night." She had wanted her friend to stay. Her mother explained to her that sleepover dates are for more grownup girls in their teens, and added that grownup means being able to study, use books, read, and be promoted. She told the child that she would not be promoted if she did not work. The child became silent and prepared for bed. Before going to sleep she told her mother the first detailed fantasy that she had ever reported.

"There was a little girl. She was naughty. Her mother told her she would punish her by not letting her go to school, and went to school to tell the teacher. The girl followed her. When they got home, the girl fired down the house. The mother was killed. When the father came home he saw the house fired down and he asked the girl what happened. He didn't punish her because she told the truth. They moved to another house. A stepmother came, but she didn't stay long. Then the girl and the father moved away to a new house where they lived together."

In this fantasy we see the characteristic shift from the primary object to a substitute. The child is represented by a little girl. All the major people in the child's life are represented, and yet the child does not recognize herself. The anger at the frustrating mother in reality appears in thin disguise in the content of a story told at bedtime. The real mother hears the story but the anger is not directed at her. Rather, she is to be entertained by her child's inventiveness. The consuming flames that "fire down" the house and kill the mother in the story represent the anger transmuted into a symbolic story element.

Such fantasies are the normal products of the structure of latency that help the child deal with unbearable wishes in relation to the parental figures. In prelatency the wishes are expressed directly. In adolescence, substitute objects are sought or the wishes obscured by regression. In latency, these wishes normally find expression in fantasies and their derivative, play.

A prime example of such a fantasy is the well-known "plumber" fantasy of Little Hans (Freud 1909), which can be seen as an attempt to resolve an oedipal conflict during early latency. Hans had fear of castration. He produced the fantasy: " 'The plumber came; and first he took away my behind with a pair of pincers, and then gave me another, and then the same with my widdler' "(p 98). Hans's father interpreted to him that the replacement organs were bigger than those removed.

Hans agreed. Freud commented, "With (this) fantasy the anxiety which arose from his castration complex was also overcome, and his painful expectations were given a happier turn" (p. 100). Through the use of the structure of latency, Hans set aside his conflicts and anxieties. His improvement was less the result of gaining insight than of a shift of his defenses from those producing phobias to those producing the state of latency.

It must be kept in mind that such fantasies are normal in latency. It would have been inadvisable to return the child described in the first case to the original situation of anger at the mother. In this child, insight was present in excess and was a source of anxiety that sapped the capacity to function and to learn. It is important to encourage the development and maintenance of the latency-state ego in children on the borderline of latency. On the other hand, neurotic children who are well able to enter the state of latency may benefit from the interpretation of their fantasies. This is illustrated by the following clinical example.

A 10-year-old girl insisted on playing out a game in the session. She did her best to dislodge some clay that she had driven into a corner. She told of the difficulty of removing it. She spoke of the great value it had because it had been in the "cave" so long. When asked about constipation problems, she spoke of her parents' concern with her constipation and of long wrangles with her grandmother about drinking prune juice. She got more attention when she was constipated. But her symptom was a mixed blessing, for she paid for her pleasure in retention with gas pains, stomachaches, and painful bowel movements. She was able to question her behavior, understand her motivation, and gain relief from her constipation. For this neurotic child, the interpretation of her fantasy opened a mine of information which she had formerly withheld. In such children, the interpretation of fantasy results in an understanding of her relationship with her parents and the nature of her fantasies. In contrast, in the borderline latency child such an interpretation would have stirred up massive aggression in response to the anxiety that the latency fantasy had formerly quelled.

The mechanisms and techniques of fantasy formation in latency are characteristic of the period. If we define the ego as the group of functions that regulate the relationship between the id, the superego, and the world of reality, we must acknowledge that the ego of the

latency child is different from that of the adult in content, conforma-
tion, and degree of intensity with which certain mechanisms of defense
are used. This can best be illustrated by describing the mechanisms of
defense in latency.

The child of 5 is struggling to cope with unresolved conflicts over
instinctual urges. He cannot fulfill his oedipal wishes, for he cannot
kill his father; nor can he have intercourse with his mother. But his
sexual urges in relation to his parents have an exciting quality. Of
course they are not seen by the child in the same light in which similar
feelings are viewed by a healthy adult. To the 5-year-old, the world of
excitement and gratification is frightening and overwhelming. Like
the explorer whose leap into the unknown jungle is edged with fright,
the child views the step into genitality as a thing of wonder and of fear.
Society provides neither gratification nor explanation of this unknown realm. The child's attempts to solve the riddle, to experience
this new world, are met with frustration, threats of castration, and fear
of loss of love. He responds by repressing his drives.

When perceptual awareness is withdrawn from the arena of oedipality and genitality, attention cathexis may be shifted to such reality
activities as athletics. Alternatively, there may be regression to prior
stages of development at which earlier drives and conflicts, now safely
negotiated, were experienced. The child may return to the sadomasochistic, smearing fantasies of the anal stage. This is one reason that
parental aggression so stimulates children during latency: they are
more attuned to aggression than to oedipal sexuality even though
genital sexuality is the underlying problem defended against by the
regression to anality.

Since the child is older and has further developed his techniques
for dealing with his anal drive energies, clinically he looks quite
different from the younger child he was when first confronted with
these urges. As a latency age child, he now represses and sublimates
them. He develops obsessive-compulsive defenses such as counting,
obsessional thoughts, and the collecting of stamps, coins, and rocks.
Reaction formations are developed and strengthened, so that we see an
industrious child who is aware of reality. Clinically, at this point, the
child is capable of producing states of latency.

Oedipal, aggressive, or sexual situations arise which may stimulate the child to the point that his impending reactions are unacceptable to him or to caretakers, parents, or teachers. Acting on such
impulsive reactions may occur (failure to enter latency). In children
with sufficient defenses, there are two alternatives to such behavior:
regression may occur to an anal-sadistic level of drive organization, or

the increase in related aggressive drive derivatives may shatter the latency state if the defenses against aggression are overwhelmed (regression to the prelatency state). The second alternative uses the structure of latency as a safety valve. The overstimulated drives of the child are channelled into fantasy, regression is prevented, and the state of latency is preserved.

Fantasy formation may be used to quiet the stirrings that would otherwise shatter the mental equilibrium of latency. At first, the stressful situation is remembered with full force. Then it, or its traces, are repressed. The remembered situation—for instance, unexpected nudity in the home, seduction by an adult, sustained and unjust punishment—is fragmented. (Only parts of a stressful situation are represented in any one latency fantasy.) The fragments are displaced onto symbolic representations that are then elaborated and synthesized into a series of coherent conscious fantasies. These fantasies discharge the drives and protect the mental equilibrium of the latency state. Here the structure of latency is at work. The preservation of the state of latency is one of its three main activities.

The primary mechanisms of defense characterizing the ego structures that institute and maintain the latency state may be summarized as follows.

1. In dealing with oedipality and genitality: regression to anal-sadistic drive organization; reality cathexis; repression.
2. In dealing with the regression to anal-sadistic drive organization: sublimation; obsessive-compulsive defenses (doing and undoing); reaction formation, repression (it is this second group that may be called "the latency mechanisms of restraint").
3. In dealing with breakthroughs of the anal, genital, and oedipal conflicts once the latency state has been established: repression; fragmentation; displacement; symbol formation; synthesis and secondary elaboration; fantasy formation (it is this third group that I designate the "structure of latency").

The development of latency is strongly influenced by society. There are primitive cultures and subcultures in which latency is not encouraged and sexual activity is encouraged, as in Case 2. Malinowski (1962) describes such a society:

[A]mong the Trobriand Islanders 'Sexual Freedom' is considerable. It begins very early, children already taking a great deal of interest in certain pursuits and amusement which come as near sexuality as their unripe age allows. This is by no means regarded as improper or immoral, is known and tolerated by the elders, and abetted by games and customary arrangements. Later on, after boys and girls have reached maturity, their freedom remains the same. [p. 5]

Here there is no latency as we know it. Since there is no biological obligation to enter latency in human beings, a parent in our culture, through his or her behavior toward the child, may lead him to manifest some infantile drive. The most common example of this is the parent who stimulates the child's aggression. The result may vary from stable latency with occasional temper tantrums to a fully disorganized child with no capacity to delay need gratification. The disorganized child may apear psychotic because of the degree of disorganization. Such a child rarely hallucinates, and when hallucinations do occur they are of the superego type. Should the condition continue untreated, the child in some instances will mature and even settle down, but he will never become all he is capable of being, since so much important basic learning time has been usurped by the excitement of an interrupted latency. The child who continues to be stimulated by the parent aggressively or sexually turns intensely to fantasy formation, as in the third case above, in order to deal with the overwhelming excitement that stirs within him. Direct gratification of body needs short-circuits the achievements that the interposition of delay would provide. There is interference with the ego functions required in learning skills. Frequently this is at the root of emotionally derived learning and reading disorders.

A clinical situation that is the mirror image of the one just described is that of latency-age children who enter physiological puberty prematurely (idiopathic isosexual puberty). These children can produce a state of latency in spite of premature pubescence. Parental and social influences, as well as phase-specific psychological development, are sometimes used to explain the fact that psychological stages develop independently of the flow of hormones (Krim 1962). This is further exemplified in adolescence by girls with Turner's syndrome (Hampson, Hampson, and Money 1959). In these children there is no puberty in the early teens because of gonadal dysgenesis. Still, under the influence of parental, societal, and peer expectations they become interested in clothes and boys, and experience all the trials and tribulations of adolescence. In idiopathic isosexual puberty, in Turner's syndrome, and in the onset of latency, cultural factors outweigh the biological ones in determining the manifest behavior of the child in latency and adolescence.

From the standpoint of culture, latency is necessary for the formation of civilization. Latency provides the period of time in which children can learn the complicated skills needed in the society. The child learns to accommodate himself to the world. Sexual gratification and oedipal feelings are allayed so that the child can live in peace with those people who love him. This is vital at a time when it is necessary to have someone care for him because of his economic dependence and his need to learn social skills, attitudes, and manners of living. The child can remain within the family as an accepted part of the family, and is still able to accept the authority of the parents. It is a period when the child consolidates his image of himself in relation to the world.

The latency years may be divided into two phases: from 6 to 8 (the early phase) and from 8 to 12 (the later phase). The first is marked by the child's preoccupation with himself. There is an inhibition of masturbatory activity. Fantasies contain amorphous monsters. The superego is strict and brutal. Real objects are denied to the child as drive outlets. In the early phase, fantasy used defensively is the primary means of adjusting to emotional stresses. Fantasy becomes a defense. The child uses reality only to disengage himself from untenable and unfulfillable drives and fantasies. Cathexis of reality, for instance, in school or sports, serves as a guarantee of the secondarily autonomous functions of the ego (Rapaport 1958).

The later phase of latency is marked by increasing availability of the outside world as the source of objects through which fantasies may be gratified. Masturbatory activity becomes less proscribed. There is a softening of the superego. Fantasies contain figures that resemble people: the monsters and ghosts of early latency are now changed into witches and robbers. In effect, the child's thoughts and fantasies begin to dwell upon gratifications with objects that resemble human forms. He can accept his oedipal urges a little more, and so can represent the parents with symbols that are somewhat less disguised. As a result of maturation the child becomes more aware of the world, his place in it, and his relationship to the future. The cognitive reorganization of the ego functions which occurs at this time lays the groundwork for the onset of adolescence. This period is therefore of importance if the origins and events of early adolescence are to be understood.

In the second phase of latency as cognitive function and reality testing improve, the mechanism of fantasy formation becomes less tenable and weakens. By the time the child is 11 or 12, he usually forsakes fantasy as a means for drive discharge and begins to integrate reality. The fantasizing function of the structure of latency comes to serve future planning by providing fantasies with reality content. Parents become more real as sexual objects. The child develops new techniques to deal with his incestuous feelings. Infantile drives, once dealt with through repression and fantasy formation, gradually reassert themselves because of the growing strength of reality testing. Latency wavers as puberty and parental encouragement of teen-age interests become manifest. The structure of latency crumbles as a defense, and the child is thrown into the chaos of adolescence.

One might well ask if fantasy is given up completely at the end of latency. The answer is obviously no; fantasy merely ceases to be the preferred means for expressing the drives. More mature object relations with the real world are developed in its stead. There are, of course, exceptions. In neurotics the persistence of fantasy is manifested in the development of symptoms. Freud (1911a) tells us that the artist has persistence of fantasy and is able "to mould his fantasies into truths of a new kind, which are valued by men as precious reflections of reality. Thus in a certain fashion he actually becomes the hero . . . [and] favorite he desires to be without following the long roundabout path of making real alterations in the external world" (p. 224). For the average person, the skill of weaving fantasy to cope with drive needs and experiences of humiliation is harnessed to that area of ego operations which may be called future planning. Reality elements replace psychoanalytic symbols, and plans for tomorrow replace fantasies of the moment.

From the point of view of development, late latency is a period of transition. The structure of the ego is transformed and the instincts are withdrawn from fantasy and are articulated with real situations and real objects. Since we are dealing with an exposition and elaboration of Freud's concept (1911a) that in latency a closer connection arises between instinct and fantasy (p. 222), it would be useful to pursue what lies behind the loosening of the connection.

In prelatency, the child had been buoyed by feelings of omnipotence and indestructibility. The introduction of castration fear, fear of loss of love, and the incest barrier made unbearable all fantasies which involved the parent in sexual and aggressive contexts. The poor reality-testing and the level of cognitive function of the child permitted the use of repression, fragmentation, displacement, symbol formation, and synthesis of symbols into story patterns to be used for the production of fantasies which could serve as safe means of drive discharge, avoiding danger to loved ones. In youngsters in the state of latency, situations which stir up the core fantasies of prelatency are thus resolved through the formation of seemingly unrelated conscious fantasies.

The configuration of ego functions that produce this activity becomes an important part of the structure of latency. Formation of benign fantasy provides a buffer permitting the continuation of the total ego structure in latency. Failure or default of these mechanisms may result from excessive stimulation of sexual or aggressive drives. School regression and aggressive outbursts in latency children are explained by this phenomenon. In the absence of such stimuli, the child may continue to use fantasy for vicarious problem solving, and thus guard against the incursions of drives and their demand for objects.

However, latency is not endless, and at the age of 7½ to 8 years, improvements in reality testing and cognitive function begin to impair the child's use of fantasy for solving problems. The marked improvement in cognitive function includes maturation of the capacity to appreciate cause and effect relationships between objects which are concretely present (Piaget's concrete operational thinking; see Woodward 1965, pp. 74–75). There is also greater objectivity. Reality objects become less assimilated to the subject's wishes. By the age of 12, this process reaches its height. Words can no longer magically change the relationships among real things and real people. Reality becomes an arena for the discharge of the drives. The stage is set for the turmoil of adolescence. The demands of the world and of prelatency fantasies are now to be faced and resolved.

Summary

Clinical data support the position that the latency state is a socially guided configuration of ego structures, and the related view that drive strengths are sustained during the latency period. In the state of latency, fantasy formation is used as a means of problem solving in which conflicts are played out in thought, rather than in reality. This spares the individual a conflict with real objects in the environment and diminishes the impact of drives to the extent that maturation and sublimation are facilitated. In this way the relative stability and diminished drive pressures typical of the period come into being. In later latency, when maturational improvement in reality testing gradually minimizes the defensive effectiveness of manifest fantasy formation, there is a gradual shift to the use of more reality-oriented defenses. This sets the stage for adolescence.

The specific cognitive organization used by the latency-age child to deal with the processing of drive energies while awake is sufficiently foreign to the ways of the adult and late adolescent that it may be understood why memories based upon or encoded in these experiences of thought do not find their way easily into the free associations of patients in later years.

Chapter 3

Normal and Pathological Development

Scientific support is lacking for the idea that there is a diminished sexual drive during the latency years. If anything, latency-age children are normally capable of manifesting a good deal of sexually excited behavior. This usually alternates with the ability to calm down in suitable settings, even in the face of highly stimulating and otherwise overwhelming situations. The ability to settle down is a product of the strengthening of those areas of the personality that control both the drives and the excitement that unbridled drives produce.

Such a strengthening in the latency years is the result of a process whose consistent intrinsic characteristics involve ego functions. This process of ongoing development during the latency years may be defined in terms of the normal and pathological aspects of both functional and maturational elements. Clinically, these normal and pathological characteristics may be delineated and may be of use to the therapist in evaluating the underpinnings of aberrant behavior. An explication and organization of these characteristics is the purpose of this chapter.

The idea of an ego structure during latency which produces states of latency calm makes it possible to include in the concept of normalcy a polarity manifested in intermittent periods of excitement and drive activity alternating with calm. Pathological behavior during latency may be construed as exaggerations of this polarity, manifested in either consistently inappropriate calm or consistently inappropriate excitement.

The form taken by clinically observable behavior during the latency age period is influenced by at least three factors:

1. behavioral expectations on the part of caretakers and peers;
2. normal maturational unfolding; and
3. the development, between the ages of 6 and 12, of the capacity to enter into a state of latency.

During the latency age period, therefore, behavior reflects the influence of an amalgam of maturational steps. Foremost among these is the status of the capacity to enter into a state of latency.

This chapter will describe the normal and pathological manifestations of characteristic defensive personality structures of the latency-age child. In addition, it will discuss the contributions to behavior of cognitive development, physical maturation, and the social organization in which the child lives.

Defensive Structures in Latency-Age Children

We turn first to the characteristic defensive personality structure that produces the state of latency in the latency-age child. This structure consists of those defenses that deal with anxiety by means of fantasy. Such fantasies are the child's responses to humiliation or to overstimulation of sexual and aggressive drives. As such, they are expressions of drives which demand fulfillment in areas where fulfillment is socially proscribed or biologically impossible. Both social proscription and biological inability to achieve satisfaction produce anxiety. The child who wants a bicycle, or anything else that may be well within his grasp, need use no defenses. On the other hand, when confronted with intense fantasy wishes for the impossible, the child must defend himself from his own fantasies in order to control the humiliation or anxiety stirred up by frustration or fear of punishment for forbidden wishes. For instance, it is really not possible for a latency-age child to act on a wish fantasy to beat up a much bigger person, especially if that person happens to be his father. Similarly, no matter how intensely sexual excitements may be felt, it is not possible for most latency-age children to achieve complete gratification of their sexual drives, since they are not orgastic.

When confronted with such realistically inexpressible fantasies, the latency-age child must resolve them intrapsychically. If his defenses are not sufficiently developed or implemented to provide for intrapsychic resolution, the level of his excitement can reach a point at which behavior becomes hectic, impulsive, and disruptive. When this happens, the child may be described clinically as either unable to enter a state of latency or experiencing an interruption of the capacity for latency states.

Typical Fantasy Contents of the Latency Period

By and large, the child is least likely to be able to live out fantasies that have to do with the relationship between himself and parents or other adults in the environment. Jealous, sexual, and aggressive interrelationships with adults and siblings provide the basic fantasy content around which most of the defensive activity becomes engaged. If one wishes to become more specific in describing the fantasies against which the child's defenses are mobilized, one finds a march of age-specific fantasies associated with each passing year.

Each fantasy, in its turn, is based upon the new and unfolding problems that the child is brought to ponder as a result of cognitive and social maturation. Thus certain fantasies and certain types of fantasy activity normally and characteristically begin at each phase of maturation. For instance, at the point at which the prelatency child is able to differentiate himself from the outside world and from his parents, and can conceive of himself without his parents, his emotional reactions revolve around comforting himself to counter the pain of expected separation and loss. When the child reaches the age of 3, he is able to differentiate the sexes. His thoughts then deal with sexual differences. When he reaches the age of toilet training, his thoughts become involved in bowel and urinary control. Anger at being controlled appears, and usually the anger is displaced to sadistic fantasies involving sibs (Blanchard 1953).

There are typical thought preoccupations and fantasies processed during the latency age period, as well. At the beginning of the latency period preoccupations revolve around an issue that the child has been dealing with since the age of 3. At that age he recognized that there was a couple in his life (his parents) who were leaving him out of things. They had activities of their own, in which he played no part. When this realization occurred the child began to develop fantasies about what the couple was doing. He began to have fantasies of taking the role of one of the parents in whatever they were doing without him, whether these activities be sexual, going out together, or entertaining people. The child assumed the role of first one parent, then the other, in a fantasy molded by his own interpretive recapitulation of parental actions. This is called the Oedipus complex.

As a child reaches 6, the capacity to experience guilt develops (see Chapter 6). At this point fantasies of taking the role of either parent may become associated with guilty discomfort. The fantasy itself no longer is experienced directly in consciousness. Rather, it must be dealt with through the use of certain defenses. Specifically, symbolic distortions help to hide the meaning of the original fantasy by creating a new, less threatening fantasy upon which the mind of the child can dwell. It is characteristic of the thinking of the child in early latency that he develop a masked way of thinking and fantasizing about experiences and observations he is trying to master.

In a child younger than 6, ideas were presented directly, as in the following example.

A 4-year-old girl looked at her grandmother. She admired aloud a beautiful pin that the grandmother was wearing. The grandmother stated in a rather direct and matter-of-fact fashion, "When I die, I'll leave it to you." The child responded in equally direct fashion, in a manner typical of the prelatency child, "Oh Grandma, I know it's wrong to say, but I can hardly wait!"

The latency-age child, when confronted with such a thought, will activate defensive processes to hide it from his own sight. The following vignette will illustrate.

A boy of 9 was in treatment for disruptive behavior in school. His mother reported that his father had scolded and slapped the boy on the day of the session here described. When the child arrived for his session, I had expected that he would tell of this experience and of his anger at his father. Instead the youngster spoke proudly of his father's new car, emphasizing its technical advances (e.g., wide track). None of the father's scolding or beating was mentioned. The youngster eventually turned the content of his session to a description of a fantasy of a war in which he killed the general.

Emphasis on the new car worked as a defense because it filled consciousness, blocking distracting, uncomfortable memories, intense affects, and unconscious content that strive to reach the zone of awareness. The uncomfortable memory in this case was the beating at the hands of his father. The mental mechanism created a shift of attention cathexes. Such a shift of cathexes from an emotionally uncomfortable object of contemplation and response to a more neutral one is an example of the mental mechanism called displacement, or "establishing a countercathexis." As a result of this phenomenon, the child produces for himself a life image shorn of painful reflections on the truth of this matter. A countercathectic "illusion of knowledge" fills the memory and permits the preservation of the myth of an idealized family relationship.

Boorstin (1983) has described the impact of this mechanism on the history of man. Referring to the widespread pre-Columbian belief that the Earth was flat, he wrote, "The great obstacle to discovering the shape of the Earth, the continents, and the ocean was not ignorance but the illusion of knowledge" (page 86).

The use of the countercathectic car failed to work adequately in the above case. This resulted in a search for a more comforting discharge-oriented fantasy. A group of symbols was organized to create a fantasy involving a powerful stranger who is conquered by the child. Beware! This defensive maneuver is fraught with potential danger for the child. What if the general should win? After all, underneath he is still the father. Any manifest fantasy is free to be reshaped by inner forces. Unfixed and malleable, it is likely to be invaded by latent content. Such changeling fantasies are liable to become, in turn, the carriers of fear. The quiet streets and havens of fantasy are apt to be invaded by the very dangers the child had sought to avoid. Defensive fantasies of aggression may thus be turned into the persecutory fear fantasies that underlie phobias.

The slothful man saith, There is a lion in the way; a lion is in the streets [Proverbs 26.13].

Characteristically, the unmodified (latent) fantasies in response to stress of the early latency years deal with oedipal wishes to take one parent's place in the relationship with the other. The fantasies are modified to produce the form manifested in the clinical situation (manifest fantasies). The child is constantly exploring identifications with each parent and, in fantasy, living out the roles he has chosen. When the fantasy is pleasant, it can be expressed in unmodified form.

When fantasy thought leads to fear of harm to self or to one of the parents, it must be distorted and modified if it is to continue as conscious fantasy. "Harm to self" means physical harm and the pain of uncomfortable affects. During the latency age period, children experience any situation which is humiliating or overwhelming as harmful and as something to be mastered.

What are the tactics available to the child to master overwhelming stresses? First, the child can do to another what has been done to him; when a child comes into a therapy session and attacks the therapist, it is worthwhile to ask the child when he himself has been so attacked. Second, the child can talk about the experience directly. Third, the child can develop a fantasy to master the circumstances of the situation that stresses him. The last of these techniques takes emotional pressure off the child without affecting the environment or involving other people. With it, the child appears to be unaffected by stress and uninvolved with drives. The third technique provides support for the quiet, calm, and pliability of the state of latency.

Oedipal fantasies, combining elements in which the child re-places the parents in their various roles with fear of retribution, reach a high level of intensity during early latency. Thereafter they continue to populate the fantasy life of the individual, but with the passing of years, additional fantasy contents appear and are pushed into prominence by their pertinence to the immediate problem at hand. This results in a deemphasis of oedipal fantasy in the middle and late latency years.

For purposes of clinical evaluation, one must be able to recognize which fantasies are age-appropriate during the latency years. For in-stance, when a child begins to feel a sense of independence from the parents at about 7 or 8 years of age, the child confronts himself with fear fantasies of being small, vulnerable, and all alone in the big world. This is reflected in fear of monsters. The monsters are symbols, masked representations of the real fears. If there are siblings to support such fantasy, jealousy and vying for parental attention give rise to sibling rivalry throughout the latency period.

Beyond the age of 9 or 10, the problem of passivity becomes a major point of issue. Children at this age, unlike Peter Pan, want to grow up, take over, and run their own lives. They object very much to parental interference. Of course, this will become much more intense as they reach adolescence, but there is already clear evidence of it in late latency. The child begins to defy the parent, and asserts a desire to make his own decisions. Often he will say angrily, "Don't treat me like a baby!" but when this happens, he may find himself threatened by the loss of the parents' love, if they want him to continue to behave like that healthy, happy youngster who did everything he was told in early latency. At this point the child is readying himself in fantasy to confront his parents and to rechannel his adaptive energies from inward-turning fantasies toward demands and actions that will intrude on the world.

Some children who are conflicted about confronting their parents in this way deflect the challenge into the form of a fantasy of defiance, accompanied by guilt and doubt. As a conflict-resolving compromise these children actually develop all manner of symptoms (to be discussed below), such as urticaria, paranoid ideation, and obsessional symptomatology. Therefore, in the presence of these symptoms in a late latency child, it is wise to look for conflicts with parents in the child's mind's eye over passivity, stealing, sexual play, greater freedom of movement, and smoking. As the child masters the problem of independence from his parents, this symptomatology clears. These symptoms are usually transient manifestations marking the period from about 9 to 12 or 13 years of age.

The late latency child who is struggling for independence usually deals in his fantasies with a harsh, limiting, and condemning early parental introject as well as the real parent. The limitation placed on the child by this fantasy evokes hostility, which causes the child to distort the real parent (usually the mother) into a stick-wielding disciplinarian (the phallic mother). In direct conflicts between the child's wishes and the mother's, a great deal of hostility is generated between parent and child. The child who cannot articulate his demands in words and so change the external world develops symbols and fantasies to create a comforting inner world. Such fantasies cast the defeated child in the role of a powerful baseball player or a famous movie star.

There are other characteristic fantasies of the latency period. These have to do with the awakening of concern about sexual identity, which intensifies when children begin a growth spurt at about 9 years of age. Pinching in of the waist and evidence of sexual dimorphism creates concern in children who haven't fully decided to be comfortable with the sex to which they have been assigned biologically. Children begin to develop all kinds of concerns about sexual identity. They worry about what they'll look like as adults. They ask whether they really are boys or girls. Boys wonder if they can turn into girls and girls wonder if they can turn into boys. These are all quite definite fantasies that can be detected in interviews with children in late latency. In addition, dawning sexuality brings in its train curiosity and worries about what sex feels like, what is right, what is wrong, how babies are born, and which of all the theories they've heard describes a real means of procreation. These become major topics of conversation and concern.

Throughout the latency period the child need not heed realistic curbs on fantasy that would force him to test in reality his potential for being anything he wishes to be. Therefore there is very little of the hopelessness and depressiveness that will appear in the adolescent. By and large, as will be described later, depression in the latency age child is manifested more in terms of listlessness and somatic symptomatology than in hopelessness and depressed mood.

Defense against Fantasies in the Latency Period

We have dealt with the definition of latency, and the fantasies that predominate in response to the various latency-age developmental tasks. Some new experiences stir up preoccupations, thoughts, and questions. Others, such as observations, talks with understanding parents and teachers, and confidences shared with older children often put the child's concerns to rest. Some of the preoccupations, thoughts, and questions do not have ready resolutions or answers, and some bring the child into confrontation and conflict with parents. Often these thoughts, if dealt with directly, would be disorganizing. Therefore they require either defensive maneuvers on the part of the child's ego or reassurance through direct communication with an adult. The basic approaches in psychotherapy with these children relate to this. The therapist may help the child to elaborate fantasies in the process of mastering disorganizing experiences, awarenesses, or thoughts. The therapist may help the child to verbalize his concerns, help him to clarify his ideas and reassure him that the situations of concern will come into the province of his ability to cope as he grows and matures. The therapist may help the child by strengthening in him mechanisms of defense that are appropriate for his age.

Awareness and appreciation of the typical latent fantasies presented above are necessary in order to investigate the defenses that are used by the child in coping with them. The clinically apparent personality structures of the latency-age child are integrated systems consisting of drives, thought preoccupations, and defenses. Manifest fantasies and symptoms are products of the interaction between age-appropriate preoccupations and associated defenses.

Once a typical preoccupation or forbidden wish has been defended against and has become unconscious, it is referred to as a latent fantasy. A conscious fantasy produced by the modifying actions of defenses on typical preoccupations and wishes is called a manifest fantasy.

From 4 to 7 years of age a child develops feelings of guilt, feelings of fear, and feelings of concern with loss of love or even injury at the hands of parents. This relates to the fact that he begins playing at or fantasying himself in one of the roles of the parents as a couple who relate to each other (the Oedipus complex). This is especially likely should one of these thoughts appear directly in consciousness. The child must therefore deal defensively with the appearance of such fantasy or be overwhelmed with uncomfortable affect. Typically, the latency-age child defends by regressing to an earlier level, usually one in which fantasies of taking a parent's role in the couple relationship are replaced by urges to mess, smear, and express anger.

Once the child has regressed to this (anal-sadistic) level, he has a different set of mechanisms available for dealing with his urges. Back when the child was 2 years old, he could do little more than mess and smear or hold back his stool to get at his parents, but during the latency age he has more mature techniques for dealing with the urge to mess, such as reaction formation. With this mechanism the child turns his urges into their opposites. Cleanliness, calm, and good behavior replace rage and messing. The calm and good behavior can further be supported by the defensive technique of obsessional activities, such as collecting. Latency children are famous for collecting. They collect stamps, coins, pebbles (which are sometimes lined up and glued onto boards), and baseball cards. There is a whole world of commercial gain to be had in the collecting tendencies of latency children.

Fantasy formation also serves as a key defense. The fantasy takes forms dictated by the regressive attacking, messing urges, as in playing at being attacked by others or being the mommy who cleans up the house. These mechanisms bind the child's urges to a great degree. Indeed, it is as a result of such latency mechanisms of restraint that the highly excited children that one sees playing in the playground at recess can settle down so quickly in the schoolroom to learn and study.

For a child to complete the work of the latency period, these episodes of calm and educability are necessary. The work of this period is the transmission of culture through the acquisition of formal verbal syntaxes gained from reading, school and parents. Parent–child inter-action has an intense effect on the progress of the work of latency. The parent who spends time with the child, involving him in verbaliza-tions that encourage increasingly complex levels of abstraction and memory organization, increases his potential to acquire the knowledge and mental attitudes of his culture. Verbal neglect and intense inter-personal involvements which overstimulate the child tend to blunt cognitive skills and to limit the time and energies that the child has available for applying his full cognitive potential to the work of latency. Parental involvement that in actuality helps a child to live out the fantasy of being one of the parents, such as walking around nude, stimulating the child, taking the child into bed, or fighting, yelling, and screaming, as may happen between the parents, stirs up a great deal of drive energy in the child, making oedipal fantasies extremely uncomfortable and mandating regression.

When regression from oedipal wishes occurs, drive derivatives, affect, and excitement intensify. The content of the fantasy involved with the drive, affect, and excitement shifts to emphasize a minor component in the thought preoccupations and fantasy elements in the oedipal reaction to the parent's behavior. This usually involves the anal-sadistic (messing, teasing, stubbornness, negativism) elements. Where these anal-sadistic components are not readily at hand in the oedipal fantasy, preexisting fantasy structures of the anal-sadistic sort are called into play or intensified.

Regression to anal-sadistic content can produce so great an intensification of the urge to mess, to misbehave, and to be negative that the mechanisms of restraint are overwhelmed. Many children have no way of defending themselves against this, and a specific type of pathology appears which is characterized by an overwhelming of the latency state or a regression out of the state of latency. The child becomes then ill-behaved, hyperactive, and unmanageable in the classroom.

Children who are able to avoid this outcome are those who have a set of defense mechanisms, the structure of latency, that will buffer them against the need to regress (see Chapter 2). It serves to shift the energies of the thought preoccupations of the overstimulated child into a substitute fantasy, still on an oedipal level, in which the child masters the stressful situation while masking the meaning of fantasy through the formation of symbols. Children who have an impairment in the ability to form symbols have a resulting impairment in the ability to enter upon and maintain states of latency.

The special organization of ego mechanisms that I call the structure of latency consists of repression (the ideas pushed out of consciousness) followed by fragmentation of the fantasy in the unconscious so that the fantasy, if it were to reappear, would be difficult to recognize. This process of masking is enhanced by symbolization of the fragmented elements so that the original contents are represented by less recognizable and less anxiety-provoking forms. This is followed by the organization of these symbols into a series of manifest fantasies representing the original latent oedipal fantasies. The manifest fantasies become the familiar fantasies of playing cops and robbers or playing house, as well as the rich and unique fantasies of the latency-age child: trips to distant planets, battles with monsters, and robbers coming into the house at night when the child is going off to sleep. All have their origins in these mechanisms, and form the normal neurotic fantasy activity of the latency-age child who, in spite of the extraordinary degree to which he immerses himself in fantasy, is able to maintain a very realistic way of dealing with the pressures of school and his teachers when in the classroom situation. This is the normal condition.

Three pathological conditions may arise as a result of impairments in the development and function of the structure of latency and the associated pathways for regression and displacement:

1. The child may fail to enter latency at all because of a failure in the symbolizing function. This prevents him from attaining the kind of defensive fantasy structures necessary to maintain a state of latency.

2. In the overstimulated child, the energies conveyed through regression to the urge to express smearing, messing, aggressive, stubborn, and negative attitudes may become so strong that the structure of latency and the mechanisms of restraint are overwhelmed. Clinically, the child becomes ill-behaved and a creature of impulse. Failure to adjust at the level of anal regression using the mechanisms of restraint may produce further regressive responses such as rhythmic jumping, tearfulness, depression, thumb sucking, hair twirling, television watching and overeating. There is a tendency to obesity.

3. One finds youngsters who have been able to develop defensive fantasies and to maintain them even when overstimulated; but their fantasies are insufficient to master the situation if left as fantasy alone. The child is impelled to act on the fantasy, in a displaced gesture aimed at solving a seemingly unrelated problem.

A typical clinical picture may be drawn of each of these three states, to help in differentiating among them.

The first type of child (one who has not entered into a state of latency) usually has difficulty with verbalization and tends to be a quiet child. When confronted with stress, he tends to become extremely anxious. He reports no dreams, is able to participate passively in the dreams or fantasies of others, tends to spend much time in front of the television set, and may do such things as awakening the parents at four in the morning to get reassurance about something that is disquieting or discomforting him. These children have very little capacity for delay.

The second type of child (one who cannot adequately defend, through fantasies produced by the structure of latency, against over-stimulation) will tend to act out in an impulsive manner with destructive hostility. He may break things belonging to other children and often gets into fights with the first person he sees. There is no formed fantasy guiding such misbehavior; one never knows from which direction the misbehavior will come.

The third type of child (one who becomes involved in actions derived from fantasy content) tends to act out as a means of tension discharge. Formed fantasy guides his misbehavior. There is a repetitive and predictable quality to his misbehavior.

> An example of misbehavior shaped by a persistent fantasy would be the youngster who invited friends to his farm while his father was absent on a long trip and ordered his mother to hook the horses up to the buckboard so that all the children could go on a hayride. When the mother refused, the child hit the mother with a whip. The child had been moved much too much into the parental role and couldn't handle it.

> An example of repeated fantasy-shaped misbehavior would be the child who had noticed that his peers all had their own bank accounts, and who repeatedly took the bank book of a friend, signed most of the money of his friend's bank account out in his own name, and then deposited it in his name.

The developmentally correlated fantasies of the latency age period make their first appearance at times when developmental factors expose the child to reality situations that are to be mastered. In those situations that cannot be mastered in reality, the child must use fantasy formation, regression, and restraint. The goal is to master intrapsychically what is otherwise impossible to master in reality. The child pursues those areas which he is physically and mentally capable of mastering, and avoids those that he cannot master. Schoolwork and athletics may provide otherwise denied gratifications in reality; therefore, in the healthy child, a good deal of energy and attention is devoted to these areas. The healthy child then handles that which remains of that which he cannot master through regression, the mechanisms of restraint and the structure of latency.

Children who are on constant guard against being put in passive situations cannot pursue these reality goals of the latency-age child. This is especially so when the late latency life situation and cognitive development introduce desires for independence and peer-dominated pursuits and choices of activity. The children seek freedom from parental control and are painfully aware of the inroads of a reality dominated by people twice their size. The angry affects engendered by this painful awareness fuel the creation of an intense fantasy life which may encompass most of their waking time. This diminishes their already meager capacity to deal with reality.

Children who devote most of their time to trying to master situations which cannot be mastered in reality, and who put most of their energy and time into fantasy, produce a disorganized state. The degree of their involvement in fantasy can reach a pathological level, on a par with breakdowns in fantasy formation. They become preoccupied with fantasy, and are constantly confronted with the blow to self-esteem that a youngster faces when he cannot master something in reality. Such children attempt mastery through comments such as, "Who's the boss around here?" "Nobody can tell me what to do; I know what to do," and, "You're not me, so you can't tell me what to do."

Cognitive Development

Before we will be able to pursue more of what the latency psychic life is like in normality and pathology, it will be necessary to develop yet another theme. The first section of this chapter examined how fantasy is used to deal with reality situations; this section has to do with how that reality is perceived, remembered, and understood. It is an error to believe that a child has adult cognitive skills.

The development of awareness is far from complete as a child reaches the age of 6. Perhaps nowhere is this developmental actuality more easily to be seen than in the drawings of children in the latency age, where the unfolding of concept and improvements in motor skills become undeniably clear. These developmental events have been amply documented by Di Leo (1970) and Fine (1976).

By the time the child is 5 years old his motor skills have reached the point that he is able to copy a circle, a cross, a square, and a triangle. It is not until 7 years of age that a child is able to copy a diamond.

It is not only in copying that there is still maturational growth to be seen in the drawings of a child. If a 6-year-old child is asked to draw a picture of a man in a boat (spontaneous recall), it is not unusual or pathological for the child to draw a picture of a boat that is transparent, with the entire body and legs of the man visible. This sort of transparency is acceptable until 9 years of age; beyond this age, it becomes quite rare and, if found in an adult, is considered an indication of psychosis.

In drawing the human figure, by the time the child reaches the age of 6 he is able to draw eyes, hands, and legs by combining circles and vertical and horizontal lines. As the child approaches latency a certain amount of movement can be imparted to a drawing with the use of lines drawn in diagonals. The entire body of an animal or person is contained within a single outline at this age.

Between 6 and 7 years of age, children begin to draw figures involved in interactions with other figures. In effect, fantasy content with movement is introduced. At around 8 years 6 months, depth is introduced. For instance, in drawings of a horse, overlapping of parts of a figure without transparencies begins to appear (Fine 1976, p. 88). Details, enrichment, and adornment become characteristic. Depth through shading appears at about 9½ years, with 11 years the point at which shading and depth become important elements.

It is not only in the area of memory expressed through motor activity (e.g., figure drawings) that one can find cognitive growth in a child. There is also maturation in the symbolizing function. The child at the age of 6 is normally capable of producing his own symbols (with unconscious meanings); he has had this ability since about 26 months. He is fully able to participate passively in the symbolic productions of others, as occurs in TV watching. Passive participation takes from him responsibility and guilt for having thought up some of the ideas he is enjoying, which really are his own.

By and large, the symbols of the early latency child (6 to 8½) are amorphous and distorted. In turn, his fear fantasies are populated by amorphous, distorted, highly symbolized characters coming after him. From 8 until about 12 the late latency child's fantasies, especially persecutory fantasies, contain thoughts about realistic characters. It is not until the child enters adolescence that fears of known real people in the real world dominate his fantasies.

Although figure drawings may be used as evidence of the ongoing development of cognition during the latency years, there is too much variability between one child and another for a timetable to be established which can be used for the differentiation of normal from pathological states. Fortunately there are more reliable developmental indicators. Piaget (see Woodward 1965) has described the unfolding cognition of the child in terms of his ability to understand and explain natural phenomena. Before the age of 7 children have a tendency to explain phenomena on the basis of intuition, giving highly personalized explanations. At 7, concrete operational thinking begins; it will predominate until about 12 years of age. This is a form of abstract thinking in which the abstract operations of the mind can be brought to bear upon concretely present items of experience. It is characterized by the ability of the child to explain, on the basis of realistic considerations, a natural phenomenon. Thus the child will be able to recognize that a shadow is produced because a stick stands between the light source and the place where the light falls. This is in contradistinction to the intuitive concept of the younger child that, for instance, the shadow is hiding from the light because it's afraid. Piaget described a change in the explanation of phenomena that occurs at 12 years of age, at the very tail end of latency. At this age, there develops abstract operational thinking. Abstract thought processes can be applied to other abstractions and ideas can be used to understand other ideas in the absence of concrete representations.

The organization of the process of memory also undergoes developmental changes by which normality may be judged during the latency age period. From the first year of life, the content of a child's memory had been dominated by affects, motor experiences, and sensations. The very young child remembers what has happened in terms of the total experience (visual, kinesthetic, auditory, haptic), without the interposition of words. Words are only gradually introduced early in the second year, as the child begins to recognize that words a parent has used represent things, people, and actions. The pattern of action is remembered, the recognized word merely being a signifier of the action. As the child matures, he is able to add more words. The predominant choice of the modality for remembering experiences remains the sensory-motor medium. This is similar to the modality used in the experience of learning and memorizing that an adult undergoes when learning to dance by being shown the steps without any verbal communication. In spite of the absence of words, the adult remembers where and how to move.

By the time the child reaches the age of 26 months, words have become more useful than the totality of sensory experiences as efficient memory agents. However, the words and ideas they represent may become associated with anxiety. Repression comes into play. This results in a split between the words and the anxiety-loaded ideas. Repression is supported by the substitution of less affect-charged words for the original words. In this way psychoanalytic symbols are introduced. These are the symbolic forms which permit the child to develop the kind of fantasies that I have described as typical of latency.

Until the child is 6 these more advanced language skills are not organized in such a way that they can be used as the predominant medium for carrying memory into consciousness. Di Leo (1970) has pointed out that a child of 6 can draw far more than he can describe in words. Schachtel (1949) has noted this limitation in the prelatency child.

At the onset of the latency years there is an apparent shift to greater use of verbalization as a medium for memory, and affectomotor memory is deemphasized. If an observer considers memory and consciousness to be defined only in terms of verbal recollection of events, then the latency-age child must be considered to have an amnesia for the period before the age of latency. It is therefore within the range of the normal for a latency-age child to have an apparent diminution in the ability to remember global experiences and prelatency events which have been limned in memory in sensory and affectomotor, rather than verbal, terms. Yet another factor in this apparent amnesia pertains to the repression of the actual recall of events in words, accompanied by the substitution of symbols in the form of fantasies representing the original event. A major portion of the appearance of memory loss is associated with the shift away from the use of nonverbal memory as a medium for recall. In this shift from the affectomotor memory organization to a memory organization dependent upon rote verbal descriptions, obviously a great deal of detail is lost, but much efficiency is gained. The child is able to enter school and to learn times tables, simple poems and the acts of elementary spelling, writing, and reading by rote.

Not until the child reaches the age of 7½ to 8 does the ability to remember abstract aspects of experiences develop and become available for use at the behest of the society. This is a key maturational achievement of the latency years. As a result, such abstract aspects of experience and understandings of the intrinsic nature of things and events can then be expressed either on motor level (modeling in clay), verbal level (verbal description of events), or abstract level (metaphors, poems, and theoretical interpretations). Any of these expressions can then be examined by the subject or the observer and processed further to be reduced to a verbal concept or formula.

Abstract conceptual memory (which entails the ability to perceive an intrinsic characteristic and to represent it in memory) can subsequently be applied to concrete things (Piaget's concrete operational thinking). This is important clinically. It is necessary in making interpretations or otherwise talking to an early latency child to be sure that abstractions are related specifically to concrete events or affects. Directions for taking medication, for instance, which contain any kind of abstraction or thought process in which it is necessary to apply principles of judgement should relate to concrete situations, and should be illustrated with examples. The application of understanding and memory of intrinsic characteristics cannot be applied to abstractions until age 12 (abstract operational thinking).

The development of the abstract conceptual memory organization is necessary for adjustment in the changing environments of an industrial society. In contrast, it can lead to estrangement from one's fellows in a magical thinking–oriented society. The encouragement or discouragement of the maturation of developmentally available potentials for abstract conceptual memory is an important criterion for the evaluation of cultures, on the mass level, and the adaptation to culture, in the individual. The development of this skill will depend on the handling of the child during the latency years.

It should be kept in mind that a child can recognize abstract similarities such as those that help one identify many breeds as one species of animal in the very earliest years of life. Abstraction does not first develop during latency; what develops in latency is a refinement of the ability to perceive the abstract intrinsic nature of an object, and then to recall the abstract concept spontaneously for later use. This characteristic first appears at approximately 7½ to 8 years of age.

Failure to achieve abstract conceptual memory organization is a requirement and prerequisite for life in a society dependent primarily on rote memory and characterized by general acceptance by the members of the society of a great deal of magical thinking. Thus primitive societies tend to develop educational techniques that direct children away from the fulfillment of such capacities.

In highly technical and industrial societies, in contrast, abstract conceptual memory organization is required for the proper handling of money, future planning, and an individual life style. Failure to achieve it is a matter of pathological importance in a culture that holds in high regard scientific knowledge, technical proficiency, material rewards, and life-preserving public health measures. Leadership qualities needed in such a society are lacking in those who have not attained abstract conceptual memory. They lack the essential ability to conceptualize, organize, and carry out plans and programs. The capacity to understand theoretical concepts, acquire a college education (as differentiated from a college degree), and the abstract principles upon which professions and businesses are based also depends on this attainment. It is for this reason that many individuals brought up in a more primitive society who enter an industrialized society during adolescence find great difficulty in adjusting. Only supportive and menial employment is available for them within such a society. (Nurcombe [1976] has pointed out the failure of Australian aborigines to achieve in this regard.) Therefore, cases of school failure which are brought to the clinician's attention should be examined using tests for the presence of concrete thinking as well as tests of the ability to comprehend the abstract kernel of a given situation.

Sexual Development

It is a rare child in our culture who is involved in open heterosexual activities during the latency age period (Kinsey 1948; Sarnoff 1976). Most children are involved in masturbatory equivalents from ages 6 to 8. There is a gradual appearance of direct masturbatory activity from 8 years old on. When a latency-age child is fantasizing and acting out the fantasy with his entire body, this is a masturbatory equivalent. In doing this, the child hides the masturbatory fantasy with a high degree of symbolization, which makes it difficult to see the sexuality in the latent content of the fantasy. There are youngsters in the period of transition from latency to adolescence, between 11 and 13 years of age, who lose the capacity for masking. They act out fantasies which have direct sexual and perverse components. For instance, a youngster made slashes in his back and, when he felt the blood flow, experienced a sensation which he later was able to describe as similar to ejaculation. This would occur when he saw himself or another man dressed in an undershirt. Typically, in the shift to adolescence, the child goes from involving the whole body in acting out symbolized masturbatory fantasies to thinking very directly represented sexual fantasies while directly stimulating the genitals, accompanied by much less activity of the whole body.

The Development of Conscience

There is a major, developmentally guided reorganization of conscience during the latency age period. As a child enters the period at about 6, he normally becomes aware of the meaning of guilt. He may be asked directly, "What is guilt?" and the nature of his answer will reveal the degree to which he internalizes social demands. The extent of the development of conscience can be delineated by a study of the answers. The child, for instance, who says, "Guilt means that when you take something, you're afraid someone's going to punish you," is still experiencing an externalized conscience. The child who answers that guilt means that "You take something and you feel bad when you get caught" shows a corrupt conscience with a great deal of externalization. This is quite different from the normal sensation of guilt which first begins to be experienced at about 6 years of age, and which is illustrated as follows: "When you feel like you want to do something, you feel bad because it's wrong."

The state of latency is ushered in when the child has the ability to know right from wrong and guide his behavior accordingly. This underlies the ability of a child to size up a situation and to appreciate when certain kinds of behavior patterns are expected. For instance, if a child sees a balloon in the classroom, he knows that the likelihood is that he can be more active and noisy. He can be on his party behavior. If there's no balloon and the teacher is standing there with a book in her hand, he knows that calm classroom behavior is required. The uproarious loosening of restrictions typical of recess behavior is activated only at recess time by the child who can have in his mind's eye a behavior pattern appropriate for that given situation. The child who is able to apply appropriate behavior to appropriate situations has attained behavioral constancy, a prerequisite for attending school. It guides a child's mechanisms of restraint toward limiting acting-out behavior in support of the school situation.

Piaget (see Flavell 1963) has done careful studies of the development of conscience around the age when the latency period begins, and has noted a shift from a "morality of restraint" to a "morality of cooperation." Under the morality of restraint, the child shifts away from a world view in which he does only what he is ordered to do by his parents. Very little convincing, discussing, or talking with a child is effective until he is about 6 or 7 years of age. Until then, the parent must tell the child what is expected of him, or else the child does not respond properly. The child does not have sufficient behavioral constancy to be put on his own. Once the child is capable of latency a morality of cooperation can be set up, in which the child is informed by guilt and his capacity to judge right from wrong behavior. At this stage, when confronted with a problem, the child recognizes that others before him have had to face and solve such a problem, and that he must be able to make decisions and solve problems in cooperation with the parents, rather than in response to their demands.

As the child approaches 8 years of age, his conscience is guided by a tendency to move away from parental influence and to seek influences from outside. At this point the individuation from the parent, which in the first years of life had taken the form of simply recognizing himself as different from his parents, now moves into the realm of morality. As a result at about 8½ to 9 years of age, children enter into the phase of ethical individuation. They begin to draw content into conscience from sources other than the parents—primarily teachers and peers in school. The earliest appearance of this is the child's desire to wear what the other children are wearing, to see a movie that the other children have seen, or to get some bubblegum that the other children are getting, while his parents insist that these activities are not necessary, not required, and for that matter, bad for him.

The child begins to reflect the influence of peers in his expectations and comes into conflict with his parents. There is likely to be inner conflict, at least. The child is not only in conflict with the parent of the 9-year-old but also with the parent he knew when he was seven, six, or younger (the parent of the morality of constraint).

These images of the parent have a multitude of sources. There is conscious memory of admonitions. There are also internalized images of the parent as objects of identifications, which are established in the following way. As the child begins to regress away from, and to repress as a means of dealing with, the Oedipus complex, there is a loss of the objects involved (parents). What results is the precipitation of an identification with the parents, which becomes a very important part—often the strongest part—of the superego. Certainly it will serve to guide behavior during the return to conservatism that succeeds the period of adolescent rebellion, which in turn was the product of ethical individuation. Challenges to the authority of these internalized early parental images are usually accompanied by a great sense of guilt and doubt. Children often resolve this through the development of symptoms. Among the symptoms are paranoid persecutory fantasies of robbers coming to hurt, urticaria, nausea, abdominal complaints, obsessive-compulsive patterns, and tics. These are usually transient. I consider it of importance to differentiate between early and late latency on the basis of the fact that in early latency, the child uses the latency mechanisms of defense to deal with conflicts with parents in terms of a simple wish not to cooperate. The late latency child's challenge of parental wishes take the form of wishes based not merely upon negation of the parents' wishes, but on inputs from outsiders (such as peers and teachers).

The essential paradigm of the shift from early to late latency is the transition in the fantasy structures of the child from fantastic fears of amorphous persecutors to fantastic fears of realistic persecutors. It is in the early moments of late latency that the child begins to be influenced more strongly by the real world. This shift marks the appearance of a momentum in maturation that will increase in impact as peer pressure and ever-increasing sexual drive energies lend their weight to a call that will carry the child away from the unfulfillable fantasies of early latency. This culminates in the ability of the maturing body to seek out objects in reality for sexual purposes and for the expression of aggression. It is through this characteristic late latency process that the structure of latency and its attempts to deal with reality through the development of fantasy evolve into "future planning." In the transition to "future planning," the fantasy resolution of problems involves planning upon which future actions can be patterned. This replaces fantasy with its primarily private means of discharge of drives.

During the late latency–early adolescent period there is a shift in the symbolic forms used. The transition encompasses a move away from the use of symbols developed primarily to express an inner feeling, and hence hardly modified to entertain or communicate with others. In their place there appear symbols and associated fantasies selected not only on the basis of their ability to evoke feelings and memory elements and to resolve conflicts privately, but also on their ability to communicate and entertain others. Such communicative symbols are developed during late latency or early adolescence.

Psychopathology in the Latency-Age Period: Psychoses

Up to this point we have dealt with normal developmental stages during the latency age and variations from the norm which may be considered subclinical pathology. Within the latency age period there are clinical manifestations of specific syndromes which are recognizable as psychoses, neuroses and depressions. We therefore shall turn our attention at this point to the characteristics of psychoses, neuroses and depressions as they occur in latency.

Childhood psychoses, extensively described in a literature of their own, are by and large endogenous phenomena or manifestations of massive psychic trauma with an existence of their own, independent of the psychodynamic forces involved in latency. Therefore, we shall concentrate on the differential diagnosis of psychotic states whose dynamics can be related to latency defensive structures.

The major difficulties in differential diagnosis occur in late latency (from 11 to 13 years of age). It is during this period, as noted above, that children begin to develop paranoid persecutory episodes in response to conflicts related to ethical individuation. This is also the age at which adult forms of schizophrenia (especially paranoid forms) first begin to be recognized, and at which prepubescent schizophrenia, the last appearing form of childhood schizophrenia, begins to be manifest. Differential diagnosis is difficult in identifying these conditions.

The paranoid episodes associated with ethical individuation are relatively transient, although they point toward the development of a borderline personality in adulthood. Unlike the other two conditions, they do not point toward a major disorganization within the few months following onset of symptoms. In all three, paranoid persecutory episodes may occur.

In the paranoid persecutory episodes associated with ethical individuation, the child and the parent report a history of night fears and phobias from 5 to 7 years of age. The child usually has a history of rich fantasy life, and the persecutory fantasies can be seen to be the fantasies of the latency age child. Close history reveals a direct temporal association in late latency to conflicts accompanied by doubt or fear.

> For instance, a child was told by her friends to steal if she wanted to be a member of their group. She didn't want to do this, became frightened, and developed a fear that there were people in a gray van outside my office who were going to kidnap her. When she was able to verbalize her concern about being forced to steal and was able to talk about the fact that she had taken something and then put it back, the paranoid episode cleared completely.

The childhood schizophrenic manifesting his illness in prepubescent schizophrenia may develop paranoid persecutory delusions at this time; this is characteristic of the disease. The normal child begins to project introjects at about 4 years of age (Bender 1947) and so develops fear fantasies at that time. The childhood schizophrenic does not begin to project introjects until about 11, so that most of his persecutors are internal: voices from within, straw coming from joints, salamanders talking to him from within his throat. It is not until the age of 11 or so, when the child begins to project his introjects, that fear fantasies involving objects outside himself (external persecutors) begin to be perceived. Such children usually have poor peer relations and difficulty in school. Specifically, they have no history of persecutory fantasies during the age period 6 to 8 years of age.

Adult schizophrenia of early onset with paranoid features is particularly difficult to differentiate from persecutory delusions associated with ethical individuation. History of adjustment during the latency years gives little help. The child may or may not have friends. The disease is diagnosed on the basis of poor relatedness, decline in or poor peer relationships, and a thinking disorder manifested in predicate identifications supporting bizarre content. It is difficult to elicit a specific precipitating event, conflict or doubt in temporal relation or demonstrated causal relation to the appearance of the persecutory fantasy. The onset of these conditions seems to be correlated temporally more to the beginning of hormonal activity than to ethical individuation.

Normal cognitive maturation produces the ability to use abstract thinking in proverb interpretation at about 11 years of age. The application of an abstract concept to an abstraction now begins to differentiate normals from those who are going to have concrete thinking. The child with adult schizophrenia of early onset may have impaired abstract thinking, while the child, whose persecutory delusions are associated with an overwhelming of the structure of latency and ethical individuation, will not. It is thus wise to ask children with persecutory fantasies to interpret proverbs. Concrete responses are only equivocal indicators, while the presence of good capacity to abstract points strongly to a regressed structure of latency as the source of difficulty.

Prepubescent schizophrenia and adult schizophrenia of early onset usually produce catastrophic intrusions on the person's life and development which can be modified to some extent by management, medication, and psychotherapy. Regression in the structure of latency, in contrast, is a transient state reflecting ego weakness and/or adjustment difficulties.

Psychopathology in the
Latency-Age Period: Neuroses

The "normal neuroses" associated with latency are characterized by the transient development of neurotic symptoms.* These are usually associated with periods of adjustment to expanding awareness, the appearance of new modalities of defense, or the modification of well-established defenses. These have been covered above, but will be recapitulated briefly here.

---

*For a fuller treatment of phobias see Chapter 6.

As a child enters into early latency, persecutory fantasies develop containing amorphous monsters who haunt and threaten the child. These usually clear by the time the child is 8 or 9, but may persist, being especially exaggerated during the period of ethical individuation. Given that obsessional mechanisms are very much a part of latency, it is not considered to be a pathological sign for a child to avoid stepping on a crack in the sidewalk for fear he'll break his mother's back! This is so even though there is a clear-cut obsessional thought involved. Compulsive touching, touching three times, or counting in threes is very often seen during the period of ethical individuation, sometimes reaching proportions so uncomfortable for the child and the parent that professional advice is sought. These usually clear spontaneously, however. The availability of the mechanisms of defense that support such symptom formation presages, in certain cases, the mobilization of obsessional defenses later on in life.

Hysterical symptomatologies are subtle in this age range, the most common being genital anesthesias. Children who have experienced overwhelming sensations during masturbatory activities develop the inability to feel. This process may lead towards asceticism as the child moves into adolescence. Since these phenomena do resolve in most cases, if they are discovered they should be followed, with a psychotherapeutic intervention called for if an ascetic, markedly inhibited character is seen to develop as the child enters adolescence. To attempt to treat or shatter this defense during latency would undermine the whole process of latency. Therefore, therapy should not be undertaken unless the defense is associated in some way with an anxiety that is in itself disorganizing to the child.

Depression

Depression in latency differs from that seen in adults and younger children.* For the sake of this discussion, the symptomatology of depression may be divided into three groups. These consist of affects (severe depressive feelings, feelings of low self-worth, a sense of hopelessness, depressed facies, crying, and sadness), somatic symptoms (psychosomatic disorders and vegetative symptoms such as psychomotor retardation) and motivational impairments (listlessness, loss of will to work). A latency-age child who becomes depressed has far fewer affective symptoms than is usual with smaller children, adolescents

---

*For a fuller treatment of depression see Chapter 7.

and adults. Rather, emphasis in depression during latency is on somatic symptomatology (Sperling 1959). The diagnosis of depression is therefore often bypassed in favor of a diagnostic nosology that takes into account the predominance of the other aspects of the symptomatology.

Affects do not dominate in depression during latency because the latency-age child has ego mechanisms to deal with affects. Depressive states involve the evocation of affectomotor experience associated with object loss and with the marked variations in sensory stimulation that occurred during the early years of life. The three differentiated components described above appear together as part of this process. Usually there are associated latent fantasies in response to object loss and the experience of humiliation. These are dealt with through the defenses associated with the structure of latency, this results in a weakening of the affective component in the depressive process.

The fantasies that occupy the child during latency, and which are regressed from or repressed, are defended against because they are associated with uncomfortable affects such as anxiety, fear of loss of love, or fear of castration. They activate the mechanisms of restraint and the structure of latency. The affect of depression has a similar result. Therefore, affects of sadness and depression are experienced by a child only briefly. (An exception is mourning, in which reality is so overwhelmingly strong.) Depressive affects are experienced only briefly, and then are processed by the structure of latency to the point that they become unavailable to consciousness. The other differentiated components of depression persist. Therefore, it is wise to suspect the possibility of depression whenever, during the latency years, symptoms and signs appear clinically which relate to the motivational or somatic components of depression. The characteristic symptoms and signs that accompany depression in latency are generalized pruritus, sleep disturbances, eating disturbances, intestinal disturbances such as vomiting and diarrhea, a fall-off in school work, malaise, listlessness, and, to a much lesser extent, crying, sadness, sad facies, and an affect of depression. Low self-worth and hopelessness typically are not found. The absence of hopelessness relates to the fact that the child's sense of reality does not develop strongly enough until he becomes about 11 or 12 for him to understand that there may not be a correction or turning-around of disappointing processes or events. The latency-age child usually has hope.

The events that precipitate and support depression during latency are primarily object losses, especially loss of a parent or friend. Loss is the key element. This is another factor that differentiates latency depressions from adult depressions. In adult depressions the precipitating cause often cannot be detected. The severe depressions of childhood (those lasting more than three months) are usually specifically related to an event which can be detected merely by asking the child what has happened, or from getting a history from the family which then may be confirmed by the child.

Summary

Despite a certain neglect in recent years, the concept of latency as a developmental stage in child development has persisted. This, I believe, is because the term and concept describe a discrete clinical phenomenon which must be taken into account if the nature of childhood is to be comprehended in its entirety.

When it was first noticed that adults in analysis do not bring to their sessions associations reflecting on the latency time period, the pioneers of psychoanalysis observed children of this age to see whether the factors that make the difference could be discovered. At first explanations of latency emphasized ego function. In time, observations of these children revealed periods of calm, quiet, pliability and educability to which the term latency, originally associated with the fact that memories from this period remained "latent" in adult analyses, was then transferred. Calm was then equated with latency. At one point a diminution of sexual drive was incorporated into this concept, markedly changing the meaning of the term *latency*.

Normal and pathological aspects of defenses, conscience, sexual development, the march of fantasies, the ontogenesis of symbolic forms during the period leading up to, through and beyond the latency years, and a general discussion of psychopathological entities found during the latency years constitute a major portion of this chapter.

In addition I have described a cognitive disparity between the memory organizations of the latency child and of the adult. This disparity results in difficulty for adults in recalling the contents stored in affectomotor memory (recall through feeling and action) and in symbolically distorted memory (recall through fantasy distortion) memory organizations to which the latency child resorts in time of trouble.

Through the creation of fantasies embodying symbols and wholebody activities (memory in action in latency-age fantasy play) the child is able to maintain latency calm, quiet, and educability in the face of stress. There is thus an intrinsic link between the paucity of verbal memories of the latency period in adult analyses and the quiet of the latency state. The tendency to maintain calm by turning uncomfortable memories into symbols and play activities creates problems in the associative retrieval of stressful memories from this period during the analyses of adults.

Part II
Psychotherapy

Chapter 4

Assessment

The latency age period encompasses the confluence of two processes: the experience of childhood and the traversal of the developmental defile from which will issue the characteristics of adulthood. Those who assess the latency-age child must be alert to impediments to and digressions from normal and effective functioning in both processes.

Normalcy

Definitions of normalcy vary from society to society. Appropriate behavior in childhood and the type of behavior that is expected to develop in the adult vary from group to group. Likewise, cultures will vary in their encouragement of maturation of psychological resources in managing the multipotentialities of personality in the latency-age child. In both the child and the adult-to-be, variations from what is commonly accepted in Western society should not, without reference to cultural norms and childrearing patterns, be defined as pathology.

Evaluation of a latency-age child requires a background knowledge on the part of the examiner of the definitions of normalcy in the child's culture of origin. The knowledge resolves into two zones. First are the expectations the society has for the behavioral patterns of the person while he is still a child as well as the expectations the society has for the person when he becomes an adult. The second of these is a knowledge of the expected influence of various types of child-rearing techniques and latency-age psychopathology on the development of the adult personality. The examiner needs background so as to be able to know whether the child's current situation is aberrant and whether it will give rise to unacceptable and pathological behavior or adjustment in adult life. A society that places the hallucinating child in an exalted position may not recognize the potential liability in the nonfunctioning adult he will become if the hallucinations are part of a deteriorating pathological process.

One must know what is considered to be normal in the culturally unique situation, as well as what is universally accepted as the average expectable range of personality organization of the normal child.

A child who appears to be functioning normally may be doing so as the result of the development of a set of mental mechanisms that produce acceptable behavior in the child, but will result in ineffective functioning in the adult. For instance, a well-behaved child in the latency age period may use fantasy to an extreme degree to cope with the stresses of living with aggressive and abusive parents. As a result of withdrawal into fantasy the child presents a quiet calm and educable image, and appears capable of coping during latency. He would be described superficially as perfectly behaved and normal. Yet this could be misleading. Fantasy as a means of coping is appropriate for a limited time only. If the fantasy world continues to dominate the child's adjustment through adolescence and into adult life, there will be difficulties. The appeal of fantasy will draw the person's energies away from confrontations with reality, and the ensuing failure to meet life and deal directly with its tasks will lead to withdrawal, unrealistic expectations, and an ineffectual adulthood.

Phenomena normal to certain cultures may mask the existence of severe pathology. While working in a clinic in an area where many children attended parochial schools, I was struck by the number of youngsters who reported hearing the voices of deities. I was told that this conformed to the teaching in the local schools, and that the behavior was honored and considered normal by parents and teachers. These voices were not pathological. They were an example of the working of culturally encouraged auditory memory potentials. Reported auditory and visual hallucinations were not to be considered as indicators of mental illness, and could not be used in evaluating a poor sense of reality in this population. Greater emphasis had to be placed on guardedness, projection, poor functioning, and poor peer relationships as indicators of psychosis.

Conversely, a primary and exaggerated use of projection during latency unaccompanied by impairment of object relations (such as fear fantasies when alone or when going to sleep), though creating much pain for the child, does not preclude a normal and healthy adult emotional life. It is difficult to predict adult pathology on the basis of manifest fear fantasies alone, including those that are adjustment-destroying, in the latency-age child. The child is still in the process of maturing and developing. Adventitious events that could shape the course of emotional growth have yet to occur. Without knowledge of these events and the degree to which they may cause immature defenses to persist, attempts at predicting the outcome of that which they influence become perilously faultstrewn. One needs knowledge of that which is to come in the child's life. There are the as yet unexperienced happenings, events and relationships of early adolescence. These will influence the transformations of the cognitive skills and ego functions of children that occur during late latency–early adolescence. The success of maturation depends on these transformations. Whether persecutory fantasies will be transformed by sublimation into art, or will cast the youngster and the adult he is to become into a narcissistically dominated world of fear, depends primarily on two factors. The first involves culturally and environmentally oriented adolescent experiences (e.g., parental or social encouragement or discouragement of removal, the adventitious coming true of a fantasy or one of its derivatives). The second is internal. It deals with the innate potential of the child to cathect reality more strongly than his own inner fantasy life. The first, adolescent experience, is unpredictable since it is so dependent on adventitious events and acts of fate. The second, reality testing, is inherent; pathology in the development of this function is a derivative of innate or internalized limitations of the capacity to cathect reality. In pathological states there is impairment in the ability to give priority to external events ahead of the seductive draw of inner-life fantasies. Magic, narcissism, and intuitive thinking are served by and support the dominance of the inner world over the sense of reality. In healthy states there is strength in the ability to give credence to the external reality one can touch and test in preference to the siren song evoked by a sense of reality that one feels within and applies to the world without. Neurotic, fantasy-dominated life patterns persist in those bound by this pathological form of apprehension of reality.

Potential impairments in the innate capacity of a child to cathect reality can be evaluated during a playroom-oriented psychiatric interview. If the child's emphasis during the play interview is on the communicative aspect of his play, rather than excluding the interviewer from knowledge of the meaning of the play, the likelihood is that an adolescence fantasy will not dominate over true object seeking. (For a full description of the clinical aspects of this point, see Chapter 13.)

In evaluating persecutory fantasies and projection in the latency-age child, the time of day at which fantasies occur has diagnostic importance. In the absence of contradictory evidence, the presence of dominating daytime persecutory preoccupations in the latency-age child points toward an impairment in the symbolizing function. One expects the fear fantasies of childhood to be better symbolized and masked, or at the least reserved for the hours before sleep and other witching hours. A lack of such reserve is a precursor of overcathexis of fantasy in adolescence. Indeed, it is considered a sign of poor functioning during latency for a child to focus his full attention on persecutors. This is especially so if the child tends to change the pattern of his life, withdrawing to hide, or to avoid teasing and persecution at the hands of peers. Isolated persecutory fear episodes require evaluation of the context of ego functioning, but the pervasive presence of projection, persecutory fantasies, and their derivatives presage a greater-than-average difficulty in attaining health through the trials of adolescence. Latency fear fantasies in which aggression is projected or expressed in poorly and inadequately displaced symbols may be early manifestations of a lifelong difficulty in dealing with one's own aggression.

Normal children recognize the bullies and seek friends elsewhere, giving little heed to the mean ones once they are out of sight. Children who have difficulty dealing with their own aggressive feelings find themselves preoccupied with bullies, occupied with bullying others, and being bullied in turn. Bullying serves only too well as a means of expression of and, through projection, as a symbol of their own aggression. These children migrate to that stratum of childhood society in which aggressive interactions dominate in the relationships between people. Such a state of affairs may presage difficult, sadomasochistic object relationships in adulthood.

The predictive value of such behavior is strong, but not foolproof. One can predict the fantasies that will dominate the adult from the dominant fantasies of the latency years, but one cannot predict acts of fate that will occur during early adolescence. External events shape the defenses and alter the emerging quality of the cognitive capacities that will influence the defensive structures to be interposed between fantasies and their derivatives in adolescence and adult life. Because these events are not foreseeable, we cannot predict with certainty the future of the child. Yet we know that the less reality-oriented the latency-age child, the greater his vulnerability in early adolescence, the greater his sensitivity to stress, and the greater his difficulty in avoiding neurotic patterns in adulthood. More specific prediction would require knowledge of the internal strength of the child's ability to cathect reality and the stress and influences of the external life events (deaths, identifications, fads, introjects, peer pressures, and so on) that will contribute to the patterns and shapes of the defense organizations of the growing child. Only that information would allow us to foretell whether persecutory fantasies will be the basis for later paranoid states, neurotic fears, philosophical systems, or a transmutation into creative structures through the interposition of sublimation.

The emergence in adolescence of an innate talent such as the ability to write or paint may shape the outcome of a sadomasochistic fantasy in adolescence. A strong capacity for artistic sublimation can provide a safety valve, not unlike the fantasy function of the structure of latency, for the expression of sadomasochistic fantasy derivatives. For instance, an outstanding novelist tells of the "paradigmatic image . . . in childhood . . . of how the larger world—the world outside the home, the schoolroom, the library—is constituted" (Oates 1982, sect. 7, p. 1). She describes an inevitable, melancholy, and tragic image, which found expression in cruel persecutions at a rural schoolhouse. She was "repeatedly—sometimes daily—tormented by older children . . . pursued across a field funnily called a playground" (p. 1). As an adult she finds herself immune to the barbs of those who are the critics of her published works, which she describes in terms of "violence in the lives of fairly normal people" (p. 1). We see that preoccupations with persecution in the latency age period may not give rise to a borderline adjustment if sublimatory strengths drain them of their venom. The successful author in question gave evidence from early on of an ability to process stressful inputs with writing. Those lacking such a felicitous endowment, and having a penchant to repeat painful traumas (strong repetition compulsion coupled with maturational lag in the shift from evocative to communicative symbols, coupled with intense narcissistic cathexis of fantasy in preference to reality) will find their lives at every turn dominated by their paradigmatic world view.

Where circumstances do not provide the culprits, neutral situations may be enlisted to serve as manifestations of the dominant fantasy theme. In the latency years the preeminent role of fantasy and the cruelty of children combine to reinforce distortions. Impressions and reactions are strengthened in the mind of the child already dominated by a neurotically informed approach to the interpretation of life experience. They become characteristic of the child. Repeated reactions based on this dynamic provide an early warning of masochistic patterns on the march, ready to assert hegemony in fast-approaching adulthood. Where persecutory fantasy is persistent and crowds out other mental content, in the absence of signs of sublimatory capacities that could dissipate the impact of fantasy, psychotherapeutic intervention is indicated. Err on the side of safety.

The Nature of Latency

The best indicator that sublimation will be strong in later life is the ability of the latency-age child to produce "states of latency." As discussed in Chapters 2 and 3, these are periods of calm, pliability, and educability, coupled with superficial asexuality, providing the emotional context for the child's acceptance of education. A state of latency is called upon when stress threatens. Though possible as early as 3 years of age, states of latency do not become dependably available until the child is about 6½ years of age. At that age there has been sufficient cognitive growth in abstract capacities to permit the child to evaluate situations and select a latency state as appropriate behavior. This decision to be calm is often automatic. It is effected through such mechanisms as reaction formation, repression, symbolization, regression, and fragmentation. The organization of a state of latency is first developed in relation to the child's confrontation with the problems of the Oedipus complex. Essentially, states of latency are induced when the latency mechanisms of restraint are enjoined to control anal-sadistic activities and fantasies. The latter are activated in this circumstance by defensive regressions in response to the dangers of oedipal fantasies. Should stimulation intensify oedipal sexual fantasies so that they threaten to overwhelm these regressive defenses, the structure of latency serves as a psychological safety valve, providing an independent pathway for the masked discharge of sexual and aggressive drives. Therefore the child who is capable of producing states of latency is able to adjust flexibly to all manner of variable stresses.

As the child moves towards adolescence, his symbols become more derived from reality elements and less derived from fantasy. As a result of this normal metamorphosis, the manifest fantasies evoked to deal with humiliation, defeat, or the intrusion of proscribed inner wishes take on more of the coloration of reality. Eventually the fantasies of the structure of latency, now constructed of realistic culture elements, become the realities of future planning.

To assess the functioning of a child, one must evaluate the strength of the structure of latency. This provides information on the child's capacity to deal with stress and the emotional factors which have become impediments to learning. In addition, one gains data for prediction of the child's capacity for future planning as an adolescent and an adult.

Any of the mechanisms of defense that help produce states of latency may falter and give rise to an impairment of function. Therefore, the evaluation of a latency-age child who is in emotional difficulty requires evaluation of the ego organization. One looks to see whether the child has entered latency at all. If not, is the failure due to a lack of social influence, an impaired symbolizing function, concrete thinking, overstimulation, or a combination of these elements?

Some children have a completely intact ego organization, yet become disorganized during the latency years. These children even give a history of having produced states of latency. Less-organized misbehavior in the child who has shown a capacity for states of latency usually indicates that there has been a regression. In these situations one should look for stimulations that have overwhelmed the structure of latency, resulting in such a high cathexis of fantasy contents that the child sees the fantasy as almost real and so moves the fantasy out of the arena of play and into the realm of action. This is to be looked for especially when there is a repeated pattern of stealing or misbehavior. The structure of latency has failed to absorb the additional pressures and there has been an intensification of the energies on the regressed anal-sadistic level. Reaction formations and obsessive compulsive defenses, employed by the normal latency-age child to hold his drives in check through the latency mechanisms of restraint, are brushed aside in these regressed children, and rage dominates.

The Symbolizing Function

Any evaluation of the latency-age child must take into account the quality of the symbolizing function. This ego function is one of the primary building blocks of the structure of latency. No matter what other mechanisms or adjustment patterns the child may have, the structure of latency provides a defense of last resort, particularly in dealing with the interface between the drives and the world. Why? Simply because the child lacks both the stature to use aggression effectively and a mature primary sexual organ to express his sexual drives.

In the latency-age child, the symbolizing function serves as an organ for the expression of sexual drives. Faced with humiliations or tasks beyond his ken, the child with an effective structure of latency can always turn inward for comfort. There he can fall back into a web of symbols, which, woven into a kind of mythic map, can be used as guide to a land where his power and self-esteem are reinstated. Thus restored, his energies are freed to pursue the business of the day. Personal fantasies and myths are evoked that may be used to organize play while releasing the child from tensions that would interfere with his capacity for calm.

A child whose symbolizing function can support latency enjoys the details in movies, plays, and TV programs. A child with impairments in the symbolizing function watches TV for the excitement of its fights and noise. To evaluate this difference, it is only necessary to ask the child to tell you about a favorite TV show or movie: the child with an immature symbolizing function will tell of the excitement, while the child with mature symbolizing will tell the story.

Children with impaired symbolizing functions may have an inability to recall dreams because they do not dream actively, which would entail producing their own symbols. One youngster I treated for failure to enter latency once plaintively asked me to give her a dream so that she could sleep at night and be good. She was afraid to sleep, dream, or fantasize because of the failure of her symbolizing function to produce symbols that would be sufficiently displaced to mask meaning and not produce uncomfortable affects. The symbols she produced were affect-porous. With affect-porous symbols, though displacement occurs, it is not of a magnitude that will take conscious attention away from the concept-linked affects that interfere with functioning. Such symbols as fire, shadow, flood, and pursuers are common examples of affect-porous symbols. Children reporting dreams containing affect-porous symbols should be interviewed with the thought that poorly controlled behavior in the waking state may be a sign of interference with latency related to the presence of these symbols. Affect-porous symbols cause the rejection of waking fantasy as defense.

Dream (oneiric) symbols and play or waking-fantasy (ludic) symbols are very similar in structure and function. Impairment in one may indicate impairment in the other. (Ludic symbols—toys and playthings used as symbols—are normally present during latency, but not after the onset of adolescence. This explains a major difference between psychotherapy in latency and adolescence: oneiric and ludic symbols can be used interchangeably with latency-age children, but the adolescent rejects ludic symbols.) The latency child lives by them. Therefore with the latency-age child, play may be adapted to therapeutic pursuits and used to encourage free association among his symbols. Thus a child with bad dreams may be induced to use dolls as the characters in his dreams to work out conflicts from his dreams in play. He can associate to dreams through the use of ludic symbols in play. Thus a 6-year-old boy, whose brother had gone into convulsions and had fallen onto the patient as he slept, was beset by dreams of a monster falling on him. He was encouraged to draw a picture of the monster. This was cut out, mounted on cardboard, and placed on a stand. For a few months, the boy played out a game in which this figure daunted and haunted a child. Repetition was associated with diminution of his dreams and eventual recovery.

The normal transition of symbolic forms through the latency period provides a further guide in assessment. At first, the symbols tend to be amorphous images whose very vagueness helps to hide the real meaning of the persecutors or adversaries. Ghosts are typical because they don't look like parents; the appearance of parents or animals at this stage as symbols is a sign of immaturity. At about 8½ years of age, the symbols should begin to become more anthropomorphic. They are seen as real people seem to look. The fantasy is woven around symbols whose sole representations are in the minds (psychic reality) of the children. The primary developmental trend of the march of symbols through the latency period takes the manifest symbolic forms away from the inner world of the child and towards a content drawn from reality. By the time the child is 12 years of age the anthropomorphic figures should be more human but still should exist only within the mind. With adolescence, the symbols consist primarily of realistic figures who exist on their own (people in the environment) who are, for the benefit of the fantasy, enlisted to play a role. Symbols that do not hew to this developmental line tend to be affect-porous and to interfere with development of the structure of latency. Obviously, the 11-year-old prepubescent schizophrenic child who sees the little green people peering at him has failed to progress in this area of development of the symbolizing function.

The way that symbols are used can be as telling as the maturational level of the symbols. For instance, symbols that evoke the moods and memories of the child with little concern for their communicative value are more pathological as the child gets older. Typically, the child who uses evocative symbols to the exclusion of communicative symbols will turn his back to the interviewer when he plays and will answer questions about the play with only a grunt or "Wait, I'll tell you later." The answer never comes. This finding is a forecaster of self- and inner fantasy-cathexes at the expense of relatedness and reality. It indicates a failure to break free of fantasy in the move toward adult life.

Superego Function

The maturational march of cognition during latency is one of the most striking and most neglected aspects of that developmental period. Cognitive growth supports changes in learning styles, symbol formation and the nature of the superego. One of the most reliable indicators of adequate cognitive competency for the development of states of latency is the comprehension of the concept of guilt. As discussed earlier, by 6 years of age a child should be able to define guilt as feeling wrong about doing or wanting to do something proscribed. The child who defines guilt as "feeling bad 'cause you got caught" for doing something wrong reflects a primitive form of superego and a weak capacity to form a structure of latency. By and large, children with latency potential have a capacity for abstract conceptualization about concrete situations sufficient to choose appropriate behavior in appropriate surroundings. Such behavioral constancy makes it possible for the child to attend school and go on a visit unaccompanied by the parent.

A developmental march also characterizes the vicissitudes of the superego in latency. Strictures on masturbation dominate from 6 to 8½. After that there is some relaxation of restrictions in general, resulting from internal cognitive changes. This enables the child to function safely on his own recognizance in new situations calling for more mature judgement. As a result of these cognitive changes, the child need no longer hold strongly to concrete verbal memories of parental demands, which produced the rigid conformity typical of early latency. As cognitive maturation progresses, abstract concepts begin to replace words in memory, and as a result more discretion and less rigidity characterize the child's decisions about acceptable behavior. In late latency, parental admonitions are joined by new influences— peers, films, and teachers—in the armamentarium of possible responses to situations. Behavioral constancy begins to look less "constant" to parents, whose ethical advice and proscriptions are more often bypassed. By 9 years of age the break may become so great between parental admonitions and peer pressures that the process of ethical individuation becomes prematurely apparent.

Parents and Assessment

There are two basic approaches to the assessment of a child during the latency years. One is the interview with the parent, the other the interview with the child. Most practitioners tend to emphasize one approach or the other. The information presented in this chapter assumes a primary emphasis on the interview with the child. In this view, perhaps the most effective use of the parent interview is to help establish the focus of the interview with the child.

Rarely can a diagnosis be established solely from the parent interview. Rather, a zone of pathology may be identified within which the approach and questions to the child can be organized. The parents' extensive knowledge of longitudinal patterns preceding pathological states make it possible early in the parent interview to detect the prodromal signs of pathological processes, and once one clue or sign is detected, other related signs can be asked about. Often, all the pieces of a pattern come tumbling out together. The subsequent interview with the child is then used to disprove or confirm the suspicions suggested by the parent interview, and to identify the seriousness of the condition.

The Spectrum of Normal Latency

Definitions of normalcy vary from society to society, and this is especially pertinent to the state of latency. Latency is not obligatory; the presence or absence of states of latency is therefore not the sole factor in determining whether the personality organization of the latency-age child and his manifest behavior are within expectable limits.

In primitive societies latency is not encouraged, and is rarely present. Its absence is part of the fabric of the culture. Without latency, the child is free to perfect the verbal concept memory and concrete thinking necessary for conformity in a society based on magic, myth, and rote recall. In industrial cultures, however, latency is invaluable. It provides the capacity to understand the intrinsic nature of the natural world and the abstractions through which the society organizes, understands, and adapts to it.

An absence of latency states thus presages limitations in function in adulthood which are a great handicap in industrial society. Inconsistent, impaired or absent latencies are common in children of certain low socioeconomic (SES) subcultures. This is not a state of pathology. It is an aspect of the transmission of culture. Though not an illness in the individual child, it reflects disorder in the body politic: some children are being shaped for limited potential in their adult years.

States of latency calm permit the child sufficient freedom from preoccupation with his own frustrations and anxieties to facilitate the transmission of culture patterns mediating success in complex societies. This is the ability to appreciate the essential and intrinsic nature of events and processes in such a way that abstract concepts are easily learned and, once learned, easily recognized even when changed in outward appearance. Thus a businessman may recognize the patterns of failure or faltering function in his business early enough to change his course of action and save himself and the business. One can thus learn from experience, and appropriately evaluate potential danger in new situations, rather than depending on rote learning, magic, and hope or fear of divine intervention. If the use of abstract thinking is not encouraged, prized, or admired, even children normally endowed with ego mechanisms and free of states of continued excitement will fail to acquire it. They will instead acquire the traits of adjustment of those around them, including concrete thinking and little energy for the calm pursuit of goals.

In evaluating impairments in abstract thinking which result from an aberrant form of latency (aberrant from the industrial culture point of view), one should look for causes of impaired latency states that transcend cultural factors alone. Latency, after all, may be impaired in the presence of conditions intrinsically characterized by concrete thinking (such as organic brain disease, certain forms of learning disability, and schizophrenia). Any condition that may result in impaired development of abstract thinking, abstract-conceptual memory organization, and their derivatives (deaf-mutism, stuttering, autistic thinking, identical twinning with little differentiation, severe oral character pathology, auditory memory retention difficulties, etc.) puts the child at risk for an impaired capacity to enter latency. In the latter conditions, the potential is intact for the perception of intrinsic characteristics, the creation of a body of memory data, and the use of abstract memory in evaluating new situations. There are, however, impediments to free communication with persons sufficiently differentiated and sufficiently regarded to serve as models for changing ways of thinking. The stutterer may only rarely find someone with the patience to hold lengthy abstract conversations with him. The twin may value the twinship above the world, and the autistic thinker his own thoughts and ways of thinking above the world. The person with memory retention problems values others, listens, and often finds a communicant, but the newly gained knowledge does not acrete to form a body of knowledge that may be used to comprehend the world on an abstract level. The deaf-mute and the blind deaf-mute, like the stutterer, require a teacher with great patience to help him fulfill his potential to master abstract operations in dealing with abstractions. In all the conditions described, latency and the future potential for progressive improvement in adjustment are threatened. For this reason, these conditions must be kept in mind when evaluating failures to enter latency and apparent cultural suppression of the development of abstract thinking, undermining states of latency.

The therapist who evaluates a child from a background which encourages adjustments other than latency states in late childhood must be wary of judging as pathological a pattern of emotional growth foreign to his own. In treating such a child, one must be aware that, in the course of therapy, cultural roots may be severed that would have provided in adulthood the ability to join in or empathize with the mental life of the community. Murphy and Murphy (1974) describe a tribe in which children who have been taught to abstract during years in a mission school were ridiculed upon return to the tribe until they lost all vestiges of foreign modes of cognition.

To better understand the nature of latency in low SES groups and in children from primitive social backgrounds, let us turn to a study of the characteristics of these groups.

Latency in Low-SES Groups

It is necessary to define the types of the low-SES groups whose period of latency potential we will be studying. Weekly income has at times been used as a criterion; however, there are entire nations with average incomes far below the average income of people who in our society are considered to be deprived. Their populations are not considered disorganized or in need of social assistance. This may be because they gain subsistence from hunting and farming, and their cognition fits the adult needs of the community. The transmission of culture elements necessary for adult success is built into their educational system and their parent–child interactions. They form stable societies. Their latency years are conducted in a manner consonant with their culture and the mental cognitive needs required for adult success. These groups are not referred to in the discussion here.

In discussing low-SES groups I refer to groups whose latency years provide a cognition which is discordant with the dominant culture. Their potential for cognitive development is shaped by their environment and parenting in a manner that may permanently interfere with the achievement of success as it is defined by the portion of society that organizes and rewards educational and professional achievement.

In low-SES environments there is often both a lack of example and a high level of excitability. Both militate against the calm pursuit of goals, abstraction, reflection, and ordering and reordering of priorities that come with an inspected life. There is essentially a lack of contact with the cultural elements necessary for success in the dominant portions of society and failure to achieve states of latency calm. These conditions militate against the transmission and acquisition of the personality tools needed to move comfortably and with comprehension in the world of abstractions, predictions, and economics that must be negotiated if one is to succeed.

Children at risk for culturally discordant latency years have parents whose lives contribute the following high-risk factors: low priority given to academics, verbal skills, and self reflection; single parent with insufficient job skills; parental figures chronically in conflict with the law; parental figures chronically unemployed; drug use and alcoholism in the parents (Chandler and Roe 1977, p. 26).

Biological Givens in Children Whose Parents Have High-Risk Characteristics

Many children with low-SES parents with high-risk characteristics have a biological endowment, on average, that would impede the valuing of others and would alter appropriate responses to the world. These influences on the organization of a child's behavior are obviously present long before the latency years. Chandler and Roe (1977) compared the behavior of neonates born to parents with high-risk characteristics to that of a control group. Neonates were studied in order to determine innate behavioral responses, uninfluenced by either parental behavior toward the child or social expectations. The authors found that "prenatal factors, having no obvious physiological base, associated (at a statistically valid level) with the parental social environment, may affect the newborn's behavioral outcome" (p. 25). Specifically, the children "demonstrated less (response) to pinprick, less responsiveness in cuddling, required more intervention in consoling, [were] more excitable, and [were] less successful in self quieting activities" (p. 28). In brief, they were less involved in external stimuli, had more inner excitement, and had more difficulty in achieving self-control through self-quieting activities. While not self-modulating to the average expected degree, they were also less susceptible to modulating influences from the world. It is suggested that during the latency years, cultural influences encouraging states of latency might be ignored as a result of this relative insensitivity to external influences on personality growth.

There are parallels between the profile of the neonate born to parents with high-risk characteristics and that of the latency-age child from any socioeconomic group who fails to take advantage of available ego mechanisms and to enter into states of latency. This implies the existence of factors which, in the view of industrial society, would be deemed pathogenic. In terms of the cultural subgroup these factors actually help to preserve its customs and traditions from change. Whether predisposed or not, all children of such a group are introduced to the patterns of their people. The therapist should be aware of the ambiguity surrounding these patterns of character development wherever disparate cultures are in close contact.

The parallels between high-risk groups and youngsters from low-risk groups who have failed to enter latency lie in impairment in communication skills. In both groups, there is less involvement with external influences and communicative activities than in the normal latency-age child. They are preoccupied with inner needs, and are known for their responses to inner excitements. By definition, children who fail to enter latency have difficulty in achieving self-control through self-quieting activities.

The Influence of Latency on Later Life

The structure of latency provides an outlet and safety valve for the effects of sudden, especially strong, or unexpected stimuli. Self-quieting occurs in the form of secondary fantasies containing symbols so masked that they appear to the uninformed to be nothing more than innocent play. These secondary fantasies are produced as the result of repression of primary fantasies aimed at more destructive outcomes. The primary fantasies are fragmented, and the subsequent symbolization of their elements permits their return to consciousness in benign forms which are potent in their capacity to provide discharge for drives that have been stirred up and if unchecked would have destroyed the state of latency of the child.

Without the mechanisms of restraint or the structure of latency, there can be no calm within which to practice the mental activities required for the acquisition of cognitive skills which are in turn necessary for success in our society. Children with these impairments in communication skills avert the social influences conducive to states of latency. Parents and social situations may introduce so much stimulation that the capacity to establish states of latency is overwhelmed.

Parents who become overexcited or resolve periods of conflict with outbursts of rage or intuitive responses undermine in two ways the child's capacity to achieve states of latency. First, they interfere with the production of states of calm in which the child is receptive to learning. Second, they set examples for identification with disruptive behavior that interfere with development of the capacity for calm reactions and the ability to evaluate the effect of immediate behavior on long-term goals. By example, by failure to provide precept and through the absence of the calm required for reflection, the child's potential is compromised. The capacity to resolve difficulties by thinking through to the intrinsic characteristics of a problem before arriving at a creative solution is undercut.

The child who does not develop the ability to produce states of latency is ill-prepared to proceed in his development to the more mature levels of behavioral capacity that the structure of latency presages. For instance, the gradual harnessing of the fantasizing function to reality-based future planning does not occur, resulting in a poor organization of the time sense and an inability to cope effectively with humiliations and problems.

It can thus be seen that failure to enter latency may have a marked effect on mental function in later life. Future planning, abstract thinking, patterns of thought associated with comprehension and interpretation of the world and events, delay in response to intrusion or insult, and use of symbols and fantasy as defense may all be impaired. Hence factors which discourage the development of states of latency will tend to restrict many personality skills required in competitive adult life. The culture of low-SES groups impedes such development.

The mechanisms and psychic events of latency state production are germaine not merely to the psychology of the moment. They are part of an ongoing developmental series that transcends the latency years. With this in mind, a number of writers have concluded that a successful latency is necessary for a successful integration into modern society. Hippler (1977) has stated that "the capacity to develop and institutionalize scientific thinking is . . . related to the percentage of a given population which utilizes the latency capacity, or the degree to which it is done" (p. 433). Campbell (1959) noted that "It is during the years between six and twelve that youngsters in our culture . . . develop their personal skills and interests, moral judgments, and notions of status" (p. 78). Latency is a life phase. One of its characteristics is a series of tasks involving cognitive maturation. Failure to complete these tasks may produce a disordered adjustment to cultural pressures in adulthood.

Normal and Variant Development of Latency-Based Cognitive Skills

The impact of latency development on later life has its roots in variant developmental aspects of latency-based cognitive skills including the development of self image, the handling of symbols, and the appreciation and utilization of wealth. These are discussed below.

The child from a low-SES group experiences interferences with the development of latency which, though considered "normal" in his cultural context, truncate his potential to function in modern society. It is a remediable condition. Parental and community cooperation and understanding are essential, however, should a course of action be attempted that is aimed at interdicting these interferences, especially in the area of cognitive development. Cognition as used in this context refers to the way that an individual organizes his perception of the world. The nature of this organization is influenced strongly by educational and environmental factors. Through educational contacts with the literature and epic tales of the culture, ways of thinking and moralities are transmitted. As Foley (1977) has pointed out "the epic genre encodes cultural attitudes, beliefs, laws, and customs in the action of its heroes" (p. 134). All societies convey these elements through traditional tales. In literate societies, this is done more efficiently by individuals with the skills and the latency calm to read. Indeed, through the written word, attitudes and means for solving problems may bridge, and even skip, generations. Wisdom becomes codified and catalogued. When a culture possesses written wisdom as a base, it can change, expand, adapt, and reach new levels without transgressing the bounds of its traditions. The written word becomes, in Thomas Mann's phrasing "the tablets of knowledge . . . the seed corn of future wisdom . . . everything can begin afresh from the written seed" (1963, p. 18). Latency renews in each generation the tools for reaping written wisdom from the fields of culture.

The abilities to comprehend abstractions and to read are basic tools in literate societies, making it possible to gain the mental and cognitive equipment needed to partake of culture. A subculture that interferes with latency deprives its children of the passport to the world of the dominant culture. Such tools are not the contents of his culture; they are solely a means of acquisition. The definition of a culture lies in the cultural contents (belief, laws and customs), ethics, and style of thought and cognition that children acquire during latency. In primitive societies, which require rote learning, mythological education, and ritual, retention of the verbal conceptual memory organization as the primary memory mode is a key to the survival of the culture, rigid and unchanging though it may be. In industrial societies, however, failure to achieve an abstract conceptual memory organization limits the socioeconomic mobility of the individual.

Normal and Variant Development of Self-Image

Within all societies there is social stratification. There are tiers of increasing privilege, set one above the other, with limitations on the mobility between levels. This exists whether the stratifications involve distinctions in wealth or in political power and position. Some of the most humiliating experiences that a person may undergo involve the enforcement of such social barriers. The low-SES person, being at the bottom of the ladder of privilege, must develop an awareness of these limitations and an acceptance of them if he is to live life without continuous conscious and incapacitating rage. It is during the period of latency that the child of a poverty family is first able to become aware of these barriers, to understand the position of his family in society, and to deal with the bruises of social limitations.

How is this done? At first, latency-type fantasy activity produces rationalizations heavily spiced with denial as a means of adjusting to social stratifications. Shared fantasies are evoked, such as "It's better to be poor, because all rich people are unhappy." Identification with the aggressor becomes important at this time. The child accepts his family or ethnic group as inferior or unworthy. In this he identifies with the opinion of the dominant group. These distortions of self-image may persist into adult life and contribute to a failure to try to improve oneself and a bypassing of opportunities. By way of reaction to identification with the aggressor, there is an elevation of the peer group in the mind's eye of the child. The peer group is praised through the use of jingoistic phrases and latency fantasies of grandeur. Unfortunately, the elevation is derived from fantasy sources, diverting energies from a strengthening of the child in reality. At once, two things happen. First, the group is weakened, since the status quo in reality goes unchallenged. Second, the child's rejection of the ways of the other (socially dominant) group excludes him from success on its terms. Thus the dawning awareness of status and the tendency toward denial in latency conspire to strengthen the boundaries of caste.

Until about 12 years of age, children from poverty backgrounds use denial to place their parent's holdings on a par with anyone's. This undermines motivation to work in school to better oneself. In over five years of observing low-SES children in foster home and cottage settings, my colleagues and I observed that latency-age children complained about the good food of the institutional home, while extolling the meager fare that they ate on home visits. These children might insist on returning to a home that could neither support nor tolerate them, and we found it best to delay any further visits to the home until after the age of 12. Children of this age were better able to evaluate the situation realistically. Before the close of latency, fantasy denial permitted the child to ignore the real defects of the home, and undermined motivation to do well in the agency setting. Many of the children were eventually offered college scholarships, but most declined, preferring to return to their old neighborhood. As one child put it, "I'll fit in better there."

Normal and Variant Development of Fantasy

Among poverty groups, latency-age children with the capacity to develop fantasy may still be at risk for the development of an impaired competence in the use of symbols. Fantasy formation is not always of the type that provides comfort and discharge, thus calming and preparing the way for educability. Fantasies may instead become trial actions which prepare for attempts to draw fulfillment from the world of reality. Overstimulation, from either family members or social situations, may prematurely provide real gratification. When the world provides fulfillment in response to an action produced by fantasy, normal progress towards less magical means to achieve goals will stop. Fantasy, having proven itself to be a way to control the world, takes center stage. Symbolic, magical gestures and rituals are emphasized. Intuitive and ritualized approaches are reinforced. Abstract conceptual memory organizations get short shrift.

A 10-year-old boy from a severe poverty area in Brooklyn failed to apply himself in school, though he was bright and well enough organized to succeed. He was a sturdy, good-looking youngster with a single gold ring in his right ear. His fantasy was to be a "street dude." To him this meant patterning himself after older youths he had seen who he claimed lived off the street, stealing pocketbooks from old ladies, and "selling." At the age of 10 he could live like a grownup with money "of his own." More specifically, he could live like one of the grownups he admired. Reading, school, education held no promise for him that could equal the magical short-circuit to manhood provided by acting on his dreams. His world's response to his actions had little to do with causality and design; more likely, they had to do with accidents or customs. No matter to him. He saw himself as one of the controlling masters of his milieu.

In the evaluation of low-SES children for fantasy and symbol skills, there appears another latency-age pattern. There are some children who have little competence in the use of symbols for fantasy formation. They fail to enter fantasy states, and are therefore limited in their ability to attempt the trial actions for which fantasies would have provided the plan. They need leaders or bosses to follow. Their skill levels are low. Their hopes are shallow, as are their abilities to plan through fantasy or to conceive of better ways and times. They do not seek improvement of skills to levels beyond their ken or beyond their limited hopes. Their skill levels remain low, and so they continue in poverty. I recall one such child whom I saw through a psychotic episode. Because of his poor capacity for symbol formation, his episode consisted of diffuse disorganized behavior. He spent hours beating a tree in an attempt to master beatings he had received at the hands of a foster parent. Such diffuse, poorly masked activities characterize the disordered behavior of children whose impaired symbol formation interferes with entering into states of latency.

Poor symbol formation is often the product of affect deprivation so commonly experienced by children of extreme poverty and rarely occurs alone, but rather is usually part of a syndrome consisting of concrete thinking, poor symbolization, and few reported dreams. The syndrome is, clearly, incompatible with the formation of states of latency. A child treated with a technique aimed at improving symbol formation (Sarnoff 1976) should be able to develop fantasies permitting the mastery of humiliation and providing an armature of fantasies around which to work, study, and build future planning and actions. In this way the child learns to plan and to prepare for tomorrow.

Normal and Variant Development of the Cognitive Evaluation of Money

It is worthwhile, in a discussion of poverty, to focus on the conception and understanding of money in the low-SES families described above. If attitudes and cognitive potentials are acquired and fixed during latency, then the most important aspect of latency, from the standpoint of poverty would be that attitudes which perpetuate poverty may be established and fixed in latency.

Concrete and magical concepts of money are transmitted to the child through the precept and example of parents, and are fixed through the locking of cognitive development at the level of rote memory, magical thinking, and concrete thinking. As described above, this occurs as a result of failure to capitalize on the creative potential of the child. The child is locked to the "immediate value" theory of money. In this theory only immediate value of the money is of practical use. Immediate value becomes the only value that money has.

There is a little story that illustrates this well. A man getting off a boat offered to pay a bystander for help with his luggage. The bystander refused, explaining that he did not need the money because he had already eaten lunch! Here is the immediate value theory of money at work. There is only money as cash. There is no concept of money as capital, or as a way to store energy and work in symbolic packages, so that work done today can feed one tomorrow. Hershey (1978) describes a group of workers in England who take out insurance policies, paying their premiums weekly to men who must search the policyholders down in order to collect the money. Say the policyholders, "Unless you call and get the money, you can forget about it!" (p. 27). The concept of insurance against possible future risk is too abstract to attract money away from its use for immediate gratification, (i.e., the price of ale). The search-and-force technique of saving is the main appeal of these policies, whose owners cannot save to ensure a future without duress. In many primitive societies, money has no value. Wealth is judged only in terms of ownership of the means of production, such as cows. The concept of converting the cow into money to bring the family above the level of subsistence is neither valued nor acted upon. There are people in Kenya who live in dung huts though their holdings in livestock put their wealth in the hundreds-of-thousands-of-dollars class.

A failure to achieve the abstract capacity to see money as a symbol, and as such as a means of filling in bad times with the fruits of good years, interferes with the ability to establish stock and sell for profit as well as the ability to save and invest. If an entire social group shares these ways of apprehending money, there will be interference with the creation of wealth, social advancement and interference with the creation of an internal buyer-market system. As a result the population of the poverty group becomes and persists as a unit that is eternally dependent on outsiders for goods and services.

Summary

During the latency period, cultural attitudes are transmitted and the cognitive levels of the codification of memory are organized. Children born to low-SES families tend to have an interrupted, or at least imperfect, latency. They are at high risk for being fixed at cognitive levels not adequate for successful adjustment in industrial society. Interference with the development of cognitive memory organizations needed for sophisticated planning may also result from a failure to develop strong states of latency. Therefore, in the assessment of the latency-age child, the organizations of cognition and of memory should be assessed to see if they are of sufficient strength and adequate type to provide the skills for coping in the social strata and job skill which would be expected from an individual with his personal background.

The Latency-Age Period in Primitive Societies

Our society is rather structured and permits little variation in latency-age adjustments. It is therefore of value to study primitive societies in order to find rare and subtle varieties. In this way one gains access to an understanding of the true degree of flexibility in the potential for cognitive development that—though not often used in our culture—exists during childhood. Certain developmental lines of cognition induced and detectable during the latency years, which will provide skills for survival and advancement in the adult in a given culture, may well condemn the adult of a more complex culture to a menial existence. For the therapist without much background, rare cognitions are apt to be viewed as disconnected oddities without prognostic implications. Their portent for adult adjustment is available to those who are conversant with alternate cognitions in the context of societies in which they form the basis for culturally validated adult function.

This section is intended as an introduction to an extensive but often neglected area of study. A more complete treatment of this material of interest to child therapists can be found in the works of Berry (1971) and Nurcombe (1976). There one will find elaboration of such concepts as the interrelation between childhood socialization practice and adult cognitive style, and the proposal that ecological pressures operate to integrate child-rearing practice and the dominant cognitive style.

Latency-age boys in hunting and gathering societies are introduced to different organizations of cognition and defenses than are comparable youngsters in sedentary farming, pastoral cultures or industrial societies. In primitive societies there are few assigned responsibilities and tasks for boys. Typically, children are closely cared for during the prelatency age period. Latency-age boys are permitted to run relatively free, and early latency-age girls are assigned to help their mothers.

In more evolved cultures, all children are assigned to farming or herding chores, lending whatever help they can to their parents. Traditions of the society, both technical and mythical, are conveyed through close association with parents and elders.

In literate cultures, the children are assigned to specialists in teaching for well-defined periods in order to learn the medium for the transmission of culture (reading). The acquisition of technical skills may be delayed until late adolescence.

Let us turn to a closer look at the hunting and foodgathering society. There is a distinct difference in the assigned roles of latency-age boys and girls. Murphy and Murphy (1974) described this as a classic pattern in primitive societies (p. 173). Girls stay at home with the women and learn the tribal traditions related to food raising, handicrafts, and food preparation. Inhibition of aggression and of sexuality is inculcated. Girls learn to be passive, to sit modestly, to sleep with their thighs tied together, and to remain in the village lest they be raped (Erikson 1945). During latency, women of primitive tribes learn traditions related to drive inhibition and the survival techniques of the tribe. Mythological traditions are not as important in their lives as in the lives of men, except as they relate to menses.

With rare exception (see Malinowski 1962), inhibition of sexual expression during the latency period is demanded of both sexes. Aggression, which is inhibited in girls, is encouraged in boys. Erikson (1945), Murphy and Murphy (1974), and Read (1965) emphasize the freedom of boys, their sadism, and the organization of a peer group that ranges freely outside the village, and that has its own hierarchy and social pattern. The boys usually form two groups, those 6 and 7 and those above 8 years of age. The younger group stays closer to home, while the older group functions more independently. Their activities include hunting with child-size weapons and often, as Read (1965) reports of children in New Guinea, shooting at each other. Ties to the mother are markedly diminished. At the end of latency the boys enter the society of men. Thus most of the transmission of technical and mythological traditions awaits puberty and the acquisition of the physical size and strength that will permit the child to participate

safely in hunting and warfare. At the time of the initiation rites
formally marking the onset of puberty, the traditions of the society
needed for manhood are transmitted. The media of cultural transmission are myths, rituals, interpretation of mystical experiences, pag-
eantry, and the explanation of symbolic pictures and patterns. The
ecological pressure to use this medium consists of successful hunting
and group coherence through shared beliefs and styles of thinking.
The medium of memory is dominated by verbal concepts. The ordering of perceptions and the interpretation of the world are organized
through traditions transmitted and remembered as verbal concepts
(verbal conceptual memory). This technique is encouraged by identification with group and adult patterns.

As the patterns and traditions are acquired, by girls in early
latency and by boys in early adolescence, mores are internalized. Ad-
herence to social rules is enforced, with shame as the superego's motivating affect. Primitive societies consist of small groups. If wrong is
done in the eye of the group, the entire world of the culprit knows.
Early adolescents in primitive society find themselves in a peer group
that controls through shame. This is similar to the use of peer groups
by adolescents in industrial societies to support their defiance of
important adults. In primitive societies the peer group of adolescence
is made up of mature men and women of the culture, who accept the
adolescents as co-workers and peers. This is why there is so little
adolescent crisis and rebellion in primitive societies.

Latency and Cognition in Primitive Societies

In industrial societies abstract, linear, nonmagical thinking dominates. Financial success is the ecological pressure. An understanding of
the implications for the future of current observations is necessary for
competence and survival. The media of memory is dominated by
conceptual abstractions. Verbal memory elements are too limited and
restricted in form to serve for the recognition of more than a few
concretely similar items. Conceptual abstractions permit the recognition of similarities among multiple clusters of concepts, forms, and
actions. The codification and recall of impressions and experiences is
organized around abstractions based on intrinsic characteristics of
objects and situations. This is only one possible form of cognitive
memory, called abstract conceptual memory organization. The development of abstract conceptual memory depends in part on the calm
that permits the acquisition of reading skills, which in literate societies open the door to the knowledge and customs of one's people. Of

equal importance, though, are the examples of cognitive style provided by parents during verbal interactions. Parent–child communication patterns aid the child in selecting the cognitive pattern of memory to be used in society from amongst the cognitive memory potentials (affectomotor, intuitive verbal, verbal conceptual, abstract conceptual, and abstract symbolic forms) that are available to the later latency-age child. This selection occurs between 8 and 12 years of age. If latency is impaired, its development is impaired. There is reason to believe that if this development is not encouraged during latency, it cannot be developed in later life. This would have strong implications for the future of the latency-age youngsters from low-SES groups with impaired or variant cognitive structures during latency.

For boys in primitive societies, the latency period is often one of exclusion from extensive conversational contact with adults. The children for the most part are sent to play and fight in a kingdom of boys outside the village. The sensitive moment for encouraging the development of abstract cognitive memory through precept and example is permitted to pass untouched. Then, at puberty, they are introduced to the magical rituals of the tribe. Magical thinking is emphasized, and memory elements are organized around verbal concepts. Survival of the individual is guaranteed if he shows willingness to surrender individual thought and logic to the requirement that the myths and the traditions of the culture are accepted as logically unchallengeable absolutes. Syncretically, the society itself is preserved from the danger of attack from within since the development of an inquiring, abstracting mind has been blocked. Neither the society nor the individual can long survive logical intrusions from ways of thought that produce creativity and abstract inquiry.

Not all primitive tribes inhibit sexuality during the latency years. In those that do not, the short circuit between need and fulfillment may prevent the emergence of a period of mental reflection during which abstract thinking can be developed. Amongst the Trobriand Islanders, according to Malinowski (1962), "Sexual freedom begins very early, children already taking a great deal of interest in certain pursuits and amusement which come as near sexuality as their unripe age allows" (p. 32). Here there is no latency as we know it, for in our society, children in the latency years are encouraged to deal with their sexual feelings by escaping into fantasy. Sexuality for the Trobriander is experienced for the pleasure of the moment, without reference to its place within causal chains. The cast of all Trobriand thought is of nonlinearity. This means that they codify and remember reality in a manner different from ours. Cultures, as explained by Lee (1950), codify and "experience reality through the use of the specific language and other patterned behavior characteristics of [the] culture, . . . [and] actually grasp reality only as it is presented . . . in this code" (p. 129). "The nature of expectancy, of motivation, of satisfaction [is] based upon a reality which is differently apprehended [amongst the Trobrianders]" (p. 131). "What we consider an attribute of a predicate, is to the Trobriander an ingredient" (p. 131). Linear cause and effect are unknown to them.

Thus illustration of the cognition of a society with a latency different from our own points to the association between nonlinear thinking and limited inhibition of sexuality during the latency period. Insofar as the psychotherapeutic milieu encourages the use of delay, displacement, and substitution symbols, it may create a medium in which abstract thinking, once encouraged, can develop.

Transmission of Cognitive Styles. In our society, parent–child interaction typically encourages the child to think as the parent does. This sets the stage for the transmission of cognitive styles. This can be encouraged by discussions about homework or aid in preparing for a test, the child hears how the parent or therapist solves a problem by reducing it as presented to its intrinsic elements.

The following example illustrates this process. A father and his 11-year-old son made their way to a museum after leaving a rehearsal of *Pagliacci*, an opera taking much of its content from the antique Italian theater form commedia dell'arte. At the museum they came upon a puppet display depicting the characters of the commedia dell'arte. The father, recognizing the relationship between the display and the opera, asked his son what he saw in the museum exhibit. The boy looked at the puppets and tried to create a story (myth?) that explained them and what they were doing. He finally admitted that the characters reminded him of no story that he knew. The father had encouraged the boy to make associations to that which he saw; the boy had tried to link it to preexisting verbal concepts, such as a scene from a familiar story. The father finally explained the abstract relationship of the puppets to the opera, and the boy caught on immediately. A potential way of organizing perceptions and memory was activated. In an instant the boy had acquired a piece of information and been introduced to the art of abstraction: stepping back from an experience and linking it to a prior experience through intrinsic similarities in concepts achieved through reducing each experience to a form so short that any further reduction would impair its identity (one of the definitions of abstraction). This resulted in the expansion of his ability to codify and remember in abstract categories.

At what great disadvantage is the child brought up in an excited, non-education-oriented home, where parents speak little to children? Latency in low socioeconomic groups is marked by this special form of starvation. It is the deprivation of the stimulation needed to perfect and give primacy to the skills of abstraction, codification and memory required for success in an industrial society as an adult. Poverty, insofar as it derives from the lack of skills described, may be viewed as transmitted from one generation to the next. It is not only an economic condition; it has characteristics reminiscent of preliterate traditions. Preliterate peoples live in societies in which such cognition fits well, but in our society it is a preparation for failure.

In assessing a child for therapy one should remember that his psyche is still being formed. Interpretation of fantasy derivatives, confrontation, and working-through are certainly vital as in the therapy of adults, but the fact of ongoing growth mandates a special concern in the child therapist. One must also be aware of the nature of ongoing maturation and development, and ask whether the developing functions will serve in the adolescent and adult world for which the child is being prepared. In this section, we have noted variant pathways of cognitive growth which, though leading to a style of adult adjustment that may be adequate under some circumstances, is likely to limit the potential for the adult in modern society. Hopefully the codification of these styles of cognition will provide a base for evaluating potential difficulties and for establishing strategies for the psychotherapeutic prophylactic remediation of relative cognitive deficiencies.

Clinical Aspects of Assessment

The diagnostic assessment of emotionally disturbed latency-age children requires techniques and knowledge different from those commonly employed in assessing adults. The latency period is characterized by sequences of progression and regression. There exist successive subperiods, each with its own normal pattern of mental function. Prelatency; early, middle, and late latency; and late latency–early adolescence are normally characterized by cognitive and psychological features which, if found in the later adolescent or adult, might represent marked pathology.

The clinician who assesses a latency-age child from the psychiatric standpoint must be equipped with a body of background knowledge which exceeds that required in the differential diagnosis of adults and adolescents.

Two factors particularly complicate assessment in latency. First, the organization of thought and memory in the child consists of expressions, cognitions and awarenesses that are foreign to the adult interviewer. Play, toys, drawings and ludic symbols (three dimensional items used to represent latent, unconscious thought contents) are often the source of information and sometimes the only medium for communication between child and interviewer. Second, the latency-age child, in contrast to the adult and at times the adolescent, is brought for the interview against his will; his symptoms are a weapon that, though alarming to his caretakers, may be a source of pride and attention for him. Special interview techniques are required with the latency-age child in zones of assessment not germaine to assessment in later years.

Zones of Assessment for Normalcy

The assessment of the latency-age child requires consideration of two zones of function (Sarnoff 1976): socially defined behavioral normalcy and biologically defined maturational normalcy.

Socially Defined Behavioral Normalcy

States of latency require the capacities to symbolize, to fantasize, to displace, and to delay (Sarnoff 1976). To evaluate the strength of these, one asks the parents about dreams told and fantasies revealed or played out. In the session with the child, encouragement of fantasy permits one to see if the child is calmed or excited by his play. If the fantasy communicates and leads to exploration of the child's experience, the latency is good and psychotherapy, if needed, has a good prognosis. If the fantasy is used to hide from the interviewer, the prognosis is poorer and special therapeutic strategies must be devised.

Biologically Defined Maturational Normalcy

Ludic Demise: Readiness for Adolescence as Reflected in the Symbolizing Function. The latency age period is marked by constant maturational change, consisting of a remarkable forward flow of phase-specific growth in physical, physiological, psychological, and cognitive areas. The persistent characteristic which defines the latency period psychologically is the coexistence of the structure of latency with the cognitive capacity to utilize ludic (play) symbols during waking periods, just as dream symbols are used in sleep, to master trauma and instinctual stress. When the ludic symbol is lost (at about 12 years of age), one of the most important steps (*ludic demise*) in psychological readiness to begin adolescence has taken place. Clinically, this step may be detected both in the therapy situation and the diagnostic interview: the child simply prefers to talk, and disdains or eschews use of the playroom or toys.

In my practice, I have both a consultation room and a playroom. They are connected, and free movement between them is usual. At the beginning of each session I provide access to both, giving the child a choice. The child who has moved away from ludic symbols is under pressure to relieve stresses created by object relations and the environment, and therefore the consultation room is chosen. In the ongoing psychotherapy situation, it is remarkable to see the transition that constitutes ludic demise. Though the transition is at times short, usually there is a period of some months during which the child is unpredictable in his choice of room, and may even wander between them as the forward movement of his cognition ebbs and flows. There is no question that during the transition, unresolvable stress situations produce regressions that reactivate play as defense. Yet there is a point beyond which no more such regressions are possible. At this point reactive depressions, temper tantrums, rages, and frank attempts to manipulate the environment with little subtlety begin to dominate the life of the child.

Readiness in the Comprehension of Environmental Phenomena. Before a child can be expected to evaluate and react to danger in new situations, he must have the capacity to comprehend accurately that which he sees or with which he comes into contact. Piaget (1945) has reviewed extensively the stages characterizing the development of the capacity to comprehend and theorize about phenomena. Early in latency, the symbolic-intuitive phase is foremost: events are interpreted concretely, and intuition, symbols, and prior experience form the basis for conclusions. By the age of 7, the child is able to make abstract interpretations of concrete events that are seen or experienced. By the age of 12, the child can interpret abstractions through the use of remembered abstractions about concrete things.

The Developmental March of Persecutory Symbols. The manifest forms of symbols undergo a maturation. Before 8½ years of age, symbols for persecutory forces have an amorphous quality. After 8½ they become more human in form. At 11 years of age symbols consist of realistic figures existing only in the mind. At adolescence, the realistic figures are drawn from the truly real. Real people are enlisted to live or play out the child's fantasies. Note how confusing it would be if one were to lose sight of the phase-specific normalcy of the symbolic form chosen, and judging the child by adult standards, call abnormal the normal fantastic persecutory symbol of early latency.

Assessment of Memory Systems. Perhaps the most important aspect of developmental cognition in the latency-age child, for the diagnostician who must keep in mind therapeutic strategies, is the development of the mental organizations that carry the function of memory. People with emotional problems suffer from abnormal persistence of memory, which results from impaired mastery and processing of elements of recall. Interpretations and comments must be geared to the undoing of psychopathogenetic memory elements. Clearly the therapist's interventions must be shaped by consideration for the child's level of memory organization and memory processing. Impairments in efferent, retentive, and afferent aspects of memory must be identified in the context of what is normal for the age. Interventions must be geared to the cognitive skills and memory capacities of the child. It is no use to make an interpretation to a child in a form that he will be unable to process into memory so that it will be available for use on the next day or during the next session.

There are three periods of memory organization that are present or may develop during the latency period; interpretations and interventions must be aimed to reach the child at the level at which he is functioning. The levels, in order of increasing maturation, are the affectomotor, verbal conceptual, and abstract conceptual memory organizations. At each level, recall may occur as the result of a purposive scanning of the registration of past events, or through the spontaneous calling to mind of memory elements which results from the compulsion to repeat and master.

Affectomotor Memory Organization. The affectomotor memory organization begins in the first years of life. As its name implies, it consists of motor components and affective components. The motor component, the first acquired, consists of purposeful modifications of innate patterns of motor activity. Essentially, the memory contents of this component are motor syntaxes. Affective and sensory stimuli can effect the spontaneous recall of these syntaxes. Because of the early and primitive nature of such memory responses, they are of marked use during the assessment of a child. Involving the child in motoric expression during a diagnostic interview can tap otherwise unavailable areas of memory. The silent child can be encouraged to play. The child who is asked to shape with his hands a remembered object under discussion may thus be brought into concrete motoric contact with the content of his concerns and, once focused on this representation, be able to widen his ability to represent it in words (codify for recall in words).

The affective component of the affectomotor memory organization consists of the ability to evoke recall of experienced patterns of affects, perceptions, and bodily postures which were associated with the original event. It represents the ability to organize recall around sensory experiences. These are usually recalled in their entirety. This produces a rather inefficient medium for carrying experiences into the future. Affective memory ability develops during the first year of life.

Conceptual Memory. Conceptual memory is defined as the ability to evoke recall of learned patterns in the form of verbal signifiers, such as words and related symbols. Conceptual memory may be divided into the earlier-appearing verbal conceptual memory and the relatively late-appearing abstract conceptual memory. Verbal conceptual memory involves recall of earlier experiences through socially dictated verbal schemata for naming. Abstract conceptual memory is defined as recall of experiences through verbalized abstract concepts representative of the intrinsic substance of things and events.

Verbal-Conceptual Memory Organization Early Latency. Verbal conceptual memory organization may be operative by the third year of life, and becomes the primary means of memory at about 6 years of age, with the onset of latency. The extent of its use is determined by environmental and social factors. In highly literate cultures, its use becomes intense. Verbal constructs are used for the retention of events in memory, the interpretation of perceptions, and the process of recall. The process locks its practitioners into their culture, for they cease to see or recall things as they are. Instead they come to see only the slogans of their faith.

It is the task of the child therapist to diagnose the nature of the child patient's verbal conceptual memory organization. Findings should then be applied to interpretive approaches to the child. The therapist should modify his input to be sensation- and motor-oriented with the child who records information through the sensory rather than the verbal route.

One of the therapist's goals may be to help the child develop more efficient ways of perceiving and identifying with his culture and its requirements; in this case strengthening of the verbal conceptual memory organization can be a product of therapeutic influence. The presence of the therapist to interpret action or experiences on a verbal level can encourage the patient to do the same.

Abstract Conceptual Memory Organization. Abstract conceptual memory organization is a maturational modification of conceptual memory. It appears first at about 8 years of age. It consists of the interpretation of events in terms of their intrinsic substance coupled with the retention of this knowledge in memory through abstractions which are at times wordless. A common school task of this level is "getting the main idea" of a reading passage. In life situations, the tasks of "reading people quickly" or "sizing things up" are parallel examples. By the age of 12 the accumulation of abstractions in memory should reach the point that there has been developed background to be applied to the interpretation of other abstractions. Clinically, this is tested by asking the patient to interpret proverbs, such as "A rolling stone gathers no moss." Some form of abstraction should be available by early adolescence. For instance, an answer that "A person who wanders from place to place does not make friends" is acceptable at that age, while "It knocks the moss off when it rolls" is a sign of immature, concrete thinking.

Zones of Assessment for Pathology

The latency-age child is totally dependent on his parents. Nowhere is he fully autonomous. In psychotherapeutic clinical situations he is mostly a reluctant participant.

Verbal fluency and self-reflection are only slightly developed when applied to emotions and affects; this is a phase characteristic. Experiences are just beginning to be stored in memory in the form of words. The use of reductive abstractions is just beginning. The capacity to create higher-order abstractions to be used in comprehending interpretations in psychotherapy begins to develop only in the later phase of latency, and becomes fully functional only in adolescence. Before these skills develop, conversations with children do not produce remembered abstract insights. Instead, attempts to provide logical answers and lines of association may stir up affects, which, in turn, initiate regressions to symbolic and intuitive means of recall. Excited fantasy and play swamp logical answers, creating barriers to communication that are impassible to the therapist who seeks only to dispense or acquire data which is packaged in verbal form.

Such factors and limitations shape the nature of the assessment process during latency. A poor sense of temporal continuity and hazy grasp of the past in the memory of the child forces the diagnostician to turn to responsible observers to fill in information which the child is not capable of remembering particularly in relation to early childhood. Family contexts, expectations, and ambitions are rarely available directly from the child. Even recent events, traumas, and dreams are often available only through parents. Frequently the child has processed them through the mastery tool of communicative speech (for instance, by telling his parents his dreams), resulting in dissipation and repression. In clinical interviews with the child, significant recent events, traumas, and memories often have undergone a conversion. As a result associated uncomfortable affects no longer attract consciousness; the events have been translated by the structure of latency into fantasies with low valence for attracting affect. For these reasons, the assessment of the child requires interviews with both structured components (asking direct questions) and nonstructured components (following fantasy), supplemented by reports from schools, parents, courts, hospitals, and other significant adults.

The assessment of latency-age psychopathology involves the following avenues of approach: the parent interview; the clinical interview with the child; educational and clinical testing; a report from the school; and reports of previous therapists and other professionals, including the pediatrician. The assessment of latency age psychopathology will require that the following Zones of Pathology be considered and, where indicated, investigated.

A. Social Maladjustment
   1. Separation problems
   2. Affect starvation
   3. Drug use
   4. Child abuse
   5. Sibling rivalry
   6. Lack of socialization
   7. Failure to develop behavioral constancy
   8. Ethical individuation conflicts
B. Organicity
   1. Cognitive problems (central processing disorders)
      a. Learning disabilities
      b. Cognitive social discordance

2. Mental retardation
3. Hyperactivity (with attention deficit)
4. Epileptic disorders
   a. Petit mal
   b. Epileptic explosive personality traits
   c. Fugues
   d. Temporal lobe epilepsy
5. Pavors
   a. Nocturnus
   b. Diurnus
6. Depression
   a. Endogenous
   b. Bipolar
7. Confusional states
   a. Postconcussive
   b. Tumor
   c. Hemorrhage
   d. Granulomatous Meningitis
8. Other emotional illnesses associated with physical conditions

C. Mental Illness Entities
   1. Schizophrenia (disorders of relatedness and the sense or testing of reality)
      a. Childhood
         i. Autism
         ii. Symbiotic psychosis
         iii. Prepubescent
         iv. Associated with cognitive impairment
      b. Adult schizophrenia of early onset
         i. Late latency–early adolescence
         ii. Paranoid type associated with premature puberty
      c. Miscellaneous
         i. Schizophreniform psychosis of late childhood
         ii. Regressive persecutory fantasy states of late latency
         iii. Asparger syndrome
   2. Depressions (affect disorders)
      a. Reactive
      b. Endogenous
      c. Bipolar
   3. Neuroses (consistent symptom patterns with anxiety)
      a. Phobia
      b. Hysteria
      c. Obsession compulsive disorder

D. Psychosomatic Disorders
1. Asthma
2. Hives
3. Anesthesias
E. Disorders in the maintenance of states of latency
1. Failure to enter latency
a. Poor symbolizing function
b. Impaired abstract thinking
c. Wernicke's aphasia
d. Impaired capacity for object relations
e. Impaired displacement and delay
2. Regression from the capacity for latency
a. Overstimulation
b. Affect-porous symbols
3. Characterological impulse discharge disorder

The advantage in clinical assessment belongs to the patient whose examiner has a background that informs differential diagnosis.

Interviewing the Parent

A great deal of the information needed by the examiner in his search for clues to the contribution of the child's psyche to his current problems is to be found in patterns of development. To detect these one must turn to the parents, rather than to the child, since these are areas of experience in which the growing child has been more participant than witness. Often the very reason that the child is brought to therapy is unknown or incomprehensible to the child. The information provided may help to streamline the interview with the child. One can often identify the diagnosis or problem quickly if the interview with the parents has helped to focus one's attention on the appropriate portion of the differential diagnosis. Furthermore, personal histories of parents and other family members are required in order to establish familial vesanic traits (the family history of mental illness or tendencies to mental illness). For these reasons, we start with input from the parents when we initiate the clinical assessment of the latency-age child.

This is not to imply that we cannot learn from the direct examination of the child. The findings of the direct loosely structured clinical interview are primary.

The best way to train in the differential diagnosis of zones of pathology (cognition, defenses, and symptoms and signs) in the latency-age child is to interview children after reading only a single sentence describing the chief complaint. This is followed by a direct interview with the child (see below). This in turn should be followed by a presentation by the examiner of his findings. Through a spontaneous presentation, a meta-awareness of the information gained becomes conscious. Such an awareness, stored in memory becomes a part of a body of knowledge and experience. This provides the examiner with a clinical background of observations and conclusions with which to reflect and compare when doing later interviews.

It is not essential for diagnosis that parents be seen. Those of us who have worked in foster care know well the futility of waiting for an early or even recent life or developmental history before proceeding with assessment. Often the parents are simply not available. Still, children have patterned signs and symptoms within their behavior and personalities. These await discovery, naming, and therapeutic intervention by the child therapist. They can be obtained through the direct interview with the child.

Psychotherapy requires maximum support and cooperation from parents. Thus parents, when available, should be seen early in the assessment process in order to establish a working relationship with them. This can be fostered by an interview which permits an early initial contact with the potential future therapist. In this way parents do not feel isolated and disregarded. While the child is in therapy, frequent contact should be encouraged to maintain a supportive alliance between parents and therapist. Concurrently, the parents serve as a source of information that the child tends not to bring to the therapy spontaneously, such as dreams, fantasies, traumatic experiences, experiences that have succumbed to the workings of the structure of latency, and experiences lost to recall over time, especially over vacations or breaks in therapy. Direct interviews with children bring out personality structures in extenso, while fantasy contents and structures are only detected piecemeal.

Parent interviews during assessment should blend imperceptibly into supportive interviews with parents that take place after therapy has started. The fact of parental contact with the therapist should not come as a surprise to the child. It is not emphasized, however, since emphasis tends to dilute the transference. The child is usually told in passing that there are meetings with the parents. When a phone contact is made the child may answer the phone. It is not necessary to obtain the latency-age child's consent for interviews with parents, a procedure that is mandatory when working with adolescents.

Confidentiality of the young patient's communications is not a major issue, as it is with the adolescent. The child's actual experiences usually do not go beyond the parent's knowledge. One must especially beware not to convey cute things said by the child during therapy sessions. A child may easily interpret such "harmless" revelations as a betrayal. Latency-age children love to be laughed along with. They despise being laughed at.

I prefer not to see parents and children together. There is danger that the alliance between adults (therapist and parents) derived from similarities of experience and cognition will be interpreted by the child as a sign of disloyalty, betrayal, or simply being left out. Therapy is made more difficult thereby.

Sometimes, in the initial interview, the child refuses to leave the parent. To accommodate this possibility, my office is arranged so that while the child and I are in the playroom the parent can be in plain sight through a large glass partition in the consultation room wall. The windowed wall is usually covered by a semiclosed set of blinds.

The initial assessment interview with parents should be semi-structured. This interview is not meant to fill in the blanks in a questionnaire that will automatically identify the diagnosis or the problem. Rather, it is an open-ended search for patterns to put into focus a differential diagnosis.

There are specific kinds of information to be sought from parents. The initial contact should, whenever possible, be held with both parents. The advantage to this is that one can observe areas of agreement and disagreement, conflicts, and identifications with the child. If both parents cannot be seen, the parent who more closely observed the early life milestones and the growth of the child (most often the mother) is the preferred interviewee.

What is actually done in the interview? I like to begin by getting the names of each sibling, their ages, their adjustments, and any particular problems. I ask the parents' ages and their work and educational histories. I also ask whether the grandparents are alive and where they live. This initial exchange will obviate interruptions once the parents begin to tell their tale.

Finally I ask, "How can I help you?" The answer to this question is the chief complaint. It will be used as the takeoff point for any one of a series of questions related in the mind of the interviewer to a syndrome of symptomatology or a life history. This in turn is linked to a syndrome of childhood psychopathology which has been singled out because they can be identified with the chief complaint.

The first questions should relate to any break in logic or any disorder in developmental sequence detected by the therapist in the initial moments of the interview. In these assessment steps, the findings are not diagnostic; they only point the way to areas of investigation. This is true in both the interview with the parents and the direct interview with the child.

Perhaps the child is old for his class (possible mental deficiency). Maybe a parent had a brilliant academic career but poor business or professional achievement (perhaps due to a brain syndrome following an accident or schizophrenic decompensation). A family living arrangement in which the maternal grandmother and all the maternal aunts live on the same floor in an apartment building should alert one to a developmental and life history with separation–individuation overtones. The nature, source and history of such failures is pursued.

Details of developmental milestones often yield important leads and data. A history of fecal play during the first year of life should prompt questions relating to intermittent maternal depression during that period. Delay in onset of speech or walking beyond 3 years demands investigation of possible mental retardation.

A failure to develop anxiety dreams at 26 months indicates a delayed and perhaps impaired symbolizing function; to round out the picture, parents should be asked about their children's dreams and reactions to fantasy. Findings of indicators of an impaired symbolizing function in the child's history primes the interviewer to pursue certain questions in the direct interview with the child, but the actual syndrome cannot be determined until the child is interviewed and tells his own story.

Nightmares, especially those whose content cannot be remembered the next morning, call for questions about withdrawal, auditory sensitivity, paucity of friends, poor relatedness, and other evidences of an adjustment with schizophrenic coloring. The same high level of suspicion is indicated if the child has these symptoms and sleeps well and a history of night fears in early latency is absent.

A transient obsessional symptom in late latency can be an indicator of a problem of ethical individuation implying that the child is experiencing difficulty in separating from the ethical standards of his parents. A series of questions about intergenerational conflict should be prompted by this indication. The answers may provide a detailed, to-the-point, and vital telling of problems with ethical individuation that accompany the child's entrance into the world of peers, with its new and unfamiliar ethical guides to behavior. Psychosomatic symptoms and short acute paranoid episodes in late latency may have similar implications.

Sudden unexplained destructive actions point toward hallucinations. Sometimes more than one possibility is presented, and the rules of differential diagnosis must be invoked. For instance, a child who repeatedly arrives at school without a homework assignment or money for a treat, which had been requested by the teacher the day before, could be poorly related or absentminded. He might be suffering from regular breaks in consciousness because of petit mal, and so might fail to hear the assignments. He might be hearing impaired. He might suffer from a disorder of auditory memory retention. This is a central processing disorder. In such a condition the command is heard but not remembered. Each possibility must be followed up with a search for other signs or symptoms that are associated with these syndromes, or the absence of same, which lessens the likelihood of a given syndrome or disease.

All one needs is a break in the information given by the parents in the direction of a sign of an identifiable pathology. The ideas and questions flow out and widen like a wide alluvial fan till. Though the context seems to be one of ease and conversation, all the ground is covered.

For example, a history might give clues that the latency-age child has been neglected. In such a situation, one finds in the parent interview signs of affect starvation: poor impulse control, difficulties in school, poor object constancy, and aggressive outbursts in the face of disappointments in relationships. One is thus tuned in to look for the following signs in the direct interview with the child: concrete thinking, two-person fantasies instead of three-person oedipal ones, overfriendliness, impaired symbolizing function, and auditory hallucinations (which, though rare, can be elicited with ease if present).

Similarly, the parent-derived history may point toward the syndrome of the rejected child: one who is loved and cared for, but held at a distance because of a neurotic complex on the part of the mother. Fears, phobias, obsessions, guilt, anxieties, and evening fears should be watched for in the direct interview with the child. When told of slowed cognitive growth in the presence of normal intelligence, and such subtle signs as discomfort when riding on the merry go round, one is signalled to look for signs of organicity (easy distractability, disorganized figure drawing) in the interview with the child.

Psychotic underpinnings are often telegraphed by parents in the interview. Parents may tell of vesanic traits in the family, and may recall that as a baby the child molded, instead of cuddling, when held. Such a child is usually also reported to have had poor peer relationships, a fear of separation from the mother, and an absence of persecutory fantasies in the early years of latency. The possibility of a schizophrenic process is implied, and becomes a focus of investigation in the clinical interview with the child. Guardedness, suspiciousness, the use of evocative symbols, hallucinations (which must be approached subtly, in stepwise fashion, if they are to be elicited at all), concrete thinking beyond 11 years of age, and the first appearance of externalized persecutors at 11 years of age are to be expected, or at the least pursued. Definitive pathological signs may eventually be found in the direct interview with the child, and the parent interview facilitates the search.

Since each new finding indicates questions to be asked of the parent and explorations to be pursued with the child, it is wise to jot down any question that must be delayed until it can be answered by observations, testing and queries during the interview with the child. For instance, if it is reported that the child has difficulty reading, one would add a series of reading paragraphs to the interview with the child.

The Direct Interview with the Child

Not only the assessment, but also the later course of treatment may turn on the initial clinical contact with the latency-age child. For this reason, this meeting should be arranged with the greatest care. After all, first impressions count. Unwilling, angry, defiant latency-age children may not be willing to be interviewed; they should be left with toys and observed at play. After a few such sessions, the examiner becomes a familiar person and conversation may be started on the basis of a budding friendship. This approach is most useful when the child thinks that coming for an interview indicates that he is viewed as severely mentally ill. The early latency child often has difficulty in separating from the parent for about the first fifteen minutes of contact. As mentioned above, one should place the parent in visual reach of the child, but in another room. Once the child has become accustomed to contact with the no-longer-unfamiliar interviewer, the parent may return to the waiting area. A child who is fearful of leaving the parent will follow the parent into the examining area (playroom) in the office. This is also useful at the end of the session should the child not wish to leave. A parent who begs the child to leave the office, necessitating the giving up of a newly found treasure (a playroom toy), is less effective in achieving departure than the mother who simply states that she is leaving, and goes. Usually the child follows swiftly with a whoop. If he does not, the shallow nature of the separation fear becomes grist for the diagnostic mill. It hints that the child's interest in sado-masochistically provoking his parent outweighs his fear of losing her.

A most useful assessment tool can be the drawing-a-person test. This is a good ice-breaker for the shy child, and in addition provides nonverbal access to the ego and personality of the child. Level of cognitive development, body image, sexual identity, organicity, mood, intelligence, presence of hallucinations, superego formation, reality testing, whether the child is in latency, and types of fantasy have been accessed through figure drawings, according to some authors (Di Leo 1970, 1973, Fein 1976, Machover 1958). I have found them to be useful in these ways only after years of experience. In general, draw-a-person is valuable not as a definitive diagnostic tool, but as a source of topics and questions for the interview.

Though the initial interview style is, for the most part, a function of the examiner's personal technique, there are certainly lower limits to the way that information can be sought. Bluntness and directness are often lost on the latency-age child, whose management of painful affects and experiences tends to involve displacement, masking, and diffusion of the problem. Such children are also guarded and mistrustful, for they have no real prior experience against which to compare the interview. Some effort at putting the latency-age child at ease with relatively neutral conversation is often helpful. Their tendency to use elaborate defense is less in evidence in discussion of neutral areas such as school, facts, sports, TV, and movies. When one is setting at ease the child who gives promise of a verbal interview, these areas are useful introductions to the fact that verbalization can be comfortable and is preferred.

Should the child drift into fantasy or play in a manner that interdicts further verbal communication, the content of the discussion just before the break in verbal communication should be noted. It often can be used to detect the topic that causes regressions. This can be of value in two ways. First, it tells the therapist what to avoid in order to keep conversation going. Second, it indicates areas of difficulty which must be dealt with at home and in future therapy sessions to produce a minimization of acting up behavior and other regressions. A working-through of the internalized relationships (such as parent/child punisher/victim fantasies) or latent fantasies based on traumatic situations (such as those relating to sibling rivalry or feelings of neglect by parents) can be the whole therapy in those whose problems lie in their fantasies rather than in impaired ego functions.

In any assessment it is necessary to differentiate between two sets of ideas which may inform behavior and produce acted-out fantasies. The first are reflections of an interaction, past or present, between parent and child. The second are those acted out fantasies which are distorted internalizations of past experiences. The former occurs in only one place, either the home or the school. The latter go with the child wherever he may roam. It seems to be written in his heart. The former requires parent counseling, and is seen as the province of the family therapist. The latter requires a psychoanalytically-oriented dynamic approach, and is the province of the child therapist or analyst.

This brings us to the question of the importance of fantasy in human psychopathology. Often pathology is defined in terms of ego functions and related regressions, or control of or tolerance for affect. Fantasy alone can at times be the key to understanding pathology. Knowledge of areas of conflict, often represented in fantasy, which produce regressions and activate ego pathology is vital. The therapist can apply this knowledge in protecting the patient from regression, either through environmental manipulation or psychotherapeutic working-through. Thus it is important to study fantasy to learn whether it is a causal link in the chain of factors that produce psychopathological signs and symptoms. Depression is sometimes, though rarely, endogenous in children; it is usually reactive, and in sustained cases may be rooted in an internalized fantasy. Thus the study of fantasy in the child, usually through play techniques, is an important part of the initial interview.

Fantasy is only part of the picture in the origin of psychopathology. Jones (1957) quoted Freud's comment, when asked about an assessment of the mental illness of Nietzsche, to the effect that everyone has conflicts. There are situations in which "conflicts fade into the background of the etiology" (p. 190). Chambers (1985) rings a similar knell when he states, "Play techniques are suitable for assessing fantasy and symbolic meaning, but not symptoms" (p. 696). Assuming that symptoms such as depression or phobias are products of structural pathology, that is, aberrant ego function in regression and states of stress, implies that there are times when the evaluator must look beyond fantasy to faults in the ego that give shape to the communication between memory, fantasy, and the world.

Just the detection of the presence or absence of symptoms is not enough; the interviewer must investigate the context of the symptom. Hallucinations, for example, may be detected by the following technique. When clued in by parental reports of "absences," or a child's drifting of attention in the interview, one can ask the child to talk about aggression. Then one can ask about dreaming, and ask if the child talks to people in his dreams. This should be followed with the question of whether such a phenomenon (hearing someone talking while alone) occurs while awake. If the child reports in the affirmative, then ask which side, if outside or inside the head, if on the right or left, and if the voice is a man or a woman. The localization of the voice indicates confirming information and a cognitive organization that is sufficiently sharp to conceptualize auditorization of thought (hallucinations). A child who denies hearing voices does not necessarily lack hallucinatory symptoms. Some youngsters are so disorganized that they cannot identify their pathological experiences in terms recognizable to untrained adult observers. If the child is insufficiently sure whether he thinks, hears or senses a presence, but senses that something lets him know that his whole family is dead, a blurred cognition is indicated. A study of central processing functions is indicated. If the voice is clearly identified by the child but speaks with a predicate identification thinking disorder (Despert 1948), schizophrenia should be considered.

When a child has trouble learning or reading, we are often content to stop at saying that he has a learning disability without giving thought to the fact that learning is only one of the areas affected by disorders of the central processing system (Chalfant 1969). Disordered cognition can affect the way a child responds to being touched, and the way he can remember, obey, and develop prudence, which is importantly informed by the capacity to hear admonitions and remember them before incorporating them into the conscience. A child who cannot recall sufficiently to bring money for lunch when visiting a museum, though having been told and being well intended, will suffer not only from an inability to learn but also from hunger, humiliating comments, an engendered low self-picture, and a sense of inadequacy.

There is much to be pursued in the diagnostic interview with the child. The idea of an interview that does not follow a structured form, but grows along lines suggested by previous answers is the best basis for an interview that will be sharp and thorough and flexible.

In spite of free form, the interview should yield information in the following areas:

1. Appearance and behavior, orientation and relatedness
2. Thought content and predominant fantasies and fantasy structures (including whether internalized and whether productive of regressions)

3. Organization of cognition, thought, and memory
4. Affect and mood (including the wish to hurt the self, if present)
5. Impulse control in session
6. Major interests and reported relatedness to friends
7. Future planning and life ambitions
8. Capacity to stand apart and look at himself
9. Strength of the structure of latency
10. Nature of the symbolizing function (are symbols defensive, or do affects pour through?)
11. Level of superego development
12. Capacity to utilize ludic symbols
13. Minor neurological findings
14. Status of the central processing system

Educational Testing

Educational testing can make a major contribution to the assessment of the latency-age child when learning problems are suggested. It may demonstrate and specifically delineate central processing disorders and related learning disabilities which, often hidden and present from early on, are contributors to self-image reduction and disordered function. I have seen children so sick that they did not have the cognitive apparatus to establish well-organized symptoms. This masked diagnosis. Through educational testing the role of subtle organic factors in impaired central processing can be elaborated and their understanding enhanced.

Outside Data

Much of the latency-age child's life takes place outside the home and away from structured and semistructured interviews. Many symptoms and many strengths will show up in school performance and related activities. It is desirable to obtain information from outside sources, such as schools, prior therapists, and other professionals, especially the child's pediatrician, who can often give an objective long term view of the child's family and problems.

Summary

The assessment of the latency-age child is presented from the standpoint of emphasis on the detection of the actual contribution of the personality of the child to the problem that brings the child to treatment. The influence of the opinions of informants is reduced to indicators of areas to be explored and confirmed through the direct examination of *the individual child*. In this way, the assessment of the child becomes the basis for the creation of psychotherapeutic strategies rather than for the submergence of the personality of the child in a sea of social and familial personalities. Thus an approach is opened that makes way for a therapy that will prepare the child for his own life and individuality rather than to a conformance with the demands of others.

Chapter 5

Psychotherapeutic Techniques

The therapy that will be described in this chapter is concerned in the main with the treatment of neurotic and characterological conditions and disorders of reality testing in children aged 6 to 12. These conditions impair the abilities needed for the development and organization, production, and maintenance of states of latency. Conversely, in the style of a vicious cycle, the absence of latency defenses intensifies the symptomatology of these pathologies. Learning disabilities and organic brain disease are not the targets of the treatment modalities to be described, although to some extent they may be useful in youngsters with these conditions in dealing with cognitive immaturity and social maladjustment, especially where states of calm are striven for but poorly mastered by the child.

It is essential to the maturation of any child as a social being that these states of calm be achieved. It is during such states that most social learning is acquired. The ego skills exercised in the development of the mental functions (e.g., fantasy formation) that are used in maintaining states of calm form the groundwork for the development of reality-oriented future planning as the child enters adolescence. Therapeutic attention is required for the states of disordered mood and behavior that mark failures in attempting to attain the latency state. Attention should also be directed to the deficiencies that result when the development of latency states fails.

Background

Childhood has a history all its own. It is the history of a minority too weak to defend itself and in constant need of advocates. As strikingly portrayed by De Mauss (1975), the history of human attitudes toward childhood is only now just beginning to touch the cultural horizon at which children are perceived as individuals with needs and personalities independent of parental goals, and as creatures to be understood rather than herded and manipulated. Child-oriented psychotherapy is a part of this history.

Only lately in the history of childhood has there come the discovery that there is a specific organization of the personality (latency) that imparts characteristics to the years 6 to 12. These characteristics develop independently of ordinary physical growth and are subject to pathological alterations and influences. As such, they may be enhanced or modified by psychotherapeutic interventions.

Prior to 1900, awareness that a child's behavior is motivated and that children have an emotional inner life appears in the writings of the occasional intuitive observer. The Spanish mock epic of the late Middle Ages "Lazarillo of Tormes" depicts a boy who is capable of self-reflection and remorse. In the mid-nineteenth century, Felix Descuret (De Saussaure 1946) viewed troubled children with an understanding of their needs, and wrote of the resolution of jealousy and emotional discomfort, with insight into the psychological workings of the inner world of the child. A number of other sources could be quoted to demonstrate that an awareness of the emotional life of the child has long been available. Such an awareness was occasionally used by gifted people, independent of organizations and educational disciplines.

It was not until 1896 that Freud (1950) first detected distinguishing characteristics of the latency period that set childhood apart. At first all that was perceived was a relative paucity of recollections from this period during the psychoanalysis of adults. This was apparently sufficient to call attention to the period for further study. During the first quarter of the twentieth century, knowledge of the period grew until the latency period came to be viewed as a period of calm between the early infantile sexual life and the burgeoning sexuality of adolescence. The calm attained during this period was at first explained by the growth of mechanisms of defense. These mechanisms were capable of transforming the moral demands of society into patterns of internal control that kept the drives in check, and shaped the drives when the efflorescence of bodily growth and instinctual energies that marks adolescence began. This view of latency held sway until 1926, when Freud declared that in latency "the sexual urges diminish in strength" (1926c, p. 210). From that point on, this became the most widely accepted general principle for understanding the quiet behavior of latency-age children. This theory obviated the development of concepts related to cognitive and ego growth that could be used as the basis for developing a psychotherapeutic strategy for dealing with troubled latency-age youngsters. Fortunately, some workers continued to advance Freud's earlier ideas. Recently the concept of an ego structure of latency has been introduced, reflecting the view that latency calm is the product of the maturation of ego functions. This view is forced upon us by the observations that calm behavior is inconsistent in children, and that some children experience no latency at all. This theoretical orientation provides the basis for a psychotherapy for latency-age children.

Failure to enter latency and marked breakdowns in latency calm become important target syndromes in the psychotherapy of latency-age children. The appearance of such behavior, though not necessarily discomforting to child or parent, has predictive value in relation to social adjustment in adolescence and adulthood (see Chapters 2 and 3). The adjustments in fantasy that help the latency-age child master humiliating situations are the forerunners of the future planning skills vital to individual adjustment in the older person "on his own." The skills in abstraction and delay required for adolescent and adult functioning are developed and practiced in the production of states of latency. Failure to develop or maintain appropriate states of latency may indicate that vital cognitive skills are unavailable or are being bypassed and given short shrift in the development of the child.

Among those clinicians who were aware of the discovery of latency, a growing body of knowledge about the psychology of childhood was organized. At first this had to do with reconstructions of the psychic life of children based on the analysis of adults (Freud 1905). Direct observation started as early as 1909 (Freud 1909). Papers began to appear that described interviews with children containing therapeutic interpretations based on psychoanalytic principles derived from earlier observations. Interestingly, in one such case (Ferenczi 1913a) a child was thought to have lost interest in pursuing a discussion of his wish to be a rooster when he ceased to talk about one in conversation and instead wanted to play with a toy rooster. The examiner was not trained to realize that the child was also communicating through his play.

Such blocks to the direct role of a trained therapist in work with a child were removed when psychoanalytically trained therapists who could work with children perceived that children of latency age symbolize their problems in their play, much in the way adults symbolize their problems in their dreams. Two prominent workers in this endeavor were Melanie Klein and Anna Freud. Their books *The Psycho-analysis of Children* (Klein 1932) and *The Psychoanalytic Treatment of Children* (A. Freud 1946) describe in great clinical detail their techniques that they found to be effective in reaching children of latency age who have adjustment problems. This psychoanalytic psychotherapy for the individual was developed and practiced in Europe and studied there by American psychiatrists. In 1935 Maxwell Gitelson brought the technique to Chicago, where it was integrated into the individualized approach to troubled children introduced by William Healy some decades before. Thus was dynamically oriented psychotherapy for children introduced to the United States.

The Theory of Child Psychotherapy

The psychotherapeutic approach to the latency-age child is predicated on the theory that the appearance of emotional symptoms and signs is determined in large measure by psychological influences. The concept does not in any way exclude biochemical or genetic factors; it merely creates a context that provides for psychotherapeutic leverage. Such factors as social influences, cognitive development, maturation of the organization of ego defenses, and the vicissitudes of the instinctual drives can be applied to the treatment of adjustment and emotional problems in latency-age children through these theories.

As opposed to the therapy of adults, which deals with internalized conflict and social maladjustments within a context of a stable cognition, psychotherapy with children must be shaped to fit the fact that one is dealing with a growing child. What is acceptable and normal behavior changes with age. Symbolizing function and abstract cognition in the areas of comprehension and memory undergo marked changes during the latency age period. As a result, interpretations must be framed and phrased in the context of an approach that takes into account the child's age-appropriate capacity for comprehension and memory. Mechanisms of defense, such as projection, repression, and denial, serve a different function in latency than they ordinarily do in adolescence and adulthood. In addition, there is an organization of defenses, *the structure of latency*, that is unique to latency. It channels drive discharge into fantasy during the latency years, while in itself serving as the groundwork for the ego capacity of future planning, which in turn becomes the bulwark of emotional health in adolescence. In the psychotherapy of the latency-age child, the structure of latency must be encouraged at the same time that its products (fantasy) are analyzed (and devalued should they be the source of trouble) if one is to understand the drives and conflicts that the products represent.

Acceptable and Normal Behavior

During the latency age period, acceptable and normal behavior is defined differently at different ages. The young child in latency is expected to be close to his mother, with few interests outside the home. The late latency child is expected to show evidence of independence, with plans of his own, often derived from the influence of his peers. The early latency child opposes his parents' wishes with contentless negativism ("No, I won't!"), whereas the older latency child opposes his parents by championing positive suggestions, showing that he wants to do something on his own. Throughout latency, normal and acceptable behavior is defined in terms of appropriate obedience to parents and teachers and an ability to achieve states of calm, quiet and pliability where required. This readiness for calm is coupled with an ability to let go and vent energy in appropriate times and places, such as in the gym, at recess, and at parties. A child who is younger than the latency age cannot be relied upon to have well-differentiated responses to differing situations, for he has not yet developed skill in identifying and responding to the cues in a given situation that indicate appropriate behavior. The capacity to achieve behavioral constancy (the ability to behave consistently in given social settings), is not fully developed until the latency years begin.

As the child enters late latency, ages 9 to 12, behavior is influenced to a greater extent by peers. In essence, this phenomenon, commonly attributed to adolescence, has roots that stretch back into latency. It is appropriate for children in late latency to show evidences of a process of individuation from the parent on the ethical level. This *ethical individuation* phase of late latency is a reflection of the cognitive maturation that places more emphasis on outside influences, reality, and the environment than on internal, past, and family influences. The superego demands derived from internal, past, and family influences are usually linked with guilt and indeed actuated into influencing personal behavior through guilt. The acquisition of new contents is contested by these affects of doubt and guilt. There is conflict and guilt when new influences challenge the child to seek new ways of doing things. Guilt is stirred when old ways of doing things are challenged and forbidden activities are encouraged by new influences. In marked cases of conflict involving ethical individuation, paranoid states, tics, urticaria, and obsessional symptoms of severe but transient character appear. They point to the presence of *ethical individuation conflict*, which should be explored in these instances.

Coupled with the problems of ethical individuation is the problem of passivity, which may also be marked in late latency. This is a conflict between the wish of the child to be cared for and to remain a child, and resentment of the loss of independence that fulfillment of this desire brings. Moods, temper fits, withdrawal to rooms, and challenges of authority take center stage clinically when these conflictual areas are most intense. Ethical individuation, with its emphasis on seeking new ways of doing things and new things to do, intensifies the passivity problems of late latency.

The normal symbolizing function undergoes changes during the latency time period. Most striking are the changes in the symbols used for the production of fantasy. The prelatency child has very direct fantasy symbols ("When you die, Mommy, I'll marry Daddy"). The early latency-age child populates his fantasies with amorphous figures, especially of persecutors, who frighten him, especially when it is dark. At about 8½ there is a shift from amorphous figures to real figures, who populate fantasies that are mainly lived out in the imagination or played out in fantasy play. In adolescence, real people populate fantasies, which are forced upon reality and are lived out in reality. What began as normal in early latency comes to be seen as neurotic behavior when it is carried on into adolescence.

The symbols that play a primary role in the formation of latency states are a special symbolic form, called a psychoanalytic symbol. An ordinary symbol is an object, idea, or thing that in the process of memory represents in the awareness and communications of the person another object or thing. It is a kind of convenient shorthand through which a great deal of information can be represented by a signal or sign that requires little effort. In the formation of a psychoanalytic symbol, the message to be conveyed is usually tied in with anxiety or another uncomfortable affect. To permit the expression of the message while maintaining comfort for the individual, the connection between the symbol and the original information is repressed. In this way fantasies can be created that express and discharge the urges implied in the original (latent fantasy) information package without revealing its content to the child or the casual observer. This sort of symbol becomes a highly useful tool in the process of mastery of uncomfortable experiences and in the discharge of drive energies for which the immature physiology of the child provides no other outlets. The latency play fantasy formed from psychoanalytic symbols becomes a means of reducing emotional tensions, much in the way that masturbation, some categories of dreams, sexual relations, athletics, and adult sublimations are used.

In keeping with the preponderance of inward-turning mental events in the latency-age child, the psychoanalytic symbols of the child have the characteristic of not taking into account communicative potentials in relation to possible listeners and observers. The symbols serve primarily the role of a medium through which past experiences and memories can be evoked for the discharge of drives, independently of objects in reality. The play fantasies of children, which are constructed from these symbols, resemble the distortion-filled dreams seen in the treatment of adults. In child therapy the play fantasies of children serve a role similar to that of the dream in adult therapy. Because of the similarity of function, dreams are less frequently reported spontaneously in the psychotherapy of the latency-age child than by adults. With the exception of bed-wetters, latency-age children rarely report dreams during therapy, even though dreaming is not rare. The therapist must make a special point of encouraging dream reporting if this is desired.

The characteristic which should have the greatest impact on the tactics of the child therapist is the level of cognitive maturation of the child. Symbols, fantasies and the structure of latency contribute to the content of the therapy and shape the interpretations of the therapist. Although the comprehension, appreciation and memory for events and the therapist's interpretations of them are the key to success, verbal content is not the whole story. The therapist's approach, the patient's productions, and the very form of the therapist's interventions are determined by the level of cognitive maturation of the child. Typically, a major portion of the child's spontaneous recall of events is channeled through the intuitive masked and highly symbolized medium of fantasy play. Therefore, the therapist, in order to gain access to the child's preoccupations, must encourage fantasy play and pay close attention to it. When the time for interpretation and reconstruction arrives, a change of pace is required. The therapist should keep as a point of reference the concrete experiences of the child in the therapy session. Though the child can produce symbolic abstractions, he is weak in the comprehension of and memory for abstraction. The poor capacity for the recall of abstraction by the child in early latency militates against abstract phrasing in interpretations made to these children. Though the therapist may understand and theorize on an adult level of comprehension, cognition, and memory organization to his own satisfaction, molding of these insights into interpretations following adult patterns of phrasing and abstraction will fall on the child's awareness as on deaf ears.

In phrasing interpretations the therapist should consider two primary areas of cognition: the organization of the understanding of events and the organization of the memory function. As Piaget (1945) has pointed out, children in the early latency years tend to understand the happenings about them in a magical, symbolic, and intuitive manner. It is only at about 7½ years of age that the child can use abstractions in the interpretation of concretely experienced and observed events. With a child younger than this, the therapist's interpretations should be concrete, and should be aimed at reconstructing true experiences that the child has distorted into distressing or even disorganizing fear fantasies. In the child older than 7½, interpretations may be more general and abstract, relating seemingly disparate concrete elements. It is not until the child is at the very end of latency (12½) that one can expect universally to find abstract reductions of abstractions. These can be understood at this age, and logical conversations can be conducted without breaks of attention and distractions into play by the child. In essence, it is at this age that the interpretation typical of adult therapy comes consistently into use. Such interpretations of content are used when the aim of the therapist is to help the child understand current behavior.

No matter what it is that the child can understand of his current behavior as a result of the level of cognitive comprehension he has reached, it is only that which the child can carry with him and remember in the future that will have an impact. When the therapist feels that insight and the ability to recognize repeated patterns of behavior are indicated in the therapy, the nature of the ontogenesis of memory function must be kept in mind.

The ontogenesis of the memory function is extraordinarily complex when related to the psychotherapy of the latency-age child. Every element brought into the session by the child is, in whole or in part, a product of memory. Since at least three different memory organizations are at work creating the spontaneous recall that produces the contents of the therapy session, the therapist must be tuned in on at least three levels of communication.

The earliest formed and most primitive memory organization used by the child is the affectomotor memory organization, which dominates until 3 years of age and bears the burden of the memory function until well past 6 years of age. The components of this memory organization are sight, sensations, and feelings that re-create the total life experience of the child, including associated affects. In the absence of verbal components, early life experiences can be recalled through affectomotor memory in the form of somatic sensations which are signifiers of the broader affectomotor imagery seeking representation in memory. Motor tone and posture, the selection of a broken toy that represents a recall of an old injury, angers, and sudden needs for toileting are all clinical manifestations that must be observed and interpreted to bring the totality of the child's experience into the psychotherapeutic field of view.

Fortunately for the therapist working with the latency-age child, the second form of memory organization, which is introduced at the end of the first year of life, begins to dominate the memory functions of the child at about age 6. This is the verbal conceptual memory organization. At this age, the child is able to reduce memory elements for holistic, nonlinear affectomotor total memory elements to efficient and logically organized concepts locked into verbal representations. To some extent, their scope is limiting. The limitations are traded off against the expanding usefulness of elements based on memory in the sphere of communications. Thus, the child can talk about or represent in verbal symbols that which he has experienced and must master. It is incumbent on the therapist to help the child to improve his verbal conceptual memory skills, and to help translate experience carried forward through affectomotor memory function into verbal concepts that can be shared, discussed, and mastered. While the child is in this phase (6 to 8), there is little value in converting observations into abstractions, for there is less likelihood that children will be able to carry forward abstractions than rote memory and verbally organized concepts in memory.

The third level of the memory organization involved in spontaneous recall is abstract conceptual memory. It may become available at about 8 years of age, but since it develops only with social and parental encouragement, it may be absent, depending on the home environment from which the child comes. Called the abstract conceptual memory organization, the third memory organization permits the child to recall spontaneously the intrinsic nature of things, rather than words.* As such, at this age, interpretations can be formed to take into account intrinsic relationships between related concrete experiences.

---

*This should be differentiated from *recognition* recall of similarities and intrinsic characteristics, which is present in the second year of life. Such recall is demonstrated by the child who can tell dogs from cats in a picture book.

(The application of abstractions to abstractions must await very late latency.) It is possible for the therapist to encourage the child to achieve skills in abstract conceptual memory at 8, and even for the child to show spontaneous evidences of this function at 8. It is the common experience of therapist and parents, however, that not until age 10 is there a meaningful increase in the child's interest in current events, abstractions, and short, clearly thought out conversations.

If the child has not reached a given level of memory organization, it is useless for the therapist to use its formal characteristics in the formation of his formulations and interpretations to the child, without first working to develop mature cognitions.

During latency, a number of mechanisms of defense undergo developmental vicissitudes. The pathology implied by their presence differs from that implied in a similar clinical manifestation in the adult. For instance, projection of transient persecutory fantasies serves an adaptive function in latency. Some defenses are less strong in latency than they are in adulthood. For instance, direct questions can often bring out repressed material in the latency-age child.

Repression is less strong during late latency. In dealing with an obsessional symptom or a paranoid episode, often all that is needed to bring forgotten events into consciousness is to ask some direct questions. As the return to consciousness occurs, the symptoms clear.

A 12-year-old girl refused to go to school out of fear that she would be kidnapped by a group of men in a car that was following her. She had a complete remission of symptoms when she was able to reconstruct the situation in which the symptoms had begun. The therapist, aware of the problems in ethical individuation that occur at this age, asked the child whether her friends had wanted her to do something that her parents would disapprove of. "Steal," said the girl, without hesitation. She then described stealing some gum from a candy store at the prompting of her friends. Though she had returned the gum, she was haunted by guilt, which had been dissociated from the theft and then expressed through the persecutory delusion. When the episode of stealing was restored to consciousness, the fear symptom cleared.

Projection in adults has strong pathological implications, but in latency it is one of the mechanisms of the normal "fear fantasy" neuroses. With the passage into adolescence, projection pursues a number of vicissitudes which include participation in sublimations, use as a bridge in object finding, and the projective-introjective process that contributes to modification of the superego. If the projections of latency continue unaltered into adolescence, a pathological import may be inferred (Sarnoff 1976).

In early latency, the child's tendency to respond intuitively and to interpret the world and its events in terms of his own self-oriented view of things permits him to assume that what he wishes to see or not to see should be accepted by others as a true view of the world. Any attempts to shatter denials at this age are fraught with frustration, if not danger. The child may stare right through the therapist. If the therapist brings too much pressure to bear, aggressions and even destructive behavior aimed at the therapist or the playroom may be expected. This is in marked contrast to the adult, for whom interpretations of denial usually produce new data.

The Structure of Latency

The two organizations of ego structure previously discussed, the mechanisms of restraint and the structure of latency, characterize latency and differentiate it from any other developmental period. Both are important because they are consistent in a given individual and are generally found in any youngster who is able to achieve states of calm. Both have dual functions: They help to produce and maintain states of latency and, in the post-latency period, form personality structures which are part of character. The mechanisms of restraint will give shape to the superego and the control of instincts, and the structure of latency will become the core of the ego skill of future planning.

In adolescence, humiliation gives rise to stress. Adaptation to the stress of humiliation may consist of fantasy formation, much as this process occurs in latency. Such adolescent fantasy, however, typically uses reality elements as symbols (i.e., "I'll drive a big car," "I'll do better in school," "I'll become a professional," "I'll be a sports [military] hero and when I return, there will be a parade and they'll know how good I am."). This type of fantasy serves more than the discharge function it did in the latency-age child. The action elements of the fantasies (going to school, joining a team, joining a uniformed service) are possible and even perhaps attainable. They become the inspiration or source for adaptive acts using a reality orientation. They provide more than a momentary fantasy response to a stress of the moment. They offer, in addition, a bridge to tomorrow. Since the child in adolescence is beginning to have the physical resources to make these truth-based dreams come true, there is the possibility that the bridge can be crossed. Thus is future planning born out of the structure of latency.

Since these personality structures serve to produce and maintain one developmental stage and also participate as character elements in subsequent stages, the child therapist is well advised to regard them with respect. The study of these structures will help to reveal psychopathology and clinical psychodynamics of the child, but strengthening them is sometimes a necessary goal of the therapy. This is especially so in those youngsters who show poor study skills, a short attention span, impulsivity, and explosiveness in chronic situations of psychological overstimulation.

These organized structures of the ego are best described within the context of the psychodynamic theory of latency. This is the theory that explains the fluctuations between excited states and calm, malleable states in the latency-age child. The theory deals with the means of drive control during this age. The latency-age child has sexual and aggressive drives equal to those of the child in prelatency, although not as strong as those seen in adolescence. The drives are manifested in aggressive behavior, sexual excitement, and masturbatory equivalents. Such inner forces as powerful drives create a problem for the child in a society that considers acceptable behavior to be indicated by suppression of these activities. The situation is compounded by the fact that biologically the child is no match for his elders physically and has not yet been equipped with a mature genital organ capable of expressing the sexual drives in a realistic, object-oriented context. In essence the child must seek the resolution of his need to discharge his drives, utilizing predominantly his inner ego resources.

If one adds to this situation the frequent seductive stimulation of the child by adults, one sees that the inner life of the apparently calm latency-age child is more analogous to a sessile steam boiler sometimes pushed toward exploding, than to calm bays that invite one to meditation.

When one is confronted with distracting drive derivatives (e.g., sexual fantasies), states of goal directedness and calm can be threatened. In early latency, the most common fantasy that threatens goal-directed, reality-oriented behavior is the Oedipal fantasy. This fantasy is characterized by sexual impulses in regard to parents, associated with guilt and fear of retribution.

These fantasies are uncomfortable for children. Any situation that stirs them up creates affects and excitements that threaten the external appearance of calm and the availability of quiet moments, which can be harnessed by educators as times for the transmission of culture.

Disruptions of calm need not take place. As Freud was the first to note, children who have reached the phallic-oedipal level resolve the threats involved in oedipal fantasy, whether spontaneous or induced, by retiring from the advanced lines of battle to reinvolve themselves in the conflicts of earlier ages. Usually this means that the child regresses to the anal-sadistic level. Oedipal sexual longings are replaced by more easily expressed urges to tease, to defy, to mess, and to smear. Such behavior is seen in angry, excited youngsters. Rooms in which parties are given are often left in shreds by such youngsters. Mothers who drive car pools know well the back seat society to which all children belong. It is a club which has as its main activity and shibboleth scatology and anal references piled high one upon the other.

Although such behavior and sadistic teasing leak out from time to time, the majority of children express their anal regressions in a masked manner. This masked outcome is the product of maturity. The child has a stronger and more complex armamentarium of ego defenses for dealing with anal-sadistic urges than he had when first he encountered them at about age 2. Reaction formation, symbol and fantasy formation, repression, and obsessional defenses (e.g., collecting) all express the primitive drives and channel them into socially acceptable patterns. The aggression and messing urges are turned into calm and neatness as a result of reaction formation. Aggressive fantasies replace actions, and collecting takes up energies in collecting and valuing stones that might otherwise be thrown. These mechanisms are grouped under the rubric "the mechanisms of restraint." The patterns into which they shape the drives are guided by the expectations of parents and the demands of teachers and society. These patterns carry over into adolescence, where they influence strongly the attitudes of the child toward the burgeoning drives that threaten to overwhelm. This is the patterned shape of the prior experience that guides the child when pitted against the seductive demands of the adolescent peer group.

There are children who are unable to handle their drives on the anal-sadistic level. Excitements and humiliation call for comfort rather than responses of aggression. These youngsters regress further to the oral phase, where they can be seen to comfort themselves with dreamy television watching, thumb sucking, cuddling of pets, and eating to the point of obesity. Maternal prohibitions that block phallic and anal assertiveness leave as the only outlet the establishment of a pattern of defenses with an oral cast.

The child who is successful in using the mechanisms of restraint to transmute the potential tumult of his anal-sadistic urges into a period of calm is a child who is capable of producing states of latency.

This product of the mechanisms of the ego opens the door to education and the absorption of culture.

The process of producing states of latency is dynamic. Overstimulation and seductive behavior, beatings and parental sarcasm can cause a flooding of the mechanism and a breakdown in the latency state. Aggressive behavior and regressed symbols are clinical expressions of a failure in the latency. In contrast, in situations such as parties, recess, free play, and athletics, such behavior is encouraged. These are natural safety valves well recognized by the caretakers of children. The child also decreases the pressures of humiliation, stimulation, and seduction by the use of talking, complaining, and the seeking of allies on a verbal level. This verbal adjustment is important for the child therapist. Through it he establishes a rapport with the child, and if phrasing is simple, the therapist can help the child to reach verbal comprehension of his problems. The slightest deflection of the therapist's attention from the child—as may occur should the therapist, for example, answer the phone—turns the child to motor syntaxes and other symbolic ways for the expression of conflicts.

The dynamic process of latency has yet another safety valve useful in maintaining the state of latency. This is the structure of latency, succinctly paraphrased by Donnellan (1977) as a ". . . configuration of defenses in the latency child which allow the expression of impulses through fantasy" (p. 141). The oedipal drives, with the aid of the structure of latency, are expressed through fantasy. Their energies are discharged through fantasy, instead of being responded to by regression and adding to the burden of the mechanisms of restraint. This is accomplished in the following way: The oedipal fantasy, either in part or in whole, undergoes repression. The repressed fantasy is fragmented, and the fragments are in turn represented by elements that, as the result of displacement, are divorced from the original and not recognizable as related to them. This is the defensive role of psychoanalytic symbolization. The symbols are then drawn together into a coherent series of symbols, which make up the manifest fantasy of the structure of latency (e.g., the child who wants to kill his father, kills a king in fantasy instead). The coherency of the series is due to its patterning by the tales and myths belonging to the child's culture. This ability to adapt personal memories and fantasies (e.g., oedipal) to stories that have a social and cultural source becomes yet another conduit through which the potential for producing a state of latency can be used to enhance the socialization and acculturation of the child.

In children with impaired capacity for delay, displacement, abstraction, symbolization, or fantasy formation, the state of latency is unstable. Therapeutic goals take this into account. To bring a child into latency so as to produce states of calm and prepare for future planning in adolescence is an important goal in the therapy of a child with an impaired ability to produce states of latency.

In all children with a structure of latency at all operative, the fantasies produced and played out in the therapy sessions become an endless source of data. Like the dreams of adults, they provide the key to the complexes, sensitivities, and instigators of regression in the individual child. The following case vignette illustrates the use of fantasy play in acquiring data in a session.

J.B. was 11 years old. He was a bright, handsome boy whose school performance fell far below expectations. At home his verbal abuse and provocations of his mother were severe enough to cause battles. He was brought for treatment because these matters had got out of hand.

J.B. was highly verbal and quick to deny his responsibility for home problems. He also denied that these problems existed. He related calmly to the therapist, spending most of his therapy time drawing uninvolved individual figures, recounting gunslinger Westerns, and talking about the books he was reading. He could not participate in any discussion of his family or the problems that he denied existed. During the early phases of the treatment, changes and defects began mysteriously to appear in the therapist's office. Telephones were disconnected. Paper wads appeared in light sockets. Toilet paper disappeared by the roll. For months the patient denied responsibility for these events. To get him to accept the need to analyze his sadism, it had to be demonstrated to him that he could not hide his role as the source of difficulties for himself and others. This required a fantasy some of the elements of which could not be ascribed to an external source. Some newly acquired soft clay provided the opportunity. He made a white human figure. He shoved a pencil point into its stomach. "Take that, Lancelot," said he. He pulled the pencil out and rejoiced as he filled the hole with bright red clay. "Blood!" he exclaimed. The therapist asked about Lancelot. The child claimed the story as his own. He had never heard of Tennyson or Malory. He explained that he used the name Lancelot because the pencil was a lance. His pleasure in the gush of blood was interpreted to him and was related to his excitement in telling and playing out movie plots. He was able to connect his wishes to the story he had told of Lancelot. Although somewhat abashed, he was thenceforth able to talk about his role in the provocations of others.

Note how the use of a three-dimensional play figure permitted movement and the passage of time to be introduced into the play. Such a figure is better than a drawing in permitting the introduction of these elements of story-telling structure. In this way symbols can be manipulated, and, without words being used, fantasy with the mobility in space and time characteristics of that found in a dream can be encouraged in a psychotherapy session. One is best warned (as we will expand upon below) that such activities have much vitality and high cathexis, and that it is not unusual for an interpretation of an underlying hostility in the patient to trigger a shift of the hostility from an interaction within the story to an interaction between the patient and the therapist or the playroom. Thus are desks and ceilings marred.

The Application of Latency Theory to Therapy

As we have described, analytically derived psychotherapy with latency-age children can be applied when there are problems of social adjustment, acceptance of self, and hypersensitive reactions to situations that induce feelings of humiliation. The child who has entered latency and manifests internalized conflicts in such a way that the same patterns of behavior are demonstrated in disparate situations (e.g., sibling rivalry, jealousy of peers, being picked on and teased) can be helped by therapy to direct his energies away from his fantasies and toward the resolution of reality problems. The overstimulated child can be helped by the therapy to place his relationship with adults into perspective, once the parents have been induced to stop the overstimulation. Children of parents who overemphasize needs for self-control and limit the rate of maturation of the child can be helped by therapy to bring their conflicts to the surface. This replaces battling within themselves to the accompaniment of guilt and doubt, which in turn alleviates the somatizations, paranoid symptoms, and tics that defend against the guilt and doubt.

Children who fail to enter latency can be helped by the therapist who understands the mechanisms involved in the psychodynamics of the establishment of states of latency. The therapist can construct a therapeutic strategy that will diminish the pressure on the child at the same time that weak ego mechanisms are strengthened.

In children with delayed cognitive growth, child psychotherapy can be applied with the aim of encouraging the establishment of more mature means of comprehending and remembering the abstractions necessary for school survival. Concurrently, improved cognition aids in the therapeutic process. A means is established by which interpretations can be enhanced to achieve lasting impact.

The technique of therapy entails the unravelling of the meanings of fantasies when direct verbal communication fails as a channel for bringing conflicts and memories to the arena of consciousness and communication.

In the following pages we consider specific procedures, activities and interventions which can be of therapeutic value. In essence, the process of cure will be explored through an investigation of the nature of its effective components.

The Hows and Whys of Equipping a Playroom

All therapies occur within a setting. For the therapist who wishes to work with the latency-age child, with the great emphasis on play and fantasy that occurs, the nature of the setting and objects in the room are crucial. Therapists offer settings of varying degrees of complexity and elaborateness. All have one thing in common. The equipment in the office is selected with an eye to its use by the latency-age child with the techniques he has available to use alternative media to express concepts and conflicts when words fail.

There are moments in therapy when words cannot be found to convey the concepts that the child wishes to express. There are times when the use of words conveys threatening concepts so directly that uncomfortable affects appear. In these circumstances, ego mechanisms related to the structure of latency are activated by the child to shift the concept into fantasies, graphic representations, three-dimensional figures, doll play, movement patterns, and somatic responses.

The therapist sets aside a drawer of his desk, a cabinet, a closet, a corner, or, best of all, a full room for the purpose of fantasy play, and equips it with the necessary devices. There is some difference of opinion over whether one should undertake the expense of having a separate playroom. Such a room is kept separate from the consultation room which has decorations that are more in keeping with the mature style required for treating adult patients. Some therapists claim that they do not need a separate playroom or play equipment because they have never worked with, or seen, a child who made messes, was sadistic, tore things, or became openly destructive in their office. These therapists imply that their skills surpass those of the ordinarily endowed therapist, who feels a need for a playroom.

I feel that the therapist without an independent playroom works under a limitation. He cannot encourage regression, follow fantasy undeterred, encourage the playing out of fantasy, or explore neurotic patterns that may be expressed through motor syntaxes. It is wise to have the playroom connected to one's consultation room so that the child can move freely between them. In this way, the child who is given a choice of rooms from the start can wander between the "talking room" and the "playing-and-talking room." His movements toward play are propelled by regressions, and the requirements of his need for ego distance from the latent content with which he is trying to cope.

The setting may be only a corner or as much as a room without outside views or noises, small enough and so simple of shape that the child cannot use distance or alcoves as means to hide. Whether the setting be a corner or a room, the material required to furnish and equip it share certain characteristics. They call upon the child's resources and personality in a response context of spontaneity. Patterned and organized play material, such as games with rules and games of chance are less helpful than dolls, clay, and drawing material, which at every manipulation are reflections of the inner life of the child. The basic principle is to place at the child's disposal material that can be used to express that which cannot be expressed in words. Fantasy play can reveal much while masking. Games with fixed rules mask more than they reveal, if only by dint of the fact that the time that is taken up with their formal aspects could otherwise be used for the spinning of fantasy. The child's personality is the subject, not the personality of the designer of the game or the personality of the therapist.

By the same token, when the therapist enters the fantasy of the patient as a character, he may not intrude his own fantasy or personality; he must seek direction from the child as to his role. Otherwise the child would be led from his thoughts and drives to follow a path that may gratify the therapist and reinforces the therapist's theories about the patient at the expense of true insight for both. When mutual storytelling is done, the therapist should avoid introducing his own fantasies and characters. Instead the therapist should seek elaborations of the ideas of the child.

Sometimes it is necessary to use structured toys and board games when investigative therapy is to be avoided and the therapist's goal is to provide companionship or support for coping skills that are heavily loaded with obsessional mechanisms. I have a preference for storing such games in a special place so that they are not available to be used by youngsters as a defensive maneuver when inappropriate to the therapy.

Nonstructured therapy materials fall into two groups. These serve the two major regressive pathways observed in children. The first group serves regression along the line of cognitive skills. The second group serves regression along the line of psychosexual development. The former emphasizes the formal aspect of media used for the recall of memory elements, (i.e., paper, crayon, clay). The selection of the latter emphasizes symbolic content (i.e., soldiers, cars, guns, dolls).

Ontogenetically, memory elements are first expressed without media. They take the form of affects and body parts in motion. The memory function expands its recall horizon to media when music, rhythm, bodily motion, and form are expressed in pounding and shaping clay. Rhythm, motion, and shapes come to be recognized and can be used to express and master prior experience toward the end of the first year of life. Later, during latency, active shaping and clay play will reflect regression to this stage. A playroom is incomplete without clay.

The next step in development is the addition of the expression of memory (spontaneous recall) in the use of two dimensional lines (three to four years of age) when the child begins to draw pictures. Often, hundreds of drawings will be made over a period of years, to the amazement of parents. Parents are equally amazed when this productivity ceases, and the child who had been seen as a potential artistic prodigy reveals himself to have been only going through a stage. Indeed, drawing is an age-appropriate way of using media to master experiences that is later deemphasized when pictures give way to words. In short, a playroom needs pencil and paper.

By the time of mid-latency the telling of tales, experienced both actively (in telling) and passively (in listening), becomes the primary means of mastering events. Now symbols find expression in words, rather than in plastic form. Yet the transition to the use of words is incompletely reached throughout latency; clay forms and drawings persist. Repeatedly, the child is seen to require the participation of his whole body (body movements expressing his excitement), so that symbolized fantasy becomes fantasy play. The playroom needs space to move (minimally 10' x 12'). Obviously, latency is the time when play materials are of great value. Without them, the child is limited to words. Only part of the story that the child has to tell can be told. Only words as symbols will be available for translation into words as direct communication to the therapist. Affects and motor patterns expressible only in play will be deleted from the translating process and no one will be the wiser.

I have already described progress developmentally, in the area of media for memory, and spontaneous recall in the service of mastery has been portrayed. In reverse order, regressions along this developmental line traverse the following schema. What the child can say, he will say. What the child cannot say, he will put into action and fantasy play. What cannot be put into fantasy play, can be drawn. What cannot be drawn, can be molded in clay, or, more primitively, acted out directly in aggressive acts and discharges of affect. Thus, if a child cannot tell a dream, he may be able to draw elements from it. If he cannot draw, then let him try to work in clay. If the child cannot tell about himself, then introduce ego distance by having the child tell the story through the use of dolls with assumed names.

The regressive pull in child therapy is in the direction of direct physical expression and organ language. Therefore the substitute expressions I have described present a potential danger that tempers their capacity to improve communication through placing the media with which the child is comfortable at his disposal. They can encourage too rapid regression in the borderline child. For this reason, for some children the play material is used to encourage the child to substitutions in the direction of less regressed activity. For example, there are times when the child has regressed to the point where he no longer expresses his latent contents through symbols and substitutes, but is actively involved in the expression of aggression through affective displays and discharge via motor syntaxes, using the therapist as object. This is a technical way of saying that sometimes the kid gets temper tantrums and starts punching out the therapist. At these times, substitutions should be upward, with the suggestion made that the child show the therapist what he has in mind using dolls or a punching balloon as a substitute object. Similarly, in children who have failed to develop verbal symbols of the psychoanalytic sort, it is necessary as a technique to encourage substitution upward through the creation of plastic elements, doll play, clay play, and drawing, as a means of expanding the child's media for expressing and mastering events, displacing and binding affects, and delaying responses.

A list of helpful play materials for the playroom includes clay, paper, pencil, watercolors, scissors, glue, a punching doll, plastic toy soldiers, a dollhouse with a doll family, and toy cars. Plastic clay that hardens is particularly useful because figures made from it may be used session after session as a basis for further elaborations of the fantasy or dream in which the figure first appeared. There should be a bathroom available. Often the regression to body and physical sensations takes the form of masturbatory activity or the need to use the bathroom. Water should be available. I prefer a pump-action sink with a self-contained cool water supply instead of a standard sink with hot and cold water and a head of pressure. Hot water can burn a child's hands, and a head of pressure can be most unfortunate if the child places his finger under the faucet and then places himself between the faucet handle and the therapist and directs a spray of water at the therapist.

The levels of regression that have to do with psychosexual development consist of a series of phases. The earliest is the oral phase. This finds reflection, in the latency years, in play in which bottles, caretaking of dolls, eating, and stories of dependency using dolls are pertinent. For this reason, dolls with bottles are useful in the playroom. Some therapists keep food around, recommending only small amounts. I find that the less that children eat, the more they talk about their need to eat, and so I do not recommend this practice.

The next phase is the anal phase. This finds reflection in the latency years in regressions to needs to smear and mess as well as sadistic and warlike fantasies. There are also fantasies of bombing, direct anal references, and projection. Clay and finger paints are most useful for expressing and letting off steam in this area. Toy soldiers are helpful for carrying out large scale fantasies of omnipotent power. The child needs both discharge in this area as well as analysis of content to help master prior experienced stresses. In addition, especially in dealing with the anal regression of the latency-age child, the mechanisms of restraint need strengthening. The most useful and most feasible strengthening maneuvers during child therapy sessions in this regard are techniques that encourage collecting and the obsessional patterning mechanisms that are used naturally by most children. An example of such a technique is the familiar game of "dots," in which lines connect dots to make boxes and each box completed belongs to the person who has completed it. Children may be encouraged to bring in pennies, baseball cards, and so on, and to organize them.

Doll play may be used to good advantage for the expression of anal phase material. It is important in this regard that the dollhouse be equipped with bathroom furniture. Clay should be available for the child to use to represent feces.

Next on the level of expression of psychosexual development are materials that can symbolize the elements of the phallic phase. Important among these elements are the Oedipus complex and sibling rivalry. Dolls of different ages and sexes and a dollhouse are invaluable in helping the child to portray the conflicts relating to this period. Guns are useful in helping children to express assertiveness, phallic penetrative urges, and oedipal aggression towards parents. Family dolls which represent parents and children to scale invite the child to express feelings in this area.

The important thing to keep in mind about the cognitive and psychosexual determinants of the material used in the playroom is the difference in goal inherent in the selection of material for the expression and study of each of these developmental lines. The materials used in the cognitive area are chosen with an eye to the form of the media needed for the expression on a symbolic level of latent memory elements. Motor syntaxes are learned at each phase for dealing with each medium (clay, paper and pencil, symbolic motor patterns, words). Such phase-related motor experiences and skills are retained in memory. They become the basis for building up a body of learning on which to base future functioning and development, or as a mechanism for the continued processing of trauma with an eye towards mastery. Regressions can activate them inappropriately.

The materials used to encourage play that will reflect information about the child's phases of psychosexual development are chosen with an eye towards their usefulness as symbols. They must be able to express latent, phase-appropriate memory content. The choice of material is based upon prior experience with symbols in the play of children and in the dreams of adults. Certain symbols have been found to be consistently used to express certain latent contents. Thus a doll with a bottle has oral connotations. Clay and feces, or finger paints and feces, have come to be equated symbolically. This is a convention which is constantly reinforced by the spontaneous clinical productions and associations of players and dreamers. A gun repeatedly appears in play and dreams as a phallic symbol.

There are some who challenge these symbolic equations and their use. Indeed, even the relationship of fantasy and latent thoughts to symptoms and behavior is challenged by some. If the child therapist takes such a negative stand, analytically derived child therapy becomes a therapy divested of much of its effectiveness. I recall from my college years a young man who openly challenged the theory that dream symbols could have an unconscious meaning. He challenged the class to analyze a dream he had had the night before. He started off at first to tell the dream in words. "I was hunting. I had a rifle. I went into this cave after a mountain lion. I raised my gun to shoot. Just as I was about to shoot, my gun went like this." At this point he ceased using a verbal mode for relating his dream and shifted to a symbolic motor pattern. He pointed his finger straight out as if aiming into the cave. Then, with the phrase "like this," his finger relaxed and hung limply from the knuckle. The class, which had maintained its demeanor up to this point, dissolved into laughter, while the dreamer only looked bewildered. A class of unsophisticated 18-year-olds apparently knew something of the secret of dreams, and put it to use that day. Experiences like this contribute to my certainty that guns should be present in playrooms so that phallic symbolism may be expressed.

The playroom furnishings themselves have specific therapeutic value. There should be low shelves in which play material may be placed in a casual and accessible manner, though easily available to the child. A table should be provided as a work surface, preferably with a top of formica, not wood. Within reach of the table should be a low chest for tools and equipment that can be brought out by the therapist as needed. A holder for paper, watercolors, pens, and pencils should be at hand. Many therapists have a couch on which the child can rest. A bin for each child is an excellent idea. File cabinets can be useful for this. In these bins, whatever the child works on consistently or has produced and wants to keep for the next session can be kept out of harm's way and out of the hands of other child patients with sibling rivalry problems. There should be an open, hard surface floor area on which the child can play by himself.

The treatment of walls is important. Children often want to write on walls. This cannot be permitted, if only because one child can fill one wall in one day. Yet, something is lost if the child is blocked in this. I've solved this by covering one wall with a dry marker board. Another wall, covered with cork, becomes a place where the child can proudly exhibit his achievements in drawing and design. In addition, the corkboard can be used to keep exposed and at hand pictorial symbolic products that might otherwise have been thrown away and that the therapist wants to keep in sight and available for future working-through.

The Qualities of the Therapist

Of all the elements in the playroom, perhaps the most important are the therapist's personality, knowledge and experience. The successful therapist must genuinely like children, not in the abstract but over prolonged periods of contact with individual children. If the impulse of the future therapist is to give his patient something to do while he reads, or if the potential therapist wishes to play games of chance with the child, or if the potential therapist finds himself dozing when assigned to the care of a child, the likelihood is that he should seek another profession. Gifted child caretakers and child observers may be insufficiently comfortable with children to be able to interact with them on a level that permits psychotherapeutic insight and communication. This may well explain why so many well trained child therapists give up direct work with children to take on supervisory and administrative roles.

The personal attributes of importance in the child therapist are warmth, a quiet and relaxed manner, a voice capable of modulation, and a capacity to remain cool and to think in the face of sometimes destructive surprises. When these attributes are present, the child's needs in a therapist are satisfied, for a child can be comfortable in the presence of such a person. Of no less importance is the ability of the potential therapist to accept regressions that occur during the therapy sessions. He must be able to accept regression in the child and accept the stirring up of his own drives that this entails without the mobilization of defenses that could block communication or insight. He must be able to accept the child's behavior, think on the level that the child thinks, and still not regress himself to the level of playing and interacting with the child on a regressed level. Play and interaction that express the therapist's own infantile needs will intensify the child's regressions and problems. The troubled child needs an adult as a therapist, not as a best friend. A child of his own age would serve the latter purpose better.

In essence, then, the potential therapist should be comfortable with a child's regressed behavior. He should be capable of regressing cognitively to be able to appreciate the child's communications and to communicate in turn. Consonant with these controlled regressions he must not lose the sense of distance that permits reflection, free-floating attention, and awareness of the influence and needs of society in guiding behavior.

It is very helpful if the therapist can draw, or can model clay into a recognizable representation. This will support the use of figures as interpretations and in the passive introduction of symbols to children with poor symbolizing function.

Child therapy requires neither the use of medication nor the "laying on of hands." It is a field open to child-oriented people of many professional backgrounds. The experience of the physician equips him to deal with childhood psychopathology from the standpoint of differential diagnosis and physical or organic modalities of treatment. This does not bear a direct relationship to the therapy of the latency-age child as such. The experience of the physician in the treatment of the physical disorders of mankind creates in the therapist what may be called a "feel for tissue": this implies that to administer any therapy one must be aware that the strongest forces for health lie in the natural recuperative and restorative processes of the body and personality. One must be able to put aside one's omnipotent fantasies and the search for hermetic magic in favor of choosing modalities of intervention that will not interfere with natural developmental and curative processes. One must accept limitations on rescue fantasies and feelings of omnipotence so that interventions can be tuned to the pace of needs of the patient, not the therapist. There is a great deal to be learned from any physicianly ministrations governed by the rule "first of all, not to harm" that can immediately be applied in the child therapy situation. Working with tissue on an intensive level, as physicians do, brings such skills into focus early in the career of the medically trained therapist. As seemingly distant an activity as learning to diagnose pathology slides has a bearing. There is an abdication of narcissism (jumping to conclusions) in favor of the verifiable and consistent observable facts revealed on the slide that is brought immediately to bear in child therapy. The theories and hypotheses of the therapist must take second place to the observable facts of the child's behavior.

Over time, anyone who works in child therapy can acquire the "feel for tissue." An awareness of this concept in the hands of therapists without medical experience may hurry the process.

Those who come to child therapy from backgrounds related to child caring have had access to an invaluable knowledge base. Child therapy requires that the troubles of the child at a given age be familiar ground to the therapist. Knowledge of the typical fantasies and reality problems of each age helps the therapist to know where to look for trouble and what to talk about and encourage in the therapeutic situation.

It is incumbent on the child therapist to fill in those areas in which background is insufficient as soon as is possible. It is of importance in seeking out a training program that it is designed to fill these needs rather than the needs of the institution on the level of research or earnings. A personal analysis is an invaluable source of knowledge into the unconscious. In addition, it helps the therapist deal with personal reactions, which would interfere with his capacity to participate in the therapeutic situation.

Effective Therapeutic Techniques

In child therapy, two areas, at least, are the focus of therapeutic attention. First, we focus on current stresses and humiliations that unsettle the child. Insulting and disappointing experiences trigger regressive behavior. Memory for the actual experiences may undergo repression. Defensive and regressive symptoms, as well as anxiety, appear in their stead. Personal insults are not the only current stresses that confront a child. Overwhelming of the ego by the drives, and developmental demands, also confound. Social pressures and the task of integrating newly acquired skills into peer accepted behavior can also unsettle a child. Psychotherapeutic activities must be aimed at helping the child deal with these difficult inputs and tasks, as well as resolving the use of defenses, when they are counterproductive or when their function produces symptoms.

The second group of problems consists of unresolved past humiliations and traumas that were not mastered when they first occurred. These are manifested in self-defeating patterns of defense mechanisms, and internalized fantasy structures, which dominate the child's behavior (such as sadomasochistic persecutory fantasies). They sensitize the child to turn current situations into insults.

Which of the usual activities that occur during child psychotherapeutic sessions are most effective in resolving these problems, both current and chronic? Of the many activities that take place during the child therapy sessions, only a small percentage are effective in helping a child to resolve repressions, master trauma, deal with humiliation, give up symptoms, and progress from regressive behavior.

The portal to obtaining mastery of the facts of progress in child therapy lies in the area of understanding the functioning of the ego structures of the latency-age child. When the child's defenses do not permit him to talk of adjustment problems directly, the alerted therapist is aware that the ego structures of the child still may permit communication through fantasy play. The alerted therapist encourages fantasy play since it can also serve as a means of discharge and vicarious coping with precipitating stresses.

Superficial Use of Play and Fantasy

The encouragement of fantasy and fantasy play is a therapeutic maneuver with multiple potentials. Coping, discharge, working-through, and communication of information are all possible through fantasy play. Therefore, fantasy play may be a means of helping the child to discharge and resolve in conflict areas, at the same time that it becomes a source of information for the working-through of chronic problems of early origin. Strengthening the capacity to fantasize also strengthens the capacity of the child to enter states of latency, with the attendant calm cooperativeness and pliability that permits the child to be taught and to learn. This is done by encouraging the use of symbols and requiring delayed responses. If a child speaks of events haltingly, and with little spontaneity, one may ask if there are any "make believes" that the child has in regard to it. Play objects in the playroom encourage this. Just letting the child play in fantasy, and develop the fantasy, helps the child to work through problems.

One can tell if this technique is working if the fantasies as told, gradually change. For instance, the child who starts off with fantasies that deal with fear of injury and loss of body parts, who goes on to fantasies of penetration and heroism, and the child who moves through fantasies of sadism towards siblings, to fantasies of the acquisition of objects to be used in adult occupations, are heading in the right direction. Often, little in the way of intervention is necessary on the part of the therapist. However, an occasional interpretation or discussion of a fear, coupled with reassurances, may hurry the child on his way to health. All the child apparently needs in order to progress is place enough and time to pursue his fantasies undisturbed. The effectiveness of this technique can be further checked simply by viewing the child's behavior outside the sessions. Maturation of fantasy content (defined in terms of less regressed symbols, situations, and reactions) and improved behavior at home, coupled with appropriate states of latency, are indicators that the therapy is effective.

In many cases discharge through fantasy leads to improved behavior very quickly. Parents tend to remove children from treatment at this point. It is well to forewarn the parents of this course of events. In this way, one is permitted to work through the child's problems more fully. In addition, one is saved the problem of patients who drop out and then return to find no place in a busy practice.

Direct discussion of surface problems, and indirect confrontation of problems through fantasy play, are the most important of the effective technical activities in Latency Age Psychotherapy. Progress clinically with discharge through fantasy is often sufficient to produce improved states of functioning. It cannot be depended upon to produce lasting results. The child who improves using play therapy alone cannot be depended upon to hold his gains. Remissions are common. For this reason, interpretive interventions, improved communication, and sympathetic discussion are important factors in securing gains.

Supportive Therapy Techniques

Selected therapeutically supportive activities are used in child therapy sessions. We deal here not with the technique of cure, but with the activities which are the building blocks from which cure is constructed.

Coping Skills. Coping skills are here defined as those aspects of the personality which may be used in confronting and dealing with day to day issues on a moment to moment basis. They are practical steps and manipulations used to handle pressures brought to bear by others, and to deal with tendencies within the child's own group of disorganizing defensive reactions. The child psychotherapist's role in regard to coping skills is, in essence, what one does while waiting for insight to arrive.

The emphasis on coping skills early on is one of the characteristics of child therapy which differentiates it from child analysis itself. In child analysis, manipulation through discussing coping skills is deemphasized. In child analysis, the dynamic interpretation of the internalized cognitive, defensive, and fantasy structures, that form and sometimes deform the patterns of a life, are the dominant activity. Such interpretations are also frequently used in child therapy, where they are paired with the techniques, especially nonverbal, described here. Dynamic interpretation becomes the basis for working through fantasies.

Other effective psychotherapeutic maneuvers similar to the development of coping skills (e.g., fantasy play as discharge, encouragement of defenses, reassurance, and pedagogy) are emphasized in dynamic psychotherapy but dominate in supportive psychotherapy. When a child's problems are the result of internalized structures and fantasies, child analysis or dynamic psychotherapy is the treatment of choice. Where reality situations, family problems, and insufficient training, or ego fragility are the issues, the therapy will require more and more noninterpretive procedures. Primary emphasis on the latter techniques in therapy is the basis for supportive psychotherapy.

Impaired coping skills are often in evidence in youngsters referred to child therapists. As the result either of chronic pressure from the disordered behavior of the child, or as the result of preexisting disorders of adjustment, the parents themselves often display poor coping skills. Thus, the children have poor models from whom to derive their own techniques. For this reason, there are times when the management of coping skills entails direct work with the parent as well as with the child. The parent who responds to stress by running and panic introduces the child to these techniques. If the parent is not worked with along with the child, the parent may undermine gains made in the treatment as a result of his continuing inappropriate behavior.

A sign in the office of a successful personnel manager read "When in danger, fear and doubt, run in circles, scream and shout." This epitomizes a typical behavior element of a person with poor coping mechanisms. Avoidance as reflected in withdrawal from sports and from contact with aggressive peers is another.

When working with a child who uses avoidance, the therapist should look for a parent who quiets his own inner anxiety by limiting the activities of the child. The parent who drives the child to school when the child could walk or ride the bus limits the child's future capacity to cope with situations requiring independent judgment, and his ability to evaluate and respond to potential danger in new situations.

Working with coping skills usually requires direct intervention. It makes up a good deal of the pedagogical aspect of child therapy. For example, the child who has trouble doing his homework may be invited to do his homework in the therapy session. Direct tutoring help is obviously not the object of the therapist. Rather, an appraisal is made of the child's formal approach to the work. For instance, a child who repeatedly "forgets all I know," when taking tests for which he had "studied hard" was found to have studied only to the point where he could recognize the material required. He had no ability to recall the material spontaneously. No amount of interpretation of motivation could have helped him to utilize his memory skills in a manner that was, until then, beyond his ken. Helping a child to set up schedules and to organize his approach to homework is useful in youngsters who tend to panic when they bunch all their work up to be done at one time.

The youngster who is constantly teased and picked on will find that therapy will eventually help him cease to seek out the group of children whose level of sadomasochistic aggressive energies propel them continually into constant situations in which they are teasing or being teased. They will leave this group when the conflicts (i.e., castration anxiety) that have initiated their regressions are worked through using dynamic interpretation. Early in the process, it is helpful to help the child to cope by helping him to identify those aspects of his own behavior that exaggerate or call forth repetition and intensification of teasing. The therapist may explain that provocations ("What did I do, I only stuck him with a pencil by accident!" "All I did was curse at him, why did he hit me?" "The teacher punished *me* for kicking *him* when *he* started it by moving my paper!") and hypersensitivity ("I can't help crying when they tease me," "They sometimes bring friends along to see how upset I get. It's like I'm a show.") are explained to the child as activities which intensify the amount of teasing received.

Two things happen when this is done. The child implements his new knowledge, so that the teasing decreases. The child is able to gain some distance from the situation, sees his active role in the process, and becomes more available for exploration into his unconscious motivation.

Direct intervention of this sort makes up a large part of the work on coping skills in child therapy sessions. A not inconsiderable contribution, though often inadvertant, is the stance and behavior of the therapist.

A 10-year-old boy, known for his temper tantrums as well as his tendency to respond to his teacher's questions in the classroom situation using expertly imitated French, German, or Spanish accents, came into a session in a furor. He railed against his soccer coach, who had criticized him that day. I sat quietly and listened. At one point he seized a towel rack and actually pulled it out of the wall. I interpreted his displaced anger. He responded with, "How can you sit there calmly?" "If I yelled back, there would only be a fight, and we would have learned nothing of what happened, and then we wouldn't be able to understand anything," said I. He seemed impressed by the use of calm in dealing with an angry person. This impression was confirmed by his mother, who reported that, within the week, he had used calm to deal with her. Upon returning home one afternoon she found that he had left some dirty socks on the floor of his room. She called him from watching television and began to scream her displeasure at him. Instead of his usual raised-voice response, he calmly waited out the storm and then commented to her on the value of discussion rather than yelling. She was doubly taken aback, once because of his new approach, and once because, in spite of his new leaf, he still had not picked up his socks.

In working with children who react to stress or frustration with temper tantrums, the therapist should alert himself to the antecedents and stresses that precipitate the regression, and be ready to offer the child substitute activities. Should the regression begin, the therapist could help the child to replace aggressive, disorganized regressive responses with organized motor syntaxes, which will then be converted to verbal equivalents, so that verbalization and reason can take the place of destructive rages, and interpretive work can be done.

For example, a child of 6, whenever confronted with a toy that he could not operate or a break in an object he was making out of

Playdough, began to scream, shout obscenities, throw chairs, and make a mess. During these periods he was not verbally communicative and tended to set toys poised to break on the edge of shelves and performed exaggerated movements such as the opening and closing of window-curtains. He did the latter with such force and alternating rapidity that I feared they would be broken. I noticed that he had set a superhero doll behind the curtain and then opened and closed it. Sensing that he was creating a quasi-stage for a character he sees on television, I placed a Victorian toy stage that stood on a nearby table at his disposal, showing him how to operate the curtains. He immediately abandoned the window-curtains and placed the doll figure on the stage. He added a second figure and had them play out a tale of attack and trickery in which one character hid beneath the stage while the other sought to find and kill him. When asked, he told me the story and discussed what the characters were doing. Thus was his rage effectively contained through the "socialization" of a gross motor syntax in which he had made global use of the room to express a half-formed fantasy. A bop-bag, clay, or even handing a child a toy gun might have served as well as the stage which was fortuitously at hand that day.

Encouraging Obsessional Defenses. One of the mainstays of the mechanisms of restraint that produce the calm of latency states in the face of anal sadistic drive regressions is obsessional defenses. In states of latency, the clinical manifestations of these defenses consist of controlled patterns of behavior which bind much energy. These include collecting stones, coins, baseball cards, and toy cars, as well as playing board games built around complex rules, drawing pictures based on patterns of geometric forms, and setting up dominoes with great and meticulous care so that they can fall in a row. These activities help to maintain for the child the state of calm which is part of an age-appropriate adjustment pattern.

When such behavior appears in the session it should not be directly discouraged, nor interpreted sui generis. Rather, discussion should proceed parallel to its appearance, with the therapist's awareness, at least in part, directed to the fact that the child is actively struggling to control regressive sadistic urges. The underlying problems may be dealt with without discouraging behavior within the therapy that has the therapeutic effect of strengthening the child's capacity to deal with intrusive regressive trends.

In children who have failed to enter latency, and who show

hyperactive, excited, and at times destructive behavior in therapy sessions, or difficulty in achieving states of calm at home or in school, the introduction of games and activities with structure, such as checkers, board games, counting, watching the clock tick away minutes, or penny collecting, provides defenses that help the child achieve a component of the ego organization that is necessary for achieving latency calm. This in turn permits the child to make progress in the work of maturing that must be done during the latency age period. This must be accomplished if the child is to be ready to negotiate the difficulties of adolescence and adulthood.

Interpretation

The two therapeutic activities described consist of strengthening ego function by changing defenses through encouragement or identification. They are prime representations of nonverbal activities which are psychotherapeutically effective. Now we focus on the role of verbalization and insight in the psychotherapeutic process. The emphasis turns from what to do to what to say.

The Interpretation of "Repeating in Action". Aggressive actions directed toward the therapist, such as silence, teasing, or striking, usually reflect or repeat an event of the day in which the child was the victim. In effect, the behavior of the child reflects an identification with (i.e., internalization of) a person who has behaved in an aggressive manner towards the child. The actions in the sessions serve to help the child to master the recent humiliation. The gain, though of importance, does not have much of an effect beyond the immediate session or relieving the immediate momentary distress. The child is only minimally aware that something is being mastered through the aggressions being brought to bear on the therapist. Through interpretation that causes a verbalization of the process, consciousness, consisting of verbal concepts, is widened to include an awareness of the defensive process.

Often, if the therapist interprets an attack against him with a question such as, "Who hit you like this today?" or "Who teased you like this today?" the child will stop, think, look surprised, and then explore the half-forgotten humiliation which had returned with such force in masked form just moments before. As the child begins to talk of the experience, there is no longer a need to relive it in action. Once the complex of events has been made expressible in verbal form, a kind of world-picture painted in words begins to appear on the canvas provided by the therapeutic situation. Unlike the spontaneous and seemingly random revelations in the playing out of fantasies, a descriptive process that uses words can be directed and expanded so that it can explore with few limits. It can even open doors through the use of verbal deductive reasoning that could only be reached through arduous work, using actions and fantasies brought to the therapy through associations in the nonverbal sphere.

The moment that the child's experience is translated from the world of affect and action to the world of words, there is a change in the quality of the therapy. Reflection, deduction, expanded detail, and manageable abstractions of extended events enrich the potential of the psychotherapeutic situation. Verbal insight becomes possible. Verbal memory becomes a therapeutic tool. Patterns of behavior are recognized. Conflicting, often self-defeating, activities can be considered simultaneously and recognized for what they are. Sources of anxiety in the child's own behavior, potentially under his control, are brought into focus. As a result, motivation for change may be introduced. The child who can see the origins of inappropriate behavior during sessions in misfortunes that befell him in the day just past, may have learned to look for causes in unexpected places and may be induced to use such thinking in other situations. Therefore, working-through (recognizing complexes and reactions and correcting them in all the places that they occur) may be introduced into child therapy, as it can in adult therapy.

Encouraging Verbalization

One is not always confronted with a child who takes out his humiliating experiences on the therapist. The therapeutic activity of getting a child to move his recollection of his experiences into the realm of words, does not always fall so easily "into one's lap." (There are exceptions to this in the form of quite verbal children.) It therefore becomes necessary at times to encourage verbalization in other ways. The most common such procedure is to question the child about his experiences, feelings, and fantasies in such a way that he must put them into words, thus invoking a verbal mode of communication. Questions that can be answered with "Fine," "Good," "All right," and "No" are counterproductive. A much more useful technique is to pick up the part of a child's sentences or activities that contain new elements, and ask for elaboration.

One should be on the alert for sudden changes of topics or a switch from verbalization to fantasy play. This may indicate that material has been reached with which the child cannot deal. These "switch moments" are often the hinges on which therapeutic progress turns. Two possibilities are the most common causes of "switch moments." In the first, the child may have hit material that is too affect-laden to face. In the second, the child's cognition has not matured to the point that he has reached the level of abstraction required to understand the therapist's recent adult-oriented interpretations and to remember them. In the latter case, the level of thought process needed to master the material on a verbal level is beyond the cognitive powers of the child.

There are two technical psychotherapeutic procedures to be followed in this situation. If the cognitive potential is available, the development of the child should be encouraged toward a level at which comprehension, memory, and insight can be maintained at a sufficient level for sustained behavioral changes to occur. Where this is not possible, greater emphasis must be placed on working-through in fantasy. A brief description of these psychotherapeutic processes follows.

Helping to Achieve Cognitive Maturation. The mere act of verbalizing in a situation in which the child is a center of attention for a sustained period of time has a strong influence in making a child become more verbal. Pointing out connections is an important part of this activity. Showing the child the assembly of whole pictures out of smaller units such as lines, circles, and dots, with accompanying verbalization is a useful exercise. For example, draw a few lines which vaguely indicate an animal. Explain to the child that with each new line he will be more able to recognize the image that is slowly being revealed. Add lines until the child links words to the concept of the animal conveyed in the simplest abstract reduction of its form. When a child speaks of a dream, or plays out a story, bring the nonverbal components into the realm of shared memory by having the child mold or draw the image. Then ask about details to foster verbalization. Retain the plastic form of the concept, and return to it again and again. Introduce it when concepts it represents are apparent in the associations of the patient. Concurrently, it behooves the therapist to avoid depending upon or using these communications which improve cognition as dynamic interpretations if they are well beyond the understanding and memory capacity of the child. They need not serve as therapeutic tools over and above their role in encouraging cognitive maturation. Therefore, when the job of cognitive maturation has been achieved, one must return to them if interpretive content is to be conveyed.

Working-Through through Fantasy Play

Fantasy Play as a Therapeutic Activity. Playing out fantasies even in the absence of communicative verbalizations that involve the therapist, and insight, can be of benefit in helping the child to abreact traumas and to work through fixations in psychosexual development.

> This was brought home to me strikingly by an 11-year-old girl who had come to analysis some years before, dominated by the wish to be a boy. She refused to wear girls' clothes, was very athletic, and avoided dolls and such. Toward the end of her treatment she insisted on extended periods of doll play. When I asked her the reason for this, she said that it expressed and fulfilled her need to play out being a mother. This was something she had denied herself before.

Strengthening the Symbolizing Function

At times a child has an absence of the ability to symbolize defensively. This interferes with fantasy play. Such children tend to have latency calm interspersed with episodes of marked anxiety, as opposed to excited behavior. Usually it is active symbolization that is missing. The child can passively use the symbols of others in the form of stories and TV dramas, for hours on end. He cannot, however, produce symbols on his own. Typically, such children fall into silence when they come upon material that is difficult to verbalize. This is in contradistinction to the shift into fantasy play that one normally sees in latency-age children. It is therapeutically useful to help these children to create unique personal symbols so that they can develop fantasy play for use in therapy and life for the mastery of conflicts, humiliations, and fixations. How is this done? One technique is to introduce clay figures, doll figures or drawings to represent the situation being described by the child at the moment he became silent. The next step is to ask the child what happens next, or even to suggest what may happen, using doll figures to illustrate the suggestion. As with most work which deals with cognitive growth in children, the symbolic potential of these children exceeds their functional capacity. This can be harnessed for therapeutic gain.

Fantasy as a Data Source

Fantasy, like dreams, can serve as a source for information and insights. This is even more true in child therapy than it is in the therapy with adults. Childhood fantasies often reflect the stressful events that have confronted the child prior to his coming to the session. The child who beats a punching bop-bag for refusing to eat may be telling the therapist of his own recent experiences with his parents at the dinner table. A repeated play theme of punishment for refusal to obey brings into focus the character trait of stubbornness in a child. The theme, oft repeated, of protecting oneself from having a leg cut off reflects castration fears. Stories of thefts, captures, and imprisonments can serve as signals, like buoys in a bay, that something lies just beneath the surface. In this case, most likely guilt.

Not only recent events but also chronic stresses, fixations, and unresolved conflicts are the precipitates around which the fantasy of the child crystallizes. A current stress that evokes a fantasy defense in latency is usually related in content and form to the pre-existing fantasy that it activates. New fantasy themes are rare. New fantasy content elements, however, are not. Repeated patterns of fantasies that are evoked in a child are usually related to unresolved antecedents and parental attitudes. Thus, the child who fantasizes that he is a hero in the face of being called a name that day may be expected to be chronically sensitive to being called a name because of a parental preoccupation with defects and inadequacies which had been part of his early life. As a result he is ever on the alert to conceal defects, and oversensitive to fault finding. The analysis of fantasy during psychotherapy is a topic that could fill an endless volume. Other examples of it will be found in succeeding chapters.

Judging Therapeutic Progress

There is little in the way of formal psychological testing for progress in therapy in the latency-age child that differs from the standard available psychological tests. In situations in which the behavioral problems of the child are manifestations of a poor symbolizing function, and the usually associated inadequate latency, the progress of the child's improving symbolizing function with therapy can be followed with a test recently devised by Donnellon (1977) that detects the quality of a latency-age child's symbolizing function.

Clinical indicators are reliable and easily detected. Improvement in function is the primary goal of therapy. Improvement is defined in terms of the following key elements. The child should be able to maintain states of sustained calm, quiet, pliability, and educability in appropriate social settings. By the end of therapy, the latency-age child should be capable of symbolization, and resolution of situations of stress, through fantasy play discharge. This should be strongly differentiated in the mind of the therapist from fantasy activity that seeks only to escape from reality. The eventual outcome of latency fantasy as defense is the assumption of primacy by its trial action component. Fantasy as compensatory trial action normally becomes reality-oriented future planning in adolescence. The symbols and situations of late latency play fantasies should be strongly colored by appropriate tendencies toward realistic elements rather than improbable creatures.

The child should be free of the symptoms which brought him to therapy. There should be good relations with peers, including acceptance of the child by other well-functioning children. Often the progress of a child in latency-age therapy can be traced best by following the changing nature and number of his friends. The march toward health is accompanied by an increase in the number of healthy friends, with troubled and provocative children diminishing as companions the further down the road to health the child goes.

Children Who Destroy the Playroom

A most trying situation for the psychotherapist, especially the beginner, occurs when a child reacts to approaches to insight with attempts to destroy the playroom. As often as not information to be gained from a child's behavior is both buried in the chaos produced in the room and reduced by the therapist's need to devote his attention efforts and energy to self-defense.

To introduce the situation in its most virulent form, let us watch it through the eyes and experience of a neophyte therapist. The following is taken from a supervisory session, which occurred immediately after the session in question.

The resident who presented was involved in his first experience in working with latency-age children. Jimmy was 8 years old. He came into the session with a rather negative attitude. There was a clinic rule which required that sessions be held during the Christmas vacation. The child insisted that this week was his vacation week. He could see no reason to be at the session. He was there only because his mother had said he had to be there. He claimed that he had no need for therapy.

The child's history revealed repeated difficulties. In school he broke things belonging to other children. He was known to have broken a window. Once, while at summer camp, he stole the keys to a counselor's car, started the car and, with a group of other children in tow, drove the car a distance of two blocks. The voyage ended when he smashed the car into a nearby tree. He told the other children, who had somehow miraculously escaped unscathed, that if they told the counselors or the head of the camp about his stealing the car, he would kill them. The children were victimized and brutalized by the patient for three or four days. Finally one of the children went to the camp director and told him of the incident and of his fear for his own life.

Jimmy was a particularly handsome youngster, with a winning smile. He knew well that he was in therapy because his behavior was out of control. He was on the brink of being transferred from public to private school because he couldn't be managed. Still he lost sight of his problems and of the goal of the therapy. Instead he came to see the therapist primarily as someone with whom to play, to use as a foil for teasing, and as an object for acting on his sadistic fantasies.

Severe family problems were apparent. The parents had little interest in each other. They were occupied most of the time in highly complex, multiple extramarital affairs. The father was known to have punched a hole into the wall of the living room when he felt that his job was endangered.

A psychotherapeutic approach involving individual therapy for the child was chosen to augment counseling of the parents. The primary reason for this was the observation that the youngster's behavior was not merely attributable to a tension–discharge disorder (impulsive type). There was seen evidence of pattern to his behavior. Internalization of fantasy was present.

A fantasy-driven neurotic pattern informed his behavior. He had repeated dreams in which overt castrative elements appeared. He was diagnosed dynamically as a person with marked internalized conflicts manifesting castration anxiety, which was defended against by counterphobic aggressive behavior. His behavior in the individual sessions in no way contradicted this.

He was filled with bravado, braggadocio, and flaunting of powers. When his fears and bodily vulnerability fantasies were explored or approached, he became doubly upset and angry and he doubled his sadistic activities towards the therapist.

Play therapy in which these fantasies were played out in the therapy room were accompanied by a diminution in the amount of aggressive, sadistic, counterphobic behavior in home and in school. He played out Superman-type fantasies in which he would rescue the world from dangerous attackers.

The main problem presented to the supervisor therapist was containing the energies of the child. They were being diverted away from fantasy play, which, when permitted to progress, led to insight and mastery. Unfortunately, though, the child's energies were usually diverted into aggressive, sadistic, and sometimes physically destructive behavior aimed at the contents of the playroom, as well as at the therapist himself.

For example, during the Christmas session, the child had unexpectedly stopped his play and begun to punch the therapist. This was followed by throwing a container filled with colored felt markers on the floor. He then screamed at the therapist, telling him to pick up the markers or else he would kill the therapist. He then took a wastebasket and threw it up at the ceiling, breaking one of the acoustical ceiling tiles.

Interpretations of his aggression as a defense against castration fears only stirred the child to greater anger and brought his attention toward the therapist, whom he began to pummel with his fists. When the therapist held the child at a distance to prevent himself from being further punched, the child began to kick him in the shins. The child could not be restrained. However, he kept close watch on the clock. He stopped punching the therapist to take time out to break a small metal car with a hammer. Precisely at the end of the session the child walked out.

At the beginning of the following session the child came in somewhat apprehensively. He was obviously concerned with the impact of what he had done on the therapist. He displayed immediate relief when he saw the therapist had provided a punching bag, which, the therapist explained to him, could be used for the deflection of his aggression should that be necessary in this session. The child did not show insight at that point. He was more concerned with punishment. If there were no punishment then he didn't particularly care to pursue what had happened further, even though he was asked to do so by the therapist. At one time he stated, "My Mommie pays the clinic for the sessions and you have to stay here and let me do these things." Insight was not his goal.

A regressed externalized superego marked the moment of shame that he had shown when walking into the playroom (see

Chapter 14). When the therapist did not respond by taking the role of the punishing superego, the child was able to retire his superego-motivating affects. He then began to look around the room to see what he could do or use for play.

The supervisor asked for descriptions of any prior episode which could have provided some warning to the therapist, had he been on the lookout. The supervisor pointed out that in the very initial stages of any therapy with latency-age children—especially the younger ones—there should be a phase of exploration to see the propensity that the child has for such regressions.

There are two distinct categories of children with regressive potentials.

First, the purely neurotic child has regressive potentials in the area of psychosexual development. He may go from phallically- to anally-informed fantasy activity. Fantasy and fantasy play continue to be operative during such regressions. Destructive action is not available. In response to interpretation, the neurotic child tends to change his associations in the direction of making the unconscious conscious and utilization of energies formerly used for repression in the service of healthier defenses.

Second, the child who has a potential to destroy the playroom has regressive potentials in the area of ego function and impulse control. In the face of stress he may shift from destructive fantasy to destructive action. The existence of this potential should be determined before interpretations of unconscious content are offered. In response to interpretation, the impulsive, motor-oriented child will transmute the uncovered unconscious impulses into action.

There are, of course, mixed pictures of regression, which are described in Chapter 6.

How does the therapist determine early on that such potentials exist? When working with a child whose relationships are characterized by teasing and being teased, bullying and being bullied, the therapist should be on the alert for overt physical aggression against himself or the playroom. A history of impulsive behavior also indicates such potential.

A limited ability to use words, symbols, and play is also an important clue. Be on the alert for physical aggression, too, when working with the child who prefers to work through and express himself with three-dimensional objects used in an only slightly symbolized manner. The child who would rather make swords and have duels is more apt to tear the office apart than the child who is content to sit and talk about his problems, or to spin fantasies. The following material, based on a supervisory session, illustrates the ease with which aggression assumes physical expression in such youngsters.

The therapist confirmed the fact that his patient's history and therapy behavior contained many examples of impulsive motor acting out of impulses. The therapist told of an attempt on his part to help the child to bind his energies and to slow down his responses. The therapist introduced origami, a Japanese paper-folding technique. (This gains the child's interest and deflects energy into a constructive channel.)

Upon entering the room the child insisted that he wanted to play ball. There was no ball present. The child still insisted. The therapist, who was skilled in origami, pulled out an instruction book. He soon showed the youngster that the office was not as ill-equipped as the child had thought. It would be possible to make a ball out of a piece of paper. Each took a piece of paper and began to make an origami ball.

Certainly it would have been better to have searched through interpretation for that against which the aggressive behavior defended. The problem was that the child at that moment required ego building. The antennae for receiving insight had been withdrawn and had been replaced by provocation. The youngster became fascinated by the paper-folding process. He was able to slow down his activities and his impulsive movements. There was a jocular interchange. The youngster had to have a number of corrections. He insisted upon exchanging model balls, or pieces of paper, with every mistake that he made. Camaraderie developed. The therapist began to let down his guard, relaxing and regressing away from an adult and therapeutic distance. He could now play with the youngster, losing his somewhat distant but clearly differentiating psychotherapeutic stance. The balls were completed. The first ball was completed by the child, with the therapist's help. Then the therapist lightheartedly completed his own ball.

At that point the therapist picked up the ball—very light and made of paper—and tossed it at the child, hitting him on the forehead. The youngster became enraged, humiliated, and began to grab the ball, threw it on the floor, stepped on it, and began to punch at the therapist and to throw everything on the table to the floor.

In supervision, the therapist added, "I know and understand

what happened there. I had aggravated his castration fears by throwing something at him when he hadn't expected it and hitting him in the forehead. The boy felt humiliated. I had become so comfortable with what we were doing that I forgot his propensity for destructiveness and his vulnerability and sensitivity." (The myths of childhood innocence and of the bland drives of latency are easily evoked. They are icebergs in the psychotherapeutic sea, set to endanger the unwary.) "But I don't quite understand what happened in the most recent session when he almost tore the place apart."

The supervisor suggested that they go over the therapy session in detail to see what could have happened.

"To begin with," noted the supervisor, "the youngster was very angry when he came into the session. In dealing with any youngster who has a tendency to regress to physically expressed impulsivity, anger upon entering the playroom signals danger that the room or therapist could be attacked.

There are techniques, both long-term and short-term, for minimizing the potential for patient violence during child psychotherapy sessions. One short-term technique would be to help the youngster to structure the session. Ordering the child to behave might work, but is fraught with a potential that the child as a result of admonition will see his aggression and anger as a potent expression of sadistic drives that can "get to" the therapist. This will only increase the possibility of aggressive action aimed at the therapist.

Structuring is best achieved through befriending the child. This can be done by introducing games and play material that require mutual interaction and some structuring rules. The introduction of origami is an example. One must remember not to lose distance just because the child has gained some. In introducing a game, the child's potential for action is limited to the parameters of the game. This is not insight-oriented activity, nor should it be. Interpretations that would expand access to unconscious, material, and free energies, and modify fantasies are more apt to stir up more rage and pathological defenses when directed towards an enraged child. The angry child is not receptive to insight. He must be prepared for insight, through being made calm and sufficiently distant from himself to be able to accept and make observations about his behavior.

When a child with a potential for violence comes into the session angry, one is confronted by a nontherapeutic situation. The therapy session is not set within the matrix of calm which will enable self-reflection and the pursuit of insight. Whereas adults comment that they are aware of how upset they are and wish to understand it, the child is very often immersed in his upsetness and struggling only to free himself of the discomfort. Like the dog who has been hurt, he is apt to bite the person who extends the helping hand of friendship.

Once the child is calmed enough to listen, the therapist may direct the child's activity into verbalization, for instance storytelling. Careful questioning about what has happened and what the child's plans are can reintroduce the therapist as ally and friend. The therapist should try to get the child to verbalize the reasons for his discontent. Has he been misled? Does he feel tricked? Is there a way to prevent the difficulty in the future?

Although there are what appear to be discussion topics in these questions, in each case the primary purpose is not to obtain information. It is to bring the child out of the affectomotor world of anger into the world of interactive communicative speech. Through delay and symbolization, the world of representation will provide a buffer against the world of feeling and acting. The technique is just the opposite of that used with the obsessional adult neurotic. It is also opposite in intent to the technique ordinarily used in helping a youngster find a way to communicate something that has been strongly repressed, or something for which the child has never found words.

With a child who is capable of regression to physical shows of violence it is necessary to avoid play activities which consist of three-dimensional expressions of memory. These include working with clay, and acting or living out dueling, wrestling, or fighting with the therapist. It is all right if the child fights with a bop-bag. It is all right if toy figures fight. It is courting danger, however, to permit the child to take on the therapist in hand to hand combat. It is especially necessary, during times of upset, to step aside and let the child's aggression and anger bypass the therapist.

Mansur, aged 10, decided to build swords out of cardboard with which to play out with the therapist a fantasy of swordsmen. The youngster particularly liked to play a game in which he was almost defeated and then, rising like a phoenix from the ashes of defeat, he destroyed the person who had been defeating him. This eventually was traced by the child and the therapist to a feeling of being overwhelmed by the angry yelling of his father, who apparently lost control as much as the child did. At one point during the dueling play the child let his guard down and the stereotyped striking of a raised sword which was an agreed-upon maneuver in the fantasy was not achieved. The therapist's sword fell lightly upon the youngster's arm.

The child had come into the session angry and tense. Through controlled play he was mastering these feelings. He was at the edge of experiencing and actively mastering recent painful events. Touching his unguarded arm unexpectedly in a situation which was not under his control revealed to him the passivity imposed by his age and size. Shorn of his defenses and too close to the physical as a mode for the expression of his drives, he lost control. This gave rise to tears, rage, screaming, punching, and trying to involve the therapist in a fist fight. This replaced what had been a good-natured exploration of his fantasy life, a turn of events that could be measured within the blink of an eye.

The therapist pointed out to the youngster that he was so upset that he would probably start a fight at home. The child projected responsibility for his rage onto the therapist, saying, "and it will be your fault." Thus he indicated a total loss of the prior insight. Although this particular situation was somewhat devastating and disastrous it was used in subsequent sessions to point out to the youngster the displacement derived from the interactions that he was having with his parents.

This case illustrates how quickly a youngster can shift from three-dimensional, whole-body, direct combatant play into angry fighting and destructiveness. It is much more difficult to go into this state from playing with two cardboard figures which are fighting each other on a tabletop while the therapist sits on the other side of the room, observing.

The ordinary pattern of cognitive steps used in helping a child to express that to which he doesn't have ready access requires one to follow the following rules. If a child cannot tell about it, have the child draw it. If the child cannot draw it, have the child work in clay. Notice that one goes from verbalization to two-dimensional figures (e.g. drawings) and thence to three-dimensional figures (e.g. work in clay or motor syntaxes involving aggressive, whole-body movement). Knowledge of this pattern is highly useful. It is more fully described below (Chapter 10). Working with three-dimensional units is very close to slipping into whole-body participation as a combatant in destructive behavior. When one approaches this type of activity or interaction with a youngster who has a tendency towards destructiveness, one is walking on rather thin ice. In the area of three-dimensional activities or three-dimensional story-telling, the more involved in fantasy the story-telling is, the better the outcome and the safer one is. The more direct and concrete the representation is, the more one is apt to light up destructiveness in the playroom.

The therapist at this point interrupted the supervisor to say, "What you're describing here are rather general concepts which can help in heading off destructive outbursts. They guide through the use of certain principles. They help the therapist who is afraid of the child's anger during the course of therapy. What if the therapist wants to face the anger and analyze it? Isn't it possible that the child will take advantage of a therapist who consistently avoids anger in this way? The therapist could be completely cowed. Isn't there a point at which such behavior on the part of the therapist will interfere with and even limit some of the potential of psychotherapy to help the child to mobilize information and bring it to the surface? I would think that there is a limit to the extent that it can be followed. If one decides not to follow these principles with a vulnerable child, but rather one does proceed to explore for hidden and repressed material, and the child does begin to go over the edge, what techniques do you advise to head off further destruction?" The supervisor responded by describing what he considered the most important step. "The most important thing you can do is to *distract* the child. Fortunately, for the circumstance, these youngsters are rather immature and easily distracted. At least this combination exists in children who are easily raised to anger. There are many elements of immaturity here which have parallels in youngsters with immature central nervous systems and neurological disorders.

One of the most useful distractions is a bop-bag. The very aggressive youngster will be apt to take the simple plastic one and throw it around and punch it and even tear into it until he causes the sand to pour out. More endurance can be obtained by using a sturdy cylindrical cloth punching bag on which drawings can be made in chalk. This is presented to the child when the child feels he wants to hit or punch something. Drawings in chalk can be utilized for helping the child to mobilize the fantasies which are often involved in this kind of behavior.

There is always the last resort, which is asking the child to leave the session and explain to the mother that the child is not in control. I've never actually gotten to the point where this had to be done, but have been amazed at how quickly children quiet down when the mere mention of the possibility of terminating the session is made."

"How therapeutic is this?" asked the therapist.

The supervisor answered, "Setting limits and helping the child to displace or restrict himself to cognitive patterns requiring self-restraint and verbalization when handling problems and excitements has therapeutic value in and of itself. The ego is strengthened by the experience. There are times in therapy sessions when children who are capable of destructive behavior force one into the position of helping the child to preserve his self-esteem. This is achieved through aiding the child to preserve his sense of his ability to control his own aggression, and avoid humiliation as a result of loss of control. Ego regressions and associated ego anxiety often occur in response to being overwhelmed by one's drives. It's a major humiliation for many of these children to lose control. Many are ashamed to come back. There are times in psychotherapy when long-term therapeutic goals become less important than the preservation of the child's pride of self as well as preservation of the therapist's own physical integrity and office property. Incidentally, I cushion the child for this from the start. I say to the children when therapy begins in a playroom, 'you can do anything you want here as long as it doesn't hurt the equipment, you or me.'"

The therapist then stated, "You know, I don't actually have a playroom, and it makes me very nervous and tense in working with these children. I think in the future I'm not going to work with any child who has this potential. I'll try to rule it out as soon as possible and then discharge him, because I don't think I want the cost of a playroom."

The supervisor then asked, "What kind of a setup do you have for children?"

The therapist then stated, "I have a corner of the room with a little table in it and some things to draw on and some clay and things to play with. But I have to put the table away in a closet and clean up before my next patient comes in."

The supervisor said, "There's no question about the fact that a playroom would be necessary if you were to consider working with children who have this propensity. The mere fact that you are tense will be picked up by them and will be used by them. You are becoming the target of their sadism. It's hard to be a good therapist when you're afraid that a child's going to break your favorite picture frame, destroy a chair, or cut up a couch that's to be used by the next patient. It's hard enough for a child to differentiate forbearance from weakness. It makes things harder for the child when he can really make you frightened."

The therapist asked, "Is it possible for mixed pictures to appear? Are there neurotic youngsters who have this potential? What are the typical dynamics of such neurotic youngsters?"

Answered the supervisor, "Well, I'm glad you asked that question because it points toward certain psychotherapeutic strategies to be used in working with them. There are, indeed, mixed pictures. There are two types of neurotic youngsters who behave in this way.

"*First,* there are those who have much fear of their fantasies. They have a primitive symbolizing function that makes their fantasies almost as disorganizing and frightening as raw drive energy. They become very fearful when any kind of aggressive feelings occur. Very often these youngsters will claim to hear a voice that tells them to misbehave and throw things. On the surface it looks spontaneous and impulsive. They appear to have isolated and encapsulated expressions of aggression."

I remember working with one youngster, the prettiest little 6-year-old girl who was most refined in her manner and attitude. In the middle of sessions and quite unexpectedly when something made her angry, she threw a pencil across the room. When asked, she blandly spoke of the voices that commanded her. When it was explained to her that the voices were really her rejected angry feelings and she was encouraged to verbalize her anger or to find play symbols through which to express anger through fantasy, the voices (externalization of anger) ceased.

"With such youngsters it is necessary to help with the development of the symbolizing function by substituting more and more symbols which are more and more displaced so as to help them develop a symbolizing function. This is extensively illustrated by Sarnoff (1976, Case 1).

"*Second* there are those who are well able to form symbols and to develop a rich fantasy life. These symbols and fantasies might well have been able to be used defensively to enter into latency had the child the requisite calm and lack of overstimulation in the home. These youngsters are usually very strongly stimulated by the parents, and the only way to deal with them is to counsel the parents to see that such things as wrestling with the children, bathing with the children in the nude, taking the children into bed with them, beatings, screaming and yelling, and appearing drunk before the children come to an end.

"The most frequent, immediate dynamic family problems that I have detected, especially with these aggressive children, is a pathological fathering, which consists of an overconcern with the child's sexuality in the girls, and a lack of time and attention on a one-to-one basis by the fathers with both girls and boys. In regard to the latter, the fathers come home, take naps, and watch TV. They don't spend time with the children. The children's rage is, to a large extent, derived from the sense of being deserted by the parent for whom they very often wait. Often the child will not tell you about this, and it has to be asked for, when interviewing. Look for great anger at omissions. For instance, look for the situation in which the child feels that he has been promised that he will go out with his father and then the promise which has been made is not kept. Often parents will attempt to substitute buying gifts in toy stores for the relationship that the child needs. Although the child likes getting the presents, the sharp contrast between the ready purchase of any present wanted and the lack of interest that follows creates an even greater sense of disappointment."

These potentially harmful outbursts are more commonly seen in youngsters before the age of 8 or 9. In the later years, it usually takes the form of the child getting up and stamping out of the room, or of a child smashing nails into pieces of wood with a hammer, or cutting up all of your chalk with a scissor. It's therefore a good idea to be especially on the lookout for such behavior in the youngster younger than 9.

Interferences with the Therapeutic Process

Parental Attitudes

One of the most common intrusions on the child therapy situation consist of actions by parents whose other obligations or wishes cause them to interfere with or cancel sessions. This is often an indication that the motivations and aspirations of the parents and the therapist may be quite at odds. The following clinical vignette illustrates the way in which therapist and parent may have ideas in relation to psychotherapy and its purpose that clash and create interferences with therapy.

The parents of a child who was making progress in therapy requested a meeting with the therapist in order to discuss the future career goals of their child. They were somewhat distressed by the thought that the child wanted to be a musician. They felt that this was not a sufficiently dependable or responsible a job. The reason that the parents brought the child to therapy was the mother's preoccupation with the thought that the child might grow up to be a homosexual. She voiced no concern for her child's diffuse inability to function in all areas—school, home, friends—that became apparent in the initial diagnostic evaluation of the child. In prior discussions, the mother had said that she would like to see the youngster become a physician. By this point in his therapy, the youngster had achieved a certain amount of skill in his academic work. The therapist attempted to help the parents to realize that, since the child was 10 years of age, there was still a great deal of time before career decisions had to be made. He tried to bring them to talk of the child's current problems, but the parents pressed forward with their discussion.

"I would like him to be a professional," said the mother.

"What kind of professional?" asked the father.

"Well, you know what we talked about before," the mother replied.

"You mean a lawyer!" exclaimed the father. "That's what I am. It takes a real man. That's not for him. I think he'd be better doing what you do, doctor. That's more in keeping with his personality. What do you think?" The father completely missed the implications and irony involved in the father's request that the therapist join him in the identification of psychotherapists as passive and nonmasculine.

Parental attitudes led to numerous interferences with the psychotherapy schedule. At one time during the therapy, the father's attitude informed a request that a session be cancelled because the child's masculinity needed to be strengthened and this could best be done by having the youngster go to see a world series baseball game. This, in the father's estimation, was the best way to create masculinity. The father had very little sympathy with the psychotherapeutic goal or method for achieving it. He would not have accepted as a successful resolution of the child's sexual identity confusion the achieving of the role of teacher, or psychotherapist for his son. The therapist would have considered his work well done had the patient been able to achieve the academic, social, and personality skills required for the relatedness necessary for any of those roles. A pursuit of the unconscious was beyond the father's ken. He sought instead identification with sports figures as a means of strengthening his child's masculinity at the expense of regular attendance at therapy sessions.

It was clear that the father was not particularly involved in the therapy, except to challenge it. It was the mother's wish to have the child in therapy that kept him there, even though her reasons were not the same as those recognized by the therapist as that which required therapy. It was the mother with whom the therapist needed to maintain a therapeutically supporting relationship in order to continue the therapy. The therapy of a latency-age child can function only if the parent is willing to bring the child and to support the therapy.

It is not unusual for the parent to destroy the therapeutic situation simply by engaging in intensive fights with the child on the trip to the doctor's office. It is necessary to instruct the parents of children who tend to establish sadomasochistic relationships not to engage in this pattern.

It is also advisable to tell parents to keep the therapy out of fights and family battles. It is best to keep the therapy from becoming a bone of contention. It is especially wise not to threaten the child with the loss of the therapy. Therapy should not be used as a means for getting the child to behave. The therapist should be portrayed by the parent to the child as a colleague, a guide and a helper—never as a punisher. In no way should the parent make an unwarranted assertion that information that has become available to him has come from the therapist. This will only support and intensify the common fantasies that children have at the beginning of therapy that the parent is using the therapist as a spy, colleague and agent for the assertion of the parent's wishes.

A parent became angry at his enuretic child, and told him that if he wet his pants again he would not be permitted to see his psychiatrist. The child, who had appeared on the surface to be quite confused, turned to his father and, with very clear logic said, "But isn't that why I'm going there?"

Parental Wealth

Sometimes a patient's wealth presents problems.

A man in his late forties entered his therapy session making a whistling sound, closed the door, sat down and said, "Wow, that's really something."

"What's really something?" asked the therapist.

"That car. You know the mother who just left here with that girl?" said the patient. "She was driving a Cadillac Eldorado. She only takes it sometimes. Most of the time she's got a little Mercedes Benz to scoot around in. Doesn't it just make you jealous?"

The therapist, who had no children himself, gazed at the patient with an intense feeling of awe which was in no way related to the jealousy that was imputed to him by the patient. Rather, his thoughts dwelled upon the fact that this man had a son who was a graduate of a fine college, an achievement from which he derived little in the way of pride. He related to money as power and was in awe of it.

The man's observation was—though faulty in particulars—valid in general. The girl's parents' money created problems for the therapist. However they were not problems of envy. They were problems in the child's adjustment, that he had to work with. The patient herself, aged 10 years, devoted extensive periods of therapy time to playing games involving multitudes of small dolls which lived in a big house near which lived a very poor family. The content of one therapy session after another dealt with fear that the poorer family would do something to the wealthy family out of jealousy. Once the child assigned the therapist the task of making a house for one set of dolls, while she made one for another. She kept criticizing the therapist for his lack of foresight in leaving out the swimming pool, the extra garage, the room for the giant-screen television set—all of which she felt were the sine qua non for an average home. She was led from these presentations to a discussion of her attitudes which held those people who did not have this to be disgusting and lazy and dangerous.

Homes of great wealth can make the giving of gifts meager gestures. Those who treat wealthy youngsters must be aware of the impairments to ego strengths and reality testing that occur when wealth facilitates the ability of fantasy, wish, and reality to fuse with much ease. Extra time should be spent in detecting and treating impairments in reality testing. Envy should be dealt with in oneself. On the other side of the spectrum, one must beware the aggression and patronizing countertransference-like behavior that is involved in dealing with youngsters from a poor background who are seen in clinics. Their material needs may be so great that one may lose sight of the intrapsychic. Therapy may be interfered with by the therapist's desire to provide the child with toys. With affect-starved children, this may give rise to hostility in the child when giving does not continue unabated. The therapist should be ever on the alert to recognize his own unconscious impulse to show up the parents. Children will defend against any activity that is seen as showing up the father. Latency-age children become angry and find an excuse or a reason to justify their parents' way of living.

The Child Seeks an Ally

Even though their interferences are blatant, and their discipline severe, direct criticisms of parents by the therapist are much to be avoided when talking to the child. One should speak to the parents directly, when the child seeks to get the therapist as an ally against the parent in situations as the following.

A 10-year-old child reported that the other children her age were permitted by their parents to go to see a movie that she was not permitted to see. It contained explicit sex. Her parents disapproved of such movies. The child felt very much put upon. She complained, began to yell and misbehave. The parents restricted the child from going out at all and added to this a six-month restriction on watching television. Cries of "Tell them to change. I'm right. They're wrong." filled the therapy session.

In such instances it should be explained to the parents privately that this sort of punishment is too severe. The child will soon forget his misdeed, but will remain angry at the punishment itself. Thus the ground will be laid for new provocations by the child. The duration of a punishment should not exceed the child's ability to remember the original incident of misbehavior. With latency-age children, punishment should be immediate, short, and directly related to the misdeed at hand.

The child, however, will turn to the therapist often and say, "Were my parents wrong? Look at how unhappy that made me, I can't watch television, what am I going to do? Call them up and tell them to let me watch television." The therapist should define his role, telling the child that his work and the child's work are not aimed at change in the parents. Rather, there are sessions in order to help the child to understand what the parents are doing and to comprehend what influence the parents' behavior is having on the child's patterns of behavior and will have on the child's way of behaving in the future, when they meet other people who behave as their parents do with them. Sometimes it is useful to refer to the moods of parents rather than their actions. Actions vary in content. There are fewer variations of mood. Mood can be asked about and returned to in later sessions.

Third-Party Payment

One of the most difficult situations in dealing with parents has to do with the parent of the child who is being seen in the clinic in which the treatment is paid for by a government program that does not require payment for missed sessions. Where there is no payment for missed sessions to reimburse the clinic, there is pressure on the therapist from the clinic. There is no financial pressure on the parent to bring the child to treatment when there is no charge for missed sessions. Other activities are given priority, especially those that entail an expense.

A therapist reported a multitude of misses during the treatment of an 8-year-old boy. When the family bothered to offer a reason, forgetting, other activities, inability to obtain transportation were foremost. The child behaved in a most verbal and cooperative manner whenever he did come to sessions; but he came to sessions rarely. The clinic had a rule that if there were three sessions in a row missed, therapy would be dropped. At no time did the family reach this limit.

There's an ethical conflict about discontinuing therapy with a motivated child. If neither child nor parent is motivated, one might as well drop the therapy. However, something is gained by the motivated child. When it is the parent who is interfering, it seems unfair to the child to drop him from treatment without making a strong attempt to explain to the parent what's happening. When the fee or a part of it is covered by patients, missed sessions are fewer and arbitrary misses are a matter of parental concern. Sessions for which parents are not financially responsible often create unavoidable complications.

For instance, a child entered the therapy session after a missed session. No mention of the missed session was made. There had been no phone call from the parent. The therapist commented, "I noticed that you missed the last session."

The child responded, "I had to get a new suit. Didn't my mother call you?"

"No," said the therapist.

"Well, I went to get a new suit with my mother," said the boy. "I asked my mother, 'Shouldn't we go see the doctor,' but— weren't you on vacation last week? I think that's what my mother said."

"No."

"Oh, wait a second, I remember, I asked my mother to call and my mother promised to call you. Didn't my mother call you?"

If the therapist is to answer this question honestly, he, in effect, exposes the mother as a liar. On the other hand, the child may be lying, and if the therapist says that the mother called, then the therapist is the liar. It's important to avoid revealing the parent as a liar, however, and the therapist was eager to avoid such a revelation.

While the therapist was trying to think of something to say, the child said, "Why, didn't *you* call?"

Under this pressure, the therapist told the child that he did not call and that the mother did not call. He stated that directly. Implied was the fact that the mother had lied to him.

The supervisor suggested to the therapist that in the future, should such a situation come up, he should not put himself in a situation where he is opposed to the parent. State the situation positively. For instance, one could say, "I will call your mother to tell her I feel the appointments are important." The interest in the child is reinforced. The possibility is kept open for the mother to cooperate without a polarization being created in which the mother is seen as behaving in a certain way that is wrong, and the therapist is all good.

Making Announcements

Ironically, it was necessary in the above case for the therapist to bring up in the same session the fact that the clinic was to run a summer camp. The therapist had the responsibility to ask the youngster whether or not he wanted to attend. Since they were fast approaching summer and the child was seen once a week, it was necessary to ask him as soon as possible. He might well miss the next few sessions and be unable to be informed in time.

When should the topic be broached: at the beginning of a session, with such a phrase as "Before we begin, I'd like to tell you there's a summer camp run by the clinic. Would you be interested in going?"; at the end of a session, with such phrases as "We have to stop now, and, by the way, we have a summer camp for people in the clinic; I'd like you to think about it and tell me whether you want to go, when you come back."; in the middle of the session, preferred by many, saying "There's a summer camp run by the clinic. Would you be interested?"?

It's important to make an announcement to parents first so that they are informed and can let you know whether what you wish to offer is possible or impossible. If the parents are absolutely against it, there's no use bringing these things up with a child. You may only end up pitting the child against the parent. Gifts should be approved by parents. This helps avoid a situation in which the parents reject.

Making an announcement when the therapy session starts may interfere with the patient's ability to bring in important new information. An end announcement leaves the child without any chance to associate or let you know how he feels. It's like homework.

If one is to use the initial part of the session for an announcement, one does not interfere with ongoing associations, and it is possible to follow the person's associations and responses to the announcement throughout the session. I prefer this timing for this reason.

If possible, one should provide at least two sessions of leeway in advance of an announcement. This gives one the chance to wait for an appropriate time to make an announcement. If it's at all possible to present it appropriately during the middle of the session, so as not to interfere with associations, then of course this should be done.

Countertransference

Countertransference refers to reactions on the part of a therapist to a patient's behavior or to therapeutic situations, either of which recreate for the therapist reflections of early life experiences. The therapist's behavior is obligatory, repetitive, and distracting from the primary work of the therapy. The most common situations that evoke such countertransferences are those associated with ordinary breaks in schedule. These include absences, misses, late payments, and announcements of future missed sessions. The introduction of a scheduled vacation announcement in the middle of a session, though preferred by many, tends to interfere with ongoing associations and gives more play for countertransference than either end or beginning announcements.

Let us turn to some examples of the way in which countertransference can interfere with associations and result in announcements that interrupt the flow of free association.

In the case of the youngster whose mother repeatedly missed sessions with the child:

> The child had busied himself after the interchange with the therapist about why he was absent and who was responsible for his absence; the youngster began looking around the room and

found some racing cars. He announced that he was going to play
a story about two brothers in racing cars. The two brothers were
involved in a race to see who could go faster. At this point the
therapist intervened with the announcement that the clinic-
related summer camp was available, and this put an immediate
end to further associations having to do with the rivalry between
the two brothers.

It is only conjecture that the fact that the therapist had a brother
may have influenced his intercession at this time. There is less conjecture in the nature of the countertransference in the next case.

A 30-year-old fellow in child psychiatry, a single woman, known
for her sturdy shoes, makeup-free face, and sensible clothing, presented
the case of a 14-year-old girl with an elevator phobia.

The girl worked as a candy-striper in a nearby hospital affiliated
with the clinic in which the fellow was working. She had discussed with the therapist her fear of elevators, her fear of going
up in the elevator, her fear of being caught in the elevator.
Claustrophobic problems had been talked about and worked
through. Separation–individuation and imagery relating the elevator to the womb had been dealt with. The child was now able to
ride the hospital elevators instead of walking up and down stairs.
During a session in which she spoke of the increased ease with
which she was able to carry out her tasks in the hospital, the girl
reported the following experience.
"I got all scared again the other day in the elevator. I was
riding—I got on on the second floor and I pushed the button to
go up to the third floor and the elevator went down to the first
floor instead of going to the third floor first, and a surgery
resident [who was blond, and blue-eyed with broad shoulders and
a chummy manner] got in. I got a big lump in my throat and I
hoped I wouldn't get scared. The elevator got stuck between the
second and third floors and people came running. The doctor
pushed the alarm and people yelled at us, 'We'll have you out of
there in about twenty minutes.'"
She said, "I began to get all nervous all over, and I began to
have all kinds of funny, excited feelings in my vagina."

At this point the fellow saw fit to make her first intervention of the
session. She simply stated, "In four and a half weeks, I'm going on my
vacation."

We can surmise that the therapist had expressed her own discomfort and lack of ease in dealing with topics relating to attractiveness and sexually exciting situations in a distracting thrust of irrelevant material into the session. In this way the therapist could present a well rationalized reason for interfering with problems in the life of the patient, that the therapist had not mastered in her own life.

Termination in Child Psychotherapy

As in other respects of psychotherapy with the latency-age child, termination of psychotherapy has characteristics contributed by the structure of latency.* There is a propensity for the use of fantasy as an escape from, and expression of, problems. Fantasies can express termination reactions which might otherwise have entered treatment through acting out, verbalization, or description of inner experiences and sensations.

Since, in the latency-age child, fantasy formation often takes precedence over verbalization, it can serve as a conduit through which otherwise unobtainable material relating to termination enters the therapeutic situation. At times the defensive, masking aspect of such fantasy formation will override its communicative aspect and interfere with the working through of termination. Fortunately, there are certain characteristic fantasies that occur in latency state children during periods of termination that represent termination reactions. Familiarity with the nature of these fantasies equips the therapist to recognize them as such. Thus termination reactions can be dealt with more quickly and effectively.

Children have less control over terminations than do adults in psychotherapy, and there are more frequent separations during child therapy. Children's dependence on parents in such matters as mobility, place of domicile, and payment for treatment creates more possibilities for separations, interruptions, and terminations in the psychotherapy of children. The lives of children are thus shaped by the movements, emotional reactions, and decisions of adults. Parents may have to move for occupational reasons. Parents may lose interest in therapy. Parents may feel physically overwhelmed by the task of bringing a child to therapy. Parental vacations may cause interruptions in treatment. Parents may develop negative transferences that cannot be worked through. These elements create a multitude of interruptions in

---

*This section is based on Sarnoff, *Latency*, pp. 247–261.

psychotherapy which are beyond the child's control, and may produce psychological responses in him.

There are other causes of interruptions in child therapy, such as illnesses, departures for summer camp, special school trips, and school holidays. Interruptions and "mini-terminations" during summer camp, vacations, and parental travel stir separation feelings in child therapy situations long before the actual termination phase of the psychotherapy. This occurs to a far greater extent than is seen in psychotherapies with adults. Furthermore, children can sense interruptions of therapy on the basis of parental behavior long before the separation has been announced by the parent to the therapist. A child's play may contain the first clue for the therapist of an upcoming interruption of treatment.

Latency-age children have termination experiences that parallel the classical termination phenomena seen during the termination phases of adult psychotherapy. Their specific manifest forms are often influenced by the ego structure of latency. Therefore, they must be sought in the fantasy life of the child as well as in overt emotional reactions and behavior. In separation situations in the psychotherapies of childhood, there are two interwoven areas of response: reactions to object loss and reactions to the unmasking of strong libidinal feelings in response to the expectation of separation.

Reactions to Object Loss

Reactions to object loss include fantasy activity reflecting any or all of the following: mobilization of aggression, feelings of rejection, incorporation of the therapist or of symbols of the therapist, and identifications with the therapist. In addition, a process of object replacement occurs in the real life of the child through the seeking of new friends. Ties to these friends replace the object tie to the soon-to-be-lost therapist. Such object replacement is a common indication of a strong, often positive, relationship between therapist and patient. The nature of the new objects sought can be used as an indicator of the long-range outcome of the therapy to an even greater degree than is possible in adult therapies.

In adult psychotherapies, object replacement usually takes the form of an intensification and modification of ties to individuals with whom the patient is already involved in a relationship of intimacy. Changes in friends and love objects as treatment progresses are usually seen in the young or in those who began treatment with limited capacities for object ties. As a rule, a child has greater freedom in the acquisition of close new friends than has an adult.

In the evaluation of the new relationships that the child establishes during the termination phase, the detection of specific characteristics can be useful in evaluating the effectiveness of the psychotherapy. The nature of the people who are sought out by the child and who accept the child as a friend is an indicator of the nature of the child himself.

Take the example of a child of 10 whose few friends, in pretreatment history, devalued school performance and were continually involved in classroom disruptions. His presenting problem was related to this behavior. As treatment progressed the youngster became more concerned with his school performance and began to relate to classmates who were similarly involved with achievement. Termination was determined on the basis of cessation of disruptive behavior in school. As termination approached, the boy developed a close friendship with a mature, achievement-oriented peer. The restructuring of the patient's personality was thus reflected not only in the level of insight he had attained in therapy but also in the type of peer who accepted him after the treatment.

Libidinal Response to Termination

Reactions to the unmasking of strong libidinal feelings in response to the expectation of separation are manifested in uncomfortable feelings and overt rejection of associated ideas more often than they are expressed in fantasy. These reactions are most commonly seen in children who have concern about passivity, and problems of sexual identity. Often these children respond to such feelings with panic reactions. In essence, the child who fears that he is homosexual becomes acutely uncomfortable when he perceives love and warm feelings for a person of the same sex. It is necessary to point out to such a child that the feelings he has for the departing therapist are the expected products of working comfortably with another person over a prolonged period of time. The feelings of love can be likened to that between father and son. The homoerotic implications of the feelings are thus defused. However, such a strong reaction predisposes the child to stress in similar situations which could arise subsequent to the end of therapy. The child who reacts with such discomfort is not ready for termination. His overwhelming reactions to homoerotic feelings should be worked through. In children, such reactions are tied to fear of subjection and situations of passivity. Cognates to these reactions on a deeper level consist of fear of castration and fusion.

Since the nature of childhood entails a passive, subjugated role in society, this role and the child's response to it should be addressed in the therapy of every child. Strikingly, the children who are most in need of such intervention are those least capable of cooperating in treatment. They are less able to talk about and investigate their reactions than to feel them and act on them. Phobic children and children with persecutory fantasies are most prominent among those who have such underlying complexes. This important aspect of the psychology of the latency-age child may be brought into focus by termination techniques which permit the child, especially the child in late latency, to join in the decision to terminate and in the selection of the termination date. The child's reactions and manipulations in the actual termination situation can be brought to his attention and discussed.

Most separations during the course of therapy occur as the result of decisions by either the therapist or the parents. Rarely does the child have any role in the decision-making process. Termination of treatment is the one area in which the child's will and psychic processes within him are primary in determining the timing of a separation. It is worthwhile to harness this reality. The inner events of the child's psychic life should contribute more to the decision-making process when it comes to termination than do the child's wishes. In the termination situation, it is possible for the child to learn to differentiate between the act of bowing to the will of another and the act of planning based on the limits set by reality. In this situation the reality involved relates to his own progress.

The Termination Decision

One evaluates a multitude of elements in a child's progress toward termination. For an accurate appraisal, parents, teachers, siblings, and the therapist as well as the child should be considered to be sources of data. The requirements of termination in child therapy are:

1. The presenting problem has been solved.
2. Access of fantasy to motor activity and action is within acceptable bounds.
3. The child's academic and social activities reflect success.
4. Verbal and abstract conceptual thinking is being used in the processing and solution of stressful inputs, to the extent that the child can understand his responses in terms of genetic antecedents in the parent–child interaction.
5. The child's developmental progress reflects a stage and rate commensurate with his peers.

6. The child's current friends reflect the level of healthy adjustment that he himself appears to have attained.

7. Further therapeutic work will only produce progress that age-appropriate natural development could provide as well.

It must be borne in mind that fantasy, which is a product of the structure of latency, persists as a defensive structure of the ego throughout the latency-age period. Therefore fantasy as a defense can normally be expected to persist on into the termination phase in the therapy of a latency child. The persistence of fantasy as defense is not considered to be pathological during the latency age. In evaluating a child for readiness for termination, however, the nature of the fantasies should be reviewed for pathological aberrations in the fantasizing function. For instance, excessively omnipotential fantasies manifested in hypercathexis of fantasy which produces withdrawal, or fantasy based on action outside of the play situation, are unacceptable. The presence of phantasmagoric symbols or symbols which are highly charged for the child (e.g., persecutory fantasies; see Chapters 4 and 8) are likewise evidences of a pathological symbolizing function during the latency-age period. This is especially true when there occurs a failure to achieve a shift to fantasies based on symbols derived from the environment and contacts in reality. When this failure occurs, the expected developmental trend toward the establishing of future planning suffers. A fantasizing function with impaired characteristics is an indication for continued treatment.

Once it has been determined through conference between the parents and the therapist that the goals originally set are fulfilled or near fulfillment and the requirements for termination mentioned above have been fulfilled, it is time to think about termination. At this point the child is told that this is the case. He joins in the decision-making process. He is asked if there are still any areas or problems for which he feels he needs help. The child is not asked to give an immediate answer; he is told to think about the important question of ending therapy and to respond as soon as he can. Usually the period of self-searching lasts a few weeks. During this time the child and the therapist discuss the child's thoughts on the matter. They establish the date on which they will talk specifically about whether or not they are ready for termination. On that date, the child, in concert with the therapist, sets a termination date or decides to put off termination for a while. Often the termination date is put off repeatedly as a result of the child's heightened awareness of his problems. The fact that he is soon to lose the skilled help of his therapist adds to his diligence. One problem after another is brought into sharper focus. One youngster, who repeatedly devalued the therapist and insisted that his sports activities should be given priority over his treatment sessions, came to one of the decision-making sessions with a concerned look. He had reviewed all of his areas of progress and had found little wanting. Yet he seemed apprehensive. Said he, "I think I'm okay now. Do you think we have taken care of all the problems?"

The time of preparation for termination is not one of passive waiting for the therapist. Rather, an intensification of therapeutic activity marks the period. Increased transference feelings energize fantasies and reactions that may be usefully mined to therapeutic advantage.

Reactions to Passivity

Primary among the reactions that may be worked with psychotherapeutically during the termination period is the negative reaction to situations of passivity. Passivity may especially be activated as a problem when a child is involved in responding to, handling, and dealing with natural processes. A child can become frustrated when dealing with the intrinsic time sequences of natural processes. He is engulfed in a sense of passivity because his desire to control the world is frustrated. The child who has problems in dealing with passivity will often be unable to agree with any date that has been set by the therapist. No matter what date the therapist may have suggested, the child will insist on an alternative. When it is decided by the child and the therapist that a termination date should be set in earnest, any date beyond two weeks from the date of the decision can be used as a termination date. Latency-age children have an emotional time awareness of about two weeks. Events more than two weeks off have less import on them. Typically, the child with passivity problems will choose a date which differs from any first agreed upon by the therapist. For instance:

One youngster, in a session in late September which was set aside for deciding on a termination in October, suggested October 10 as the termination date. The therapist readily concurred. The child immediately changed the date to October 12. Again the therapist agreed. Again, the child changed. This time the therapist asked what was happening. The child replied, "I want to decide. I don't want you to have anything to do about it."

An inability to accept guidance should be explored with the child. If a problem in dealing with passivity is deemed to be present, then the final date of termination should be put off until the child is capable of shared decision making. The child's difficulties in this area can be interpreted to him in terms of associations and fantasies which are developed from the child's attempt to process and master the problem of accepting natural and parental influences on his behavior, plans, and decisions.

Fantasy Related to Termination

Now we turn to the role of fantasy formation in the evaluation and detection of conflicts associated with separations, interruptions, and terminations in latency-age psychotherapy. The psychological responses of the latency state child to termination and separations can rarely be elicited by direct questioning. If one listens to the child's fantasies, however, one is often able to detect the presence of conflict-laden material. Such fantasies point to therapeutic approaches and suggest areas of conflict that might not otherwise be considered. The fantasies produced immediately prior to any interruption in treatment convey information about the child's reaction to the upcoming separation. These fantasies prepare the therapist for dealing with the related intense responses of the child at the time that an actual termination date has been set and is being approached.

Fantasy as defense which is free of impairing characteristics is an acceptable ego mechanism in latency, and an important precursor of mechanisms in later life that will contribute to creativity, future planning, and the enjoyment of culture. It is not the purpose of psychotherapy to interfere with this important step in the maturation of the child's ego. A successful therapy leaves the child's fantasizing function intact; in many cases it must strengthen it. Much of the emotional reaction to termination in latency remains detectable through the child's fantasy productions.

The following case histories illustrate the use of fantasy and fantasy play as tools for detecting underlying emotional reactions to interruptions, separations, and terminations in latency age psychotherapy.

Ellen was a 9-year-old brought to treatment because of depressed moods ever since the traumatic loss of her father the year before. She was able to work in school and had a few friends. Yet her days were joyless, and her eyes constantly filled with tears. She was repeatedly overcome with the desire to run from the house and go in search of her father. At night she would dream that he came to awaken her or that she heard his voice. She would search the house for him to no avail. She sometimes believed that he was dead, and then spoke of killing herself to join him.

Ellen's mother was an attractive woman in her late thirties, herself quite depressed. As she described her daughter's behavior there were no tears, but she lacked the spontaneity one would expect of a person emerging from mourning a year after suffering a personal loss. She had often hit her daughter to control her behavior. When she realized that this technique had no effect, she brought the child for treatment.

The story of the father's disappearance was told in separate versions by the child and the mother. According to the child, the father had taken her and her sister on an outing one Saturday in October. Mother had stayed home to study. They had intended to visit an aunt, have lunch, and then spend an afternoon watching a puppet show in a local park. While at lunch, they met a friend of the father who was also going to the puppet show. The father turned his children over to him, explaining that he wanted to get home to watch a football game on TV. This was unusual for him, since he usually spent his Saturdays on family outings. (The child emphasized this to illustrate her closeness to her father.)

When they were dropped off at home, Ellen and her sister both noticed that their parents were very quiet with one another, "like after they have a fight." The following Thursday her father awakened her very early in the morning by kissing her on the cheek. She did not show that she was awake because she was frightened by a strange wetness on his face. She fell back to sleep. Later in the morning she awakened to her mother's calls for her father. She kept calling his name. There was no answer. Her mother seemed upset, but not surprised.

The child stayed home from school and watched her mother call her father's office, relatives, friends, and hangouts. Each negative answer and each passing hour tightened the noose that strangles hope. At the end of the day the mother announced to the children with a tone of certainty that their father had disappeared forever.

The mother's story parelleled that of the daughter. She added details which explained the certainty and final tone of her pronouncement. The father had, in fact, returned home early from the outing. Upon entering the house he went directly to his bedroom where he found his wife in flagrante delicto with the gardener. The gardener left the house without confrontation.

When Ellen's mother turned to her husband, he responded to everything that she said with a quiet "I understand." She waited the hours through in expectation of an outburst. Days passed and still she waited for some response, perhaps a smile or some break in the grim silence. That Thursday morning, when she awakened, he was gone. He had spent the four days liquidating his assets, and when he disappeared the family was left without means or reserves. One friend reported that he had said he doubted the children were his.

In the therapy, the child was encouraged to verbalize her feelings. Her difficulty in expressing her anger in general had blunted her capacity to express feelings about her father's desertion. In her play fantasies of a family which she played out, she cast me in the role of the father. At times she struck out at me. She was often preoccupied with sexual fantasies, and liked to tell "dirty jokes." Although her sexual preoccupations suggested that she knew of her mother's encounters, at no time did I find any corroboration of this, direct or indirect. Her excitement was directly traceable to her mother's constant discussion, of information couched in scientific terms related to emunctory functions and reproduction.

The patient felt guilty about wanting to love a man other than her father. In part she used her preoccupation with her father as a way of avoiding her budding sexual feelings for boys. As she became more aware of the reasons for involving herself exclusively in the fantasies about her father, she became less tearful and more able to involve herself with peers.

With the emotional reactions that had necessitated psychotherapy resolved, it was time to introduce the idea of termination. Because a separation problem was primary here, the idea of termination was introduced. At the thought of termination, the child became emotionally brittle and angry in response to any comment or suggestion related to the subject.

When I asked her to set a general termination date, she suggested a date a year and a half in the future. In the next session she was sullen and silent. While in school she had heard my voice again and again, saying, "There are other things." I pointed out her difficulty in letting me go. She carried me with her in fantasy. I related this to her difficulty in letting go of her father. Gradually she began to have fantasies, limited in content to reality possibilities. She fantasized that I would attend a piano recital in which she was to participate and that she would introduce me as her father. Sometimes she would see a man on a streetcorner and develop the fantasy that she could not be sure if it were I or her father. We spoke of the potential that a young person has to find someone new to take the place of a father companion. She became more content, and began to tell more jokes about boys and girls. Her interest now turned to her sexual development. She was free of symptomatology when she left psychotherapy.

In this case, the fantasies involving the therapist gave a clear picture of the motivations that dominated her response to her father's disappearance. Most of the work in depth with this child dealt with reactions of which she became aware as the result of reliving, in transference fantasy, separation reactions during the termination phase. In this case the fantasies lacked subtlety.

In the next case, the reaction to separation was subtly conveyed in fantasy, and was unexpected. It is a prime example of a termination reaction that is solely detected through fantasy.

Arnold was 7 years old and very handsome. He had dark hair and features that were strong and manly for a little boy. Arnold engaged in disruptive behavior in the classroom. He also developed acute episodes of loss of temper and anger at his parents. This was manifested in destructive behavior, including dropping and breaking a lamp on the kitchen floor. The child was brought to a clinic where I was a fellow in child psychiatry. While I did not understand the nature of latency at the time, in retrospect it is possible to see that this was a youngster with a good structure of latency who had been overstimulated by a family situation.

The father had given up his role of authority by default. The child was in very close contact with his mother, who overstimulated him in her own search for emotional support and companionship. The father's presence interrupted the child's relationship with his mother and mobilized his aggression. It was soon seen in the therapy that Arnold's acting out was based on an oedipal hostility that had been displaced from his father. Direct hostility to the father would have been too dangerous for him.

The child played out fantasies in plenty. He established a positive relationship with me once he discovered that aggression directed toward me was not destructive. He established a nonsadomasochistic relationship with me. Very little insight-oriented therapy was done. Most of his gains involved achieving a balance in his relationships with men and women. Since I provided a male object to whom he could relate, the amount of object libido directed to his all-too-willing mother diminished. This lessened his guilt, his excitement, and his hostility.

After seven months of our work together, I had come to the end of my training at that hospital, and military commitments forced my relocation to another part of the country. It was necessary, therefore, for him to be assigned to a new therapist who was a year behind me in the training program. Little working-through of termination was advised because the new therapist was available immediately. During our last session, which followed a meeting with the new therapist, Arnold thanked me for my help and said he hoped his new doctor would be more comfortable to be with once he got to know him. I interpreted this attitude as a manifestation of his anxiety at being assigned to a new therapist, but he ignored my remark.

He placed a chair on a low table, and put a carton in front of the chair. He sat down and pretended to drive. When I questioned him about his fantasy, again I received no response. I noticed that from time to time he pulled the imaginary steering device toward him and then pushed it away. I asked him if he were flying an airplane. He did not respond directly, but now began to make low, humming, airplane-like noises. In order to enter the game I held an imaginary microphone to my mouth and said, "This is the airport contacting Arnold's plane. Please answer; I want to give flight instructions." He immediately picked up his own imaginary microphone and responded, "This is Arnie, what do you want?" As so often happens in these situations, after the child responded I didn't really know what I could say that would avoid possible contamination of his fantasy. I asked where he was going, and fortunately got an answer. He said, "I'm going to California. I'm flying there." I asked him, "Where in California? If I want to send a letter to you, how would I reach you?" He responded, "That's easy. Just write to me care of the orphan's home."

The session was near an end. The explanations of the necessity for my going into military service at the end of my training had had no impact on this youngster. He saw himself as rejected and became subtly aggressive through his fantasy, in which he actively left, excluding me. I communicated information on the nature of his attitude to his next therapist. It was possible for the new therapist to handle this material or relate to the child who rejected him. The child refused to continue treatment with this therapist and dropped out of treatment after three months. With the cessation of treatment, the child returned to his old behavior patterns.

This case illustrated a number of points: fantasy can carry the attitudes of a latency-age patient; the technique of changing therapists in training centers is fraught with difficulty; more attention should be paid to the impact of such changes on a child.

Children do not respond strongly to separations and terminations until about two weeks prior to actual separation. Usually a child knows that he is going to go to camp or away for summer vacation on the day that he starts treatment. This does not become a pertinent element in the treatment situation until about two weeks before the termination or separation actually occurs. This is not an irrelevant point. At time, therapists discuss termination or separation with a child from four to six weeks in advance. They handle the immediate response and assume that everything has been taken care of. Even a few weeks before the separation, when the event is pressing, the child will not verbalize any difficulties. He's busy processing them into fantasies. It is only through observation of the fantasies and through heightened awareness during the two weeks before the actual event that it is possible to see through the fantasies to the fact that the child is troubled. The following case will illustrate.

Betsy was 8 years old when she came to analysis because of a shyness which caused the parents great concern. She had almost no friends. She was quite explosive at home, and had difficulty in separating from her mother. As her treatment progressed, it became very clear that her mother also had difficulty in separating from her.

While telling me about her phobias the child began to dwell on a recollection of a camp to which she had been sent a few summers before and to which she was to return the following summer. There was a large stand of dark trees in the camp; it was right behind her bunk. When she first came to treatment, she was sure it contained all kinds of monsters and demons that would barge in on her. As she grew older, these turned into robbers and kidnappers. At the time of the sessions presented here, Betsy was more able to accept the prospect of going to camp for the following summer. In part she could consider camp because of the supportive nature of our relationship; she felt she could come to me if she became troubled and that I could help her to understand the reality of the situation and the inner origin of her fears. She appeared to have the camp situation well in control.

Approximately a week and a half before the interruption of sessions for her summer vacation, she began to tell stories of a hunter dressed in buckskin who carried a large knife and went into the woods in search of Indians. It seemed clear that she was attempting here to take an active role in fantasy and to master the fear of the fantasy people in the woods behind her bunk. I began to approach the fantasy from this aspect. She provided me with an imaginary satchel to carry and told me that I was her assistant who would help her with the hunt for the Indians. She found their camp, but no Indians were there. She was jumped on by the Indians. She fought the Indians off. Finally, she trapped an Indian and, uncharacteristically for her, told me that she was going to eat the Indian and that I should eat my own food. She then proceeded to kill the Indian and to prepare him to be cooked.

At this point I was alerted to the possible meaning of this fantasy by a previous fantasy in her treatment. I shall go back to the session in which the earlier fantasy took place, for a brief digression. In that session, the child, who had a food fad in which she refused to eat fish, had taken a wooden sculpture which had a mild resemblance to a phallic symbol and, calling it a fish that her father had caught, devoured it in fantasy. At that point I interpreted to her the confusion she had between her father (the fisherman) and the fish. Her desire to devour her father made her uncomfortable about eating fish. She developed a feeling of nausea in the session. She mastered this by gobbling down the wooden figure again. She then turned to me and said that she didn't think she'd have trouble eating fish any more. Her mother reported to me that the food fad had ceased after that session. I therefore was prepared to see the devouring of the Indian as a kind of active fantasy in which she played out her cannibalistic wishes toward her father.

With this thought in mind, we now return to the preseparation session. I turned to her and asked what part of the Indian's body she was going to eat. I entertained the thought that she might be made more aware of her wishes to devour the father's penis. However, her response did not relate to any part of the fantasy figure which had undisplaced phallic associations. She said, "I would like to eat his brains." It should be noted that in the hunting fantasy I had been assigned the role of a rather dull helper. It could have been easy to rule myself out as the latent content of the Indian symbol on this superficial basis. However, the role assignment in a fantasy of a given character, whether it be therapist, patient, or parent, does not negate his role as the latent content of another character. I could have been the latent content of the Indian. Since this was a session that occurred in a preseparation period, I was especially on the alert for incorporative fantasies, such as the fantasy of incorporation and devouring that is so typical a human response to separation. I therefore asked Betsy whether the Indian represented myself. She said that she wished that she could take some of my brains with her when she goes to camp, because she was still frightened of certain things and would have liked very much to be able to talk about these things with me when she was frightened about them.

The recognition of fantasies of devouring brains as a possible incorporative fantasy opened the way to a specific focus in our psychotherapeutic work. By making this connection, it was possible to get her to verbalize her feelings. I then asked what she was worried about. She talked about walking to the camp bathroom at night, the dark woods, insects, and girls who might not like her. She especially feared that one of the children in the camp would begin to cry during the first days. This was especially threatening to her because of her feeling that if somebody else cried, her own wish to cry would break through. I pointed out to her that although she could not take my brains with her, it would be possible for her to discuss these problems and the origins of fears involved with them before she went away. She shifted from fantasy at that point to the direct discussion of problems that she was concerned with, although from time to time, when she became blocked in talking about what troubled her she turned to fantasy as a means of elaborating her problems.

Summary

The psychotherapist who works with the latency-age child requires special training because of the unique nature of the executive apparatus of the ego in this age group. This ego function, when operating well, can often mask problems that should be solved lest they menace adolescent adjustment. It is important to approach latency children as individuals, rather than to succumb to the use of modalities that put all children into one category, and create a buffer between the patient's needs and the therapist's response. This situation can be produced by the use of such disparate modalities as drug therapy or dynamically oriented therapy in which the source of interpretations are abstract theories rather than the associations and fantasy play elements of the child. Individual children should not be forced into the molds of a preconceived notion, constructed from the latest therapeutic fad.

In child therapy, the associations of the child should be the measure of all things. This is not meant to criticize the substance of current theories. What is criticized here are therapists who would use any single theory to explain the processes in many different children. Advances in theory should expand, not limit, the number of psychotherapeutic possibilities and strategies. Latency-age children should especially be protected from theory-boundedness. They cannot defend themselves. Unfortunately, therapists with the least training, who are most apt to fall back on ready-made interpretations, are frequently assigned to work with children. This is a product of the myth that latency-age children are little adults, with little ego psychological development and diminished drives. Therapists of latency-age children should be specially trained to understand latency ego development.

In this chapter I have dealt with the technical strategies required for a psychotherapeutic approach to children in the latency-age period. Attention has been given to the effect of the state of latency on the ability of the child to cooperate in treatment. There is yet another aspect to the age of latency: the developmental process that marks this period influences the manifestations of certain clinical phenomena, producing characteristics that require special approaches in diagnostic and therapeutic situations. These are discussed in the following chapters.

Part III
Psychotherapeutic Strategies in Specific Contexts

Chapter 6
Phobias

There are few childhood psychological aberrations that appear as suddenly and dramatically as phobia. As often as not, a quiet evening is shattered by frightened screams from the child's bedroom, or a pleasant outing or vacation idyll gives way to the chaos of a child cringing at the sight of seaweed or at the sound of distant rolling thunder. There is a sudden dissociation of the child's sense of reality from the reality testing of the observer. Because of this, phobia is easily recognized as mental illness. Even the most antipsychological or psychologically unsophisticated parent recognizes that here is a situation beyond his prior experience. There are immediate signs of the child's distress, and there is behavior beyond the control of the family. Discomfort to both the child and the family, and the strangeness of the symptoms, are often enough to bring the parents to a child psychiatrist in search of help.

The parents will see the phobia as the primary problem, and relief of it the only goal. When this relief is obtained and the acute phase has passed, parents without knowledge of such matters may see no need for further treatment. The phobia is regarded in retrospect as though it were a recent cold. Once gone, it is considered cured. The neurotic underpinnings, which form the nest from which such symptoms may again be spawned, are left for the therapist to warn about and to ponder.

A 10-year-old boy could not get to sleep because of intense fears of a monster who, he feared, inhabited the night. He would enter his parents' bedroom and keep them awake with tales of his feared imaginings. In play therapy the boy drew a picture of the monster. The picture was cut out, mounted on a backing of cardboard, and used by the child to ambush families in cars on their way to holiday fun. Within ten sessions, this play theme was linked to a real family situation. The boy's father was known to call home on a Saturday to tell his son to wait for him there, rather than go out to play with his friends. The father had repeatedly disappointed the child, keeping him waiting for as long as five hours without a call to tell him that important business had come up. This was anger-provoking for the child. I encouraged the father to keep the appointments he made with his son. I told him not to set up interferences with his son's play dates with friends unless he, the father, was actually with the child. This relieved some of the pressure to be angry, which had been projected onto the fun-killing monster of the child's imagination. Swiftly the symptoms cleared as the child shifted his arena for the expression of his now-attenuated fears from home to play therapy. Within eight weeks of the start of therapy, the father left a message during the session before his son's therapy session to inform me that the child had improved, and that the session scheduled for that very day would be the last.

Unfortunately, relief of symptoms is not cure. The experienced clinician knows that the capacity to produce phobic symptoms during latency will, in other times and climes, bring forth other painful symptoms. In keeping with the age and level of maturity of the patient, old wine will find its way to new bottles.

In the case above, the child's aggression took the form of feared fantasy figures. His father's behavior was shielded from the child's anger and direct criticism by a family-social context that permitted anger only if it dared be spoken in phrases derived from the cryptic language of symbols. The path to symbols and symptoms was traversed because of this external inhibition and because of the existence of preexisting neurotic and disordered cognitive underpinnings. These supported access to the use of fantasy derivatives so strong that there could be maintained an avoidance of confrontation with reality. These fantasy derivatives were the child's only means of processing and mastering the stress of his father's behavior. When fantasy derivatives are manifested in symbols that persecute, and are responded to with avoidance, the clinical condition is called a phobia. It is to a study of such conditions that this chapter is devoted.

Definitions

In common parlance, *phobia* refers to a fear of a specific object or situation. This fear is sufficiently great to cause the subject of the fear to try strenuously to avoid contact with the feared object or situation. Such avoidances as that which results from fear of horseback riding after a fall from a horse could be fit into this definition.

The specific medico-scientific term *phobia* implies the existence of a more complex condition than such a phobic avoidance reaction. In psychoanalytically informed terminology, *phobia* implies the existence of a fear whose object is unknown to the subject of the fear. The subject, or patient, has his conscious awareness cut off from the feared object by repression. In place of the feared object, and hiding it, there appears a symbol. This manifest symbol is related to that which is hidden through some cryptic, often abstract bridge. Avoidance of the symbol makes possible continued contact with that which is the true object of fear.

Thus the characteristics of a true phobia are:

1. an avoidance reaction;
2. a symbol or symbolic situation that is avoided;
3. a true object of fear, which is represented by the symbol;
4. repression of the link between the symbol and the truly feared object, which the symbol represents;
5. sustained affect (anxiety, fear) that has been transferred from the truly feared objects to the symbol;
6. the phobia protects an endangered object relationship or activity.

The role of psychotherapy in dealing with phobias places emphasis on uncovering the nature of the true object of fear. This makes it possible to work out false ideas about the object or to accept unacceptable aspects of a life situation that threaten its continuation.

The phobias of latency-age children satisfy the requirements of a true phobia, but they have their own peculiarities that set them apart from true phobias found in adults. These differences are useful to know in working with phobic children. Phobias in children are easier to work with. Repression is not as strong. The true object of fear is more easily detected. The parents are still present in the life of the child. Therefore the child's gains from the phobia are primary gains. The earliest relationships are still extant and are represented in the phobia.

In the adult, in contrast, the phobia is sustained by a link to secondary social gains. Reliable parental love has been either locked in by dependence generated by the phobia or replaced by an unhealthy relationship of interdependence. In the latter case, the gain is the neurotic interaction itself. Few of the social graces and skills required to establish a healthy relationship are present. The phobic symptoms may have become so linked to a lifestyle that the symptoms have lost much of their status as reactions to conflict and have become autonomous sources of behavior. For this reason, in all childhood phobias, and especially in those that appear in adolescence, direct confrontation with the feared symbol is indicated to avert the fixing in place of the phobia.

There follow descriptions of adult and child phobias.

Anna was 31 years old. She lived on an island that was connected to a nearby city by a bridge. She lived with her parents and earned her money by operating a typing service from her home. She longed to date, live in the city, and have a full life. Unfortunately, she had a bridge phobia. The only way that she could cross the bridge was with her mother, who served as her companion. She could not leave to make a life for herself.

Bart was in his mid-50s. He ran a small men's clothing store in a transitional neighborhood. One day an intruder entered his store, bound him, held a gun to his head, and took his money. Bart was told by the intruder that he should not call the police for two hours after the intruder had left the store. He complied.

After the episode, at first he was filled with fear. He took a few days off. Then on the day he was to return to work, he experienced severe chest pain. He and his sister went to their family physician, who found no physical abnormalities. Bart was convinced that he was having a heart attack. How could he return to work?

His wife now supported the family, which consisted of the couple and Bart's sister. When Bart first came to my office, his wife and sister accompanied him. He explained that the only way that he could travel was with a companion. His wife was his phobic companion. (The companion is a frequent feature of phobia. It is less often detected in childhood phobia, simply because the parent as companion is phase-appropriate.)

In Bart's mind, the heart pain and the robbery were things apart. He told of each separately. Two facts, however, soon became apparent. The pain prevented him from going to work and he was fearful of another robbery. Any connection between these thoughts were obscured in Bart's mind by the justification provided by the pain. I decided that the traumatic aspects of the neurosis should be worked through through abreaction, (repeated telling of the traumatic experience). It soon was apparent to Bart himself that whenever he spoke of the robbery, he clutched his chest and changed the topic to his "illness." He could see the connection, and confronted the resolution he had dreaded. He would sell his store, move to another neighborhood, and go to work in a cousin's shoe store.

With this insight, the working through of the trauma, and the social situational adjustments that had to be made, Bart's chest symptoms cleared completely. He became able to travel without his wife. He was still accompanied to sessions by his sister, however. I asked him if his problems could be considered to be resolved if he still required his sister as a companion. "Oh!" he said, "That has been going on since she was a girl. She's phobic. I'm *her* companion."

Jim was 7 years old. He spoke of monsters that he feared. He had seen them in a movie on TV, and they had reappeared in his dreams and awakened him. Now he was afraid to be left alone at sleep time because they would come after him. He often checked the bedroom to make sure his father was all right. In the games that he played, he covered his head with his sweater and threatened his friends as though he were the monster.

The symptoms resolved so quickly that it was hard to determine all the dynamics. One of the monsters in the dream was very big. In association to questions about the large monster, Jim told of thinking that his father was a giant after hearing the bedtime story "Jack and the Beanstalk." The traumatic element in seeing the movie monsters merged with a projection of his hostility onto his father. This produced a situation in which Jim felt the relationship with his father would be threatened by the hostility felt to be a characteristic of either person. The monsters as carriers of anger for both father and son made continuation of the father–son relationship possible.

These cases illustrate the differences between adult and child phobia which have already been described. There is an additional difference that deserves our attention. That difference takes into account the venue of the phobic symbol. The phobic experience in the adult is polarized toward symbols encountered in the physical world. For the phobic child, the venue of phobic symbol is polarized toward the world of fantasy and dreams, with a touch of the real that brings the condition to the attention of the parents. This is a developmental characteristic.

In adults, psychoanalytic symbols are normally found in dreams (oneiric symbols). The symbols that mediate neurotic symptoms are patterned after them. The symbols of adult phobias are limited in content by the requirement that they have a physical world locus.

In children psychoanalytic symbols are normally found in dreams (oneiric symbols) and in the plastic elements available in playroom settings and toy stores (ludic symbols; Piaget 1945). There is a naturally wider choice of symbols, associated with repression (psychoanalytic symbols), for use in the formation of childhood phobias. This results in the tendency for the symbols of latency-age phobias to cluster in a polarity dominated by play, dreams, and imagination.

Armed with this information one can understand the free interchange that occurs between dreams and play. In child therapy contexts, dream figures can be turned into play figures with ease. Just make cutouts or clay models. Thus play can be manipulated to include sensitive material. Interpretation can be made using play objects. Most important is the fact that foreknowledge of the extent of the lair of the phobic symbol helps to organize questions in diagnostic interviews. The child who denies fears in reality situations may have phobic symbols to fear in dreams, in play, in fantasy, and in the darkening hours that follow "the children's hour."

Not all fears are true phobias. The same feared object may be a reality to be feared for one person, a reminder of a trauma for another, a true phobia for yet another, and a precipitant of psychotic symptomatology for yet another. Fear of flying is such a symptom in adults (Sarnoff 1957). School phobia is such a symptom in children. This sort of spectrum of disease patterns occurs most often when there are obligatory occupational situations.

Fear of Flying

Real Cause

Paula was 28 when she noticed that someone had neglected to remove the panel that excluded dust from the engine of the aircraft in which she sat ready to take off. She voiced her fears, to the gratitude of everyone.

Recall of a Trauma

Fred, a pilot, was 23 when he began to vomit before each flight. The vomiting was a product of a conscious fear engendered when he saw the plane of his wingman hit a tree during a low-level flight exercise.

True Phobia

Arvin was 21. He was in basic flight training in the Air Force. He began to have trouble landing his aircraft after he began to solo. The difficulty was attributed to a loss of depth perception. He apparently could not judge his distance above the ground and therefore bounced his plane when he landed. No physical impairment could be found to explain the difficulty. When confronted with a promise that he would get a waiver for his deficiency, he had an acute anxiety attack. Note that the air forces of the world take disciplinary action against pilots with fear of flying. The social stigma is so great that the fear may be repressed and impeding symptoms introduced.

Psychotic Reaction

Phillip was 32. He was a pilot. He experienced erections, ejaculations, and hallucinations when flying. He refused to fly.

School Phobia

Real Cause

Jane was 15 when she developed infectious mononucleosis and was forced to stay home from school for six weeks. When the time came to return to school, she began to cry and simulate her old symptoms. In a diagnostic interview, it was determined that the week of her return was midterm week. She was not prepared. Tutoring and later reentry were recommended. This regimen was followed, and Jane returned to school without mishap.

Recall of a Trauma

Timmy was 5. He had just entered kindergarten. His expectation was great, and so was his eagerness. His mother was quite surprised, therefore, when in the second week of school he feigned illness and refused to go to school. "Help! Help!" he screamed, as his parents tried to pull him out from under a couch, whose farther leg he was grasping for dear life. When he was quietly asked what troubled him and reassured that he could speak freely, he told of threats by a bully on the bus to cut off his hand. The bully was spoken to, and Timmy learned to read.

True School Phobia

Lee was 7. Trembling and crying each morning, she refused to go to school. She sneezed repeatedly and claimed that she was afraid of school and too sick to go. Her mother was overwhelmed by this behavior. Not only did she have to get Lee off to school, she also had to take care of the toddlers left when her friend and neighbor of many years had suddenly died. In therapy it was determined that Lee feared to leave her mother's side because she was afraid that her mother, too, would die.

Psychosis

Lil was 11. She insisted on coming home from school when she realized that her mother had placed a radio transmitter in an aspirin her mother had given her that morning. At times she heard the chewing of dinosaurs outside the classroom window.

The material below will be devoted to true latency-age phobias, those associated with repression and symbol formation.

The Implications of Latency-Age Phobias

Most of the phobic states that occur during the latency age period are as transient as latency itself. For this reason there is danger that such symptoms will not be taken seriously. The implications of the appearance of a phobia in latency are twofold. One is immediate, and involves the response of the unsophisticated observer, often the parent. The other is long-term. It engages the expertise of the therapist to whose attention the symptom has been drawn.

Because of their transience, childhood phobias tend to be considered normal and to presage little long-range danger. Indeed, the immediate effects of phobia (e.g. anxiety and parental discomfort) can be adjusted to or ameliorated as soon as the phobic symptoms pass. The long-term implications of a latency-age phobia present a much greater magnitude of concern. The underpinnings of phobia persist after the symptoms have disappeared, predisposing the child to manifestations of their influence in the mature years that are to follow.

From what has been said, it must be clear that while the therapist should be concerned with the immediate effects of childhood phobias, as are parents, it is necessary to emphasize the long-term effects that could be the products of failure to treat the underlying pathology. This emphasis is required to counter the fact that the hidden nature of phobic underpinnings invites neglect. The childhood phobia often serves as a barometer indicating the inner tempests that brew during the psychosexual and cognitive maturational phases of childhood. These in turn were spawned by pathology in past development. They presage future storms.

Immediate Implications

The discomfort wrought by childhood phobias on family and child are often sufficient to bring the parents to the child psychiatrist in search of help. The phobia is portrayed as the primary problem, and its relief as the only goal. When signs of distress and behavior beyond the control of the family clear, no further need for the therapist is felt. (See case on pp. 187–188.)

Rarely does parental concern go beyond the immediate discomfort of the child and family. Therefore, it is wise for the therapist early in the treatment to educate the parent of the phobic child in understanding the impact of phobic underpinnings as well as information to be used to recognize them.

Long-Term Implications

Epiavoidances. Rarely is thought given by parents to the eventual effect of the interferences with learning and the inhibitions of social grace acquisition that accompany childhood phobia. Only very informed parents voice concern for the implications that transcend the immediate difficulty. Specific phobias may result in specific deformations in future function. For instance, a child who fears water may not learn to swim. In the case of school phobia there is an interference with functions that are extremely important for later life—not only academics and learning skills, but many social experiences as well. Thus, phobic epiavoidances may interfere seriously with development and educational progress.

An 8-year-old girl clung to her mother's skirt, sucking her thumb intently. She gazed at the children with whom she had been playing just moments before, until to her dismay a large dog had appeared on the scene. The others petted the dog. Only after it left did the child rejoin her friends. They teased her. Within the power order of children, she fell to last place. Her socialization and choice of friends shifted to few and fearful children like herself.

Underpinnings. The long-term effects of the underpinnings of childhood phobia are not always as easily discernable as the long-term effects just discussed. These underpinnings are by nature unconscious and therefore not easily perceived. Their implications for the future are often too abstract for those lacking in experience to understand. Each phobic child should be studied to determine the degree to which severe pathological and psychopathogenic distortions of ego function are present.

The presence of a phobia in childhood could in some cases be a predictor of health. First, in order to form a phobia, the child has to be capable of projection of introjects. Theoretically this capacity precludes the presence of childhood schizophrenia. If so, it would follow that childhood phobia and childhood schizophrenia are mutually exlusive before the age of 10.

Second, the development of the ability to project contributes to the development of social contacts in adolescence. The child can follow fear fantasies about peers into relationships with those peers. One is drawn in body and in attention to those whom he fears. If a child has the ability to separate the sense of reality (i.e., fantasy—the reality one feels) from reality testing (i.e., physis—the reality one can touch), then projection may form a bridge to peers and be a useful mechanism in adolescent adjustment (Sarnoff 1972).

The presence of a phobia in childhood can in some cases be viewed as normal. Healthy young minds are capable of repression, condensation, displacement, projection, and denial. These are the mechanisms at work in producing a phobia. At any time, these mechanisms can produce a transient phobia or a frightening dream. The mere existence of a childhood phobia does not indicate or predict a fragile or pathological adjustment in adult years. One must, in the evaluation of the phobic child, look beyond these defenses to detect possible personality weaknesses.

The presence of a phobia in childhood can in many cases be a predictor of future emotional problems. Specific types of ego weakness that predispose to the development of latency-age phobia contribute to adjustment failures in later life. The therapist who works with the phobic child must evaluate these ego weaknesses to decide whether extensive therapy, with goals beyond the alleviation of the phobic symptoms, is indicated. Some of these weaknesses are:

1. A poor symbolizing function with heightened cathexis of fantasy priorities. These youngsters dwell on their fantasies, leaving reality to shift for itself. They are unable to separate that which they sense as reality from that which in reality can be tested. They often seem unaware that their perception is unusual or even bizarre.

A nurse on an adolescent ward tried to help the patients to be less gullible. "You wouldn't believe it if someone said they saw green men, would you?" she asked. A child of 11 responded, "When I look in the mirror, sometimes my face is green."

A child avoided school because she heard the sound of dinosaurs outside the classroom window.

Healthier types of symbols in phobia formation include animal phobias, amorphous creatures (before the age of 8½), and symbols drawn from current social emphasis. An example of the last follows.

A child of 7 was brought for treatment because of his fears that he would be eaten by goblins. These fears were quickly dispelled when it was learned that he had been teased by a sibling, who threatened him with being gobbled up by the goblins. These goblins were at the time everywhere illustrated as a harbinger of Halloween. A few weeks later the boy returned with identical fears. With Halloween now past, the symbol seemed bizarre until I asked him if he had seen one of the goblins. He said he had. I asked him to draw what he had seen. He drew a picture of a bird with a striking resemblance to a turkey. He had confused the slang term for turkey (gobbler) with the gobbling goblins of Halloween. Thanksgiving, and its promises of gobblers to come, had reignited his fears, with reality supports in the form of pictures and promises of the coming of the "gobblers."

2. Long-term effects of the experiencing of oneself as small, passive, and vulnerable. Phobia undermines confidence. There is a trauma with lifelong implications involved in imagined humiliation while experiencing a phobic reaction in childhood. One's self-image

in later life suffers from the experience of sensing oneself to be a passive object of aggression.

3. Premium given to the sense of reality over reality testing throughout life. In evaluating a phobic child it is necessary to determine if the break in reality testing implied by the existence of the phobia is limited to the current episode or is part of a lifelong pattern. The latter is pathological, indicating the presence of a mental fault that can permit symptom development unlimited by the constraints of reality. Such a lifelong pattern requires treatment that emphasizes reality testing. Phobias that are activated in the evening, at night, or under conditions of decreased sensory stimulation are less pathological than those that occur in broad daylight. The former occur during conditions of a decrease in the sensory guarantees of primarily autonomous functioning of the ego in relation to the id. Phobias in broad daylight indicate weakened reality testing. A lifelong pattern of weakened reality testing can be seen clinically in a history of failure to learn from experience, or an episode such as the following:

A boy of six gazed in awe at some seabirds that sat upon the sea within easy reach of the sailboat in which he rode. Finally he spoke. "Look at the chipmunks," he said. The kindly skipper explained that those were seagulls. Later a fellow passenger heard the child mumble to himself, "They are chipmunks!"

4. Pathological introjects. The nature of the introjects involved in the projections from which the feared objects of the phobia are derived should be studied. One should study the behavior of parents and primary objects who may have been the models for introjects in early life. Their current behavior may be supporting and reinforcing a hostile, distorted object image as an introject. Family-oriented therapy is indicated in these cases. Study of the origin and maintenance of the introject is only half the study of the introject in latency-age phobia; one should also study the degree to which introjection of hostile projections (projective identifications) in early childhood has played a role. Such a process is an indicator of poor reality testing. When introjects wear the coloration of the aggressive drive to excess, there is the possibility that the original introjected object was falsely perceived. The fantasied (elaborated) persecutor is now falsely perceived as unduly hostile as a result of an old false perception.

These underpinnings are part and parcel of a chronic personality defect that just happens to be expressed through phobic symptoms in latency. Let us focus for a moment on a problem created by these unseen aspects of childhood phobia. Now that medication can be used to make anxiety manageable, psychotherapy is not always thought of for childhood phobia. One should not use medication without evaluating the severity of the underlying personality defect and its future implications. The existence of frequent infection responsive to medication does not rule out the requirement that diabetes be considered in the differential diagnosis. On the contrary, it mandates such a differential diagnosis. Childhood phobia, with its tendency to be cured by any and all modalities (including the passage of time), likewise requires a differential diagnosis, including those diagnoses that presage crippling emotional conditions in adulthood.

I have had occasion to follow for as long as twenty years individuals with latency-age phobias. My impression is that the phobias of early latency when they are limited to night fears are quite normal and presage no severe pathology in adulthood. If the phobias are sufficiently charged with energy that actual changes in family plans are necessary, or if night phobias continue into the day, one should be on the alert for later depressive states and adolescent shyness. Night fears occurring in late latency and accompanied by great aggression and difficulty in shifting attention cathexes from inner fears and personal fantasies to the outside world presage borderline functioning in the adult, which will be manifested primarily in fear of close object ties in the early twenties. Yochelson (1976), in his study of the criminal mind, spoke about the typical childhood psychological adjustment of the adult criminal. "His [the criminal's] parents may remember that early in his life the criminal child had more fears than the other children; he was the one who needed the night light the longest; he was the least tolerant of pain and the most afraid of the doctor. Criminal children fear thunder, lightning, water, heights, goblins—almost anything. . . . Many are so fearful of the water that they never learn to swim. . . . Although the fear is initially strong, running away is so deflating to the youngster's self image that he decides to stand fast and try to hold his own. The fear is replaced by a desire to win and dominate" (p. 206). Yochelson describes how the victim becomes merely a pawn in the plans of the criminal, with little concern on the criminal's part for the feelings of the victim or the victim's sense of life or property.

The Role of the Therapist

The job of the child psychiatrist confronted with a phobia in a latency-age child is to respond to the parent's awareness of the child's symptoms and the effect that the symptoms have on current functioning. He must explain to the parents the effect of phobia on future skills and functioning, and interpret to the parents the less easily perceived implications of phobia for unconscious areas of functioning, subtle interferences with maturation, and cognitive impairments. For the immediately evident aspects of these conditions, the child psychiatrist brings to his work sympathy, support, compassion, and the mitigating aspects of therapy. The occult aspects of phobic conditions require one to educate and inform the parent, and direct the therapy toward reconstructive techniques that will strengthen the ego, give the child insight, and improve his potential for the future.

The Differential Diagnosis of Childhood Phobia

Cognitive, physiological, and psychological factors contribute to the origins and times of onset of phobias and avoidance reactions. We will describe here those factors, as well as therapeutic approaches, differential diagnosis, and prognosis for phobic states during latency. In addition, we will consider the implications for maturational and developmental growth of the states that predispose a child to phobia formation.

Night Fears

"Night fears," probably the most common of childhood phobias, are the periods of fear that occur when latency-age children go to bed. They may begin at as early an age as 26 months, when the capacity to form psychoanalytic symbols (where what is represented and what represents is, as the result of repression, no longer connected in the awareness of the child) first develops. Night fears become most intense at 6 to 8 years of age. Then repression becomes stronger. Oedipal fantasies are repressed. The need to discharge drives must find other symbols for expression. For instance, a 6- to 8-year-old boy projects hostility that he feels for his father onto his father. This hostility is a manifestation of oedipal wishes. The father is then seen as a persecutor. Fearing the pain of being hated by his father, the child displaces the hostility from his father to symbols in the form of amorphous monster-like objects, which the child sets in the real world. In the most limited sense night fears occur only when the child is going off to sleep. Monsters, robbers, skeletons, goblins, and demons populate the world of these children. They want the night light on, the closet door open with the light on or shut. The hall door must be open, or the hall light or bathroom light must be left on.

The appearance of this type of phobia is directly related to the high sensitivity to sensory deprivation that typifies this age period. Eruptions of id-dominated material in response to loss of guarantees of the autonomous functions of the ego in relation to the id are possible at any age. At no time is the process more sensitive to changes in stimulation than during latency. J. M. Barrie, in *Peter Pan*, immortalized this fact when he wrote, "Neverland . . . when you play at it by day with the chairs and table cloth, it is not in the least alarming, but in the two minutes before you go to sleep, it becomes very nearly real. That is why there are night lights." These phobias may therefore be considered normal for the most part. When occurring in the absence of other pathology, they serve as an indicator of cognitive maturational events, which for a brief time have provided a rather explicit conduit for the manifestation of psychosexual conflict.

Such phobias require a healthy precursor. Children have to have experienced introjection of lost objects. Projection of these introjects is a component of phobia formation. Such projection can occur as early as the second year of life. At the latest they should begin by 4 years of age. In childhood schizophrenia (see Bender 1947), it is not uncommon for such a process to begin only in the eleventh year; such a delay is pathognomonic of childhood schizophrenia. This evidence suggests that night fears in latency-age children, especially those in early latency, reflect a normal maturational process (the normal neurosis of latency). The absence of such symptoms suggests a consideration of childhood schizophrenia in the differential diagnosis.

Waking Phobia

When the child's phobic reactions occur when the child is fully awake—as in "I'm afraid to go in the water; I might [or will] be bitten by a fish or by a crab," fear of thunder, fear of robots, fear of shadows, fear of the dark, fear of lightning, fear of the wind—we are dealing with a process of greater seriousness than that suggested by night fear. The mitigating presence of an altered ego state introduced by the sensory deprivation implicit in darkness and aloneness is not present. What is present is a serious hypercathexis of persecutory fantasy to an extent that environmental reinforcements of reality testing are overwhelmed.

There are many phobic states that occur in latency-age children in broad daylight that do not involve fear of repression supported psychoanalytic symbols. In this section I limit the topics to deal with uncomplicated waking phobia, such as a fear of stairs, tunnels, bridges, seaweed, or people in masks. In uncomplicated simple phobia psychoanalytic symbols are involved. Fears based on separation, as in symbiotic psychoses or avoidance maneuvers associated with psychotic delusions such as those that produce school avoidance fall into another category, which will be described in later sections.

The waking phobia that involves psychoanalytic symbols in childhood is similar clinically to phobia seen in the adult. Usually these states indicate an overstimulation of the child by the parents, caretakers, or other children. Latency-age phobia may respond rather quickly if parents are advised not to take the child into bed, not to beat the child, and not to walk around naked in front of the child. Taking showers or baths with children is also often involved when this symptom occurs. Such immediate pressures are related to the onset of these symptoms.

Why does this symptomatology appear with latency and disappear when adolescence comes on? This is the pattern in a majority of cases, without treatment and in spite of the persistence of seductive behavior on the part of the parents. The answer lies in the ego structure of latency. The "structure of latency" functions to a large extent through the creation of latent fantasies. These are the product of the projection of conflict-filled core fantasies that have been molded into occult representations through the use of masking symbols. These core fantasies are worked on through further displacement to produce manifest fantasies. The symbols of manifest fantasies have less valence for attracting affect. They can therefore appear in consciousness and be used for the discharge of drives by being communicated to another person, much in the way that talking to a therapist can calm emotional turmoil.

The structure of latency may be burdened with too much stimulation. The symbolizing function of the child may be immature or defective, producing symbols porous to the affect against which they are supposed to defend. These symbols appear in manifest fantasies associated with anxiety. When this happens, the affect-masking effect of the symbolizing and fantasizing function fails. Although the identity of the original feared object continues to be hidden, the affect associated with the original object persists. The persecutor and the persecuted of a masked story give way to new protagonists. The child as the persecuted one is returned from the zone of repression. The venue of the persecutory symbol is shifted so that the identity of the persecutor is hidden while the uncomfortable affect is reinforced. A raw tale of fury is produced. The discharge-oriented play fantasy of a peasant leader who kills a cruel king in a distant land is replaced by a lived-out fear of a persecutor whose victim is the child (as in the fear that the "dog will bite").

The structure of latency continues to play a role into adolescence, a role that is a far cry from its function in latency. The symbol representations through which it works shift from fantasy symbols to reality elements. This is one of the cognitive maturational changes that accompany the transition from latency to adolescence. The role of the structure of latency turns to future planning (a reality-oriented ego function). Regressions and phobic reactions involved in the fantasy function of the latency-age child are mobilized in the direction of object relations. Drive organization shifts for its drive discharge from fantasy objects to objects in the environment. Phobias may then be developed in relation to social situations, while the fantastic persecutors of latency lose their preeminent position. Phobias in early adolescence tend to give way to shyness, introversion, asceticism, or withdrawal. Adult phobias usually first appear during the late teens through the early twenties (Laughlin 1967, p. 566).

One may therefore expect latency-age phobias to clear with age. Laughlin quoted Menninger to the effect that "about twenty percent of college students have or have had phobias in early years which sooner or later disappeared spontaneously" (p. 566). Regression of the symbolizing function, and the prelatency fantasies that sensitized the child to the behavior of others, find different pathways for expression. They may even produce new phobias. In effect, the bottles in which psychopathology appears change during the shift from latency to adolescence; within the new bottles one finds the same old wine. If we take the view that the waking phobias of latency will heal with time and medication, we will probably be right. But what is gained in curing the phobia but not the child? Psychotherapy in latency has value. Latency is a good time to get to the ego defects and psychosexual sensitivities and fantasies that lie beneath the troubles of latency and can give rise to other forms of psychopathology in adolescence and adulthood.

In confronting a child with a waking phobia psychotherapeutically, one must be on the lookout for an overstimulating parent, a defective symbolizing function, a low level of anxiety tolerance, or a diminished stimulus barrier in considering the factors in the differential diagnosis. Treatment must be geared to the underpinnings of the diagnosis, as must the determination of prognosis. The primary technique for dealing with "waking phobia" is a play therapy technique that strengthens the symbolizing function.

Pavor Diurnus

Pavor diurnus, or day terrors, are waking fears that occur in individuals whose histories reveal the presence of night terrors (*pavor nocturnus*) before the age of 6, and sleep walking during latency. There appear to be at least two factors involved in their appearance in latency-age children. First, they occur during periods of psychological stress. Second, there is a physiological predisposition, as manifested in a disorder of arousal as described by Broughton (1968).

In cases of night terror the parents describe a peculiar type of nightmare characterized by hypermotility, confused automatic behavior, motor control that appears to be volitional, and awareness of the surround, with retrograde amnesia for the behavior and thought content during the attack. Kales (1969) did electroencephalographic studies of children during these attacks. He discovered in the EEG a hypnogogic hypersynchrony during rousal from fourth-stage sleep, signifying a disorder of arousal. A typical clinical history consists of an alternation of rare attacks with periods during which attacks come in series. The latter usually occur during periods of emotional turmoil. In latency, sleepwalking often starts with an accompanying decline in the night pavor. In most cases, by 9 or 10 years of age all symptomatology clears, including the immature sleep record on the EEG. In a small group of patients, the *pavor* continues unstintingly. For those with persistent *pavor,* memory for the dream content becomes possible. This has negative prognostic significance in adolescence. As adults, they may have sustained attacks or episodes patterned in bursts. In studies of the adjustment of these patients (Fisher 1970) there were reported difficulties in the setting up of appointments because of intercurrent psychiatric hospitalization.

Pavor diurnis is a disease that was well known in the nineteenth century. Macnish (1834) wrote of such waking terrors in adults, and Still (1900), publishing in *Lancet,* described day terrors in children. There were periods of extreme anxiety occurring during the waking period of a child's day, accompanied by hallucinated threatening figures. The last mention of it is a description by Ernest Jones (1931) of *pavor* states occurring during wakefulness. The probability is that the condition has recently been grouped with acute hallucinosis in childhood. I mentioned this in my book *Latency,* and apparently clinicians were thereby alerted to the condition. There soon appeared referrals for consultation with youngsters who had an early history of *pavor nocturnus* or sleepwalking and, later, phobic reactions while awake, which contained *pavor*-like material. Many of the children functioned well between episodes. Youngsters who had definite *pavor nocturnus* and some episodes of *pavor diurnus* could be helped with dynamically oriented psychotherapy aimed at diminishing the seriousness of interference with function that derives from the presence of *pavor diurnus*.

Here is a classic example of *pavor diurnus*.

Helen was 10½ when seen. There was a history of *pavor nocturnus* in early childhood. She said, "When I was younger I would wake up and walk downstairs. I started talking nonsense about my dream and running around." Although up she was not fully roused and had no recall for *pavor*-dream content or what she had done while walking about. Recall for *pavor*-dream content began at age 8. "More and more I remember the dreams since I was 8½." At 10½ she reported that during the day she got "these effects of things getting bigger and coming at me. My mother and father's face flashes up and gets bigger—it's kind of scary. If I don't fight them, the scary things continue into the night." She fights them by concentrating on other ideas. "It gets better 'cause I fight it. If I don't try to fight it it wouldn't get better." If she is concentrating, the images do not occur. She must work hard to keep the images out of her mind. For instance, once a visual image appeared in her head—a silver man on a playing field. He just stood there. He even had a shadow. "I made him friendly and walk around. He looked so creepy. I was frightened by the thought." She never has these images when she is having fun with friends or working in school. When relaxed, riding in a car, reading, relaxing at night without music or people to listen to, she has to expend continous effort to keep from being overwhelmed by these affect-porous symbols that make her so anxious. She maintains a phobic avoidance of the situations in which she might experience such episodes.

Another child's *pavor diurnus* consisted of a mouth that appeared in the wall and made fun of her.

Diazepam (Valium) obliterates fourth-stage sleep, and the elimination of arousal from fourth-stage sleep should be, and usually is, accompanied by a cessation of *pavors*. Some of the parents of children with *pavor diurnus* have reported good results with diazepam. I have seen improvement in a hospitalized 15-year-old girl with *pavor diurnus* and irritability and paranoid states while awake. All three of these symptoms cleared. She became less disturbed but on discharge was no less impaired in her ability to relate to others than before receiving medication.

The description in the case history of the need to concentrate to avoid the hallucinations is important. *Pavor diurnus* is an example of intact organs of perception being overwhelmed by intrusions of fantasy material. To avoid these intrusions the child is forced to struggle to maintain primary contact with external world realities. There is no sensory deprivation, as occurs in the case of night fears, that encourages an inward turning of the organ of consciousness. Rather, there is a faulty ability to rouse to contact with reality and defend against the intrusion of fantasy. The underlying problem here is more physiological than psychological. Techniques to minimize strong affects of anxiety and depression are useful in helping these people maintain distance from the intruding affect-porous symbols that threaten to sap their efficiency, at the least, or even their sense of reality.

Phobic Reactions of Late Latency

Differential Diagnosis from Psychotic States

As the child passes from latency to adolescence, there is a period when persecutory fantasy accompanied by phobic reactions or phobic symptoms present difficult and far-reaching differential diagnostic problems. As reality testing becomes stronger, the symbols selected for fantasy formation by the structure of latency call increasingly upon reality elements from which they can weave their contents. The closer to reality the symbols are, the more likely are they to become fear producing when they (the symbols) attract underlying hostile wishes. The condition, in essence, does not differ from the regressions in the structure of latency that occur in early latency. The later regression is a product of any factors that impair the capacity of the structure of latency to diminish anxiety. Usually the manifest symptoms of the later regression take the form of fear of robbers, rapists, kidnappers, or murderers who are out to get the child. The symptomatology may expand to include a need for a companion, fear of school, or fear of shopping centers where the feared events might occur. Night fears, with the need for night-lights and the like, are rekindled. Typically these youngsters had night fears while younger, have many friends to whom they continue to relate well, and develop abstract thinking normally, with no thinking disorders. Regression in the structure of latency requires treatment that deals with underlying conflicts about accepting budding conscious sexual urges and ameliorating the poor symbolizing function that has been revealed.

Sometimes it is hard to differentiate these paranoid states, which present as phobic reactions and follow maturational changes and regressions in the structure of latency, from the schizophrenic diseases accompanied by persecutory delusions and phobic reactions that first appear at this age (adult schizophrenia of early onset and prepubescent schizophrenia).

Adult Schizophrenia of Early Onset

Adult schizophrenia of early onset may present with phobic symptoms, such as fear of persecution at parties, manifested by avoidance of social situations. These youngsters have thinking disorders and a flat affect. In the realm of object relations, they usually have had few friends during the latency years. Some have had friends but begin to have problems with object relations at this time. They often demonstrate engaging personalities in a psychiatric interview. For these, it is easy to confuse this state with regression in the structure of latency. Early onset schizophrenia has the same prognosis as the adult form of paranoid schizophrenia.

Prepubescent Schizophrenia

Prepubescent schizophrenia comes on after age 11. Typically the child has external persecutors, which may be responded to with phobic avoidance. Before this, the persecutors were within, as would be expected in a condition in which introjects are not projected until 11 years of age. There is a history of poor object relatedness; marked concrete thinking is evident. The feared symbols are bizarre. The primary modality of treatment is medication. An example of the symptomatology of a prepubescent schizophrenic episode follows.

A boy aged 10, who avoided pizza because it gave him a bad stomachache and who often feared going to school, explained to me that in addition to the pizza allergy, he had pain in his "axis." The axis was a metal bar that fastened his heels together. The pain was very intense unless he directed his attention to his stomach, which then hurt instead. In addition, he had periods of "absence" while in school, during which he descended from his classroom 200 miles into the earth, where he sat with a group of other people while the devil talked to him. The stomach pain cleared up after one session. The father interrogated the child about my interview and, discerning that the "devil" had the face of a girl, who teased the boy while in the bus, instructed the boy to beat up the girl. He did.

Differential diagnosis between these conditions, any one of which can appear to be a phobia, is important because of the differing therapeutic indications and prognoses.

Phobic Reactions Related to Ethical Individuation in Late Latency

After about the age of 9, children begin to derive the contents for the aspects of the superego that control behavior from peers as well as from parents. The result can be marked conflicts between behavior considered permissible during late latency and the superego contents that persist from early childhood. I like to call this aspect of late latency *ethical individuation*. During this period, reality influences and introjects both lay claim to control of ethical decisions. A phase-specific interface is introduced, and around it intrapsychic conflict can evolve. This is especially so for those who can form new wishes on the basis of new experiences, but at the same time are subject to strong reinforcements of the internalized introjects of early childhood. During this period, obsessions, transient tics, hives, night fears, and phobias occur at the time of heightened confrontations between peer pressure and parental introjects.

A 12-year-old girl felt terror at the thought of the end of the session. She feared men intent on kidnapping her. I had to accompany her through the "phobic zone" to her parents' car. This was accompanied by bad dreams, night fears, and continuous fear of kidnappers. I inquired into her recent activities. She had been induced to steal by her friends. This put her in conflict with the internalized dictates of her parents. She became overwhelmed with guilt. The kidnappers were her way of expressing guilt. She was able to address her conflict and the phobia disappeared as quickly as it had appeared.

Rarely are these conditions brought to a child psychiatrist de novo. They are of such brief duration that only the very sophisticated parent would consider them to be of any significance. If the phobic symptom appears in isolation, insignificance is probably an accurate appraisal. The therapeutic considerations involved in symptoms related to ethical individuation, including phobia, require the parents to lessen the effects of their influence through early introjects when appropriate. As in the preceding case, analysis of the conflict is both possible and fruitful.

These people, by dint of the balance that they strike between the demands of reality and the demands of their introjects, are prime candidates for conflict-ridden periods of adjustment during new situations. They tend to be symptom-prone rather than given to developing anxiety or acting out.

Phobic States Associated with Maturational Moves in the Symbolizing Function

Because of the frequent developmental changes in the defenses and cognitive functions of latency, symptom changes often occur. For this reason, one must be on guard not to attribute a new symptom to the nearest stress.

A child of 8½ was transferred from his public school to a parochial school. On arrival at the new school, he developed a phobic reaction to school attendance. When taken to school each day, he refused to enter the classroom. He insisted on waiting anxiously in the hall. Logic dictated to those who had worked up the case that the child's school phobia was a reaction to the move, the new environment, and separation from familiar haunts. Investigation of his history, though, revealed that he suffered from chronic night fears, which had cleared completely with the onset of the school phobia. It was recognized at this point that rather than being an acute problem of school phobia, his phobia was of long standing. The symbol venue had changed, shifting from amorphous fantastic objects of fear to a specific external object of fear. The attention of the therapist could then be directed to the chronic stresses that underlay the symptomatology, once the chronic nature of the illness was identified.

This case illustrates the change of object chosen for symbolization and incorporation into a fantasy from an amorphous, internally conceived monster (the night fear) to reality elements used to actualize the fear and rationalize it with external reality supports. This shift in symptom often occurs. Most commonly, it gives rise to the agoraphobia of late latency–early adolescence. However, it occurs at its earliest with the cognitive shift in the nature of objects used as symbols, which occurs at 8½. [In this regard, see also Anthony (1959) and Piaget (1945).] The move is necessary and normal, and presages a normal shift into adolescence. These patients must, however, be followed to be sure that they will move to the next step, which is the replacement of the fantasy-laden real people feared by reality-oriented real people. This is a normal step, but fixation at the point of transition to the feared real object is crippling.

Summary

Phobic symptoms, phobic avoidance reactions, and the persecutory fantasies that often hide beneath phobic behavior should not be merely noted in an evaluation. Differential diagnosis should be undertaken with an eye to the impact of the total pathology on long-range functioning and adult adjustment. Childhood phobia may be likened to the pulsing musical theme one hears in movies in advance of a shark appearing suddenly from the ocean depths. Sometimes it's just a false alarm. Sometimes the shark appears. If one were in the water, it would be a good idea to look around.

Chapter 7

Depression

During latency, the presence of a sustained depressed affect and mood is not a mandatory feature for making the diagnosis of clinical depression. A depressive affect is often present in these conditions and, when present, is a bellwether in making the diagnosis. It is possible, however, to recognize depression in a child whose clinical condition is limited to the following diagnostic criteria: frequent crying for no apparent reason, lassitude, declining attention to school work, complaints about other children, loss of appetite, constipation or other gastrointestinal complaints, loss or shrinkage of the future autobiography, hypochondria, itching all over, difficulty in separating from parents, nightmares, frequent awakening, suicidal gestures, and accident proneness. Even in the absence of a depressive affect these are signs and symptoms of depression in childhood. These clinical findings should alert a clinician to the possible presence of depression.

How can there be a depression without a depressive affect? Such a situation is not foreign to adult psychiatry, in which such conditions are labeled masked depression. In these conditions, the affect "depression," the name used to identify the entire syndrome, need not always be present. Depressive affect is only one component of the syndrome that bears the name depression. Other aspects of the syndrome, though, may dominate the clinical picture.

In adults, there are depressive affect equivalents, such as elation, hypomania, and somatic symptoms. There are also phobic symptoms, vegetative symptoms, and motivational impairments. These psychological symptoms, which mask the depressive affect, are in fact the products of defenses which defend against the affect. When these dominate, and as a result make the affect not apparent, the syndrome *depression* may still be present.

The situation is somewhat different in the child. Depression is more often buried than masked during latency. The mildly depressed latency-age child can master the depressive affect by processing it through fantasy. States of latency may be produced in which no apparent problem is to be seen. As often as not, adult caretakers are grateful to see the child appearing happy, and comfort themselves with their misdiagnosis. More severe forms of depression in latency-age children may present with depressive syndromes resembling frank adult depressions, as well as adult-type masked depressions whose manifest forms resemble common neuroses.

Heuristic Axioms

There is an axiom applied to the study of childhood psychopathology, which states that depression is rare in childhood (Despert 1952). This belief is the product of the burying and masking functions described above. The goal of this chapter will be to explore why the axiom appears to hold for children 6 to 12 years of age, and to understand the mechanisms that produce this phenomenon. In so doing, various principles of psychopathology will be explicated, and these can be of advantage in preparing psychotherapeutic strategies.

The observed rarity of depression in childhood is a result of the common tendency to judge children by adult standards. Symptoms from the world of childhood are overlooked in the search for that which for the most part belongs in the domain of adult psychopathology. If one seeks to describe a clinically manifest depression as we see it in adults, then "depression in childhood" is rare indeed. It should be kept in mind, however, that because of the different organization of the ego that exists during the latency phase, symptoms during that period tend to constitute their own characteristic groupings, or syndromes. The childhood syndromes of depression are no exception to this. If we search for full-blown adultiform depressions in the child, few will be found; in actuality, depression during the latency-age period is masked in its own way, but is not excessively rare. The style for the handling of affects in latency is different from that in adulthood. Therefore, we can expect that even in situations in which depressive affects do begin to appear, alternative symptomatologies will be introduced to a much greater extent than in adults.

Clinical Manifestations of Depression

What are the clinical manifestations of depression in adulthood, against which the symptom complexes of the child are so often judged? They are vegetative *signs*, such as psychomotor retardation (a slowing of speech and motor movements); tearfulness; constipation; poor appetite; disturbed sleep patterns (multiple awakenings, insomnia, early morning awakening); facial pallor; difficulties with partings, especially when leaving a clinician's office (Japanese psychiatrists refer to this as *stickiness*); suicide attempts; and such mood *symptoms* as malaise; ennui; depressed mood (sadness); a sense of low self-worth; suicidal ideation; negative-content hallucinations; self-recrimination; a sense that the depressed state has always been present; anxiety; guilt; an empty feeling in the stomach; a sense that current time is all the time that there is, and a feeling that one is living in a black box. In the absence of any major stress, one should especially beware the presence of itching and of psychomotor retardation associated with a family history of depression. This last set of symptoms indicates an endogenous depression, which requires medication and further workup to rule out the organic conditions that produce depressions (i.e., brain tumor of the temporal lobe, endocrine abnormalities, pancreatic cancer, and pernicious anemia—the latter two are quite rare in children).

As an expression of a disordered personality state over a sustained and continuous period, such adult symptom complexes, even in part, are hard to find in children during latency. It is not till patients reach the age of 14 or 15 that one begins to see depression in its adult form. In the clinical practice of the author, there has been an uncanny number of girls in whom symptoms of sustained depressed mood first became apparent at exactly 12½ years of age.

Let us review the clinical manifestations of depression during the latency period. They are: listlessness and lassitude; a decrease in school performance; moodiness; general unhappiness; being hard to please; rapid changes of mood; a tendency toward crying; clinging behavior; a return of thumb sucking; somatic symptomatology involving the digestive tract (diarrhea and vomiting); generalized and often intractable pruritis; complaints about other children; loss of appetite; loss or shrinkage of the future autobiography; hypochondria; difficulty in separating from parents; nightmares; sleep disturbances; accident proneness and other forms of aggression directed towards the self, such as suicide attempts; hallucinations with negative content and, rarely, the mood changes found in adult depressives.

The sharp descriptive difference between adult and latency-age depression presents a difficulty: If depression as we know it in adults is so rare in childhood (specifically during latency), how are we to define a state in childhood as *depression*? Obviously, it is required that we search out the fundamental elements and the nature of depression at different ages, so that we will not be misled by the fact that surface symptomatologies differ at various stages of life. This principle is not new, but the application is perhaps unique. For example, one can identify a person as being past middle age when the surface symptomatology is that of an involutional depression.

It is likely that the appearance of adultiform depression at adolescence is the result of a cognitive change associated with puberty and successful resolution of a psychological phase of development, with a transition into a new phase of ego organization. We shall return to this in later chapters devoted to the cognitive changes that accompany the shift from latency to adolescence and to details of the transition to the new phase of personality development. The interesting observations by Spitz (1946) of prelatency children who unquestionably suffered from the physiological and psychological signs of the adult form of depression rule out the idea that there is a primary physiological change that produces adultiform depression upon the appearance of adolescence.

Diagnosing Depression in the Absence of Depressive Affect

How can one determine that a clinical syndrome free of depressive affect and occurring in childhood is depression equatable or similar to depression as found in adults?

What is required is to discover the nature of depression. The extrinsic forms, consisting of many varied syndromes, symptoms, and signs, which represent the outcomes of varied psychological situations in early childhood, are too protean to help us define a common intrinsic characteristic. This must be found in dynamics and origins. There is a general principle in the field of pathology, that human tissue has specific and, at times, age-geared responses to trauma. This applies to psychological as well as physical trauma. In the psychological sphere, trauma from any age or time can be carried forward by the function of memory into later times, when the remembered trauma is responded to by the cognitive styles and defenses of the later age. These age-specific responses can be observed and described; they are more accessible to study than were their antecedents. They tend to over-shadow the flow of the underlying psychological processes that pro-duce periods of clinical depression, progression, and regression through cognitive and genetic psychological phases. The antecedents of depression shape the reactions of later times. Ego functions geared to the cognition of the age shape responses. In depression, responses involve sensitivity to loss of objects, loss of self-esteem, shortfalls in the pursuit of the ego ideal, the mobilization of guilt, and the internaliza-tion of conflict. These responses produce, in each phase, specific reactions that constitute depression for that age.

Thus, in approaching depression in the latency-age child, we must keep in mind that his depression will have the characteristics of the condition as it is seen in latency, not those of depression as seen in an adult. We should also remember that the term depression describes a multitude of emotional states and their equivalents. There is no one depression; therefore, there is no single description or explanation of those states related to adult depressions as they occur during the latency period. Masked depression, or *depressive equivalent,* can be diagnosed in both adult and child. What the clinician describes may, on the surface, appear to be a phobia, a psychosomatic symptom, or a sleep disturbance. How is it possible, then, to draw the conclusion that a psychological manifestation is a symptom that masks and represents depression, rather than a clinical phenomenon sui generis, i.e., a true phobia or obsessional neurosis? If we find components of depression in a clinical state, we consider the possibility of depression. If while we analyze someone for phobia, the phobic defense is lifted and a depres-sion appears, we are justified in saying that the phobia masked a depression, or at least that phobia and depression are variant manifes-tations of the same underlying psychological conflict or processes.

Reconstructing the Antecedents of Depression

The appearance of depressive equivalents indicates the presence of something so intrinsic to the state of depression that a diagnosis of depression can be made in the child in the absence of clinical depres-sive affects. There is a general axiom in studying psychopathology that underlying causal processes may be shared by disparate manifest symp-toms, and that these causal processes and their sources are the antece-dents of the manifest symptoms. If we apply this axiom to depression, we can say that a depressive equivalent shares origins with frank depressions. It follows that we can identify a depressive equivalent as depression if we can detect the antecedents of depression in the history of the patient. To do this, we must have a reconstruction of the antecedents of depression against which to compare our clinical findings.

A number of approaches are available to us in reconstructing the antecedents of depression. They provide multiple clues to the psychological origins of depression. These clues in turn offer insights that are useful in approaching depression from the standpoint of psychotherapeutic strategies and prevention.

One approach, which reveals a common early life history for the child and the adult depressive, is the technique of reconstruction of the early childhood experiences of patients who have manifest depression in adult life. Another is reconstruction derived from the play of depressed children. Comparison reveals similar roots. A related approach has been direct observation of patients with depressive states in early childhood with subsequent following of these patients into latency and adult life to see if common roots produce different specific symptom groupings at different ages. Yet another clinical approach studies the dynamics of the various depressive symptom clusters for evidence of similar dynamics.

We turn first to the workers in adult psychoanalysis who reconstructed the antecedents of depression. Abraham (1924) described the precursor of depression as an early childhood object loss. The experience of depression in an adult was seen to be the reexperiencing of the feelings that occurred with the loss of the breast (maternal nurture and tenderness while nursing). Abraham's concept is that the loss of an object along with the affects associated with it (paradigmatically the loss of the breast/mother) can be seen as the primal experience from which depressive experience and feelings are derived. He concluded that suckling, eating, introjection, and fantasy, all oral-phase activities, are associated and that they play a role in the formation of depressive states. Therefore, depressive states have these factors in common whether or not depressive affect is present. Symptom variation results from the interplay between these factors (dragged from the past to the present by memory) and the age-appropriate organizations of defense.

Lewin (1950) described the paradigmatic prototype of depression as lying in infantile sensations while sucking at the breast, falling asleep at the breast, and being "swallowed up" by the breast. Clinically this would be manifested in eating, sleeping, and angry fear of having one's identity swallowed up as a result of a psychological fusion with another person. Withdrawal into fantasy associated with denial of problem stimuli is one of the elements that characterizes depressive states.

Freud (1917) noted that aggression turned on the self was the basic characteristic of depression. This leads us to the conclusion that aggression turned on the self, such as accident-proneness and self-destructive activities (e.g., suicide attempts), can be considered as depressive equivalents.

Depressive States during Infancy

An important contribution to the understanding of depression is derivable from the work of those who have studied directly the age period to which psychoanalytic investigators have assigned the psychological origin of depression. A. Freud (1936), Spitz (1946), and Mahler (1969) have focused their attention on the periods of early life at which individuation and separation first occur. Separation experiences at that time have been implicated as psychopathogenetic by those who have studied depression in adults. In turning to their work, we move from those who have reconstructed the childhood antecedents of depression to review the work of those who have done direct observations of the very phases in which the precursors described are being generated.

With the separation–individuation phase introduced by the experience of separation and stranger anxiety, the child gives evidence of an awareness of the absence of the mother. The child, not yet able to reconstitute an image of the mother to comfort himself, becomes very anxious at separations. This is one of the prototypes of depression. As the child approaches 18 months, he gradually develops *object constancy* (a term introduced by Anna Freud). This is the ability to evoke the image of the lost object and to comfort oneself with this object-image. Many depressions occur in individuals who either fail to develop a consistent capacity to recall the comforting object's image or who had, and still recall, inconstant objects from the start. We say such people have poor object constancy. They feel a sense of loss. They feel deserted, and develop a low sense of self-esteem. In trying to re-evoke earlier object relations, ego states, and affective states, they find themselves confronted with a disappointing comforter.

These concepts have been strongly reinforced by Spitz (1946) in his work on hospitalism and anaclitic depression. He discovered that after the eighth month of life the substitution of poor mothering for a good mother results in a marked change in the child. Over a period of months, the child gradually develops a depressive affect, a slowing of movement, tearfulness, and what appears to be a full-blown depression manifesting the characteristics of depression in adulthood. The child is characterized by "weeping, tears running down the face, shaking of the whole body" (p. 315). There are also insomnia, loss of appetite, loss of weight, and retardation of movement. The clinical condition described is comparable to that of adult depression.

Reconstructions of the early life experience of the adult depressive have focused primarily on the influence of the events of separation during the first year of life (i.e., reconstructions and direct studies of the origins of depression in the oral phase). Bibring (1953), however, went beyond this. He pointed out that depressions associated with and derived from the oral (separation–individuation phase) are not associated with guilt; rather, they are responses to separation and loss. Depressions with guilt, which deal with loss of self-esteem in terms of falling short of an ego ideal, derive their characteristics from the affects of the period when punishment fears come to relate to internal punishers. When this context is internalized, aggression turned inward is allied with conscience; and painful guilt and depressive affects are then the clinical manifestations. Thus, during the phallic part of the oedipal phase, depression associated with guilt finds its origins and the paradigms for later expression. Therefore, a person whose depression is derived from a sense of object loss associated with the oral part of the oedipal phase (this is the point at which the child is aware of the parents as a couple who have left him out) usually has a sense of low self-esteem associated with depression, but not guilt. A sense of guilt in depression is seen where castration wishes and fear of retribution from the father are important elements. As the child enters latency, these feared attack-oriented elements are internalized to fuel the superego-motivating affect of guilt.

Depression during Latency

We have reviewed three areas: theories of origin for adult forms of depression, reconstructions of the sources of depression which are rooted in early childhood, and depressive states in early childhood. We turn now to the direct study of frank depression and equivalent symptomatologies in latency-age children. In this way, we can establish diagnostic principles with which to identify these conditions. Once they are identified as a group, their origins and their differences may be studied as a unit. Thus we can confirm the underpinnings and antecedents of depressive symptomatology in latency. The intrinsic nature of depression in its many manifest forms is allied to this understanding.

In the studies done with youngsters who have exhibited some form of manifest clinical depression during the latency age period, at least three distinct clinical entities appear: emotional acrescentism (affect starvation), frank depression, and depressive equivalents.

The Affect-Starved Child

Emotional acrescentism (affect starvation resulting in failure to grow emotionally) is a term introduced by L. Sachs (1962), who studied latency-age children who had been markedly deprived and neglected in early childhood. In them she discovered a tendency toward concrete thinking, hallucinations, high degree of verbal skill, and an engaging personality. These youngsters tend to form very quick and close attachments with older people. They appear to be very loving, but they have one remarkable characteristic: they appear incapable of remembering the good things that were done for them by the people to whom they attach themselves. One such child punched a nurse when she spent extra time with a new arrival on the ward. She had even planned to adopt the puncher until that time. These children do not appear to be depressed in early latency, but they become resentful, angry, and depressed in late latency. Although they seem gracious and well-relating, this is a misleading observation.

In actuality, they have a poor ability to establish a consistent, reassuring image of a new object. The resulting limited ability to change their view of people, even after contact with loving caretakers, leads to a view of people as lacking kindness, reliability, or trustworthiness. This leaves them in unremitting recollection of a deep, unfulfilled object hunger that is only slowly modified by reality experiences, if at all. They rarely achieve a relationship close enough to produce a sense of loss that would limit hostile, demanding, regressive states. Therapists confronting such children need to be aware of the unmoored nature of the child's object ties. These children are as unreliable as landless wanderers and marauders. A therapeutic goal is to provide an anchoring relationship. There is a need for consistency over extended periods of time.

These children's sense of that of which the world consists is hopelessness in the search for a reliable harbour from loneliness and a sense of betrayal. This gives these young people the makings of depressive symptomatology at any age—infancy, adolescence, or adulthood.

Latency's unique dynamics hold the depressive symptoms at bay. The affects can be defended against by the fantasy structures produced by the structure of latency. If followed to late latency, their object hunger and manifest use of the mechanism of denial and fantasy become apparent. At about the age of 11, they change markedly. Fantasies of magical gratifications give way to disgruntled awareness of their hopeless reality as they feel it to be. They may begin to steal. They begin to show marked aggressive acting out. Suicidal ideation and manifest depressive affects soon follow. Rare is the person in this group who has depression with guilt. This is a prime example of a depression with marked oral features. These children are usually identified and brought for treatment, either when they explode briefly during early latency or during the period of decompensation that occurs at about 11 years of age.

Sachs (1962) felt that she was describing here those children who have had the early life experiences observed by Spitz in his work (1946) on anaclitic depression (i.e., severe emotional deprivation and poor object relations). She described the affect-starved child in early latency as follows: clinging object relations, outgoing, charming, crying pitifully when frustrated (p. 637). In late latency, after about age 11, she describes poor superego development, marked sullenness, moodiness in passive individuals with unpredictable flareups, suicide attempts, and an absent sense of guilt.

Frank Depression during the Latency Age

Connell (1973), Sperling (1959), and Bemporad and Kyu (1984) have written about their observations of children with clinical depression. Three symptomatically depressed latency-age children were identified by Sperling in her clinical practice. Twenty cases seen by Connell were identified and gathered as the result of a request that children from all over Australia who manifested signs and symptoms of clinical depression be sent to her hospital for a research study. The relative rarity of overt symptomatology is evident from the sparsity of cases observed in both private practice and research settings. There was remarkable agreement between Sperling and Connell in regard to the description of their clinical findings. It is striking that Connell discovered four patients who were unusually depressed and responded to Tofranil (imipramine), indicating that the rudiments of the two types of depressive illness seen in adults (endogenous and exogenous) are recognizable in childhood. Contrary to the usual findings in adults, the endogenous depressions (depressive affect and mood, severe vegetative signs, response to tricyclic amines) were associated with easily identified precipitating causes. Whereas in adults the precipitants of depression are easily detected only with exogenous depressions, in children visible precipitants are an almost universal phenomenon.

The symptomatology of the clinically depressed child bore similarities to that of adult depression, although there was not a perfect concordance. In the child with masked depression, this discordance is greater, the main point being the primacy of the depressed mood in the adult. Sperling felt that this discordance in symptoms might be the source of the apparent rarity of "depression" in children. As she pointed out, "Depression is not rare in children. However, it's not easily recognized because its overt manifestations are in most cases different from those of adults" (p. 383).

The twenty-three cases diagnosed as depression by Sperling and Connell had manifest sustained clinically depressed moods. Inclusion in Connell's group required depressed mood sustained for more than three months. It is this symptom that is rare in childhood. Sperling felt that the diagnosis of depression could be made more often if the criterion of sustained depressed affect were eliminated. In her view, depression in childhood is indicated by the following criteria: for youngsters before the age of 4, look for listlessness, moodiness, and general unhappiness, with food intake and sleep patterns affected; in the latency-age child one should watch for listlessness, moodiness, general unhappiness, a tendency toward crying, oral symptoms such as thumb sucking, somatic symptomatology in the digestive area (here she included food intake and eating disturbances as well as ulcerative colitis), pruritis (generalized and intractable itching), and sleep disturbances. In addition, accident proneness and direction of aggression toward the self, such as suicide attempts, were not considered unusual in an extended group of youngsters with these findings but no severe sustained depressive mood. In looking for causal factors, Sperling looked to early childhood, where she found "an impaired mother–child relationship with fear of the loss of the object" (p. 393). [Note the relationship of this to Abraham's (1924) findings.] She felt that this was the condition necessary to treat in dealing with depressions and depressive equivalents in children.

Connell had little doubt that the children whom she studied suffered from a condition "involving mood disturbance that resembled adult depressive illness in some respects but also had characteristics of its own, chief among which were somatic symptoms and antisocial behavior" (1973, p. 84). Early wakening, anorexia, abdominal pain, headaches, wetting, and soiling were some of the concomitant symptoms noted in her depressive studies. The depressive mood in both Sperling's and Connell's groups was unquestioned.

Depressive Equivalents during Latency

One might be drawn to the conclusion that children younger than 4 can have depressions with all the characteristics of an adult depression. In those older than 14, one can also find the characteristics of adult depression with some frequency. There appears to be *some interposed phenomenon* during the period from 5 to 13 that alters the course of the symptomatology of clinical depression in the majority of patients, so that overt depressive moods become rare and short-lived and the patients manifest their depressive illness in masked and cryptic forms.

The interposed phenomenon must be a factor that deals with uncomfortable affects in a way that removes them from awareness; and one such phenomenon might be the structure of latency. The latency-age child has an organization of ego defenses that deals with uncomfortable affects through repression of the fantasies associated with them. There is fragmentation of the fantasies and displacement of their parts into symbolic representations less porous to the affects associated with the original concepts. These displaced symbols are regrouped into pleasant or mastery-oriented fantasies. They can be used for the discharge of drives and the mastery of humiliating experiences without clinically manifest uncomfortable affects. The structure of latency and its fantasy products thus become defenses against affects. Depressive affects are amongst the uncomfortable ones that can be dealt with in this way. Therefore, even severe depressive states during latency show less depressive affect than is found in their adult equivalents. For this reason, during the latency period, depression is less important as a symptom of psychopathology than it is in adults.

Depression as a symptom in latency tends to be a transient affect, fleeting in its availability to consciousness, and attenuated as the result of the defensive mobilization of fantasies and depressive equivalents. Depressive affects may be found to underlie persecutory states, unsuccessful attempts to adjust to new peer groups, psychosomatic responses, obsessional states, hyperactivity, and oral regressive states accompanied by overeating and overweight.

"Normal Depression" in Latency

In the latency-age child, sustained manifest depressions are most often seen in normal situations such as mourning and related reactions to loss. Object loss is processed through identification during mourning, introjection, and finding new objects, as in other age groups. The latency-age child also has a *structure of latency* to call into service.

Through this group of ego functions, the child is able to create fantasy by which the experience of loss can undergo a catharsis, much as adults experience catharsis when seeing dramatic performances.

Periods of manifest depression may also occur when a child has fallen short of the demands of his superego, producing anger directed at himself. The superego has three primary groups of functions. These are the ego mechanisms that enforce the superego demands, the superego demands themselves (a sort of book of rules), and the superego-motivating affects. The last are the driving force for acting on the demands of the superego; they may also limit actions. Behaving in accord with superego demands brings pleasant affects, whereas running counter to them evokes displeasure. These affects, in effect, dominate human social behavior. Uncomfortable feeling states are created in a person equipped with an immature superego. These are triggers for depression, and may serve as the equivalents of depression. Usually a person is guided to acceptable behavior by the threat that these affects will become manifest. Self-control brings equanimity. Loss of control brings discomfort and reactive depression in those states in which behavior falls short of one's own expectations. It is in the area of the superego-motivating affects that unconscious guilt and unconscious depression serve as constant watchmen and guides.

In addition to the superego-motivating affects, a second form of unconscious affect guides intentional behavior—affect that has been experienced on the surface of consciousness and then been repressed. It has been held in repression by the mechanism of displacement and maintained there by riveting attention (cathexes) onto substitute ideas and symptoms. In this second form lies the mechanism for the development of the aspects of depressive symptomatology that diverge from depressive affect.

Depressions often signal the presence of an immature superego. Such a superego is commonly understood to be sadistic and cruel to the person of whose personality it is a constituent. In part, painful depression is a sign of its cruelty. The mature superego guides behavior while recognizing the wisdom of responding to id wishes. There is the sense that nothing that is human should be considered foreign, whereas the immature superego is brutal in its criticism. Immature parents engender immature superegos in their offspring. The immature superego does not cause depression, but it colors the quality of the depressive reaction in a child, thus causing depressions to be more severe. The more immature the superego, the harder is a person on himself in situations of disappointment.

A common source of depression is a situation that stirs anger and at the same time frustrates its expression. Another source is any situation that humiliates the child. A child's small size renders outwardly directed anger futile—the world does not change in response to little howls or to the beating of tiny fists. Latency-age defenses convert anger into the signs and symptoms seen when a child is confronted with such situations.

The specific mechanisms used to deal with angry feelings (the aggressive drive) are twofold: projection and actualization. Both defenses effect a mastery of humiliation through living out a displaced victory over fears or memories. Peers or other reality elements serve in the way that play symbols do. They "actualize" (i.e., make real) fantasies in which the child succeeds.

In addition to mastery through fantasy, the thrust of these defenses is to shift the drive cathexes from the self, drawing energy away from an inward turning of the drives. Such inward turning of the drives on the self is the characteristic mode of energy discharge associated with the production of depression in adults (see Freud 1917). When there are overt evidences of depression akin to that of the adult in the life of the latency-age child, there has been a failure of these latency mechanisms and the latency-age ego organizations (e.g., restraint and the structure of latency). As a result of these failures, aggressive energies turn inward, and depressive symptomatology is released.

Before the issue may be considered closed, it will be necessary to explain the emergence of the adult form of depression with the onset of adolescence. We have noted the fact that failure of the defense mechanisms of latency will release depression. Frank depression and the state of latency are mutually exclusive. The defense mechanisms of the latency period begin to crumble in late latency as a result of an improvement in cognition. The resolution and working through of stressful situations by means of fantasy passes when the ludic symbol is no longer available to the waking child. In the latency years, it is possible for a child to avoid confrontation with his problems as a result of the ability to redirect his energies and change his world through the manipulation of symbols. Once he reaches adolescence, the child must face his affects. His attention is called to the irritants in his real world.

There is a useful clinical insight to be derived from this shift from an internal resolution of conflicts to one that requires the cooperation of the world. Latency calm in the child lessens the chance that there will be meaningful communication between child and adult during adolescence. Parents tend to take a child's peace of mind for granted during latency. The calm of latency with its ability to turn off affects, as though the child is no longer bothered by a trauma, fools parents who are all too eager to believe that childhood is a time of blissful ignorance. A parent who is aware that either his actions or other circumstances are affecting a child may well have considered a heart-to-heart talk "next morning" to help the child deal with (confront and master) the problems. Perhaps the parent plans to cancel another activity to make time for the discussion. If the structure of latency has done its task, then at the time of the planned talk, the child will appear comfortable and content with his play. Thereby, the chance to set up or continue the parent–child line of communication is not taken. The child seems well, the parent is content. Each goes his separate way. With the coming of adolescence there is a return of sustained awareness of affects. A sharp focus on identifying the sources of emotional discomfort could support discussion. Because no provision for sustained communication had been established in latency, the separate ways continue. Parent and child grow apart. The conflict of generations in adolescence can be seen as a residue of the capacity of the ego structures of the latency-age period to mask problems and affects, leading to a decline in the interpersonal skills that detect, defuse, define, and resolve problems through open discussion.

Depressive Elements in Late Latency–Early Adolescence

The period of late latency and early adolescence is a time when the person races forward toward individuation and social maturity. The pace is set by peers and society. The child, confronted by tasks beyond his ken or by situations that are foreign to his experience, is often at a loss. There may have been insufficient time to develop an identity upon which to fall back. A sense of being overwhelmed, lost, and rudderless confronts the child. The sense of inadequacy that ensues may be warded off by a regression to a state in which maternal nurturing is evoked to comfort and guide the perplexed child. This state of orally regressed dependency is accompanied by depressive affects and equivalents. Children in this state can be seen clinically to spend all their time watching television while eating and growing fat. Beware allergies, asthma, and hives in these young people, for upon entering adolescence, the depression that is inherent in the adjustment of these youngsters may be unmasked.

Such states can be prevented by early encouragement of the child to become independent of the parent. The ego function that is the ability to evaluate potential danger in new situations should be developed by permitting the child ever-increasing freedom of movement in consonance with the experience of other children. Overprotective parents tend to cause this sequence of events to take a pathological turn.

It is important to take into account dependency and aggressive and regressive needs to understand adolescent depression. All three elements come jointly into focus when we remember that two of the three primary tasks of adolescence are the achievement of removal (separation from parents as the primary objects for drive gratification) and coping with passivity. Natural urges push the child toward removal. Social wants "sin against the strength of youth" and keep the children home in the *best* of circumstances. Adolescents are all dressed up with adult bodies, but without the right, or the money, to have a place to go. Parents control the roost; the child must accede to parental will. Anger is the result of this forced dependency. The child may either fight or flee into a regressive surrender. Storms of depression accompany these battles between the generations. Estrangement from the parent may give rise to strong reactions, in which parental images are introjected and added to earlier imagoes as a means of dealing with the loss of the same rejected parent. This is bound to intensify the conflict and the depression, which without the structure of latency can no longer be masked.

The *introject* is an important concept in understanding adolescence. In essence, parental images and characteristics become part of the child's inner experience of himself. Depression arises when there is conflict between the ideas, wishes, and pressures of peers and the internalized wishes of the parent of early life. The introjected, harshly punishing parent is transformed into the cruel immature superego and—in the context of our topic—the impetus, spirit, and soul (psyche) of depression.

The development of identity and the regulation of self-esteem are also primary tasks in adolescence. If children may become depressed when they fall short of their own expectations, imagine what a quandary a child would be in if the expectations themselves were uncertain as the result of a fluid identity. This occurs in the affect-starved child and also in the normal state of changing and vacillating identifications with parents, peers, and culture heroes that is part of the adolescent scene in our day. It is no wonder that suicide is the fourth leading cause of death among young people aged 15 to 19. Aside from the fact that it is during this period that organically (e.g., endogenously) based depressions make their first strong impact (marijuana/quaalude suicidal depression, suicide through substance abuse, monopolar depressions, schizophrenias) and inexperienced drivers first take to the road and drive as though they were immortal, there is the problem of passivity. Children want independence, and parents are loath to let them go. The more primitive the parent, the harsher the superego of the child and the deeper the hurting potential of the depression. Suicide is a possible vent for these forces.

Fantasy Denial and Depression

Fantasy and depression are distinct and different entities. During latency it can be seen that they can achieve a function in common, in that their presence obviates the need for response to problems in reality that require direct handling. Other mental processes that share this function are denial, dreaming, and promises made to oneself, often during therapy or analysis, that the problem will be resolved. In all five of these mechanisms, a problem that requires attention can be put aside as a result of a mental activity. Of vital importance is the fact that the problem persists in spite of a facile sleight of the ego's hand. Examples follow.

Denial

A 7-year-old boy, who often railed at therapy and refused to admit that there was any need for treatment, presented a therapeutic problem, in that there was nothing to talk about. This was in spite of the fact that his mother manhandled him, threw him bodily into water, and often left him for extended periods with inadequate caretakers. One day, he began his session with the announcement that a funny thing had happened on the way into the office from his mother's car. Said he, "I just got all better." His denial obviated the need for further intervention while it blocked pathways to insight into the cause of his disruptive school behavior.

Dreaming

A man in his 40s, who was quite hostile to his wife and often wished to leave her, developed anxiety episodes, almost daily, in response to her criticisms and intrusions into his plans. He felt free of tension after a dream in which he saw a plane containing his wife crash in flames. The effect of the dream was to help him reset his affects. He was less tense after discharging his anger at her through the dream. The problems with the wife had not been confronted.

At times, and especially in children, dreams like this one are linked with so much anxiety that the child awakens. Such REM nightmares are by nature more constructive than ordinary "resetting" anxiety dreams. Instead of clearing the air of affects, they alert one to the fact that there is a problem to be solved. These dreams are depressive equivalents.

A child of 5, who had witnessed his brother having a convulsion, awakened repeatedly from a dream in which a large monster attacked him. In therapy, a cut-out doll in the form of the monster was used repeatedly in play to help the child master the memory.

In this case, there was no reality to be changed. There was only a memory to be mastered or defused. However, the principle of using a dream element, which has been converted into a ludic symbol (a paper doll), as a tool for diffusing the impact of a stressful situation is well illustrated. When the stress entails a current reality, dream elements can be used in a similar fashion. The appearance of an anxiety dream signals the presence of a stress that is not being dealt with directly. A doll used to represent a dream element may be employed to encourage fantasy from which one can identify the stress. Then the child's attention may be drawn back to the problem and techniques developed for resolving the problem directly. In this way, parental abuse or situations with peers that are the products of character traits in the patient can be brought to the surface for adjustment or analysis.

A child of 10, with an anxiety dream of an attacking monster—from which he did not awaken—alerted his therapist through the dream to neglect on the part of the father. This insight was reached through paper doll dream associations. In a dream, the monster attacked a car full of picnickers. Each member of the party was constructed as a doll and placed in a car. The members were then identified by name and relationship. The father's tendency to yell at the child and to break appointments on weekend days was reached. Work was done with the child and the parent to correct the situation directly.

Promises Made—Often, In Therapy. When a person has clear insight into the source of his difficulties, lying in either the behavior of another person or repeated self-destructive behavior, a promise to correct the situation through an obvious direct intervention, such as a diet or divorce, often puts the mind at ease without solving anything. More praise is merited by the disclosure "I started a diet last Wednesday" than by a promise to "go on a diet tomorrow." Many marriages remain intact because promises to oneself to leave the marriage provide a reminder of the fact that all is not hopeless and that there is an alternative to remaining in a bad situation. Hope is the comfort that such promises offer, though on the surface they appear to be constructs for future planning. There is an apt saying, "If wishes were horses, beggars would ride." In dealing with affects that are strong, it is wise to keep in mind that planning and fantasy are close kin.

Anxiety dreams that awaken the dreamer interfere with the defensive dream processing of core problem areas. If the dreamer were to continue to sleep, then the problems might be mastered for the moment. However, since no change in insight or personality has occurred, it remains only a matter of time before the problem reappears. If the dreamer awakens, the problems are saved for analysis and possible resolution with insight.

Fantasies serve functions similar to those functions of the dream that would reset affects to calm while leaving intact the propensity for repeating the difficult situation.

Fantasy. Of all the functions that serve to distract the personality from the task of dealing directly with problems, fantasy is the leading one during latency.

> A 9-year-old who was dependent upon adults to drive him about, and was affected severely by limits placed on visits with his divorced father, conducted a continuously running fantasy of being a used-car dealer.
> Another child, who was rejected by his peers, bragged of his gang, who lived in a distant city and whom he planned to bring to his hometown to revenge wrongs done to him.

Through fantasy, magical adjustments to problems become possible. In latency, this is necessary for the most part because of the limited physical and sexual equipment of the child. During later developmental periods in life, when cognition will no longer permit fantasy to hold sway, the role played by fantasy is retained as a legacy of latency. However, the functional elements for carrying out this role are those available in the later phase. Dreams, denial, promises, and depression take over the role played by fantasy. A healthier derivative of latency-age fantasy is future planning. This is a form of fantasy that utilizes realistic elements as symbols from which the fantasy is derived. It should be obvious from this that an important approach to depression in the postlatency period is the harnessing of fantasy to the needs of future planning.

Depression. Depression and fantasy have similar effects during the latency years. A digression from the task of dealing with and resolving problems is the product of their presence. Clinically depressed latency-age children can, for the most part, identify the precipitants of their depression. Psychotherapeutic tasks are best served by focusing attention on these precipitants. Aggression turned inward should be identified and the true objects of the aggression discussed. Most often, children with overt depression have both impaired symbolizing functions and parents who give mixed messages and demand very high levels of achievement from the child. In situations in which masked depression (somatic symptoms, nightmares, etc.) is detected, the child should be dealt with as though a depression or a richly elaborated fantasy defense is present. Often, working through of problems with the child is insufficient. The parent(s), whose expectations and demands, thinking disorders, and doubly crossed messages confuse and bewilder the child into a state of mind that requires escape into fantasy or withdrawal into depression, must be advised, or sent into treatment in order to clear the way for a positive result in the child's therapy.

Summary

During the latency-age period, manifest depression characterized clinically by the presence of intense, continuous, and pervasive negative affects is rare. There is no lack of conditions that share with the prelatency, postlatency, and adult periods mental preoccupations and historical antecedents usually associated with manifest depression. However, the defenses of the latency age oppose and vanquish affects through the use of the countercathectic powers of symbols and fantasy.

Depression is most closely linked with the aggressive drive, both theoretically and clinically. It is appropriate, therefore, that the next chapter deals with the developmental vicissitudes of the aggressive drive.

Chapter 8

The Aggressive Drive and Its Vicissitudes

Often one hears some symptom that causes distress to both parent and child during the latency years devalued as an object of psychotherapy with the simple phrase, "He'll outgrow it." Within this phrase lie half-concealed the uniqueness and complexity of the ego of the latency child.

The ego organization of the latency-age child is different from the ego organization of the adolescent and adult, so much so, in fact, that the symptoms and behavior that are a product of its function can be depended upon, to a large extent, to disappear with the transition to adolescent and adult ego forms. This developmental process is of little comfort to bewildered parents faced with no recourse from years of unremitting pressure from such chronic (but transient) symptoms of childhood as tics, stuttering, bed-wetting, nocturnal anxiety, and temper outbursts. The phrase "He'll outgrow it" offers only limited reassurance. From the objective standpoint of an experienced clinician, who can bring to bear a linear perspective derived from observations encompassing a wide span of years, even the accuracy of the prediction is limited. What will the child outgrow: The symptom? The immature or aberrant personality structure that provides the substrate that makes the symptom possible? The family or emotional stresses to which the symptoms are a response? Or the conflicts and fantasy structures that so sensitize the child to events in his life that ordinary stresses require balancing by symptom formation in order that *some* adjustment be made possible?

Obviously, in the light of the questions posed above, disquieting symptoms and behavior in a child reflect the presence of a variety of possible impairments. These are the underpinnings of aberrant symptoms and behavior, and few of them are likely to be dispelled by the passage of a few short years. Though the symptoms may be outgrown, their underpinnings persist to inform and shape the symptoms and behavior of later years.

Even in such a condition as hyperactivity, which responds to methylphenidate hydrochloride (Ritalin), and in many cases will clear with adolescence, it is worthwhile to explore the circumstances of onset of episodes and related interpersonal problems. In this way, one avoids the possibility that medication will serve as a buffer or wall between definitive intervention and psychopathogenetic factors that could generate psychological problems over a lifetime.

The latency years are not without their influence on later psychopathology. Problem areas may be passed over and the underpinnings of psychopathology preserved when symptoms are produced that distract child and parent from the problem core. This will be covered in the next section.

Also treated in this chapter are the shaping of certain problem areas; emotional imprinting leading to later psychopathology; the development of the superego; and the genesis of masochism. Because the operative organs for the discharge of aggression are much more developed during latency than are those for the sexual drive, teasing and rough fantasy play provide a good venue in the search for the antecedents and underpinnings of adolescent masochism.

The Impact of Regression, the Mechanisms of Restraint, and the Structure of Latency on Symptom Formation and Behavior during the Latency Years

The state of latency is the product of an active process of organization of ego functions in response to social demands. The latency age is a time of dominance of dynamic defensive structures. These respond to the needs of the child and the limits placed by society. The child experiences a complex reorganization of the defensive structure of the ego. The state of good behavior, educability, and pliability is maintained as the result of an ever-changing equilibrium between defenses and drives.

The ability to produce a state of latency is contingent not only upon the ability to interpret social cues; rather, human evolution and the ontogenesis of the mechanisms of defense that can produce it are also important. Thus, regressions that follow genetic pathways and failures to mature in psychic development can be brought into the context of therapeutic approaches to states of behavioral abnormality in latency-age children. Failures to develop mature symbolic forms or behavioral constancy are notions that may be used in conceptualizing the origins of a difficulty in a latency-age child and in constructing an approach to its remediation.

The state of latency is the product of a development. Latency grows out of the resolution of the phallic phase, the conflicts of which are settled for the moment by defensive structures rather than problem solving. The phallic (prelatency) child is immersed in oedipal fantasy. It is theoretically possible that such fantasy could continue in manifest form through the latency years, but observation proves this not to be the case. Oedipal preoccupations seem to decline in intensity during the latency years, only to reassert themselves in early adolescence. In their place, preoccupations with anality and, later on, passivity come to dominate latency-age fantasy. When these preoccupations are defended against by mechanisms that produce periods of calm, states of latency are said to present a response to the dangers (loss of love and castration anxiety) inherent in oedipal fantasy.

The shift from phallic to anal-sadistic drive organization and fantasy structures is characteristic of the latency age. It colors the behavior and typical fantasies of latency-age children.

Special ego organizations channel these anal-sadistic energies. They convert the child's behavior from the undifferentiated massive drive discharge patterns typical of anal-sadistic regressions into the range of control that makes possible learning in the classroom.

The child, having made a defensive regression to anal-sadistic energies from oedipal fantasy, is confronted with an intrapsychic situation that differs from that found in the original anal phase. There are new, and more mature, ego mechanisms of defense to use in dealing with anal-sadistic drive energies. Anal sadism is, therefore, not immediately woven into fantasies and actions and impulsive-appearing behavior. Rather, states of calm assertiveness appear.

This modification of aggression results from the interposing of a group of defenses that I should like to call—for obvious reasons—the *mechanisms of restraint*. Among these defenses are sublimation, obsessive-compulsive activities, doing and undoing, symbol and fantasy formation, reaction formations, and repressions. It is their activation that produces the psychological state of calm, pliability, and educability that characterizes latency. This aids in the adjustment of the child, which requires that he adapt to a world that demands social compliance and the ability to acquire knowledge.

In a latency-age child capable of entering the state of latency, the aforementioned defenses are available to hold in check otherwise disruptive id derivatives. The child at this age has little choice other than to regress away from oedipal fantasies. He is too small physically to express his aggressive drives effectively in his relationships with adult caretakers. Latency-age children are, with few exceptions, similarly limited sexually. There is little in the way of a discharge pathway in reality for drives in latency.

Fantasy, reaction formations, and carefully monitored socially accepted behavior patterns (i.e., school recess and athletics) become the primary outlets for aggression. (Fantasy formation using psychoanalytic symbols and regression serve as the primary techniques for coping with the sexual drives.) The child is expected to surrender and to attempt to please by learning well what is respected by his culture. The patterns of defense established with the mechanisms of restraint form a template in latency, which influences the permissible expression of the drives during puberty. The latency period has a role in the shaping of the adult personality. There develops, as a by-product of the formation of the latency ego, a deformation of possible derivatives and expressions of the drives during adolescence and adult life.

The defenses that help to produce the state of latency may be overwhelmed in the situation in which the child's drives are strongly stimulated by seductive behavior, either in a direct form or in one that stimulates sympathetic activation of the drives. So that these defenses may continue to maintain the state of latency undisturbed, a safeguard is provided to preserve their function in the face of seductions and traumas. A child who has a normal symbolizing function and capacity for symbolization organizes a *structure of latency*. Through this structure, the child quells the humiliation of trauma and the excitement of drive activation through seduction by dismantling the memories of the traumatic events or seduction and the latent fantasies that they stir up. The child actively reorganizes and synthesizes them into highly symbolized and displaced stories. Disquieting affects are quelled. In effect, there is a safety valve on the pressure cooker we call latency. By reliving events couched in the symbols and stories of latency play, the child is able to find an outlet for his heightened drives and yet maintain a state of latency. Thus, he gains comfort or revenge without threatening the situation in which he hopes to function well (i.e., school) or interfering with his emotional equilibrium or adjustment. Mechanisms similar to those involved in actively producing discharge fantasies and symbols, in which the hero can be covertly identified with the child's own self, may be utilized for passive identification with the myths and legends provided by the child's social group. From this we can glean yet another view of the influence of latency on later life: The developmental defensive events of latency contribute to the mechanisms for social group identification. The ego organizations derived from the structure of latency that lend themselves to the passive development of group identification persist beyond latency. Through them, the individual can acquire, and continue to acquire, the images for cultural patterns of behavior, ritual, and belief that will guide his life and form his mores, his opinions, and his social reactions for as long as a lifetime.

The functioning of the structure of latency introduces into the psychic life of the latency-age child a mechanism with great potential for subterfuge, which deceives the observer who seeks to understand the workings of the emotional life of the child. Whenever a child can escape into fantasy, the following are possible: unpleasant experiences will seem to have had no effect; uncomfortable affects will seem to have gone unnoticed; depression will be masked, and symptoms which appear at a time remote from their precipitants will be judged to be related to other than psychological causes. Worse yet, there may develop a theory of the psychology of the latency years that fails to take into account regression and fantasy as defenses. As a result, certain conditions will be considered to be pathological when they are not (e.g., daydreaming and intense fantasy play), while others will be considered normal when, for that society, they are pathological (e.g., the cluster of aggressive behavior and stubbornness in the presence of extreme concreteness, and a poor capacity to form symbols in fantasy play).

It is of interest to stop for a moment and ponder the latter cluster of signs, symptoms, and behaviors. Many people who have the power easily to say that a child will outgrow the poor behavior associated with this cluster may not be fully equipped to evaluate the intensity and appropriateness of this group of personality traits from a developmental standpoint. In a 2-year-old child, the cluster is normal. In poverty environments, it is not unexpected. In the latency of an American middle-class child, the cluster has high predictive value for future troubles in adolescence and adulthood. Failure to enter latency means poor preparation for the handling of such elements as group identification through concepts, future planning, and high-level memory for abstract concepts.

To tie all this together in a clinical context, it may be best to focus upon the answer to the question, "What is the relationship of symptom formation or behavioral pathology in the latency age period to the mechanisms of restraint and the structure of latency?" The answer, simply, is: when these mechanisms fail to develop or function adequately, there is impulsive behavior, acting on impulse and dare, unrestrained pressure brought to bear on parents and teachers, and sexual acting out in the form of exposure, sexual exploration, and sexual contacts. There is no buffer to deal with the drives. This is coupled with the frustrations of reality. Rarely do such youngsters produce neurotic symptoms.

One youngster, aged 6, was brought to me with complaints that he failed to learn in school, was disruptive, provoked fights, and claimed that he was being picked on by his peers without cause. In the sessions, he sought to provoke by spilling things, breaking toys, removing drawings by others from the walls, and messing up the well-arranged doll house. At the end of sessions, he refused to leave. Some insight into his aggressive behavior could be seen from his comment to me at the end of one session, "What does it take to make you angry?" He was made uncomfortable by aggression. His latency defenses were poorly developed. Any therapeutic strategy would have to take into account a series of activities aimed at encouraging or enhancing latency-producing skills. In the absence of the latency defense organization he had organized his adjustment around the defense of actualization. In essence, he justified his own anger, which he rejected, by mobilizing aggression in others. This was followed by attributing his own anger to an acceptable response to an "unprovoked" attack. The trouble was that only he believed it. Interpretation of this defense was not adequate by itself. The most important therapeutic stratagem had to do with the development and strengthening of the latency ego structures. Second to this was work with the mother to reduce her seductive and abandonment behavior toward him, which stirred fears of desertion and mobilized the aggression with which he was so uncomfortable.

Where do neurotic symptoms come in? Such symptoms often appear when the structure of latency is constituted from mechanisms of defense that are immature in quality. Of what use is a masking symbol that fails to block out the affect associated with that which is latently feared? Such a situation exists when the potentially defensive fantasy of a battle won becomes a battle lost.

One child, aged 7, with an impaired structure of latency had a recurrent daytime fantasy that a thousand snakes led by a bloody-headed ghost were pursuing her. Just as they were about to reach her, they turned from her to attack someone nearby. Her respite from terror was short-lived, for she soon became aware that the dying substitute was her mother. While in school, she defended against fear of her mother's death by obsessional rewriting of her name on test papers. A therapeutic approach that strengthened her symbolizing function made her comfortable. Her anxiety was lessened, and her symptom cleared. She might even have out-grown her problem without therapy if maturation had inter-vened to place at her disposal a more mature structure of latency. The same gain cannot be expected in relation to the sadomaso-chistic latent fantasy structure that underlay the painful fantasy. She provides an excellent clinical example of sadomasochistic latency-age regression, reinforced by severe fixations on the anal-sadistic level of drive organization. In the sessions, she delighted in making mixtures of clay, paint, and glue, which she called "duty messes," and threatened to pour on my office carpet.

What does a child outgrow? A child will appear to outgrow only elements that have to do with the structure of latency and social and biological limitations on drive discharge. The latent material (fanta-sies, regressive trends, interpersonal problems) will persist after these phase-specific phenomena are no longer active. In what form will they persist? Where will they go? They find expression in new modes of disorganized behavior, sexual acting out, or a search for latency calm and timelessness through drug use. Old wine will find new bottles. The song will end, but somehow in the postlatency years the melody will find a new singer and a new song.

The Latency Years as a Period of Emotional Imprinting Leading to Psychopathology

There is clear evidence that the organization of mechanisms of defense in adult life is shaped by the stresses of latency. There is also evidence that parental, social, or internal emotional pressures during the latency years can interfere with the phase-appropriate acquisition of thought processes and memory organizations that utilize high levels of abstract thinking. Someone asked to diagnose a latency-age child would be well warned to avoid the reassurance that a child will out-grow retardation in these areas without closely investigating the emotional pressures faced by the child and the intactness of the states of latency he is able to produce.

If psychopathogenetic imprinting takes place during the latency years in areas apart from cognitive styles and cognitive skills, there is implied the possibility that new areas of psychological sensitivity and new volatile fantasy structures and systems can be acquired beyond the age of 5. This would mean that unusual and traumatic experiences during the latency years should not be minimized as a source of future psychopathology.

This is not to deny the importance of the first 5 years of life in these matters. One often sees quite clearly that the cognition of the 6- to 12-year-old may regress to a level of function like that of a much younger child. In these states there appears to be a sensitivity to stimuli that would permit a molding of the memory on a par with that of early years. The child in such a state perceives surrounding events in terms of total feeling and experience. The episode is not bound and neutralized by being converted into words before being committed to memory, and thus the pressure to recall it is especially strong. Reparative masteries and repetition compulsions associated with these experiences are like those related to the memories of early childhood. Most codifications for memory of these events are cast in the total affectomotor experience of the event. Such codifications leave room for ambiguity; memory may take the form of somatic symptoms, psychological symptoms, affects, dream, or character.

In view of this potential to add new memories to the store that mauls the mind's peace, it seems to me that even in those years beyond the age of 5, the book is not yet closed to new and psychopathogenetic influences. Some later-appearing psychopathology may well be traceable to roots in fantasies aimed at mastering traumas of the latency years. These should be differentiated from traumatic neurosis, in which the memories are exact reproductions of traumatic experience.

The following case contains the hint that led me to draw this hypothesis.

An 11-year-old youngster did poorly in school, felt picked on, and was strikingly effeminate. He had recently moved from Oregon to Texas.

In his analysis, the effeminacy was worked through. It disappeared. The following data were recovered from repression about the time that the symptom disappeared. He had not been effeminate until age 7. It was then that his mother had surgery for a benign ovarian tumor. Because the mother suffered from an emotional illness, there was a delay of many months prior to surgery. During this time, the mother became increasingly nervous, abusive, and disturbed. By the time the tumor diagnosis was made and surgery was recommended, the child had been exposed to an emotional battering, both at the hands of and at the sight of the distressed mother. He was in an anxious, indeed overwhelmed, state at the time that he was told that his mother was going to have surgery and that there was a chance that she would not survive. He handled it calmly at first (the structure of latency masking the emotional response and minimizing its effects to the observer). He developed a fantasy that his father had given his mother the tumor through sexual intercourse. The tumor was equated with a younger sister whose gestation was related to the appearance of symptoms in the mother. This was clearly an oedipal fantasy with sibling rivalry overtones. On the surface, he swore never to have intercourse so as never to give a woman a tumor. At about this time he became effeminate, expressing on a motor level his attempt to master the unexpected loss of his mother through incorporation of her mannerisms so that, as he verbalized in his sessions, she could live through him. Other problems were present, which had much earlier origins. However, a latency trauma had had a dynamic influence on a symptom.

One must not underestimate the power of a trauma in latency, especially when its first impact seems to have been dealt with quietly. The structure of latency starts off with repression of affect and then goes on to produce defensive fantasies which, if heavily charged with drive energies, can invade the action and behavioral levels of the personality.

Maturational Vicissitudes of the Superego during the Latency Years and Impulsive Behavior in Latency-Age Children

It is a postulate in the field of child development that the superego is formed, quite complete, as a result of the internalizations that accompany the passing of the Oedipus complex and related ensuing psychic object losses. This happens at age 6, and is concurrent with the onset of latency. These internalizations carry only superego contents to be used for ethical decision making. Youngsters who have such contents are still prone to outbursts of impulsive behavior, even though they know that what they are doing is "wrong."

To understand this impulsive behavior during latency, one must also take into account other aspects of superego structure, with origins and acquisitions that differ in location and timing from superego "demands." The superego can be viewed as a tripartite structure. The presence of ethical protocols is not sufficient to produce consistent socialized behavior. Also required are affects that motivate the implementation of superego demands (e.g., guilt, shame, anxiety, pride) and an effective part of the ego involved in the implementation of superego demands (e.g., mechanisms of restraint and the structure of latency). The superego has a number of parts, from various sources. The parts are acquired at different times. Therefore, although under the best of circumstances the superego may function consistently and effectively beginning at 6 years of age, it is not unusual under poor circumstances for the superego to become fully or intermittently effective only years after latency begins, and perhaps never.

Clinically, the three factors separate with remarkable clarity.

Superego contents are acquired from the earliest years. From the time the child can control his movements, he knows it is wrong to touch or break certain things. Soiling and wetting activate shame in the second year of life. Masturbation and sexual fantasy, especially of the oedipal type, are forbidden and proscribed after 6 years of age. Violation of personal property and theft are known to be wrong as early as 4, and certainly by 6. Then, after 9 years of age, new contents derived from peers begin to push aside the admonitions of parent, church, and state.

Foremost among the components that produce the effectively functioning superego are the affects that motivate the implementation of superego demands. Any child from 4 to 15 years of age will tell you that stealing is wrong. All that this tells us is that the child knows right from wrong, but not how deeply internalized the admonition is. Does the child feel he must behave to meet demands from outside, or does the child feel that the demands come from within himself? This can be uncovered by finding the time at which the child feels sufficiently uncomfortable about angry thoughts, the wish to steal, or other activities that threaten life, limb, or reputation to limit or alter these thoughts or activities—

Is it before the wish becomes conscious?
Is it when the wish is conscious?

Is it after the deed is done?
Is it only when caught and questioned?
Is it only after responsibility for the deed has been proven?

Clinically, one may either ask questions to establish these points or just listen and assign the person to the proper category. Rarely is a person completely dominated by the attitude from a single level. Certain acts are considered worse than others, and are subject to earlier intercession from the portion of the ego that inhibits action in the service of superego demands. The further down the list, the earlier and more primitive is the superego from the standpoint of the location and the source of superego affects.

Examples of the superego in its most primitive form would be the following.

The boy was 15. He asked me after three sessions to call his parents and tell them he was cured. He had been able to rephrase my words from an earlier session to his satisfaction. He had changed the meaning of my words to convey the concept that I felt his only problem was schoolwork. He had earned some good marks, and thus he suggested that I tell his parents that he was cured. I pointed out that I was aware that his mother knew a good deal about therapy and would recognize the falsehood. "Oh!" responded he, "I didn't think you knew that. Okay, you better not tell them."

A boy came into treatment for depression at age 12½. On the surface, he thought his depression was caused by his small stature. Shorter than others around him, he felt puny. He had a need to compensate by doing things to impress others. This resulted in a good deal of impulsive behavior. He ignored the implications of his actions. From age 11 through 13, he was involved in drinking until he became ill, transporting and selling drugs, jumping motorized dirt bikes at high speed, and provoking teachers. Impulsive behavior was also experienced by him as a means of dealing with depressive feelings related to his experience of an overwhelming fear that accompanied episodes of commotion during his grandfather's tumultuous final days. At times he was left alone to care for him. Then, too, he felt puny and overwhelmed. They key to understanding his impulsive behavior lay in part in its use as a defense against the sense of puniness. It obliterated the puny feelings for the moment. This could not, however, be considered the sole cause. Fantasies of greatnesss might have worked as well in dealing with a sense of puniness. "Greatness in action" was the product of a failure of superego maturation that resulted in regret only when he was caught in the aftermath of the outcome. He felt discomfort when he careened into his home drunk, confused, and vomiting, when failing grades came in, and when he was apprehended for selling drugs. He did not feel guilt early enough to prohibit himself from the acts. Once, during a transition period in the therapy when he was able to limit his drinking, he noted that he was still riding a motorcycle. He realized that its ability to blunt the feeling of puniness overrode the dangerousness of his action.

Variability of the motivating affects of the superego in regard to specific superego demands is an important characteristic of the superego in latency, although this characteristic is not limited to that period. This is strikingly seen in the following case.

A child of 10 had been brought to treatment for stuttering, present since the age of 7. A multitude of therapeutic techniques had been tried. He came to me as a last resort, and was accepted for treatment because there were treatable additional symptoms present. He teased, and was being teased, and he had poor peer relationships, poor school performance, and a low self-image. It soon became apparent that the stuttering was variable in intensity. The variations could be traced to episodes, especially with his sister, in which he was belittled or humiliated. He would become angry; however, he despised and denied his anger. He pushed it from consciousness, and became involved in subtle provocations of his peers. The anger pushed for expression. He presented a picture of ambivalence, at once angry and peaceful. When he tried to speak of neutral things, the presence of anger could be detected in the stutter. He stuttered most when telling jokes intended to trick the listener. When he was encouraged to ventilate his angry feelings and accept his anger, he became disdainful of the therapist. Superego control of direct hostility interceded before content reached consciousness in the case of anger related to his sister. Provocation of peers in school was intensified during these times. There was no inhibition of these aggressions. Internalized aggressive inhibitions involved anger at his sister and humiliations at the hands of adults. Peers and the therapist were fair game. With the working through of the attitudes toward specific angers in response to specific humiliations, the stutter came under conscious control.

Maturation of internalization of superego affects sometimes comes late if at all. One should be as wary of saying, "He'll outgrow the impulsiveness," as one should be of ruling out this outcome. Therapeutic techniques involving confrontation can speed up the internalization of superego affects.

We have already dealt with deficiencies in superego function that relate to the ego functions that implement superego demands, namely, the mechanisms of restraint and the structure of latency. Although the contents of the superego may direct the flow of moral behavior and the affects (guilt and shame) of the superego may give force to the demands, the limitation of aggression and impulsivity during the latency years has limits of its own. Unless there are rich enough and strong enough ego mechanisms and structures, there will be no means for the limitation of aggression and the enforcement of superego demands. The internal inhibition of aggressive urges (id) depends, for instance, on the capacity of the structure of latency to provide fantasies as safety valves through which the aggression can be allowed to escape.

The Underpinnings of Masochism in Latency-Age Children

Childhood may be visualized as a map. Where one finds latency and diversion of aggression to useful tasks, there are the civilized areas. There is also a part of childhood that might be described as the jungle of masochism. This is located within that stratum of childhood society where differences are settled with fists and communication abounds in insult cruelty and degrading gestures and positioning. A child whose adjustment requires a setting consisting of those who dwell in this stratum can take the role of the oppressor or oppressed depending on his strength in relation to others.

To study the nature of masochism in latency, we shall study a 10-year-old boy presented to the author in a supervisory session.

The therapist in presenting the patient introduced him by describing his predicament in trying to treat the boy.

"I don't know what I'm going to do. This kid comes in and tells me nothing's wrong, that he gets along with everybody and that he likes the teacher; but when he goes out to have lunch the kids pick on him. When he leaves to go home from school they 'book him,' which means that they knock his books out of his hands so he's left with the books on the ground while they are running away. He claims that nothing's wrong, but is constantly complaining to his mother about the misbehavior of the children in the school."

In the session, the child repeatedly asked the therapist what to do. The therapist gave him some rather direct advice in the form of a recommendation that he not respond to the children and not show that he's being "gotten to," that he not cry, and that he not punch back but walk away. The child complains that he can't do this because the table he has to eat at contains these children.

To try to focus on the experience of the therapist, the author asked the therapist what the child does during the sessions. In this way he hopes to be able to help the therapist to bring the teasing aggression of the patient into the treatment communications.

Without realizing it, the therapist had described his suffering at the hands of a withholding and self-contradictory patient.

The therapist described the child's tendency to pick up a pen and then pick at the cork wall in the office. At times the child picks up and plays with some glass figurines that the therapist has in the office. The play is provocative, for the therapist has expressed his concern lest the glass be broken. In essence, the therapist feels provoked, but is unable to recognize that the child is behaving in a most teasing and provocative manner toward him.

This is a classical presentation of such a child. They complain of being teased as though innocent, while demonstrating to the therapist the way in which they inform the world through their own teasing that they are members of childhood's brotherhood of pain. They invite partners to tease.

As his parents describe him, the child comes from an essentially intact home with parents who are quite concerned about his progress. He has a left-sided tic involving his lips. His parents' chief complaint is that when "the child gets angry he turns on others"; although he doesn't attack his parents physically, he insults them, but he has been known to hit other children, to fight them, and to hurt them. He takes his anger out on himself, too, by hitting himself. He never scarred himself or mutilated

himself in any way; and when faced with any kind of disappointment on the part of the parents, in terms of a promise or a hoped-
for treat, he will blow up, he's very irritable. He has few friends,
children in the neighborhood are known to hate him, and he is
described as eating alone at school.

In the initial interview with the child, the therapist had found
him to present himself as one who was more sinned against than
sinner. In the interview there was no eye contact. He began the
session by telling about talking to himself when he feels afraid
and doesn't know what to do. His main problem, he says, is that
though he is a perfectly good person and doesn't hurt anyone, he
is constantly at the mercy of others and is teased by them. He
becomes miserably uncomfortable. He tends to be irritable. He
blows up at home at people who try to help him. A high degree
of verbal facility in expressing himself and talking about his
feelings was noted immediately. He spoke of work with a previous therapist who had helped him to realize that he should
hold in his fears rather than cry, so as not to communicate that he
could be taken advantage of. He denied punching other children,
saying he didn't want to be blamed for punching—"I let them
punch me so they'll get in trouble." He went on to say, "when I
get very mad I punch myself and I slam the door."

"Sometimes I get so angry," says he, "that I can't think
straight."

Youngsters with this sort of behavior pattern have difficulty in
dealing with their aggression. They have a low self-image, and turn
their anger on themselves through actualizing the anger. *Actualizing*
refers to the technique of making one's fantasy real through the re-
cruitment of peers to play a role in the fantasy. Through getting other
children to behave in a punishing fashion toward them, these children—who do not like themselves—can deny the fact that they don't
like themselves, or that they are angry. They can manifest their self-
directed anger through the behavior of others. They say they are not
provoking this; rather, they are the ones provoked. Therefore it is
difficult to get to this material if one asks them directly. A comment
related to this material by indirection was made during a therapy
session.

The indirect comment was, "You don't like yourself." At this
point he said, "That's 'cause there's something about me I never
told anybody, something I wanted to do to someone but I didn't

do. But I didn't, and I felt ashamed." At this point the therapist/
diagnostician entertained the possibility of being able to outdis-
tance all other therapists the child had seen and to get information that the child had never given to anyone else.

The temptation was thought to be worth seizing, and so the
therapist asked that he be told what this thing was. It turned out later
on to be something quite inoffensive—a wish to say to his former
therapist that he liked him.

The child made a great deal of it, saying, "I don't know whether I
can tell you, . . . I can't tell you, . . . I'm not sure." The therapist,
alerted by his prior experience with the child's provocations,
rather than becoming upset or angry at this, or pushing the child
for more information, or saying "please tell me," said, "I think
you're using the information that you have to tease me." The
youngster said, "Yes, I tease a lot. I tease kids because they get on
my nerves, so what I do is, at lunch, if I want to be alone, I say to
them, 'I have this, nyah nyah, and you can't have it.' That's when
they punch my food or try to take my lunch." He then disclosed
that when he watches television he enjoys seeing the good guys
hitting the bad guys and he likes it when the bad guys (sic) win.
The way was opened to deal in treatment with the child as the
source of his problems.

This highly verbal youngster had great difficulty in the production of fantasy. Thus, his only means for discharge of the manifestation of a fantasy of low self-image was to provoke other people into
hurting him. He told the following story:

"This boy, he had a dime and then he dropped it. Someone else
found it and closed the door, so he had to walk home without the
dime. After that he got a dollar. The kid had a plan. He gets a
dime back in exchange for a counterfeit dollar. He got so much
money he was able to buy a toy. If you stole something and there
was a contest and you put it in and you got a prize and you lost it,
a person who found it and kept it was guilty. He didn't feel that
good." The last paragraph contains his definition of guilt.

The patient was so verbal that he had no time to play. Even his
stories seemed to be directly related to the fantasy of stealing from
people, taking from people, and teasing people.

It is important to keep in mind that one of the roles of latency fantasy is the working through of the fantasy content of the sadomasochistic aspects of the prelatency stage. When a child enters the latency age period, he has the opportunity to master or process these fantasies. If they have been truly mastered, they will not be available to contribute to character in adolescence. If, however, as in the case of this youngster, a fantasy pathway is not present and he is compelled to cause his peers to live out the fantasy actively, the experience is recorded as a new trauma, and adds to the psychopathogenetic weight of the child's latent fantasy life. There is little hope for the kinds of resolution that are possible in adolescence when actualization may be normal.

Parental behavior and environment may deter or speed the process. If there were no children with whom to play out the fear fantasies, most likely he would be unable to manifest them in the way that he had. Parents who actually live out the role of persecutor because of something in their own personality draw the child away from the capacity of manifest fantasy to help the child to master a sadomasochistic latent fantasy life. The child will retain this influence on character as a result of the influence of actualization on the fantasy discharge function.

Manifest fantasy is normal for the latency-age child. It is the only outlet for children in dealing with the aggressive drive and latent fantasies.

In approaching masochistic children psychotherapeutically it is important to detect and to demonstrate to the child the internalized nature of the conflict that lies behind the apparent teasing that confronts the child from other children. It is necessary to see the way the fantasy is actualized and be able to demonstrate this to the child. The child has to find cooperative peers in order to play these fantasies out. The child must enter into the world of those people who look for the expression or reception of hostility in the school setting as their means of expressing anger. A therapy demonstrates this to the child.

In keeping with this, the best sign of improvement or resolution, rather than submergence of these fantasies in the child, is amelioration of the child's functioning as manifested through a change in the friends. A turn to comfortable, healthy children who do well in school; whose work and orientation are primarily toward the organization of useful energies applied in a neutral fashion for dealing with realities, and who avoid provoking people of the real world into taking a role in which a child is beaten or punished, is a positive sign.

Conclusion

The age period in which the structure of latency is set is equipped with as complex a set of mechanisms and structures for adjustment as any other phase. Symptoms may be transient, but the juggernaut of unresolved earlier conflicts, neurotic underpinnings, personality weaknesses, and newly acquired developmental aberrations rolls inexorably toward the precipitation of adult psychopathology. Should one be tempted to conclude in regard to latency-age psychopathology, "He'll outgrow it," one should give a moment's reflection to the fact that there is more to the latency age and state than meets the eye.

Chapter 9

The Sexual Drive and
Its Vicissitudes

The sexual drive undergoes a remarkable degree of maturation and development from birth to about 15 years of age. In the first years of life, drive energies are involved in a search for pleasurable discharge, concentered all in self. In early childhood and latency, drives find outlet through channels dominated by fantasy. At puberty, an organ system specific for the drive matures, providing an outlet channel to conduct libidinal energies toward love objects, which are beyond the limits of the self. Finally, in late adolescence, there is a chance to establish an articulation of the drive and organ system with the needs of the object.

The capacity for object love is not the product of the birth process, but rather of years of development. The therapist who works with children and younger adolescents requires a background in normal child development against which to compare the child, so that pathology can be identified and progess gauged.

What follows is a theoretical schema based upon clinical observations and a patchwork of theoretical concepts derived or adapted from the literature. The primary thrust will be the developmental explication of the vicissitudes experienced by the sexual drive in the developing child. Material relating to the latency period may be found in more extensive form in my book *Latency* (Sarnoff 1976). Guiding the detection of such vicissitudes is the concept that maturation of the drive discharge apparatus precedes and forecasts the form that object relations (libidinal drive discharge) can take at a given age. This principle leads to the following cognate clinical aphorisms: (1) clinical states of sexual object relatedness reflect the level of function and maturation of the sexual drive discharge apparatus, and (2) clinical progress can be identified as structural maturation of the drive discharge apparatus. This maturation is reflected in changes in superficial clinical manifestations.

The Early Years

All drive energies are present as concomitants of a mature physical apparatus or organ for discharge at birth (e.g., hunger drive has the mouth, respiratory drive, the lungs). Syncretism involving drive and organ is mandatory. Failure to achieve this is incompatible with survival.

Aggressive, sexual, and neutral drive energies (those energies reserved for the maintenance of the promised psychic structures of maturity) must each await the maturation of specific organs for discharge. In this, they differ from all other drives. Each is capable of delay in discharge, and each may be displaced to organs, and purposes, foreign to their eventual place in the healthy adjustment of the individual. Of all the instincts, the one that can be displaced most far afield is the sexual drive. Temporally, its potential for protean manifestations is set in the longest delay of any drive for the maturation of an effector organ capable of mutative involvement with the object world.

All the while that the neutral and aggressive drive energies are involved in keeping objects at bay or seeking objects as liaisons in the service of nutritive needs, comfort, and growing cognition, sexuality and the sexual drives must undertake the peregrinations to be expected of the unrequired and unrequited. The primary tasks of the earliest years of life are survival and physical and mental growth. Before puberty, procreation is not merely low on the horizon; rather, it is not even in sight.

Areas for the Displaced Discharge of the Sexual Drive

During the earliest years, the sexual drive lacks a primary organ for its discharge. Sexual energies are involved more in exploration and development of means and tools for discharge than in seeking, finding, and holding objects. As the means and tools are mastered, they become the accessways to finding objects for drive discharge in ongoing social contexts during growth. Among these means and tools are thumb sucking, fantasy activity, humming, rocking, and latency play activity. They will influence the expression of the sexual drive in maturity. When appropriately processed for retention in memory, these immature forms may intrude into and shape adult object relations. In this way, they serve as templates for regressive sexual behavior during adult life; and thus, for the therapy of adults, as well as that of children, a knowledge of the developmental course traversed by sexuality in its search for a form and then an object is of importance.

It is postulated that immediately at birth there is no object in psychic representation; only the self exists as an object for the sexual drive. All libidinal energies are, thus, expressed through the organs and experiences of the infant's own body. This state of total self-orientation is referred to as the stage of *primary narcissism*. Libidinal gratification is achieved through manipulation of body parts or participation in the function of an organ. This was illustrated by Freud (1905) with an example of the reconstruction of the experience of a child while nursing. Said he, "The child's lips . . . behave like an erotogenic zone, and no doubt stimulation by the warm flow of milk is the cause of the pleasurable sensation" (p. 181). He called the phenomenon *autoerotic*. This early manifestation of the sexual drive has an organ for expression. The absence of capacity for psychic representation of a libidinal object rules out the possibility that there is a true libidinal object. Like a burr caught in the hair of a horse, the libido is moving with no other goal or object save moving, and it takes its direction from the process on which it hitches a ride.

In autoerotic activity, the sexual drive is discharged through the use of a nonsexual body function (e.g., eating) carried out by a nonsexual body organ (the mouth). Manipulations of parts of the body, the skin, and the mucous membrane during later years represent attempts to recreate this experience of using one's own body for drive gratification. Piaget (see Woodward, 1965), who theorized in terms of unfolding cognitive maturation and mutual influences between cognitive growth and experience, offered a basis for conceptualizing the displacement of drive discharge from the use of one activity to another. He posited that organized motor patterns of activity could be linked to one another. He called this the *coordination of schemata*. This coordination could result in the following: If an activity that is used for autoerotic purposes is habitually associated with a second activity, then the second activity can become a pathway for the discharge of libidinal drive. This could well be the mechanism of the search for the ultimate means and tools by which libidinal discharge is accomplished. The coordination of motor activity schemes when permanent is called by Piaget a *primary circular reaction,* exemplified by the "reciprocal (and mutual influence) between grasping and sucking" (Woodward 1965, p. 62). The sexual drive energies initially linked with the sucking reflex, as described in Freud's concept of the autoerotic, find gratification through both grasping and sucking as a result of the coordination of these reflexes. When sucking is withdrawn at weaning, the other part of the paired reciprocal activities, rubbing with the hand or fingers, continues as an available activity through which to discharge sexual energies.

Upon differentiation of self and object, psychic representation of objects becomes possible. At that point, we say that the stage of *object libido* has been reached. Then the rubbing fingers are involved in gratification of the sexual drive with the first external object. Those who watch nursing children will recognize this in the grasping of hair or mother's clothes during nursing. Thus hair twirling and rubbing fingers over velvet-fringed blankets also come to serve for expression of oral drives. Through the coordination of reflexes and schemes of activity, pathways for displacement are established, and thereby, with the withdrawal of the bottle or the nipple, the search for comfort takes forms other than closeness to mother as a differentiated object.

During the first months of life, autoerotic activity serves as a medium for drive discharge and comfort derived from the self. There is no alternative to this state of affairs until the second half of the first year of life, when self–object differentiation begins. Sources of pleasurable sensations are then resolved into two spheres: that of two-point sensations, consisting of feelings emanating from the sensing organ (mouth) and the part of the child's own body with which he comes into contact (thumb), and the sphere of single sensation, consisting of feelings emanating from the sensing organ (mouth) in contact with an object (breast) external to the child (that is, non-"I"). For the libidinal drive, which is discharged through motor activities involving both spheres, self–object differentiation first comes to the child's awareness through the differentiated sensations of the two spheres. Two-point sensation is missing with non-I objects. These sensations are less intense. In addition, they are not under the total control of the child, as are two-point sensations. As self–object differentiation develops, there is a continual shift between the two spheres as discharge pathways for the libidinal drive. The activity, it should be noted, remains the same—what changes is the cognitive capacity to apprehend the presence of an object.

When an object is perceived, the activity is called masturbation. There is only rhythmic motor activity at this early stage; there are no elaborated fantasies. From the onset of early object differentiation, during the second half of the first year of life to eighteen months, drive gratification is achieved through such activities as rhythmic touching, sucking, and rubbing soft parts of the body. This alternates with cuddling, snuggling, and warm interactions with differentiated parental figures, the last of which leads to a consistent object tie with an animate responding object. Subsequent losses of the object may be followed by a regression, often with the result that the child seeks a part of the self (thumbsucking, rocking), a body product (fecal play), or some external thing (for instance, a doll or other object to be handled) as a substitute object. In this preverbal and prefantasy world of the earliest years of childhood, a multitude of schemas of motor activity are coordinated with thumb sucking and hair twirling in the service of the discharge of the libidinal drive. The search for and harnessing of rhythmic motor activity become patterned and structured. The first tool for the discharge of libidinal drive energies is produced.

Early in the first half of the second year of life, an ego function begins burgeoning. The capacity for fantasy begins a march towards centrality, which will reach its peak in latency. The first stages in this march include the further development of primary process thinking that accompanies early stages in the maturation of symbols, concept formation, and speech. A very early use of these skills is the interpretation by the child of the substitute objects mentioned above as undifferentiated, concrete, conscious representations of lost objects for libidinal drive gratification. At this point in development, primitive concrete conceptualizations accompany, and are coordinated with, motor schemata bent toward libidinal discharge. These are the primordia of elaborated masturbation fantasies; they are tightly integrated with motor activity. The beginning of a new dimension in the means for libidinal drive discharge is found here.

Much grows from this small beginning. The fantasizing function as the organ for sexual discharge, so important in latency, originates as an appendage to rhythmic motor activity.

As the potentials of the fantasizing function increase, masturbatory fantasy participates in and harnesses maturation to the purpose of drive discharge development. Pertinent cognitive maturational events, such as the development of symbolic play (Piaget 1945) and physiognomic thinking (Werner 1940) enrich the wellsprings of a child's potential for masturbatory fantasy.

Symbolic play refers to the ability of the child to let a play object retain its original identity while representing something else in play. There is a move away from concreteness and the requirement that the substitute object have a direct connection with the original object in this situation.

Physiognomic thinking is the ability to consider things as "animate, even though actually lifeless." [Werner 1940, p. 69]

A zone of thought and activity interposed between drive and need-satisfying object develops. The child can now "pretend" while seeking physical outlets for his drives. The circumstances of sexual gratification can now be represented in the brain conceptually, and expressed verbally. Words, formerly used for naming alone, are now employed so that they represent and express drives through displacement. The child enhances his skills for the discharge of sexual drive in this way.

Once concepts can be involved in fantasy formation, and through primary symbolization and physiognomic thinking consciously changed, the way is open for prospective, expectant, future-selective fantasy contents. This is the point in ontogeny when fantasy and play can become operative, and when conscious mental acts can create a psychic reality independent of the reality that can be tested. As Huizinga (1950) has perceived, "Play only becomes possible, thinkable and understandable when an influx of *mind* [his italics] breaks down the absolute determinism of the Cosmos" (page 3). In this regard also, Hartmann (1958) has said: " . . . the sharper differentiation of the ego and the id . . . in human adults makes for a superior, more flexible relation to the external world; [concomitantly it] increases the alienation of the id from reality. In the animal neither of these two institutions is so flexibly close to or so alienated from reality" (p. 49).

This point in development was also described by Winnicott (1953) who stated that "at some theoretical point early in the development of every human individual, an infant . . . is capable of conceiving of the idea of something which would meet the growing needs which arise out of instinctual tension" (p. 239).

At this stage, it is possible that masturbation fantasy contains distortions of the psychic image of reality that can be fitted to pre-established pathways, mostly motor- and oral-dependent, which have served for the gratification of drives. The contents of masturbation fantasies are products of the transmutation of objects and the world into instruments for the expression of drive energies. After this step, during the second year of life, ideas and objects can be distorted, through the malleability of their mental images, to fit designs suitable for sexual gratification.

The Toddler Years

By the first half of the third year of life, an additional cognitive step provides for enrichment of the fantasy that accompanies masturbation. Prior to this, fantasies consist of conscious wish and metaphor, but now psychoanalytic symbolization becomes possible. Briefly, in the formation of such a symbol, the link between the signifier and the signified has been repressed. With this step, there is a major shift in the potential of fantasy to afford a pathway for gratification of libidinal drives. Fantasy content will be expressible in verbal rather than action or organ experiences once its full meaning can be cushioned by symbolization associated with repression.

The richness newly imparted to fantasy by these emerging skills makes fantasy more attractive for masturbatory use. At first repression is thin, and masturbation fantasies—which are first reported in 3-year-olds to have form and syntax—tend to show little masking. Blanchard reported that children of that age masturbate with sadistic destructive fantasies about brothers and sisters as well as about parents. "Fantasies so often are concerned with injuring, torturing and killing people whom they love as well as hate" (1953, p. 30). Masturbation in the form of thumb sucking, rhythmic movement, and genital stimulation persists. When needed, masking fantasy is invoked. Then, with the intensification of the potential for repression that ushers in latency, fantasy formation becomes dominant. Therefore, although mechanisms for the production of masking fantasy are present in the prelatency child, the prelatency child tends to express drives directly in word and deed. "Mommy, when Daddy dies, I'm going to marry you" is the kind of expression often heard in, and common to, prelatency. It is rare in the latency-age child. For the prelatency and early-latency child, direct fantasy and genital play are the elements of expression for the sexual drives.

The Latency Years

The state of latency occurs when mechanisms of defense such as reaction formation and obsessional behavior are used to control the anal-sadistic activities and fantasies that are activated by defensive regressions, which in turn are responses to the dangers of oedipal sexual fantasies in the 6-year-old. Should stimulation cause oedipal sexual fantasies to increase, another safety valve, the structure of latency, is available in addition to regression. It is a group of defenses that produce a characteristic cognitive style. Among its characteristics are the development of masking symbols, which aid in the establishment of distortion-filled fantasies. Such fantasies are then used as the conduit for the discharge of drives during a time when drives are strong and sexual expression is forbidden by custom and limited by organ immaturity.

For the child aged 7 or above, latency-state cognitive styles mold the motor and fantasy components that express sexuality into forms in which latent meaning and original intent are lost to conscious awareness. The child's fantasy activity undergoes a transformation through the masking of meanings and distortions which produce manifest fantasies without detectable relationship to latent fantasy.

Motor activity, such as direct genital stimulation, is inhibited and displaced into diffuse whole-body activity, which may or may not be correlated with fantasy activity. Thus, the link between fantasy and masturbation is broken during the latency state. Either motor activity or highly masked and symbolized fantasy—or both combined, as in "cops-and-robbers" play—can serve as the vehicle for the relief of tension and the discharge of drives in the latency state. Extensive use of masking fantasy and fantasy play is available to the child as an independent pathway for the masked discharge of sexual drives. The sort of ego equipment that produces this state is quite appropriate for a group expected to live up to the social myth that they are devoid of sexuality, or at any rate have very little sexuality. It is utterly incompatible with the adult goal of procreating the next generation. Therefore, fantasy as the sexual organ of the person in a state of latency is only a waystation for the sexual drive. There is a whole stage of development still to be traversed in gaining the tools and techniques of the sexual drive on the way to maturity. There are biological and cognitive underpinnings to be discovered in understanding this final phase of the maturation of the sexual instincts.

Overt Sexuality in Latency

From the biological standpoint, there is something to be gained from a study of genital stimulation in latency-age children. This includes masturbation as well as activities with older peers and adults. According to Sorensen (1973), 7 percent of all adolescents have had sexual intercourse at the age of 12 or younger; that is, 10 percent of all boys and 3 percent of all girls. During the latency years, boys are capable of erection (Sarnoff 1976). Orgastic sensations are frequent, but ejaculation is rare (Kinsey 1948). In Kinsey's study, sexual relations in latency were rare in college-bound youngsters. On the other hand, for those who were not going to college, or for that matter not going to finish high school, the percentage of participants in coitus was large. The number of different episodes and partners for this group was also greater.

The categorization of individuals involved in prepubertal coitus into two statistically significant groups (college bound and non-college bound) is roughly congruent with the two groups that one encounters clinically. Youngsters who are involved in frequent coitus with a number of partners continue this pattern with the onset of puberty and in adolescence. They appear to be comfortable with their physical needs, and capable of finding partners with whom to express them. Usually they are not high academic achievers. Youngsters whose prepubertal coital experience is limited in frequency and involves but a single partner tend to withdraw from coital activity at puberty, and pass through the same transitional period of orientation to the expression of their bodily needs in society that is experienced in age-mates who have not yet engaged in overt expressions of genital sexuality.

In technical terms, one would say that the group that experiences coitus at high frequency has had no latency, or at least a frequently interrupted one, whereas those with the occasional experiences suffered breaks in their state of latency followed by immediate reconstitution. With the coming of adolescence, the latter share with the majority of their peers the experience of the transition from latency defenses in dealing with sexual drives to the set of mechanisms used by adults in finding sexual expression. This transitional experience characterizes the sexuality of adolescence. Before one can achieve this, however, one must undergo some physical maturation. The 7 percent who engaged in coitus in the latency years still had immature organs and poor access to orgasm. Often, soothing and calming aspects of stroking were what was sought. There is, indeed, little physiological or biological readiness of the organ system destined to become the organs for the sexual drives.

Adolescence

Biological Factors in Puberty

Before one can pursue the cognitive maturation that provides the basis for the shift from fantasy to objects as the targets of sexual release, it is necessary to bring into focus the biological developmental events that create the organic background that propels, limits, and directs the psychological maturation of sexuality during adolescence. The most prominent factor in this area is the appearance of secondary sexual characteristics, with enlargement and maturation of the genitalia and increase in the sexual drives to the point that the mechanisms of defense of latency cannot cope with them. The most important factor in this process, but by no means the only one, is the appearance of increased levels of testosterone and estradiol in the years immediately preceding puberty. Faima and Winter (1972) stated that in boys "between the ages of six and ten years . . . there is a gradual but significant rise in the mean level (of testosterone)" (p. 34). "Between 10 and 17 years there (is) approximately a twentyfold increase in plasma testosterone" (p. 36). "The most marked testosterone increments occur between ages 12 and 14" (p. 38).

"Estradiol is undetectable in the serum of most . . . prepubertal girls" (Faima and Winter 1972, p. 40). Its cyclical appearance in the blood stream accompanies the appearance at about 11 years of labial hair and subareolar breast buds. This phenomenon precedes the onset of menses by from 12 to 30 months. We may conclude that in boys and girls there is a period of years before sexual maturation becomes apparent when preadolescent children must deal on the psychological level with sexual physiological stresses that approach the adult level. The psychology of adolescence and adolescent sexuality begins before puberty, if puberty is defined by the appearance of menarche and the first ejaculation. This is consonant with the clinical observation that precocious puberty is usually preceded by increased sexual interest or even sexual acting out on the part of the child. Through the period of rapid growth in latency and adolescence, the growth hormone, in addition, contributes to the level of sexual drive experienced (Nielson and Thompson 1947).

Besides changes of hormone level, increased sensitivity of target organs, increased body weight, and changes in the sensitivity of sensors in the hypothalamus, which detects levels of estradiol and testosterone in the blood stream, are all part of the network of factors that propel the child away from latency fantasy and toward sexual maturity. There is evidence that although the strength of the drives has some degree of correlation with the level of hormone that is released by the gonads, the "capacity to fall in love" (defined as the ability to articulate the expression of one's sexual drives through fantasies, planning, situations, and conditions that take into account the needs of the partner) is mediated through a hypothalamic mechanism independent of the pituitary gland and its hormones. Briefly, what is implied is that this cognitive maturation of the fantasizing and/or planning function of the ego matures independently of the maturation of the hormonal releasing mechanisms of the hypothalamus (Money 1972). Thus, when a patient with Kallman's syndrome (a condition in males marked by failure to produce the pituitary hormone that activates the testes to produce male hormone, coupled with a failure of development of a sense of smell) is given hormone injections, he does not develop a capacity to love, but rather develops aggressive and primitive styles of approach to sexual encounters. Such a finding militates against Piaget's concept of reversibility (defined in terms of the objective world becoming more important than the ego at age 8) as the source of the object emphasis of the capacity to fall in love. Apparently the capacity to fall in love is linked to the maturational steps that produce hormone, but is not dependent upon the hormones, like, for example, breast development. There are changes, such as weight gain, sensitivity to low hormone levels in the hypothalamus, and cognitive shifts, that are part of the initial stages of sexual maturation. They may be independent of each other.

That cognitive developmental steps parallel to the maturational changes of puberty—such as hormonal flow—is not an isolated phenomenon. Witelson (1975) has clearly demonstrated, in a large population sample, that the localization of the central higher cortical process of spatial orientation to the right brain, which is operative in boys by age 6, in girls is delayed until puberty. This function is known not to improve in girls with untreated Turner's syndrome.

The physiological changes in early adolescence are accompanied by concurrent changes in cognition. This has far-reaching implications. For psychoanalysts and psychotherapists, it means that there is a whole developmental continuum to be watched for and compared against in evaluating the developing adolescent. We must be sure that cognitive growth which supports personality maturation in adolescence and is independent of hormonal manifestations is progressing appropriately. When there is a lag, the lag must be coped with, or the patient helped to mature.

So far, I have listed two cognitive changes that could be involved in this process. These are a change in the nature of the object seeking and localization of spatial cognition in girls. This is offered as an indicator that cognitive maturation participates in the general growth surge associated with the onset of sexual maturity.

Adolescent Sexuality

With the beginnings of adolescence, sexual fantasies rooted in memories of earlier experiences begin to reassert themselves through relatively undisguised forms similar to those seen in the prelatency years. Alterations in cognition mandate that there will be changes in emphasis, choice of symbols, and the organization of defenses brought to bear on the latent content of the fantasy. The earlier experiences are seen through more adult eyes and shaped into influential memories that propel the child toward fantasy and behavior consonant with the cognition and expectation of the peer group. These fantasies are carried forth into the creativity, sexuality, and dreams of adult life. One should, therefore, be careful in reconstructing the events of early childhood from the associations of an adult; and one must keep constantly in mind the alterations that the verbal memory organization of adolescence work on the affectomotor experiential memories from early childhood, which are reasserted in adolescence when the power of the latency defense organizations begins to ebb.

Although the physical changes of maturation (orgasm readiness, genital enlargement, etc.) make satisfactory sexuality possible and provide the sexual drive with an organ for discharge to be used independently of other functions, mature sexuality is incomplete without the social contexts (and the fantasies and planning that go into their production) that provide the settings and conditions for acceptable sexual encounters with love objects. Mature sexuality is first seen in adolescence as a product of fantasy. The nature of the fantasy is different from that seen in latency, for the fantasies are frankly sexual and contain considerations for the needs of the loved object. Indeed, the symbols in these fantasies are so close to reality figures (the closer the better) that they might better be called future planning than fantasies. However, their roots in unconscious drives make their inclusion in the category of fantasy mandatory. What renders them close to reality planning is the extent to which the real world participates in it. The nature of the fantasy and the resulting behavior is in turn influenced by the nature of the cognitive changes and the degree to which success in achieving these changes occurs in the developing adolescent. Other cognitive changes that occur at this age and contribute to this process include:

1. The shift from evocative to communicative symbols in fantasy formation and creativity;

2. The appearance of tertiary elaboration; and
3. The assumption of dominance by communicative speech.

Common to these three is an impact on the shaping of latent fantasy into conscious fantasy. The shaping produced is dominated by a need to communicate to reality "objects." Awareness of the need to temper, change, and conform content to the point that it will be understandable to peers and partners dominates. Should the fantasy become the source of action, socially compatible behavior characterizes the resulting interactions.

4. The shift of the adaptive function of the mechanism of projection from persecutory nocturnal fantasies to sublimatory activity, exploration of social situations, and projective–introjective processes leading to modifications in the demands of the superego;
5. The impetus given to object seeking and reality orientation by the organizing influence of the first ejaculation and menarche, and
6. The final step in the use of symbols as objects. (This refers to the ultimate stage in a continuum which begins with the concrete symbolizations of early childhood and ends with the use of objects in reality as symbols of primary objects. It is achieved through the acting out of fantasies in life situations.*)

These cognitive changes are developed in temporal congruity with sexual maturation. They influence sexual behavior and related fantasy formation in adolescence.

The Work of Adolescence

Let us develop a clinically oriented description of the transition into adolescence involving the sexual drive through which will be threaded references to the physical, cognitive, and psychological factors referred to before.

In the sexual sphere, the work of adolescence is the undoing of latency constraints, disengagement from latency fantasy activity as an organ for sexual discharge, and the integration of thought, action, a new organ, drive, and object into an acceptable pattern. One of the

---

*This is covered extensively in the chapter on cognitive growth in *Latency* (Sarnoff 1976).

primary steps in this process is the rapprochement of sexual fantasy and genital masturbation so that both occur in concert. In addition, masking of intent through the use of symbols lessens.

With adolescence, there is not only the increase in sexual drive, but also a lessening of the restrictions associated with latency defense organizations. There is an increase in the reality orientation of the child. Fantasy becomes less effective as a means of discharge of sexual drive. Fantasy symbols normally complete the shift from amorphous beings to real beings conjured up in the mind. Direct sexual content replaces the distorted fantasies. Girls may write themselves letters from young men and even mail them to themselves. Boys begin to try on their mother's or sister's clothes. Fantasy gives way to behavior. Familiar objects are seized upon for sexual use. Letters and clothes give way to a search for sexual objects. At first, there is a heightened excitement in things visual. Sexually oriented photomagazines become an object of attention. Girls stare at themselves in mirrors, boys delight in telescopes and binoculars whose focus often wanders from the stars to neighbors' windows. The mechanisms of restraint that held the regressed anal-sadistic messing urges at bay begin to weaken as the finely ordered rooms of latency-age children give way to rooms with desks so laden with random books, papers, and gadgets that its adolescent owner must do homework on that part of the floor from which the ever-present layers of dirty clothes can most easily be pushed aside. Sexuality in the child is recognized and responded to by the child. At times, the biological sexual assignment runs into uncertain acceptance. Confused about their identities, the children develop bisexual fantasies. Those in conflict may even develop impairments in abstract thinking. With menarche or the first ejaculation, the sexual die is cast on the physical level. For most, the question is answered and the conflict over; for others the rejection of the biological sexual assignment persists.

> One lad played out a great variety of fantasies during latency. At the joint between latency and adolescence, he began to play out in his mother's clothes the role of a seductive girl.
>
> Another boy controlled erections that resulted from seeing men in undershirts by cutting the skin of his back with a razor till he bled. After his first ejaculation, his masturbatory fantasies involved girls in sadomasochistic situations.

The first ejaculation, like the menarche, is an organizing experience that serves increased contact with reality and the object world. It is one of the maturational pressures that impels the individual toward a redissociation of adolescent masturbatory fantasy from masturbatory activity and into an increased articulation of the drives with objects in the surround. At this point the influence of society and the needs of the partner are brought to bear on the child. Syncretic with this process is the deployment of the group of related cognitive skills referred to above as communicative speech, communicative symbols, and tertiary elaboration. They produce an impact on latent fantasy that causes its shaping into conscious fantasy, whose form is dominated by an awareness of the need to temper, change, and conform content so that it will be understandable to people, peers, and partners. This is less in evidence in the discharge-oriented fantasies of latency play and of cryptic dreams.

Concomitant with this cognitive shift and the maturation of organ function is the burgeoning internal affect phenomena of sexuality. The newly dawning intense physical response is awesome and requires "getting used to." A period of orientation to these feelings is required. Masturbation ceases to be a soothing activity during periods of excitement, and becomes the arena in which the reorientation takes place. Alone and in sole command of the stimulation of feelings, the masturbating child masters the unknown world of intense orgastic feelings at a pace commensurate with his or her own individual tolerance.

Once the "self" has been explored, the child is ready to carry this mastery into new areas. The march of sexuality in search of an object for gratification of drives proceeds through the self (through autoerotism) to masturbation, to fantasy, to latency fantasy play, to masturbation dominated by discharge gratification, through orgasm involving a primary sexual organ, to a final step found in the use of the sexual organ with a loved partner. Planning and acting in the area of sexual drive discharge is still very much fantasy-dominated, with the fantasy itself strongly influenced by the needs of the partner. Where primitive fantasy components persist, the needs of the partner must be excluded, or very special partners with congruent fantasy-dominated sexuality sought. Libidinal cathexes are then said to be directed more toward one's inner fantasies than toward loved objects. This state of pathological narcissism in adult life parallels the distribution of cathexes of libidinal energies seen in the phase of secondary narcissism. Fixations and regressions anywhere within the developmental continuum that have been described here can contribute to pathological sexual adjustments in adult life.

Summary

The evolution of sexuality from infancy to adolescence has been presented through a study of the transmutation of sexual drive derivatives from one manifestation to another with each unfolding developmental stage. Readiness of the body's drive discharge apparatus precedes and forecasts the form that object relations and libidinal drive discharge can take at a given age. In early childhood, motor activities serve such survival tasks as alimentation and excretion and only secondarily serve a simultaneous role in sexual drive discharge. During the latency years, the symbolizing function is enhanced and takes over primacy as an organ for sexual discharge. The manifest symbols used in this pursuit become more realistic as the child grows older. As a result sexual drive discharge becomes more involved with objects in reality. Concommitantly maturation of primary organs for sexual drive discharge, and the development of a cognition that permits the inclusion of another person in one's consideration and planning produces the ability to fall in love. Progress in reality testing, maturation of organs and cognitive growth in concert enable the establishment of a lasting sexual relationship.

Chapter 10

Developmental Considerations in the Psychotherapy of Latency-Age Children

In this chapter, aspects of the development of cognition that are pertinent to psychotherapy during latency will be explored. An attempt will be made to integrate developmental cognitive information into the theories of personality that are used as the basis of psychotherapies for children aged 6 to 12.

For the most part, the psychotherapies of childhood are derived from a model with roots in adult psychopathology. Since adulthood is characterized by a relative cognitive fixity, adult therapies pay little attention to cognitive changes. This attitude is brought to the training situation, along with other aspects of the adult therapy model, by the budding child therapist whose prior experience has been limited to adults. Similarly, theoreticians apply current theories derived from adult therapies to children. Rare is the child therapist who continues to treat children through the many years it will take him to become a recognized theorist. Memory of experience rather than experience itself becomes the source of data; theory breeds theory. The theories of child therapy, therefore, tend to become adultomorphic. Since adults, by definition, are individuals who have completed development, adult-oriented psychotherapy is designed to deal primarily with emotional conditions that reflect disorders in the workings of the defense ego. Emphasis is placed on faulty function involving repression, affects, and reminiscences rather than on developmental factors. These emphases spill into child therapy.

Workers in cognition, in contrast, are oriented toward child development, with little orientation towards therapy. They have concentrated on memory, mentation, and the explanation of events by children at the moment of happening, with the result that cognitive psychology and dynamic psychotherapy exist at arm's length. Intuition, not theory, guides the child therapist in dealing with the cognitive aspects of communication and pathology in children under treatment.

There have been some exceptions, however. Switzer (1963) devised tests to determine the timing of maturational changes in cognition from verbal to abstract conceptual ways of perceiving and remembering. I have blended these data and clinical observations to produce a theory of the relationship between changes in memory organization and the state of latency (Sarnoff 1976).

There has as yet been little attempt to understand the impact of developmental change in cognition on the technique of child psychotherapy and child analysis. Such developmental changes are reflected in an important observation made in the early 1920s by Vygotsky (see Luria 1974). He described it as follows: "Although a young child thinks by remembering, an adolescent remembers by thinking." (p. 11). The young child experiences memory. The adolescent tends more to discover his past through words. Essentially, the purpose of this chapter is to study the possible impact of Vygotsky's phenomenon on the technique of child therapy and child analysis during the periods of transition between young childhood and adolescence (latency).

Psychotherapeutic techniques depend for their effectiveness on the memory organization used by the patient. Memory function especially is involved in the process of free association and in the ability of the patient to recall interpretations. As Vygotsky, as well as Switzer, has observed, memory organization changes with maturation. Changes in the way memory is organized have their effect upon free association, interpretation, and the possibility of retaining insight in the psychological treatment of the latency-age child.

Forms of Free Association in Childhood

The experienced psychotherapist of adults who comes to the treatment of the latency-age child for the first time expecting that the child will free associate in the manner of adults will be quite disappointed. Although free association does occur in children, it does not take exactly the manifest form that one finds in adults. In adults, conscious effort can be enlisted to put into *words* insights into self, memories, latent contents, the past, and verbalized abstractions. The flow of words reflecting unconscious motivation and determined by psychic factors conveys the stream of consciousness that reflects the inner workings of the personality. Children may, indeed, use a flow of words so contrived in this way; however, other conduits tend to predominate. The content of the play of children also reflects unconscious motivation and is determined by psychic factors. In this regard, the flow of the play and fantasy productions of children may be considered the equivalent of adult free associations and dreams. Cognitive development through the latency years is reflected in a shift from *play to words* in free association.

To understand the psychology of latency-age children, one must master the subtleties presented by the metamorphic nature of their free associations. The changes involved are maturationally based. Examples of such metamorphoses are to be found in the shift of emphasis that occurs in the processes of communication and retention of unconscious content. Two of the metamorphoses are salient. In the first, the child in late latency moves the area of free association from unfocused fantasy play to verbalization and dream reporting. In the second, there are changes that occur throughout the latency years in the organization of the thought processes involved in memory (the developmental aspects of memory function.)

From Fantasy Play to Verbalization and Dream Reporting in Late Latency

Typically, during early and midlatency the spontaneous reporting of dreams lags behind that of late latency, adolescence, and adulthood; instead, fantasy play is predominant in symbolic communication.

Fantasy Play

The latency-age child is capable of bringing to play therapy the kind of symbols found in dreams. Fantasy play contains such symbols. One might infer that fantasy play lives next door to the dream. In play, toys and actions take the place of visual dream imagery. Contained within the flow of fantasy play are reflections of latent contents as well as regressions in the face of stress. These regressions, one finds, are similar to those in the verbal free associations of adults. There is a direct relationship between the mental activity involved in the fantasy play activities of the latency-age child and the mental mechanisms involved in dreaming. The symbolic forms (ludic versus oeneric—see Piaget 1945) are almost identical.

Fantasy play as a form of psychic activity is available from late in the third year of life to the end of the latency period. Its beginnings can be roughly correlated with—and most certainly follow upon—the ontogenetic appearance of distortion dreams at this time. Both fantasy play and distortion dreams are characterized by the presence of psychoanalytic symbols, which mean that the latent content is not available to the conscious awareness of the dreamer or player at the time that the manifest form of the symbol is being experienced. Maturation of the cognitive skills that support adjustment through discharge in fantasy and the development of the ego organization that I call the structure of latency combine to provide a drive outlet through the use of dream symbols in fantasy play. This persists, and may divert energies from dream reporting until late latency, when further maturation strips fantasy of much of its discharge potential. In addition, play (ludic) symbols mature. They become less evocative and more communicative. With adolescence, they practically disappear. As a result, primacy shifts to the dream as the vehicle through which evocative psychoanalytic symbolic contents are borne to the therapist in adolescence.

Concurrent with these developmental events during the latency years is a shift of emphasis in the memory function of spontaneous recall. Recall through feelings and the manipulation of objects gives way to remembering through the use of verbalization, which influences the nature of children's productions during therapy sessions.

The capacity to recall latent content on the level of verbalized abstractions derived from intrinsic qualities appears in late latency. By this one may explain the predominance of ludic fantasy symbols (play form) in the content of the productions and the relatively rare spontaneous dream associations of an early-latency-age child. The younger child is more likely to present his associations to events, recent humiliating experiences, dreams, and therapeutic interpretations in the form of indirect fantasy symbols and activities requiring play objects, than to use words for the expression of his latent concepts. Older children in states of anxiety that require defensive regression may regress to the use of these early modes of cognition. The behavior patterns thus produced in psychotherapy sessions appear to be failures in free association. In actuality, this is a regression resulting in a failure to produce adultiform verbal associations. The play and fantasy symbols that are produced in these circumstances are rich in reflections of latent content associated to an event, interpretation, or dream which has preceded it. Knowledge of the nature of the symbolic forms produced by the immature symbolizing function of the latency ego, especially in regard to the "when" and "where" of their activation and function, may be helpful in the analysis of fantasy play, late-latency regressions, and the occasionally reported dream of the early-latency child. Instead of giving up in the face of such symbolic forms during a therapy session, one should adapt one's technique in order to use them. Insight into the intricacies of these symbolic forms and their times of appearance aids the therapist in helping a child expand the expression of his associations.

A child of seven had dreamed of a snake-like monster, but could give few verbal associations, was encouraged to extend her associations to the dream by making a semipermanent clay representation of the monster. This play symbol was then used in subsequent sessions in a multitude of fantasies and contexts to expand insight for the therapist. Fantasy content can be expanded in this way (see Sarnoff 1976).

A midlatency child who was troubled about her classroom situation found herself at a loss for words in describing very threatening experiences while in school. She was able to expand her expressive skills to reveal a fantasy of an armed murderous revolt against the teacher when she was encouraged to draw pictures of the participants. The pictures were cut out, glued on boards, and turned into puppets. These could be used session after session to reflect her unfolding day-by-day experiences, as well as the invasion of her recall and interpretation of the school events by the internalized fantasies that dominated and distorted her interpretation of the people around her.

Such an approach becomes less necessary with the late-latency child who is beginning to seek objects for the discharge of his drives in real action, using real objects, in his peer group. Such a child tells of his dreams more readily; he tends to stop and think more about what has been said and then to associate to it verbally. Should the older child block in the face of this advance, fantasy play can be encouraged to maintain the continuity of free association. Such encouragement, though, runs counter to development; it is intrinsically infantilizing and should therefore be limited in usage. Verbal free association is more efficient and makes dream reporting possible.

Verbalization Including Dream Reporting

Dream reporting in the therapy of early and midlatency-age children is rare. Apparently, the ability of the early-latency child to express conflicts through fantasy play using dream-like symbolism is a dream equivalent. Its use obviates the need for expression of drive derivatives through the direct reporting of dreams to the therapist. Voth (1978) has described spontaneous dream reporting in a latency-age child who was very responsive to dream analysis. The child revealed his inner life and internalized conflicts through dreams. This permitted a working through of his problems to an unusual degree for a child receiving psychotherapy twice a week. Such an approach cannot, of course, be generalized to all children. In the sparse literature devoted to children's dreams and concerned with children's ability to work with free association during the latency age period, there is evidence that these problems have been approached and worked with on a theoretical and clinical level. Dream interpretation at this age has been discussed in my book *Latency* (Sarnoff 1976). A. Freud (1927) and Lippman (1956) have reported on the usefulness of dreams in child analysis and child therapy. The contribution of the former, given here, is the most complete and most graphic.

> We have in dream interpretation a field in which we can apply unchanged to children the methods of analysis of adults. During analysis the child dreams neither less nor more than the grown-up, the transparency or obscurity of the dream content conforms as in the case of adults to the strength of the resistance. Children's dreams are certainly easier to interpret. We find in them every such distortion of wish fulfillment as corresponds to the complicated neurotic organization of the childish patient. But there is nothing easier to make the child grasp than dream interpretation. At the first account of a dream I say 'No dream can make itself out of nothing; it must be fetched every bit from somewhere'—and I then set off with the child in search of its origins. The child . . . follows up the separate images or words into real life with great satisfaction. I have conducted . . . analyses (of unintelligent children) almost exclusively using dreams. [p. 18]

The potential usefulness of dreams in the psychological treatment of children had been established at the very beginning of child analysis. The frequency and actual usefulness of dream reporting in latency-age children became the main area in which differences of opinion occurred. Sterba (1956) found, in a dream frequency study involving more children and more therapy hours than any other available in the literature, that in five phobic children, only three dreams appeared in 1,000 treatment hours. She concluded that "[dreams] are found to play a surprisingly insignificant role in the treatment of children" (p. 130).

Drawing on her general experience, Sterba (1955) noted "one exception to this, i.e., in cases where direct instinctual gratification of one erotic zone plays a dominant role, as for example in *bed wetters . . .*" (italics mine). "In such cases one may see repetitive dreams around one subject, such as, for example, dreams of water or fire in the wetters . . ." (p. 131). Conclusions in regard to the frequency of dream reporting in the literature imply that it is uncommon in child therapy sessions. Actually, dream reporting is not rare, and occurs frequently in certain groups, such as bed wetters.

There is controversy in the literature as to the actual clinical usefulness of the dreams that are reported. Voth (1978) implies an unequivocally positive impression about the usefulness of dreams. One of his patients was able to free associate to the dreams verbally and to search out unconscious meanings. In my own work (Sarnoff, 1976), I have found that there are children who can cooperate in this way and others who cannot. Voth (1978) suggests that the primary factor to be considered in explaining this difference is age. He states, ". . . it may well be that younger patients do not associate as well as did this very bright eleven year old boy" (p. 255). Age and levels of cognitive skill are important in determining how well a child can free associate in words.

A. Freud (1927) described clinical incidents in which children in the latency age period reported dreams during treatment, after which "associations to the dreams fail to appear" (p. 18). Ferenczi (1913), in detailing a report of a 5-year-old boy who crowed like a cock, made one of the earliest references in the literature to the poor verbal free association skills to be found in early-latency-age youngsters.

Immediately on entering my room his attention was attracted by a small bronze mountain cock among the numerous other objects lying about; he brought it to me and asked 'will you give it to me?' I gave him some paper and a pencil and he immediately drew a cock. . . . But he was already bored and wanted to go back to his toys. Direct psychoanalytic investigation was therefore impossible. [p. 244]

Unfortunately, Ferenczi did not follow up the other conclusion to be drawn from his description. Children have other ways of remembering, and therefore associating to, concepts and memories. Among these are the capacity to play or to draw pictures of the concepts and memories. Sterba (1956) concluded from her aforementioned study that in latency-age children, dreams and free associations are limited.

It may well be that the ability of the child to express conflicts through fantasy play using dream-like symbolism is a dream equivalent, and obviates the need for expression of drive derivatives through reporting of dreams. As stated before, this kind of fantasy activity is available from 3 years of age to the end of latency, and begins with (or certainly follows upon) the ontogenetic appearance of distortion dreams. As I have pointed out (Sarnoff 1974, 1976), "Dreams which contain psychoanalytic symbols have not been reported prior to the first half of the third year of life. Until then, there is no distortion in dreams. Before twenty-six months, dreams are wish-fulfilling dreams. Anxiety dreams occurring before this time contain direct reproductions of anxiety causing situations met in recent daytime experience. The appearance of these events in dreams is an attempt at a mastery through repetition identical to that which is seen during traumatic neuroses in adulthood and latency" (Sarnoff 1976, p. 27).

Even the shape of dream reporting has an ontogenetic history. Wish-fulfilling dreams continue to go on throughout life. Distortion and symbol formation contribute to dreams and fantasy beginning with the third year. Maturation of the cognitive skills that support adjustment through fantasy and the development of the state of latency provide a drive outlet through the use of dream symbols in fantasy play. This persists and may divert energies from dream reporting until further maturation strips fantasy of much of its discharge potential during late latency. This later step in maturation puts dreaming into a position of primacy as the vehicle through which the dream symbol is conveyed to the therapist. It explains the relative paucity of dream reporting in the psychotherapy of early latency-age children. It leaves unanswered the question of the relative failure of children who have reported dreams to associate to the dreams verbally after the dreams have been reported.

Dream symbols are but an item on the developmental timetables for the tools through which children express for the therapist the latent memory contents that press for representation in the therapy. Capacity to recall latent content on the level of verbalized abstraction appears in late latency. This offers an additional explanation for the dominance of fantasy symbols in play form within the content of the associations of an early latency-age child. The younger the child, the more is he apt to present his associations to dreams in direct fantasy symbols and activities requiring play objects rather than words for expressing latent concepts.

There are differences in the ways that awareness of self and memory of the past can be conveyed by children to therapists. The differences may be noted from child to child and from one age to another.

These differences relate to the unfolding of cognitive skills in the area of the organization of the memory function. Factors influencing this unfolding fall into three distinct groupings. These are: psychogenic, developmental, and innate. The developmental factors in memory organization and their influence on therapeutic interventions are the topics of the rest of this chapter.

Developmental Aspects of Memory Function: Influence on the Psychotherapy of Latency-Age Children

Memory finds consciousness through signs, signifiers, metaphors, *symbols*, feelings, and affects. These elements shape the presenting face of those psychic events which involve memory. Memory can only be perceived by the outside observer through these representations. In this context, the symbols that appear during psychotherapy sessions represent memory. Since developmental modifications occur in symbols during the latency years, one could get the impression that the memory function represented in symbol formation has been comparably modified. This impression should be rejected, for it is untrue and it casts discord on logic.

In therapy with adults, an intact and mature memory function is taken as a "given"; *i.e.*, it is taken for granted that what is said will be remembered. Further, it is taken for granted that all that is worth remembering can, and will be remembered in verbal form. Regressions to the use of sensations and affects as conduits for memory elements are recognized as special cases. The visually oriented symbols that occur in dreams are an exception, which goes unemphasized in the mainstream of current theories regarding ego function. The intact and mature memory function of the adult psychotherapy patient is a clinical verity. Its presence explains why it is that little time is spent in discussions of psychotherapy and psychoanalysis as applied to adult patients, on problems in therapeutic progress created by inefficient, immature, or nonfunctioning memory organizations. During the latency years, active developmental changes in memory function and organization force modifications in techniques of diagnosis, listening, and interpretation. For this reason, experience with adult patients in psychotherapy provides insufficient theoretical resources for understanding the free associations of children.

In working with a child in the latency years, one must understand the developmental aspects of memory peculiar to the age. In addition, developmental aspects of the formation of symbols that communicate the contents of memory to the therapist must be separated from memory function itself.

To facilitate the separation of the stages of symbol development during the latency years from the phases in the development of memory function during that period, it was necessary to spell out in advance, in the introduction to this chapter, the independent developmental modifications we might expect to find in the symbols we observe during psychotherapy. In this way, the study of memory development can stand alone.

The Development of Memory Function

Memory function matures and changes during the latency years. This has far-reaching implications for the nature and effectiveness of activities undertaken in child therapy.

There is little reflection of the development of memory function in most discussions of the theory of psychotherapy during the latency age period. The topics covered in such discussions are usually confined to the latest findings in research in early infant development or the current fads in adult psychotherapy. As a result, discussions of specific problems of latency-age development are neither broadcast nor pursued.

Concomitantly, the fact that memory function matures and changes during latency is rarely focused upon in approaches to the psychotherapy of the child. Yet, the importance of memory limitation in child therapy can be simply illuminated if one only thinks about the following fact: A child who has not yet attained a level of memory organization that will permit the retention of abstract concepts may nod his head in agreement to an interpretation framed with such thought, and yet be little able to understand—and less able to retain—the concepts for use in comprehending his behavior or holding insights.

Spontaneous Recall

Memory means many things. It is worthwhile, therefore, to define the functions of memory to which I shall be referring. I have specifically in mind the capacity for the *spontaneous recall* of experience, perhaps best illustrated as the differentiated function used in answering "fill in the blanks" questions on tests, in contradistinction to multiple choice recall through recognition. Spontaneous recall can occur without external prompting, as happens when a tune is suddenly recalled, an unaccomplished responsibility pops into one's head, or when a free association occurs during one of the psychotherapies. Spontaneous recall can also occur in response to a suggestion or request that something be recalled: such is the case in the "fill in the blanks" questions, and in the response to a question or interpretation by a therapist. There are other forms of recall, such as *recognition recall*, in which a representation of the experience or the thing to be recalled is shown to the subject and is recognized as part of a previous experience. Recognition recall may be used to activate spontaneous recall, which is the activity involved when the nonintrusive therapist permits the patient to free associate. *Free associations* are spontaneously recalled thought elements.

The unbidden appearance of organized patterns in free associations consisting of nonstimulated spontaneous recalls led to the theoretical concept that there are drives that impel memory elements back toward representation in consciousness. These representations are shaped by the form of the media for representing past experiences appropriate to the age and culture involved. They may be actions (as in fate neuroses), words (as in adult analyses), affects (as in mourning), or symbols (as in dreams and fantasy play). There appears to be compulsion to repeat prior experiences (see Freud 1926a). This is especially so in response to experiences that have been uncomfortable, traumatic, humiliating, or incomplete (the Zygarnik effect). The repetition appears to serve a mastery function. Rarely is the experience recalled without some modification that favors the person involved. For instance, the person who has recently had his fender dented in an automobile accident can think of little else for a while. During this period the number of other cars with dented fenders that he notices increase incredibly, in keeping with his need to have a sanctioning experience which will help him master the recent trauma. Or consider the following case.

A 10-year-old boy came for his appointment within a hour of a confrontation with two older boys who demanded that he buy marijuana from them. They threatened to kill him if he told anyone that they had approached him. He reported their action to his parents, after spending half an hour hiding from the boys. He could speak of nothing else during the session. However, the pressure to master the experience caused him to present himself as a hero, and to leave out the part of the story in which he hid in fear.

There are many ways to remember. Which experiences will activate an ongoing spontaneous recall? Frankly traumatic events lead. For children, humiliating events are important factors. An apparently benign experience may not be exempt, however. This is the case in situations that reopen for the person highly charged fantasies and complexes and their associated anxieties which had previously been mastered.

Let us consider the ways in which spontaneous recall is manifested during the latency age period. There are two types of recall, distorted representation and direct representation.

Distorted representation entails recall through symbols that mask meaning. This form of representation persists throughout latency as a memory moiety that gives to the latency state its most striking identifying characteristic, that is, the existence of the structure of latency. Distorted representation changes in form in concert with developmental changes in symbolic forms.

Direct representation entails the rote recall of events and information. It undergoes a series of developmental changes in its intrinsic nature because of the existence of three discrete forms of memory organization: the affectomotor memory organization, the verbal conceptual memory organization, and the abstract conceptual memory organization. The therapist must contend with these in dealing with the latency-age child.

Distorted Representation: The Structure of Latency as a Memory Moiety

When a child has been exposed to a trying experience, the repetition of the experience can color his mental life for years. Direct recall of such traumatic and overwhelming events repeatedly over a period of years would be counterproductive. There is no mastery in the recall of one's own weakness and impotence. Let us not forget that for adults, the need to recall and master may help to propel the thinking of the subject away from an amotivational state of withdrawal and into a state of heightened tension during which activities and planning that take into account one's potentialities overcome humiliation, strengthen the self-image, and initiate future planning to benefit the subject. Such a healthy response is not possible for the latency-age child. "The latency age child is too small physically to express his aggressive drives effectively in reality. Latency age children are, with few exceptions, maturationally incapable of achieving orgasm and ejaculation. . . . Children of the age period are therefore unable to express sexual drives effectively" (Sarnoff 1976, p. 153). Adultiform behavior in response to the compulsion to spontaneous recall of disquieting memory elements is not possible. Planning and actions to make sure that it will never happen again is beyond their skills. "There is no way out and no possibility of a face saving victory in reality for this biologically celibate soldier-dwarf" (Sarnoff 1976, p. 153). The child comes to terms with the compulsion to recall what is painful through the distortion of the memory through the use of symbols in a form that can be more easily handled. There are produced fantasy situations in which the uncomfortable affect is masked, modified, encapsulated, and even isolated. This protects the child from being overwhelmed and makes possible the establishment of extended periods of calm. It is the group of mechanisms that produce this cushion for calm that I call the structure of latency.

An example of the structure of latency functioning as such a memory moiety was presented rather graphically during a recent supervisory session.

The supervisee was just beginning his child therapy training and had been assigned the evaluation and treatment of a youngster whose sole problem was a failure to advance with others of his age in school. A central processing disorder had been identified, and the child had been classified as having minimal brain dysfunction. He was a compliant and cooperative youngster. However, there was very little in his conversation to hold the interest of a student. He said little spontaneously and responded to questions with a well-modulated "fine" or "O.K." As the student prepared to leave my office, with the suggestion that he continue to follow the child until he had been assigned to a learning disabilities specialist, he turned to me and asked, "Oh, by the way, I had meant to ask you what I should do about the binoculars, but I forgot." "What binoculars," asked I. Said the student, "The boy wants to know if he can bring in binoculars, and I want to be sure that it's proper and won't interfere with the therapy." I assured him that it would not, and suggested that he ask the child why he needed them. The child made it clear that he wanted to look at the chimneys of the nearby hospital that could be seen through the window. The need to look had a sense of urgency, a touch of fear and an air of mystery. No amount of questioning could elicit more than the information that there was something there that the child had to look at. I finally suggested to the student that he ask the child to draw a picture of the smokestacks.

The child did, and indicated that there was something behind the
smokestacks that he wished to see. He studied the smokestacks
hard. The next suggestion was that clay figures of the smokestacks be made. The child made such a smokestack with a hole in
the top, and a little hole was also made in the base of the
smokestack. When questioned about this concrete representation,
the boy told of snakes that went into the hole and of his need to
watch them. He commented that if his brother could see the
stack, he would say it looked like a penis. Two years before, the
child had had penile surgery for the correction of a mild congeni-
tal deformity. Whatever residual memory he had of his response
to the surgery was now involved in his fear fantasy involving the
smokestacks. Some approach to his surgical experience could be
made through the smokestack made of clay. Essentially, this
child was psychologically asymptomatic. The curiosity of the
therapist had led to the revelation that the child, along with
thousands of others his age, was in the process of working
through the spontaneous recall of a tramatic past event through
the use of masking symbols.

Nondistorting Memory Functions:
Their Development during the Latency Age and
Their Effect on the Nature of Interpretation

Although willing to cooperate, the child in the case of the smokestacks
could not respond to verbal questions about his earlier trauma, which
probably was neither experienced nor remembered by him verbally. He
could not even associate to his two-dimensional drawings, which were
abstractly reduced representations of his visual experience of the symbolic smokestack. Only with the three-dimensional clay figure was he
able to represent and talk about what was out of sight, and thus
unavailable for verbalization. He brought it into sight, and was able to
verbalize what was concretely before him. Free association of adult
form was obviously not available to him. However, once the therapist
had found the key to the level of memory organization from which the
child was drawing his symbols, and concurrently found a means for
stimulating associations (interpretation to activate spontaneous recall), the hiding place of the child's thoughts was revealed and secret
sufferings and fears stood ready to unfold, directly and undistorted,
from his memory.

We are now ready to move from the role of symbols as a tool for
adjustment (through repression) in the latency-age child to those

direct-recall aspects of memory during latency that undergo developmental modification and underlie the latent contents that may be directly represented, or find their way to consciousness, through masking symbolic forms.

Clarity of memory is defined in terms of the type of memory organization being used by the listener or observer. Thus, a person who speaks only French will find the English-speaking person totally unclear in his ability to help recover an element from the past. In like manner, a person who expects a patient to remember and to free associate in words will consider the use of visual symbols in free association to be neither memory nor free association. For this reason, the categorization of the material here to be presented as nondistorting memory implies that the observer–therapist is aware of the developmental aspects of memory during the latency age period and recognizes that more than words may constitute the manifest content of free association.

The developmental steps are, in order of increasing maturation: affectomotor memory organization, verbal conceptual memory organization, and abstract conceptual memory organization. There is also a form of memory organization involving abstract topographic memory, but this is rarely developed in those outside the field of mathematics. The names describe the primary means through which the world of experience is apprehended and carried forward in time in memory elements. Motivation to recall may occur as the result of a purposive scanning of the registration of past events, or the spontaneous calling to mind of memory elements that results from the compulsion to repeat and master.

Affectomotor Memory Organization

The affectomotor memory organization consists of two components, motor and affective. The motor component is acquired first. It consists of purposefully modified patterns of motor activity. Piaget describes the earliest acquisition of the motor component in the first year of life in the process of exercising of schemata and "circular reactions." Essentially, the contents of memory of this component are motor syntaxes. Affect, as well as sensory stimuli, can activate the spontaneous recall of these syntaxes. Because of the early and primitive nature of these memory responses, they are of great use to the child therapist. By involving the child in motoric expression during a therapy session, otherwise unavailable areas of memory may be tapped. The silent child can be encouraged to play. Thus, the child who was asked to shape the object of his attentions, the chimney, with his hands was able to be brought into concrete motoric contact with the content of his concerns and, once focused on a representation of his concern, to widen his ability to represent it in words (codify for recall in words).

When a child moves to motoric memory elements spontaneously (a regression), the therapist should be wary. If the regression involved is not limited—and one can only predict this at the time in a patient one knows well—there is a danger that all verbalization potential will be lost and that the child will begin throwing things. If this is the case, or is suspected, further regression can be blocked by introducing a miniaturized representation of the room, a verbalization, a symbolic play object, or any element that will take the child away from further regressed motoric activity. Interpretations at such a time should be approached with great care and should always offer strong defenses or support against anxiety, if accurate, they will push the child further into regression and action.

> An 8-year-old boy who was very much concerned with cleanliness noted that he had stained his coat with chalk. He tried to brush it off. He turned then to play with clay in the room. At first he formed a snake. Then he announced that it was not a snake but a messy "duty." He then began to pound the snakelike form. The therapist interpreted that he wanted to beat away the "duty" the way he wanted to beat away the chalk stain on his coat. The child picked up the clay and threw it at the therapist, hitting him in the head.

The affect component of the affectomotor memory organization consists of the ability to evoke recall of learned patterns in the form of affects, perceptions, and bodily postures associated with the initial experience. It represents the ability to organize recall around sensory experiences. These are usually recalled in their entirety, and thus is a rather inefficient medium for carrying experiences into the future. This ability develops during the first year of life. Piaget (see Woodward 1965) suggests that acquisition of the sensory image, as the vehicle of the ability to represent an object symbolically in the absence of direct sensory stimulation from the object, occurs at the end of the sensorimotor period (about 18 months).

Affectomotor memory organization persists in creative geniuses to the extent that they have whole worlds that they can bring into focus as adults, which they then draw upon in the creation of works of art.

Proust made this famous in his description of the evocation of an entire town recalled to mind by a bit of biscuit. Traumatic dreams carry this skill into the realm of possible manifestations in the area of emotional health.

Conceptual Memory

During the last half of the first year of life, words are acquired. At first they serve to please parents and to name things; but not long after, speech is harnessed as a potential signifier of sensory memory contents with a greater capacity to transmit the content efficiently. By 18 months, symbols in the form of things begin to take on this function. At 26 months, repression comes into play. Psychoanalytic symbols are activated, and interpretations of the unconscious become possible. The harnessing of words as a potentially more efficient medium for the recall of experiences introduces memory organization on the conceptual level.

Conceptual memory is defined as the ability to evoke recall of learned patterns in the form of verbal signifiers, such as words and related symbols. Conceptual memory may be divided into the earlier-appearing verbal conceptual memory and the relatively late-appearing abstract conceptual memory. *Verbal conceptual* memory involves recall of earlier experiences through socially dictated verbal schemata for naming. *Abstract conceptual* memory is defined as recall of experiences through verbalized abstract concepts representative of the intrinsic substance of things and events.

Verbal Conceptual Memory Organization. Verbal conceptual memory organization is present, and available for use, by the third year of life at the latest. It is not the primary means used for memory until about 6 years of age, when latency begins. The extent to which it is used is strongly determined by environmental and social factors. In highly literate cultures, its use may become so intense that verbal constructs are employed in the retention of events in memory and in the interpretation of perceptions, as well as in the process of recall. Individuals who operate in this way are truly locked into their culture, for they no longer can see or recall things as they are, but can only see the slogans of their faith. The child therapist must diagnose the nature of the child patient's verbal conceptual memory organization in his verbal approaches to the child, and modify his input to be more sensation- and motor-oriented in working with the child who records information through the sensory rather than the verbal route. In addition, one of the goals of the therapist may be to guide the child to more efficient ways of perceiving and identifying with his culture and its requirements.

The development and primacy of the verbal conceptual memory organization is influenced by environment. It is not wholly dependent on cognitive maturation. The level of verbal conceptual memory that one reaches is a social phenomenon. Primitive tribes block abstract conceptual memory. A culture that is preliterate limits verbal concept memory while encouraging sensory-affectomotor memory. Mack (1976), in describing his interviews with Arab tribesmen of the desert, noted that they had acute and detailed memories for events:

> Perhaps this is due to absence of literacy, and the dependence on recollections through sight and sound, when communication is achieved orally. "Their very illiteracy has trained them to a longer memory and a closer hearing of the news," Lawrence of Arabia once wrote. [p. 206]

The development of high levels of skill in the use of the verbal conceptual memory organization is sometimes a product of therapeutic influence. It may happen just because there is someone (in the form of the therapist) to interpret the action or the experiences on a verbal level and to encourage the patient to do the same.

Abstract Conceptual Memory Organization. Abstract conceptual memory organization is a maturationally based modification of conceptual memory. It first appears between 7½ and 8½ years of age, and consists of the skill of interpreting events in terms of their intrinsic substance and retaining this substance in memory through abstractions, with or without words. The most common area in which such interpretation takes place is in "getting the main idea" during reading. In life situations this is sometimes called "reading people quickly" or being able to "size things up." Piaget (see Woodward p. 65) describes as *concrete operational thinking* such skills in relation to the interpretation of concrete events, things, and experiences. Abstract conceptual memory goes beyond the level of interpretation to the level of storing for future use, that which has been learned. By the age of 12, the accumulation of abstractions in memory should have reached the point at which abstractions can be applied to the interpretation of other abstractions. Clinically, this takes the form of being able to interpret proverbs.

As I have said, literate societies tend to encourage the development of abstract memory skills, whereas primitive societies discourage it, encouraging instead rote memory for verbal concepts. In this way a gathering of abstractions in memory, which might topple simplistic myths, is averted. This is necessary for the maintenance of a society controlled through magic and myth.

Luria (1968) described a mnemonist who had a perfect memory for visual and verbal percepts. This man achieved his remarkable capacity for total recall by "converting meaningless sound combinations into comprehensible images" (p. 45). He actively sought to recall through images and was very successful. He was fixed at the sensory-affectomotor level of memory organization. He recalled word images primarily, but had poorly developed the capacity to gather abstractions in memory so as to create a bundle of abstract conceptions against which to compare new experiences. Never could he develop the abstract conceptual level of memory organization. "Thus, trying to understand a passage, to grasp the information it contains (which other people accomplish by singling out what is most important), became a tortuous procedure for S., a struggle against images that kept rising to the surface in his mind" (p. 113).

Clinical Applications

We shall concentrate from this point on the clinical applicability of the foregoing material. In children, who tend to defend through using symbols—which mask—to serve as the elements in consciousness through which memories are activated (the structure of latency as a memory moiety), free association of the adult form is not to be expected. This is also the case for those who regress to the use of motor syntaxes to serve as associations. Free association of the childhood kind (as already described) can be followed, understood, and interpreted when working with such youngsters, if the therapist is alert to the way in which symbols and action are used in free association.

When an interpretation is to be made to a child who uses symbols and actions (reflecting an operative memory organization between the affectomotor and the verbal conceptual, and an interpretive level between the intuitive–symbolic and concrete operational thinking—see Piaget 1945), the therapist would do well to note that his personal way of understanding the child may take a form (i.e., getting the main idea and forming an abstraction) that the child cannot use. Such children experience recall through symbols that represent sensory recollections.

This is far removed from that which the therapist experiences. Rather, the therapist records an abstract interpretation of the cryptic symbols that are the products of the child's recall. This is a common source of misunderstanding—the therapist's abstract interpretations might as well be written on the wind. Though heard, they will not be understood, or if understood by the child, they will not be encoded for memory in the abstract form in which they are presented. The goal of providing insight that will endure beyond the boundaries of the session is beyond reach.

To achieve therapeutically effective communication, the therapist has two choices when establishing a psychotherapeutic strategy, either modification of his approach, to put himself in touch with the cognitive and memory level of the patient, or assisting the child in achieving a more mature level of memory organization. For the child younger than 6, the first approach is primary. For the child older than 8, the second is mandatory and therapeutic, since it coordinates with the expected thought processes of our society. The skills of the first approach must be ever at the ready to deal with regressed states and the structure of latency.

Movement, Affect, and Play Object Symbols as Free Association

The following clinical vignettes illustrate the therapeutic approach to the child who is capable of verbal recall, but who free associates through recall that is immersed in movement, affect, and play object symbols. Note that the main purpose of the technique is to get the child to use a more mature form of communication and memory organization in his associations.

Converting Action into Fantasy

A youngster, aged 9, stopped talking to the therapist and began to play by bouncing a ball against the wall. The therapist watched to observe if there was any fantasy involved. He searched especially for signs that would reflect an associated thought content, and noticed that the child was repeating numbers as he played. "What are you playing?" the therapist asked, "Are you keeping score in a game with yourself or with someone else?" "With my father," the child said. "Quiet, I'm winning."

Unlocking the Fantasy to Reveal the Problem Within

A 10-year-old boy in the third year of treatment began a session by picking up sticks and guns from all over the playroom. He locked some play money in a box and hid it. He announced that it was a box of doubloons. He gave me a gun and told me that they were going to rob the bank where the doubloons are kept. Stories of robberies and being captured were standard fare for this child; they were usually brought up when he felt guilty about something. I asked about this. The boy explained, "I really like stories about robberies and being captured. Nothing special happened (to stimulate the fantasy)." He then proceeded with the story, in which he played the chief and I, a henchman. In the course of preparations for the robbery, he walked from the playroom into my office, where he planned the crime while sitting at my desk and swiveling in my chair. This was a change from the routine story. I pointed it out. "I'm the 'Godfather'," said he, "I need a big desk." I pointed out that I've noticed that people his age always go to my chair when they come into the room. What did he think the reason was? He explained, "When I was little I could use the table in there as a desk." He then described in detail his need for objects in reality to fulfill his fantasies. "Now when I want to feel like a big shot, I have to have a real desk." I asked, "What else do you do when you need to feel like a big shot?" "Have some gum," he said. "You chew gum?" I asked. "Sure," said he. "Did you ever smoke?" "No," I said. "I'm going to smoke," he said, "'cause then I'll feel sharp like a grownup and when I'm 20 I'm going to buy a stick of marijuana and try it. Do you know what marijuana looks like? Today someone said, 'a penny a piece or 100 for a dollar.' I bought one." He went to his coat pocket and took out a "punk" and asked if it were marijuana. He seemed relieved when I told him it was not. We spoke about drugs till the end of the session.

Even though the boy began the session by playing out a fantasy, the therapist was able to bring the child to a discussion of developmental changes in his defenses, as well as bring into focus the question of fear of drug usage, which was the problem behind the fantasy evoked. He had mobilized fantasy as a defense (structure of latency). The original conflict of the day was reconstituted by calling attention to a change in the content of an oft repeated fantasy. The stress of the conflict had resulted, in this lad with an obviously well-organized abstract conceptual memory organization, in a regression to affecto-motor expression as a defense against feelings of guilt and smallness. He chose action involving the desk, chair, and role of the "Godfather." This was associated with chewing gum, which symbolized adult-type relief from tension in the form of smoking. The therapist's verbaliza-tion encouraged the child to shift to verbalization. His concern that his search to feel like an adult would lead him into drug usage could then be pursued on the level of verbal abstraction.

Verbal Conceptual Memory Elements Converted into a Meaningful Communication

Let us now consider what impact is produced on the therapist's activity by comprehending a child's level of cognitive function during an initial interview. The client is a 7-year-old whose mental life has reached only the level of verbal conceptual memory. We illustrate the modification of approach required to put the therapist in touch with the cognitive level of a patient who has learned to remember by rote the essential nature of the experience remembered, without neces-sarily comprehending it on an abstract level.

A 7-year-old boy was brought for evaluation because of anxiety, hyperactivity, and excessive anger. At the beginning of the ses-sion I asked why he had come. He explained that he had "behav-ior problems." "What are they?" I asked. He had difficulty with this, finally explaining that he knows what to do, but it just comes out bad. He answered questions freely, and in a short time I had determined that he heard his own voice telling him to misbehave. It seems that words like "behavior problem," "excite-ment," and "I want to do better" were rote repetitions of things he had heard his parents say. Not knowing of the voice, they had theorized an explanation. The child knew that he would be rewarded if he used the words of the explanation; however, he could not explain the abstract meaning of the phrases as they had been used. When asked, "What will you do when you are doing better?" he answered, "I forget what I do wrong. I never done it twice. I try not to do it." "What?" I asked. "I want to behave better," said he. He could not tell what that meant, or when he had misbehaved or what he had done. He could use words for effect, but not for meaning. He said his mother said he misbehaves when he is "excited." I then asked him, "Do you know what it means to be excited?" He tried to find words. He had a concept but no words. He began to jump up and down. He stepped aside and, pointing at the place in which he had been jumping, said, "Like that." Thenceforth he said, "you jump up and down," whenever he wanted to say excitement. By using the same phrase, I was able to question him about situations that excite him and the things he does when he "jumps up and down."

He could not recall his "make-believes," but he did remember that he had dreams of monsters. He said, "I pretend monsters come in dreams and kill me." I asked what a monster looked like. He said that he didn't know. He could feel the monster, but not see it. I asked him to draw it. He said, "I can dream a monster but I can't draw it. I asked, "Can you make one out of clay?" He responded, "Sure." I gave him Playdoh. He made two pylons, then another two. Those, he explained, were legs. He made two more legs and began to make a body to put on them. As the clay monster took form, he became afraid of it. He could not continue his work on it. I found that though he feared the three-dimensional figure, he could continue to work with a less threatening, two-dimensional picture. I had drawn a picture of the legs of the clay figure. He looked at it and peering at the clay figure drew into my sketch a body and head. He then drew a line from the monster's head to the ground.

I have chosen these vignettes from this initial interview to illustrate:

1. the affectomotor recollection of a concept (jumping for excitement) followed by the establishment of a verbal description as a signifier of the concrete act. The verbal conceptual mode of expression was then used to explore the experience of excitement. Surely this child thinks by remembering.

2. the observation, which I have noted repeatedly, that an early-latency child can draw what he has difficulty describing and can mold what he has difficulty drawing, or can fill in another's drawing. This knowledge may be used by a therapist in encouraging an otherwise noncommunicative child to associate further when blocked; it is done by using phase-compatible materials to encourage associative expression.

Treatment of the Child with Delayed Abstract Conceptual Memory

In dealing with the problem of the late-latency child who has not achieved full usage of abstract concepts as the medium for retention in memory, the goal of the therapist is twofold. In addition to seeking phrasings for interpretations that are compatible with the patient's style of thought and memory function, the therapist should seek to help the child achieve an abstract conceptual memory organization.

To some extent this problem may be found in each child who is newly arrived in the late latency. To the extent that this is so, the brief recommendations that will be presented are applicable in many cases. One should be especially on the alert for this condition in youngsters who present with symptoms based upon the use of motor function and body organs or orifices. Such conditions as enuresis, stuttering, encopresis, and thumb sucking have, in my experience, often been accompanied by difficulty in school work and limitations in abstract conceptual memory organization. A cardinal sign of this condition is a combination of extended fantasy play with answers to questions that consist of the word "fine" or a distracted grunt. Other clues are extended and detailed reports of dreams or television shows. The latter reflects the presence of an extraordinary verbal memory, such as that possessed by Luria's mnemonist.

> One such youngster 10 years old asked me if I had seen the "Wizard of Oz." I asked him to tell me about it. To my amazement, he presented the script almost verbatim, or so it seemed. He took two sessions to do it. When I asked him afterwards what the story was about, he could not tell me.

In dealing with youngsters who have this problem, one should continually refer to earlier fantasies or events, with abbreviated phrases. In essence, one lends ego by introducing an "abstract" or symbol that the child will be able to recognize as a part of the whole. Sometimes the child is so delayed that word exercises are not sufficient. Then, it is best to use a medium for recall of memory that the child is capable of handling, for instance, clay figures or drawings. Clay figures which represent an element in a fantasy can be made. They are preserved and kept in a safe place. They can be brought out in session after session. They can be used as reminders of earlier and similar fantasies when a derivative fantasy based on the same latent fantasy as the earlier fantasy is presented. Pictures may be used in the same way with children who are at the level at which two-dimensional items are usable for activating spontaneous recall. Often a bulletin board to which drawings can be attached may serve as a substitute memory. The figures can serve as an interpretation. When they are accompanied by words, the use of words for transmitting abstractions in memory is reinforced and furthered, as in the following case.

A 10-year-old boy had a fantasy about an army tank. He was not capable of elaborating on it. I suggested that he make one for us to use so he could tell me about the fantasy by acting it out. At the next session, he brought in two enormous shipping crates from which he built the tank. He was so concrete in the memory organization used in his fantasies and free associations that he could not play out his fantasies with the slight degree of abstraction needed to reduce the size of the tank. When he found his "tank" unwieldy, he welcomed my drawing of a tank and went on from there.

In treating youngsters who have difficulty in word representations and drawings it is sometimes useful to draw a background of houses or the out-of-doors and to place figures in the picture, inviting the child to add his own answering figures. The fantasies involved here are not necessarily the child's alone. The process is not aimed at uncovering material, but encouraging free association on a more mature level than otherwise possible.

One youngster, aged 10, who was subject to episodes of breaking things, accompanied by diurnal enuresis (EEG findings were negative), drew some pictures of "the breaker" when asked why he wet. He could tell no more than this. After a year of play therapy, in which most of the techniques described were used, plus exercises in drawing figures in story contexts, the child was able to elaborate a context for the breaker that reflected his inner experience of the voice. The child was able to tell me when I pointed to the picture of "the breaker" (which I had cut out and pinned with a firm backing to the cork board on the wall) that whenever he wet and broke things, he had heard the voice of "the breaker" telling him to break. There could be no resolution of the symptom until it was understood in its entirety, and it could be interpreted to him that the voice was a projection of his wish to revenge himself on his father whenever the father scolded him.

In the case of this youngster, as with many others, intensification of the symptom occurred when confronted with fantasy elements that required phallic aggressiveness. Reactive regressions to anal-sadistic levels were manifest; for example:

> An 11-year-old stutterer stuttered most during the sessions when he asked me if a particular thing, which he wanted to use, was in the playroom. If he could be prompted to order *me* to get the item, he could say the entire command without stuttering.

A state of doubt in the face of aggressive parental figures who interfere with the child's comfortable expression of phallic competitive strivings is a prime psychological factor in the retardation of maturation of the abstract conceptual memory organization. It should be looked for in such cases. Interpretation of it, using the child's level of memory organization, will enhance the abstract memory, as well as ameliorate the overall state of pathology.

Treatment When the Child Has a Competent Abstract Conceptual Memory Organization

In treating the child with abstract conceptual memory skills, the approach is similar to that of the treatment of adults. Both groups "remember by thinking." Up to approximately 12 years of age, abstract concepts should be applied to concrete events. At 12 [with the development, as observed by Piaget, of abstract operational thinking (see Woodward 1965)], the application of remembered abstract insights to abstract situations can be expected and utilized.

Summary

An investigation of the role of memory in free association has been presented. The mode of registration and recall (sensory images and/or words and/or abstractions) differs in the child of latency age from that of the adult. During the latency age period, the child's cognitive processes undergo a marked series of developmental changes in the elements used in memory organization. To the extent that these differences in mode of manifestation of memory exist, there are differences between the free associations of the child and those of the adult. Children do free associate. It is necessary to understand the principles that govern age-appropriate memory elements in the child before these free associations can be used therapeutically.

By helping the child to develop the capacity to store abstractions in memory, the therapist also helps the child to gather a context of abstractions through which to interpret his behavior. In essence, the abstract conceptual memory organization is the carrier of the capacity to step back from oneself and take the role of the observing ego. Strengthening of these functions furthers the results of child therapy. In this chapter, related memory organizations, memory modes, and the theory of their ontogenesis were presented, and followed by clinical examples of the application of this theoretical material in the psychotherapy of children.

Chapter 11

Memory and Fantasy in the Psychotherapy of the Latency-Age Child

The main focus of this chapter will be on a search for an understanding of the psychopathogenetic role of past experience and memory in sensitizing a child to find affect stimulation in current situations. Experience is carried through memory into the present in a form, a pattern—*sensitizing latent fantasy*—that may be adapted to create misinterpretations of new situations and experiences. An attempt at mastery of past experience takes place through reexperiencing in the new reality. The process is a dynamic one, with its driving force coming from the pressure of unresolved traumatic events of the past. The forces of mastery and repetition seek the new experiences to serve as symbols for past traumas. The result is a distortion of reality, which takes the form of misunderstandings, manifest fantasies, or defensive (masking) fantasy play in children. The process may progress to such a degree that defensive energies are mobilized at the expense of neutral energies needed for the pursuit of healthy growth. Child therapy takes advantage of this process when the therapist recognizes that the play of the child contains a use of toys to express and master trauma.

The Role of Fantasy in the Psychic Life of the Child

In children with impaired capacity for delay, displacement, abstraction, symbolization, or fantasy formation, the state of latency is unstable. Therapeutic goals take this into account. To bring a child into "latency" so as to produce states of calm and prepare for future planning in adolescence is an important goal in the therapy of a child with an impaired ability to produce states of latency. In all children who have a structure of latency that is at all operative, the fantasies produced and played out in the therapy sessions become an endless source of data. Like the dreams of adults, they provide the key to the complexes, sensitivities, and instigators of regression in the individual child.

The fantasies produced by the structure of latency are the highly symbolized, defensively constructed manifest fantasies that are played out in symbolic latency fantasy play. They mask latent fantasies, which are *not* merely passive unconscious symbol patterns, awaiting a cue to come forth and give some shape to the manifest fantasies of play. Actually, their presence is part of an actively motivating system of psychical forces, which are ever at the ready to alter the child's behavior. They bring unresolved experiences and traumas from the child's past into action through distorted interpretations of new experiences, and overreactions in action as well as fantasy. Thus, the child whose latent fantasies are tied up with jealous feelings in regard to his parents quite likely will be stirred by seductive behavior to the point that the structure of latency is moved to produce an oedipal fantasy in play. Failing this, there may be a shift in a regressive direction. This portends aggressive behavior unless further mobilization of the mechanisms of restraint can bring the aggression under control.

The mechanisms of restraint deal primarily with regressions from oedipal fantasies. The latency defense of the structure of latency is less specific, since it is often called upon to deal with a multitude of possible complexes, sensitivities, and instigators of anger, overwhelming excitements, humiliations, and the many putdowns to which the psyches of our patients, as children, are prone—and heir.

Though there are times when the child can tell us what troubles him, it is not rare to find that the child has tucked away the memory of troubles and set out in pursuit of masking fantasy in their stead. Often one must derive the hidden content from the child's activities in the playroom.

Translation of a play fantasy into the recent trial or trouble that it represents requires an interpretive technique similar to dream interpretation. The recent trouble is like the day residue of a dream, in that it is the source of intensification of a sore spot in the child's sensitized psyche. The sore spot represents old unmastered experiences (for instance, infantile memories of deprivation or trauma) that provide a pattern—a sensitizing latent fantasy—which new traumas reawaken and into which new experience is forced, to produce a new synthesis in the form of a manifest fantasy. The process is dynamic. The forces of mastery and repetition seek new experiences to serve as symbols for past traumas; the events of today call forth memories, and the result is a distortion of reality that takes the form of misunderstandings and produces manifest fantasies and defensive (masking) fantasy play in children.

The child who talks directly of his current problems presents difficulty to the therapist only in gauging the level of cognition at which to aim a comment or interpretation. Content is focused by the child.

Recall through fantasy adds complexity. Because of the presence of sensitizing latent fantasies, current experiences tend to activate fantasy contents that lead the observer away from recent events and toward seemingly unrelated residues of past experience. The therapist must try to differentiate between the two sources of content and decide which one to pursue. The child who immerses his troubles in a sea of fantasy presents a problem to the therapist akin to a puzzle box to which a key must be found.

Phase-Specific Fantasies

For the child therapist, an understanding of the nature of the phase-specific, typical sensitizing latent fantasies of childhood is useful. It helps in alerting him to pertinent possibilities and in recognizing what may be troubling the child on a deeper level in cases where recent events dominate the manifest fantasy. Knowledge of latent sensitizing fantasies assists the therapist in identifying that which may be motivating manifest play elements in play therapy sessions.

The explication of sensitizing fantasies is not difficult. They are not diffuse; they have a discernible pattern. There is a march of fantasies through the years, against which the latency defenses of the child are mobilized and from which their manifest fantasies are derived. Each fantasy in its turn is based upon the new and unfolding problems that a child is brought to ponder by the expanding awareness that accompanies cognitive and social maturation. Certain fantasies and types of fantasy activity are characteristically invoked to resolve the specific problems that are introduced with each specific phase of maturation. Their appearance denotes attempts to explain or resolve universally experienced phenomena. Persistence of these fantasies colors the fantasy life and sensitivities of individuals throughout life.

Preoedipal Fantasies. When the prelatency child is able to differentiate himself from the outside world and from his parents, and conceive of himself without his parents—and therefore alone—he is primed for emotional reactions that revolve about problems of aloneness, separation, and loss. When the child reaches the age of 3 he is able to differentiate sexes, and his thoughts thenceforth deal with sexual differences. When he reaches the age of toilet training, his thoughts become involved in bowel and urinary control. These relate to the already well-known and accepted timings of the pregenital stages of development. The presence of siblings introduces rivals and patterns of sibling rivalry that may last a lifetime. Parental preferences for a child of another sex, or feelings of weakness in the face of drives which the child feels could be dealt with better if the genital apparatus of the opposite sex were present, can introduce womb or penis envy, which if unresolved contributes a warp to the character in later years.

Universal Fantasies in Latency

Early Latency: Oedipality and Guilt. Certain thought preoccupations and fantasies are processed during the latency age period as well. Awareness of their typical times of appearance primes the therapist to be alert for them as possible sources of difficulty that beset a child at a given age. At the beginning of the latency period (5 to 6 years of age), thought processes and fantasy preoccupation revolve about certain aspects of the Oedipus complex. As the child reaches 6, the capacity to experience guilt develops. Fantasies of taking the roles of either of the parents at this point often cease to be the source of pleasant musings and instead become associated with guilty discomfort. These fantasies (oedipal) give rise to fear situations when the child is dealt with seductively. They are defended against by fantasies of theft followed by imprisonment or ones in which a peasant leader kills the king in a galaxy long, long ago and far, far away. Such fantasies are the predominant fantasies of the latency period, but they may persist to populate the fantasy life of the individual thereafter.

Middle Latency: Loneliness and Separation. With the passing of years, additional fantasy contents appear. They are related to the problems of the child at the stage of latency-age development at which they emerge. Their pertinence to the immediate problems at hand pushes them into prominence, resulting in a deemphasis of oedipal fantasy in the middle and late latency years. For instance, when a child begins to feel a sense of independence from the parents at about 7 or 8 years of age, he confronts himself with fear fantasies of being small, vulnerable, and all alone in the big world. This is reflected in a fear of being alone. A fear of monsters develops. The monsters are symbols of the impotence children fear, masked representations of their defensively mobilized aggression.

Late Middle Latency: Passivity. Beyond the age of 9 or 10, the problem of passivity becomes a major issue. The sense of independence has grown in these children to the point that they wish to break free of parental control. They object to the passive role that they have to take in relation to the decision-making parent. In many ways this is a recapitulation of the 2-year-old's demand to know, "Who's the boss of me." These children—who, unlike Peter Pan, want to grow up—would like to be able to take over, and run, their own lives. They object to parental control and interference on an ever-widening horizon of activities. Eventually this trend becomes so intense in adolescence that there is little else to be seen.

Clear evidences of it are to be found in late latency. Children begin to defy parents, and confront them with a desire to make their own decisions. Often they angrily say, "Don't treat me like a baby!" When this happens, the child often finds himself threatened by the loss of the parent's love. The child feels, and the parents often concur, that the parents want the child to continue to behave like that healthy, happy youngster who did everything he was told to do in early latency. At this point, the child is readying himself in fantasy to confront his parents and to turn his adaptive energies from inward-turning fantasies, which solve problems through the manipulation of symbols, to demands and actions that will intrude on the world. The children become especially sensitive to situations in which their decisions are challenged or their immaturity emphasized.

Late Latency: Ethical Individuation. The child's sensitivity leads to feelings of humiliation and inferiority when faced with ethical conflicts with parents in reality. This may include activities as simple as crossing the street alone, and as ominous as peer pressure involving stealing, drugs, and sex.

One defense is to generate fantasies through the structure of latency. Thoughts about being movie stars or champion athletes, or owning motorbikes take center stage in these fantasies. Some children who have conflicts about such confrontations with their parents deflect the challenge into fantasies of defiance. These often take the form of fantasies of theft and crime, which are at times acted out. Often a sense of preexperienced guilt imbues them with a feeling of permission. Others accompany the fantasies of defiance with doubt and guilt, and this often blocks the ability to manifest the fantasy in play, thought, or action. As a compromise to resolve the conflict, children may shift into symptom formation. Urticaria, paranoid ideation, and obsessional symptomatology are common in this circumstance. In the presence of these symptoms in a late latency child, it is wise to look for conflicts with the parents in reality or with the parents as they appear in the child's mind's eye over such issues as passivity, stealing, sexual play, greater freedom of movement, and smoking. As the child masters the problem of independence from parents and can accept individuation from parents in the ethical sphere, the symptoms usually clear.

The late-latency child, who is struggling for independence, usually deals with a harsh, limiting, and condemning parent in his fantasies, as well as with the real parent. This fantasy of the hostile parent places limitations on the child's activities, which in turn evoke hostility in the child. The hostility so evoked causes the child to further distort the real parent, usually the mother, into a stick-wielding disciplinarian (the phallic mother). Parents respond with hostility in return. Escalating anger and a deteriorating situation ensue. Therapeutic leverage is in the hands of the therapist who is aware of the potential of fantasy to distort the relationship between parent and child at this age, and who is ready to help child and family recognize and work through the problem.

Late Latency–Early Adolescence: Sexual Identity Crises. There are other characteristic fantasies which mark the latency age period. These have to do with the awakening concern about sexual identity, which intensifies at the point that children begin a growth spurt, at about 9 years of age. Body changes, though too slight to be detected by a casual observer, alert the child to the sexual dimorphism that defines the adult sexual assignment. Evidences of such sexual dimorphism create concern in the child who has not fully decided to be comfortable with the sex to which he has been assigned biologically. Children begin to develop concerns about sexual identity, and to worry about what they'll look like as adults. They ask whether they are really boys or girls; boys wonder if they can turn into girls, and girls wonder if they can turn into boys. These are often well-defined fantasies, which cause the children concern, stir up other fantasies and castration fears, and are detectable in interviews with children in late latency.

Therapeutic Strategies

What should be the approach of the therapist in dealing with the fantasy life of latency-age children? The therapist may help the child to elaborate and play out the fantasies. This helps when the child is experiencing the fantasy as a means of repetition, or mastery and discharge. It is also useful when manifest fantasy deals with disorganizing experiences and disquieting new awarenesses or thoughts. The therapist may help the child to verbalize his concerns, to clarify his ideas. Reassurance may be given that the situations that concern the child will come into the province of the child's ability to cope as he grows and matures, and the child may be helped by the therapist's strengthening in him the mechanisms of defense that are appropriate for his age.

The fantasies described so far are universal in latency-age children. They relate to universal experiences associated with common growth phenomena, such as the shared maturations of cognition, which bring potentials into view and ready the child for independent functioning. The structure of latency when brought to bear on these stresses produces the fantasies described above.

Fantasies to Manage Trauma. Therapy with children in the latency years would be incomplete if therapeutic interventions were limited to common or universal situations and the reactive fantasies associated with them. There are experiences that are relatively unique in individual children. These too are defensively processed into fantasy by children. To identify these, the therapist does not have such guidelines as the brief outline presented above for the common fantasy-provoking situations of latency. Unique psychopathogenetic past events and situations must be detected and reconstructed as the result of continuous attention and interpretation. Generalizations are not possible. There follow clinical vignettes to illustrate some of these.

It is well to keep in mind the following rules for recognizing that manifest fantasy play is being used to process a unique experience or is related to some item of aberrant past behavior. The older the child, the more is he apt to act out the fantasy without recourse to verbal representations. Anger, shame, guilt, and sexual excitement in a fantasy play situation indicate that the child is dealing with a strategic memory based upon a traumatic experience. Memory is selective in these matters: events selected for retention, recall, and working through are by their very nature attractive to the sexual and aggressive drives. For the small child, these drives find little in the way of realizeable outlet. Stimulating these drives forces the child into an untenable position. The child becomes "overcharged," with no place for release save recourse to discharge in fantasy.

Trauma-Based Mastery Fantasy

An 11-year-old kept coming home drunk. He had come to treatment for depression, which occurred only in winter. The experience of getting drunk was eventually related to his mother's reaction to the death of her father, who had died on a winter's day. She had become drunk during the wake and had lost control of herself and the situation. In drinking, he was acting out the fantasy that he could handle the situation better than his mother had. His grandfather had died at home after a series of acute situations of near-death, which the youngster had witnessed, sometimes as the only one present. He was able to describe his feelings of terror at those times, and of fear for his life. With the working through of this material, the depression present at that time cleared. It did not occur during subsequent winters.

A 6-year-old child was brought to the clinic for evaluation of an apparent absence of conscience. His mother presented as a point of history of great importance to her the fact that when he was 4, she had left him and his less than 2-year-old sibling alone in the bathtub while she ran out to buy some cigarettes. When she returned he announced that the baby wasn't moving. She rushed to the bathroom and saw that the younger child had drowned. In the direct interview with the child, the youngster conveyed no verbal recall for the incident. I did not ask him directly about his brother. About the middle of the interview, the child asked me for a piece of paper because he wanted to draw a picture of a favorite uncle. He drew the uncle in a swimming pool. The uncle was described by the child as "drowning a boy."

Treatment Approach to Trauma Based Fantasy

Jimmy* was 8 years old. He was brought to treatment because of provocations on his part in home and at school. His mother brought him for treatment out of a sense of guilt, at the time of a

---

*I am grateful to Margaret Moxness, M.D. for calling this case to my attention.

separation from her multiply unfaithful husband, who had left the family home to take up residence with his mother. The child's situation had been unique in the following regard. His mother would beat him and only scold his younger brother when she was angry. She took out on him her anger, rage, despair, and spite for his identification with her husband's family. This was no fault of his. His father's family identified him as one of their own, while losing sight of the role of the mother in his birth. The mother had suffered toxemia at his birth and had remained in the hospital for a few weeks after his discharge to his paternal grandmother. The father's mother prepared the religious naming ceremony, which was celebrated on the very day that the child's mother left the hospital. In an oversight considered by the mother to be reflective of the attitude of the parental family, the mother was not invited. She learned of the ceremony after the fact from her own outraged mother. Thus the child came to be identified with the father's family in the mind of the mother. As a result, he became the proper target of her wrath. (Such attitudes are not unique. Another patient once reported the story of a visit to her mother-in-law. The dining room table was noted to be set with three extra plates instead of the four indicated for her family. When her husband asked about the absent plate, his mother regarded his wife with disdain, saying "Why should I cook for strangers?")

Clinically, the child appeared to be depressed. He refused to talk about his problems or concerns. At the end of the sessions, he put on an expression that was interpreted by the therapist as pride that he had held out and not talked as requested. He was not silent. He loved to play. He would sit at one side of the table with the therapist on the opposite side. A short wooden building block was given to the therapist. The boy took a long one. The edges of the table were the goals, and the blocks were the playing paddles in a game that used a mother doll from a family doll group as the ball. Points were won if the mother doll could be hit in such a way that it was forced over the edge of the table. The child, who admires wrestlers who fly into their opponents, called out a lengthy play-by-play description of the battles involved in the game.

Attempts at intervention other than cooperating in the game were futile. Such techniques as interviewing the mother doll or the players during halftime were brushed aside. This represented an attempt to get the child to discuss his problem at a removed level. The objective is to distance one's comments as far into fantasy as the ego of the child has removed himself, and removed his area of concern. Usually one can judge the nature of the original nonremoved concern by listening to the topic of conversation in which the child was involved at the time he stopped talking and began fantasy play. Since this child had refused to talk, recourse to another source of ideas was necessary. Here the topic about which he was to be asked was indicated by the game and the history that had been given by the mother. Obviously, the child was dealing with anger at his mother and an identification with her aggression and her hitting him when he was younger. The mother doll could have been asked if she had had any prior experience at being hit or hitting someone else. ("Did anyone hit you like this before?" "Did you ever hit anyone like you are being hit?") The child rejected all communication, save the hitting game. In spite of this failure to achieve verbalization, on either a direct or removed level, there was consistent improvement in behavior at home and at school.

The Theory of Therapy. In dealing with such a child in need of therapy, two levels of help are possible. One can either help the child by encouraging him to play out his fantasy (evocative play) or one can lead the child to talk about his problem at its traumatic root (communicative play).

Evocative play. The continuation and encouragement of evocative play provides through the therapy a controlled and guided outlet for tensions and a theatre for the cathartic discharge of tensions associated with traumatic memories. Such play can be introduced and encouraged in a context that is nonthreatening to both the child and the therapist if a playroom is used and the child is told that he can do anything that does not hurt himself, the therapist, or the equipment. The lowering of tension thus achieved will often discharge tensions to the level that the child can produce periods of latency calm. In these latency states there is produced a new behavioral niche in the social ecological system of the child. If the mother has changed, as the result of experience, education, or maturation, there is opened a door to the learning of a new style of relationship between parent and child. Often, concurrent interviews with the parent succeed in encouraging and directing the parent to behavior that welcomes and shapes the newly revealed potentials of the child. At times, interpretations during play do not result in direct communication about problems, but rather, as good interpretations do, in changes in the content of the fantasy play which expands the area and content of the catharsis; and sometimes control and limitation of behavior in sessions suggest, or strengthen, defenses that provide for stronger latency states outside of the therapy situation.

Communicative play. Communicative play uses the child's play fantasies as a tool for discharge as well. However, if the child will cooperate, then questions may be asked that will take the child back to the roots of the problem. Actual trauma can be discussed and misinterpretations clarified and corrected. In this way, there is conscious mastery, and dissipation of the trauma that is sensitizing the child to a current experience.

A child played out a situation in which she was the master and the therapist a slave. She would scold him furiously. In response to the question "Did anyone ever treat you like a slave and scold you?" the girl, aged 8, reported that her mother was hiring a new housekeeper, who was to arrive at work that week. The girl was very anxious, because once they had had a maid who hit her while her parents were out, and forced her to go to bed very early so that she (the maid) would be free to read; she threatened the children with death if they described her actions to the parents. The child came to realize that this was her present concern, or at least contributed to it. She was able to discuss this with her mother, clear the air, and plan with her mother steps to reassure herself that such a situation would not arise again.

Summary

The treatment of latency-age children revolves primarily about manifest fantasies derived from drives that have been stirred but cannot be discharged. These fantasies are universal and typical. They are the products of masking modifications of latent fantasies evoked by universal situations and experiences, which could not be resolved at their inception and are carried as extra baggage in memory. They are brought out on every possible occasion in an attempt to master and resolve them. The manifest fantasies of latency have origins in the child's early fantasy interpretations of the events, experiences, and mysteries of early childhood.

However, treatment of the latency-age child is not limited to work with universal latent fantasies (e.g., drive-influenced distortions) or the phases of unfolding awareness that occur during the latency years. There are facets to latency-age fantasy life that are best understood if the origin of the fantasy is recognized to be an actual trauma.

Latency may be seen as a phase organized into coherent developmental substages. It has a structure of its own and work to accomplish if the child is to reach emotional adolescence. Emotional health is aided if problems of adjustment to these subphases are recognized in their masked reflections in the mirror of fantasy.

Analytically derived psychotherapy with latency-age children can be applied to problems of social adjustment, acceptance of self, and hypersensitive reactions to situations that induce feelings of humiliation. The child who has entered latency and manifests internalized conflicts so as to have the same patterns of behavior in disparate situations (i.e., sibling rivalry, jealousy of peers, being picked on and teased) can be helped to direct energies away from fantasies and toward the resolution of reality problems. The overstimulated or traumatized child can be helped to place his relationship with adults into perspective after the parents have been induced to stop the overstimulation. Children of parents who overemphasize needs for control and limit the rate of maturation of the child can be helped in bringing their conflicts to the surface instead of battling within themselves to the accompaniment of guilt and doubt. This in turn alleviates somatizations, paranoid symptoms, and tics, which defend against the guilt and doubt.

Children who fail to enter latency may be helped by the therapist who understands the mechanisms involved in the psychodynamics of the establishment of states of latency. The therapist constructs a therapeutic strategy that will diminish the pressure on the child at the same time that weak mechanisms are strengthened.

In children whose failure to enter latency is associated with delay in the maturation of the cognition required to establish a state of latency, child therapy may be applied with the aim of encouraging the establishment of more mature means of comprehending and remembering the abstractions necessary for survival in school. Concurrently, improvement in cognition aids the therapeutic process. There is established a means to enhance interpretations, in terms of improving the child's level of understanding, in order to achieve a lasting effect.

Chapter 12

Repetition Compulsion and Reparative Mastery

Psychotherapy of children is aimed at achieving repetition and mastery of remembered past traumas through the analysis of symbolization, play, and direct recall. Through this is achieved resolution of early- and latency-age conflicts, during latency.

This chapter will provide an in-depth presentation of an important cognitive developmental step, that is, the shift in the polarity of symbols from the evocative to the communicative mode. This is an early sign of the shift from latency to adolescence.

Repetition Compulsion and Reparative Mastery

Repetition Compulsion

The structure of latency and the fantasy play of the latency-age child, to which it contributes strongly, are primary outlets for discharge of tensions in the child. Adults have reality objects with whom to express drives and live out fantasies or lives. Younger children are more direct in their demands. Latency, though, is uniquely the period in which fantasy has primacy as a technique for drive discharge and mastery of stress. As such, the latency age period becomes a time in which the repetitive use of fantasy for discharge dominates and seems to the observer to be exaggerated.

The first historical description of drive discharge through childhood fantasy play was based on an observation of an 18-month-old child by Freud (1926a). The child was observed throwing a reel with a string attached to it, far from him. By pulling the string he retrieved it. Freud saw throwing and drawing back as childhood repetition aimed at mastering an unpleasant experience. The structure and function of such a repetition are similar to that seen in the repeated traumatic dream. Freud postulated that there is a compulsion to repeat those life events that are experienced as unpleasant. From the standpoint of drive theory, such activity may be viewed as the discharge of an aggressive drive which has been turned on the self. It can also be seen as a regression to a paradigm derived from the earliest narcissistic position (primary masochism). This consists of the self-cathexis imposed by that early state in which there is no psychic differentiation between self and world. Then there can be no object in the mind's eye.

When there is only discharge of drive without resolution of fantasy or trauma, each pressure to regress starts a repetitive pattern. Ever and again, the drive discharges. Pain repeats. The memory for the painful experience becomes the obligate pathway through which the drive, bereft of external object, finds moments of release. As occurs while traveling, the journey can usurp the attention at the expense of the goal. It has been said, "Getting there is half the fun." In this situation, the repetition of the fantasy becomes the sole purpose and provides only the reward of misery. The resolution of the fantasy and the finding of a new and contemporary object are forgone while attention and energies go to affect and process rather than to resolution and object-seeking.

To paraphrase Freud (1926a); patients of any age "cannot remember all that is repressed and what cannot be remembered may be precisely the essential part of it. . . . [The patient] is obliged to repeat the repressed material as a contemporary experience" if an adult, or to employ symbolic masking in the form of repeated play fantasies, if a child. Such ever-repeating fantasies, which evoke past events and moods while hiding antecedent meaning, predominate in the repetition compulsions of latency. They are closely related to dreams. This is especially so in regard to the symbolic forms used. It is of interest that spontaneous dream reporting is relatively rare in latency-age children, even though dreams are not. They use the ludic (play) symbols, which are cousins to oneiric or dream symbols, in their therapy play and therefore do not require dream symbols to evoke their moods. The situation changes as the child enters adolescence. Ludic symbols disappear (ludic demise). Adolescents shun the playroom and toys. Now, dreams bear the brunt of providing discharge symbols for the repetition compulsion, until, as part of the march of cognition that follows the evolution of the capacity to fall in love, peers in reality are wielded as the symbols to serve in fantasies that the person is compelled to repeat.

Reparative Mastery

There is an alternative form of fantasy play that we see in latency-age children which bears a surface resemblance to the fantasy play of the repetition compulsion. This form of play is used to recall, process, discharge, and permit the child to shed the memory of a trauma. I call such play *reparative mastery play*. The memories dealt with are recent, for the most part. Under the pressure of internal emotional guides, the play fantasies of children in latency drift toward the symbolic depiction of the more distant past.

The point of departure in differentiating the two sorts of play fantasy lies in the concept of mastery. Repetition compulsion repeats endlessly: reparative mastery, once experienced, ends the mnemonic hegemony over life events and conscious awareness that had been held by the traumatic events depicted. Obviously this is an important distinction. The encouragement of reparative mastery play is a potentially effective psychotherapeutic maneuver. It should be considered in the protocol of any psychotherapeutic strategy. In a similar vein, repetition compulsion should be discouraged or converted to reparative mastery play. The means of differentiating these types of play and the means of converting repetition play to mastery play will be described in what follows.

Clinical Examples

Reparative Mastery

The reparative mastery fantasy in latency is characterized by constant form, with changes in details that reflect ongoing involvement with teachers and peers. The symbolizing function uses ludic symbols to express fantasy during play. There is regular and sometimes impressively swift improvement in behavior outside the session, an improvement that seems to correlate with continuous use of fantasy play and the inclusion of verbal communication to the therapist during play activity. The child is frequently quite verbal, and permits exploration of content and extension of fantasy.

The Massive Transference Shift

A common form of reparative mastery is the massive transference shift. A late-latency-age girl in analysis entered the room briskly. She went to a table and began to play with some toys. I asked her about the play. She did not answer. I watched her play, and prepared to interpret. As I spoke, she said, "You're contaminated, I won't talk to you." I thought a bit and then asked, "Who called you contaminated?" "My sister," said she. "She had a friend over and they wouldn't play with me and they called me contaminated." She continued her stance for the rest of the session. At the end of the session, she felt better and the episode was never repeated. I served as a symbol of the sister and her friend. Her vengeance vented, she had mastered the humiliation and could go on from there.

The Ludic Symbol. More typically, the mastery fantasy takes the form of a fantasy of punishers, cops and robbers, or heroes scaling heights. The following vignette depicts such a mastery fantasy in which the classical ludic symbol is used.

The patient is a 9-year-old boy who had recently been transferred from a therapy of one year's duration in which no progress had been made in controlling poor behavior, poor peer relations, and bullying of peers. In that therapy, the child had been exposed to interpretations of his drives equating phallic exhibitionistic behavior with the wish to expose his genitals to the therapist and to seduce the therapist. Such interpretations might be effective; in this case, defenses were bypassed. Drive energies were stimulated rather than helped toward control. At one point, the boy stamped on the roof of the therapist's car after a session.

When he came to the first session in my playroom, he went directly to a punching bag and began to beat it fiercely. At one point, I asked him whom he would like to hit like that. He immediately gave a confusing answer, in which he revealed that his father was the target of his wrath. However, it was made clear that he was not beaten by the father. Rather, he had observed his father beating his sister. Here, the transference shift used a bop bag as a symbol of the sister and himself as the father. Fortunately, he had not chosen to have me serve in the sister's role, an activity that he suggested to me a few sessions later.

I called the mother after these sessions of bop bag beating to ask if there was any change in his behavior. She described improvement reported from the school and observed greater tractability at home, though he teased his 15-year-old sister when a boy came to visit.

During the sessions the beatings continued for three more weeks. At one point, the punching bag burst and had to be replaced. He continued the beatings. He answered all questions. It became clear, though, that most of his experience in the session was on the level of affectomotor discharge, with a minimum of verbal structure. The action and affect were repeated almost ad infinitum.

Then one day he said he was bored. He asked me to show him my gun. I asked where he had gotten the idea that I had a gun. "Aren't you afraid of robbers?" He walked to my consulting room and opened my top drawer to look for the gun. As he looked, he said, "Dr. L (his former therapist) has a gun for robbers. He showed it to me." I explained that I had no gun. He repeated the question in subsequent sessions. Each time I explained that I had no gun (and thought to myself about his prior therapist's interpretation of phallic exhibitionism).

After about a month, the fantasy content changed. He took a Superman figure and bound it with rubber bands onto a doll bath filled with water. All this was done in silence. As he approached the end of the binding process he explained spontaneously, "He is bound by krypton rope and can't get away."

Note here that the fantasy play, although silent, had a communicative function. He wanted me as audience to his fantasy, and he gave me a summary to convey the meaning in his actions. Subsequently, if I asked him questions he answered freely at any time, although at times he had to think to formulate his answer. Notice, also, that the symbolic object, the tied subject, was very much a true ludic symbol as defined by Piaget (1945)—namely, a structure of matter and dimension used to play out a fantasy—also known as a toy. This ludic symbol was used with emphasis on the communicative pole in its symbolic usage.

The story did not end there. In the next session, he had Aquaman cut Superman's bonds and save his life. Superman was put aside. Aquaman was joined by Wonderwoman and Batman. They were bound together within a wide cardboard cylinder, around which tape was wound. He taped the figures together. There was an obvious change in content; I asked what had happened, and why the person who saved Superman was punished. "They stole something," he said. I reminded him that in the movie "Superman" three people had been found guilty, bound into a clear flat sheet, and shot into the universe. "You got it," he said.

Converting the Verbal Symbol to the Ludic Symbol. The next case represents an example of a mastery fantasy in which exploration and expansion of the fantasy are achieved by converting the symbolic form used from verbal symbols to ludic symbols. What is the purpose of the conversion? More extensive processing (working through) is produced.

An 8-year-old boy was brought to therapy because of refusal to "behave," refusal to go to bed when told, hopping out of bed to harrass his parents, and yelling at his parents in public. In all other areas, his behavior was exemplary. The father was capable of calling his son at the last minute to cancel the appointment that had been set at the expense of the boy's other activities.

In sessions, the youngster readily told of his bad dreams, which caused him to resist going to bed on time. He detailed a dream. In it, a father yells at his child and the child wants to hit him. The father never takes the child anywhere.

My therapeutic strategy at this point took two directions. First I advised the father to spend time with his son. The father began to take him out. Second, I encouraged mastery through play.

In ongoing sessions the youngster told a story of the boy who wanted to hit his father. I asked him to draw a picture of the people in the story. He drew the father and the son. I cut out the figures he had drawn and glued them on cardboard backs set on stands. "I'll make the whole family," he said. He drew many figures populating a world. The boy figure hit the father. Then another father figure and a boy went to a ball game. About the tenth session the mother reported that his excellent school behavior was now present at home. He was sleeping well and behaving well. During the twelfth session, the child said, "Now I'm going to draw a monster—watch what he does to the others." He drew; I mounted it. The session ended. A few hours before the next session, the father called me. He said that the child was doing well, thanked me for caring for his son, and said that since he was moving into an expensive new house, he could not afford therapy for a healthy child. "Today will be his last day," he said. When I

discussed this with the child, he said, "I have to get used to it."
We discussed his anger at the mercurial nature of the father's life
style. At the end of the session, he asked if he could take home the
figures. I put them in a box and he left quietly.

Repetition Compulsion

Repetition compulsion fantasy in latency is characterized by constant,
almost unchanging repetition of stories, ludic symbols, used in the
evocative mode, no improvement outside the session in spite of continuous use of fantasy play, and the exclusion of the therapist from the
play activity. The child may be quite verbal, but does not permit
exploration of content or extension of the fantasy.

A 10-year-old encopretic youngster, who soiled at the command
of hallucinations, played out movie plots unceasingly. He remembered the movie scripts word for word. If I tried to ask a
question while he played out a fantasy, he would respond with
the diagnostically significant phrase, "Wait a minute." I could
wait for hours and not have reason to believe he would return to
my question.

The stories that serve repetition compulsion are not meant to
communicate. They do not attempt to create a psychic reality out of a
shared concept or experience. These fantasies do not try to strengthen
reality testing by forcing the fantasy into a verbal form that would
convey meaning to another and superimpose the influence of socially
shaped verbal concepts on the loose logic of fantasy. The fantasies
could serve these purposes, but the service of such a goal is not the goal
of the poorly relating child. The ancient trauma itself is hidden by the
ritual use of a current public fantasy in the case of this child. Other
children spin out a fantasy that serves only to evoke the past, and
conveys no meaning to the therapist, except that which can be guessed
or surmised from the language of universal symbolism.

An 8-year-old boy played with a marble and a stick. He faced the
corner and hid his play from me at every turn. If I tried to see
what he was doing, he shifted his position to block my view.

A girl of 9, who was intensely jealous of a younger sister, hit her
sister at every turn, was unpopular at school, and involved in
a relationship with her mother in which she would scream,

stamp her feet, bite her hand, and flap her fingers in angry excitement. In my playroom she used many small family dolls to tell a story of two groups of children. One group had a favorite little girl. This little girl was removed from the other group by trickery. I was assigned by the child to move the dolls in the other group. As the story progressed, she moved from a communicative to an evocative symbolic mode. She handed me a group of dolls and pointed to the corner across the room. From where I sat, I could see that the favored little girl doll was being hanged. She continued to play at this for a number of sessions. There was no improvement at home. I knew I would have to convert her play to a communicative mode. Any attempt to ask questions or make an interpretation was met with, "Shh!" or "Not now," or "I'll tell you later." At times she screamed at me, "Be quiet!" After one attempt to communicate with her, she handed me some doll furniture and seven or eight dolls, and ordered me to play by myself and leave her alone.

Converting the Evocative Mode into a Communicative One

I placed one doll on a desk top, lying supine with arms crossed, and surrounded the figure so formed with other dolls. She glanced over at this somber grouping. Her face became quizzical, then disdainful. "What's that?" she asked. "He died," I said quietly. "I don't want anyone dying in the stories here," she rejoined. "I think I saw you hang the kidnapped little girl." "That's different," she said, "she was bad, she took all the attention." "Tell me about it," said I, *and she did.* Concomitant clinical improvement was reported; conversion achieved.

Catching the attention of the child is vital to conversion from the evocative to the communicative mode of symbol usage which is intrinsic to the conversion from repetition compulsion to reparative mastery.

The youngster who retold movies was engaged in communicative (reparative mastery) modes, when he was caught short by my comment to him that "Star Wars" and "The Rescuers" have the same plot. He was able to improve his capacity for abstraction in relation to this interchange, as well as to accept the interpretation that his choice of similar themes reflected a contribution from his own personality. With a youngster such as this (he was psychotic and experienced command hallucinations), one can expect to achieve communication and its attendant mastery only briefly. Longer and longer periods of communicative activity can be achieved during a long therapy.

There is a world of difference between these two cases. In one—the girl with the tale of the kidnapped child—there was intermittent regressive withdrawal into the exitless trap of the self-dominated world of primary masochism. In such cases, the child seeks to suffer the evocation of trauma alone, requiring intrusion by the therapist to restore her to her intact capacity for the communicative use of fantasy for mastery. In the other, the boy who repeated unchanged tales that had been previously told by others (movies, television stories, etc.) had a fantasy life dominated by a continuous, fixated position of rest in an objectless world of self-directed rage from which he must be drawn in gradual steps.

Although both children are locked in repetition compulsion, the first has a greater degree of potential mental health and capacity for the spontaneous resolution of conflict. From such cases it is possible to see that in this regard there are three categories of latency-age children: those whose fantasy life is devoted to reparative mastery, those whose fantasy life is dominated by repetition compulsion, and those who run the danger of shifting from the first category to the second.

Summary

Children who do not or cannot convert their repetition compulsions into reparative mastery during latency are doomed to an adult life shaped by the repetition compulsion. Those who cannot shift, or be shifted, from an evocative to a communicative mode in their fantasy and speech produce a cognitive style close to that seen in the borderline psychotic, or psychotic as adults. Failure to resolve psychopathogenetic fantasy content during latency through the use of the communicative mode leaves the postlatency individual with intrusions of content from the past that will shape sensitivities and patterns of planning and expectation to the extent that the sense of reality (psychic reality) will dominate over reality testing (the world one can touch). In adolescence and in adult life, attention cathexes will be drawn to fantasy-dominated plans and conclusions in preference to reality.

The degree of penetrance of the evocative fantasy pole in adult life may be predicted to some extent by the therapist. There is correlation of this outcome with unwillingness of the latency-age child in therapy to answer questions in self-designated, specific areas. Although specific symptoms may pass with time, the unremitting use of the evocative fantasy pole (repetition compulsion in contradistinction to reparative mastery) is one of the underpinnings of latency-age psychopathology that will persist.

Part IV

Latency Experience
and Later Life

Chapter 13

The Role of the Parents

Latency provides a pathway for an autoplastic response to frustration. This permits adjustments to stress independent of parental pressures. Parents, however, can use the structure of latency as a conduit into the child's mind for the transmission of their culture to the child. This brings parental expectations into the child's world view and contributes to his character. Therefore, the encouragement of latency should be a major priority for parents.

The direct role of the parents of latency-age children in their lives is limited by the essentially internal nature of the phenomena involved in the production of latency. The maturational factors that make a state of latency possible by the age of 6 have to do with maturational ego and cognitive changes. The areas in which the parents have influence during prelatency contribute to the strength and coloration of latency-age phenomena. Parents make indirect contributions in the form of developmental influences during prelatency. The restless, angry, shouting parent serves as a poor role model for the latency-bound youngster. Beatings, seductions, and excited behavior on the part of the parents shatter the state of latency. The drives are stirred beyond the capacity of the structure of latency to neutralize them. Conversely, the calm parent who takes an interest in his child and his child's education strengthens the state of latency. The parent who introduces hobbies and helps the child to collect pennies, baseball cards, pebbles, and the like strengthens the ego structures upon which the restraint and calm of latency depends. Encouraging the latency-age child to fantasy is relatively rare in fathers. The reading of bedtime stories and fairy tales is the most common type of such activity. Few parents reach the degree of involvement in stirring fantasy that characterized the father of Søren Kierkegaard, who responded to his child's request to go out by creating fantasy worlds in the house through which they both wandered.

The child acquires information about the world and his own relationship to society as guided by the family. The age of latency is sandwiched between early childhood (ages 1-5), when the child learns about what is expected from him in relation to his family, and adolescence (ages 13-19), when the child learns about what is expected from him in relation to society as defined by his peers.

In the latency age period, parents can define behavior and establish patterns of reaction that set the templates for adolescent drive-discharge patterns. For those adolescents in rebellion, the parental guidelines provide the armatures around which the person can reconstruct his identity in the years of maturity.

There is an introduction of parental imagoes after the age of 6, which augments the important introjects of early childhood. Patterns of speech, cognition, and memory organization mature during latency years under the tutelage of and in identification with the parents. Although the basic structure of the personality is laid down by the age of 5 years, it does not follow that experiences subsequent to that time have no effect. Parents continue to mold the child until he or she reaches adolescence, and even beyond.

One question must be continually confronted in dealing with the role of parents in latency development: Can the role of the mother really be differentiated from the role of the father? In this chapter I base my descriptions on family units in which there is a strong differentiation of parental roles. The father can be recognized because he is physically stronger, feels less obligation to take primary responsibility for the child when the mother is present, is home less than the mother, and is, in his daily work, more directly confronted with the economic and financial stresses of supporting the family. He is forced to interpret to the family reality limitations, and to be watchful for the intrinsic nature of things rather than take things on the face value of the words that represent them. This is the father's role; but there is no obligate connection between these tasks and the sexual biological assignment of the parent. Women have assumed this role as well as men, even though typically it is assigned to the father. When the mother assumes the role, it is possible that there will result sexual identity confusion in the children. In shaping the development of cognition, the father, by dint of the pressures of the pragmatic imperatives that confront him in the day-to-day process of earning a living, emphasizes the practical. He contributes heavily to the training of the child that involves the logical thought processes (i.e., magic, verbal conceptual memory, abstract conceptual memory), which are recognized by his particular society as the means for apprehending, interpreting, and recording truth. The classical mother lends greater weight to the transmission of tradition, while the father reinforces styles of cognition that mediate survival in new situations and in the market place. The distribution of these chores, so sharp in primitive societies, is blurred in ours. Either parent may contribute, but the weight of influence is the father's in any society in which the male must meet the world and wrest a living from it.

One searches in vain for a biological basis (correlate and determinant) that places males in this position (of dominating the development of abstract conceptual modes of memory and thought). The opposite actually seems to be the case. "Females, on average, surpass males in several language skills, including articulation, comprehensibility, fluent production, use of verbal information in a learning task, and rapid production of symbolic codes or names" (Wittig and Petersen 1979). Yet, these are the very skills that are developed by the father in teaching the child how to think for his world. Evolutionary reason for woman's preeminence in word usage is offered by Mead (1958), who points out that delayed puberty, which evolved in mankind before language, shortened the childbearing period and thereby prolonged the woman's life. Man still hunted and died young. Woman was able to live long enough to develop and pass on to the progeny of the tribe patterns through which the evolution of new language skills could be guided (see Sarnoff 1976, pp. 355–357). Women, consigned by childbearing and their smaller physical stature to the hearth, became the guardians of the homely crafts and traditions, while men took up the bow and confronted the world beyond and its dangers. As society evolved into a structure woven about an organized market place, and the means of making a living shifted from wielding tools of strength to the manipulation of symbols and abstractions, the role of breadwinner did not shift to the better-equipped female, but remained with the male whose strength lay in physical power, size, and the more basic "superior performance on visuo-spatial tasks, mechanical and mathematical skills" (Wittig and Petersen 1979, p. 50). Thus, the female, who is better equipped to teach nimble feats of logic, is pushed aside. The father, whose true strengths are elsewhere, is forced to hone his cognition. The classical mother is not. Therefore, the father typically serves as the intermediary between the child and the real world "out there," and conveys to the child the styles of thought that the child will need to make his or her way.

The Father and Cognition in Latency

The cognitive progressions of latency-age children are many. Here we shall focus on thought patterns associated with the child's apprehending, understanding, and coding for memory of his experienced world. Awareness that the cognition of children differs from that of adults was reflected upon by Visgotsky [as quoted by Luria (1976)]: ". . . Visgotsky observed that although the young child thinks by remembering, an adolescent remembers by thinking" (p. 11). Indeed, there are three levels of memory development that characterize the memory cognition of the latency-age child. At the earliest, the child remembers total experiences on a perceptual affectomotor level (affectomotor memory organization). With the development of the capacity for a state of latency, words and verbal symbols move into the primary position as the carriers of memory (verbal conceptual memory organization). As the child moves into late latency, about the age of 9, the ability to recall through coding, in the form of awareness of the essentials of what has been perceived, provides the child with an exceptionally accurate, undistorted, and highly efficient means of storing data for later use in interpreting new experiences (abstract conceptual memory organization). There is no requirement that this skill be developed. In many societies it is inhibited by the nature of the educational processes (see "The Work of Latency" in Sarnoff 1976). The father of the latency-age child is an important source of the pressure to develop this type of memory organization in our society. Industrial society is organized through this memory organization (i.e., keying into the intrinsic nature of problems and situations so that they may be solved through the use of prior experiences with similar situations). Religious societies are organized around the verbal conceptual memory organization (i.e., resolution of problems through precedent and ritual, establishment of truth through revelation of the word of God).

One should be alert to the hazard of confusing memories that are conveyed in words with the type of memory organization involved. All three forms of memory operation can achieve recall through the processing into words of the data that one wishes to communicate to another person; only the verbal conceptual form codes awarenesses into words for retention in memory.

Psychotherapeutic Considerations:
The Therapeutic Process as a Form of Parenting

This aforementioned differentiation is vital for the child therapist, who must at all times be cognizant of the memory modality that is being used by the child, as well as the potential of the child to use more mature ones. At times it is necessary, as a therapeutic maneuver, to bring the child to the most mature level in order to improve his ability to communicate, to function, and to use and retain the insights of child therapy.

There is a vicissitude set aside for the memories and motives of children that have been repressed before they have found their way to a form in which they can be understood and confronted. These motives grow and develop unbridled by reflection, wisdom, or logic, all of which relate to the abstract conceptual memory organization. For the therapist to bring reflection, wisdom, and logic to bear on such motives it is necessary that they be transformed into characters of rhetoric. Only then, when the concepts can be processed into words, can the logical capacities of the mind of the child in therapy be focused on them. More than words is involved. Words help to make what is knowable transmissible. Without the cognitive metamorphosis that makes motivation knowable and then transmissible, child therapy is limited to a set of simultaneous monologues; and therapy is then no more than a battle between a disciplined battalion in search of a woodland victory and a disinterested band of spirits cavorting in the forest canopy above their heads. There is no real contact.

When the therapist helps the child to find the concept and the words to express it, the role of the therapist and the role of the classical father in regard to the latency-age child become similar. To this extent, the therapy of a latency-age child transcends the ordinary goals of adult therapy. Even the ordinary pedagogical aspects of child therapy are transcended. In effect, such teaching is akin to parenting. Fulfilling cognitive potentials in a child expands the child's social and occupational horizons, as would be the case if the child had other parents.

Shakespeare conveys this meaning well, in a speech made by Prospero to Caliban (*Tempest,* Act I, Scene 2, 353). Prospero, it will be remembered, has raised Caliban from a creature of beastlike sensibilities to the level of adult human awareness. In speaking of this feat, Prospero says:

"[I] took pains to make thee speak, taught thee each hour
One thing or other: When thou didst not, savage,

Know thine own meaning, but wouldst gabble like
A thing most brutish, I endowed thy purposes
With words that made them known. . . ."

The role of the parent goes beyond teaching the child words with which to name and remember. The parent can also help the child to find ways of understanding what he sees in terms of abstract reductions of the phenomena under study, so that knowledge of the very essence of events can be coded into memory. From this grows a capacity to integrate and interpret new experiences in terms of their intrinsic nature. Past experience becomes the guide, and perceptions and interpretations based on verbal stereotyping are cast off. Because of his position in closer contact with the practical world beyond the family unit, to the father falls the greater share of the burden of transmitting and encouraging these memory skills. We have already noted differences in the roles of father and mother in this area.

Boy/Girl Differences

What are some of the factors that cause latency-age boys and girls to respond differently to training in memory through abstract coding? Boys tend to be more successful in this pursuit than girls. Why do girls lag? As Harris (1979) has pointed out, "Given their earlier and superior linguistic abilities, it is conceivable that females, more than males, tend to code visual-spatial information linguistically—and, consequently, less efficiently in many instances" (p. 52). Another factor is sex-role expectation. Boys are expected to perform better in mathematics and spatial areas, whereas girls are expected to excel in verbal skills. There is actually a pattern of results on aptitude tests that is called feminine patterning, "that is, a higher verbal than mathematics score" (Radin 1976, p. 244). Although sociocultural factors have been blamed for this difference, Harris (1979) suggests that an "exclusively sociocultural analysis of male mathematical superiority cannot stand" (p. 52). Indeed, it is a repeated finding that in the absence of the father, boys take on the feminine pattern in aptitude test scores. The boy whose father is absent experiences a lack of the parental influence and model for the identification that could encourage the fulfillment of potential, which in girls appears to be on the average not as great (Harris 1979).

Father/Mother Differences

Tolerance of ambiguity is more tolerable in the keeping of a home than it is in the world of business, where tolerance of ambiguity brings disaster. The classical father brings to the approach to new experiences a background of intolerance to ambiguity. The child who identifies with such a father has a strengthened approach to fresh and new problems. Absence of this demand for stringency in approach can lead to inexact interpretation of events and a willingness to let words and slogans influence the interpretations of events. The capacity for tolerating ambiguity, according to Radin (1976), "may well hinder the ability to solve complex problems; jumping to a solution before examining all aspects of a problem should surely reduce the child's problem-solving competence" (p. 247). The girl who identifies with her mother (the "classical mother") would then bring less stringent demands to later tasks.

The following case illustrates that parental biological sex assignment is less important in this regard than the parent's actual experience and social-role assignment.

Jimmy was 4 years old when his father lost his eyesight. Unable to deal with this sudden loss of function, the father, at age 35, withdrew from any attempt at gainful employment and took over the care of the house and the cooking, while his wife, who had been a lawyer, returned to work. The mother, who had been passive and dependent, looking to her husband to guide her steps even in matters as simple as voting, was thrust into the position of breadwinner. At first, she found herself taken advantage of in the business world, and even the object of a swindle which reduced the family's meager resources to the point of bankruptcy. The family home was lost and the children (there was one brother, aged 8) placed briefly in a normal child-caring institution. Jimmy's mother learned quickly. She stopped taking people at face value and turned from using intuition to applying reasoned-out principles based upon past experiences to solve the problems of livelihood that confronted her. Her professional skills improved. Her husband, in the meantime, carried on the household chores, protected from the pressures of the outside world. In analysis, Jimmy gave clear indication that his identification was with his mother. Problems of sexual identity loomed strongly in his analytic work. His mother's role as the "classical

latency father" transmitted to him the basis for a cognition that
greeted the world with little room for ambiguity in the way he
classified new information, and little in the way of vagueness in
his later recall of the event.

The influence of a single parent who emphasized word meaning
over abstract concept implications is to be seen in the following case.

Frank's father had deserted the family when Frank was 3. Without a father in the house, the child had identified with the high
tolerance for ambiguity that characterized his mother's approach
to the evaluation of issues and situations. The mother returned
with the child to live with her parents. Although she held a part-
time, noncompetitive job, her main source of support was her
father. At the time Frank was seen, his grandfather was living in
Florida, as he had been for a number of years. His mother had
recently remarried. For eight years he had been a one-parent
child. His own father was scarcely visible, contributing only
minimally to his support. The boy was quite rejecting of his
mother's new husband. In essence, his position of primacy in the
household had been usurped. He was consciously resentful and
took pains to disobey, provoke, and keep distance from his "new
father." When the time came to go to camp, he expected to be
sent by the new father, who was expected to provide the money
for something that was the "right of every boy" who lived in the
affluent community into which they had moved. He did not feel
that he needed to be polite or thankful. He held these views as a
matter of course, and without conflict. The fact that his real
relationship with this man, which had all the intrinsic characteristics that pointed toward a situation in which there were no ties
and nothing owed by him or to him, could not support such a
demand was beyond him. He proclaimed his right "de jure" and
complained bitterly of mistreatment when his new father requested some sign of gratitude.

An example of the transmission of ambiguity tolerance from
parent to child is revealed in the following interchange:

Q: (Therapist) What will you do for Thanksgiving?
A: Have dinner. People come to the house.
Q: Who is coming for Thanksgiving?
A: Company.

Q: Who?
A: I don't know.
Q: Doesn't your mother tell you?
A: When I asked, she said, "You'll see when they come."

"The literature on cognitive style tends to support the view that boys' approach to problem solving is influenced by their relationship with their fathers. . . . The link between fathers' behavior and girls' cognitive competence (is) negligible. Girls tend to establish a cognition in identification with their mothers." (Radin 1976, p. 249). The father who responds to his daughter according to sex stereotypes (treating her in a fashion that elicits a traditionally "feminine" reaction) may reinforce this and retard her intellectual and academic development. If, however, the father sets up a relationship in which the girl can model her intellectual efforts and achievement motivation after the abstract conceptual pattern, the father can heighten abstract memory skills in his daughter. Too much paternal warmth may interfere with such development in a late-latency-age girl whose oedipal strivings must be counteracted by withdrawal from the father.

The Contribution of the Parents to Self-Image

The image of the self and the self-esteem that is derived from it undergo a remarkable vicissitude with the onset of the latency age period. Before 5 years of age, self-esteem was associated to an important degree, but not exclusively, with the attitude of the parent to the child. This can produce a precarious situation, for the depressed or uncaring parent may not pay attention to the child. Such neglect may leave the child feeling unworthy in spite of great competence. Parental love supports self-esteem; and, in turn, parental love is encouraged by behavior on the part of the child that demonstrates the child's ability to conform to the parent's demands in the behavioral sphere. After the age of 6, although this pattern persists and continues to contribute to the self-image, an important overlay is added: a portion of the child's self-esteem begins to be derived from the attitudes of society. At first this is constituted by those areas that are preferred by the parents. Later, the influence and values of the teacher are felt. By the end of the latency years, peer pressure begins to define the skills and behaviors by which self-worth is judged. At the onset of the latency years, the large world begins to define self-esteem, making the attitudes of the parent to the child less important and, at times, least important. One thing, however, is certain: parental expectations encourage this change, as does the child's desire to avoid passivity at the hands of the parents.

When the child begins to go to school, leaving home in the morning just as fathers ordinarily do, he leaves the world of the mother and begins to explore the outside world. The behavior and the symbols that indicate success in this new world (if they are not too ambiguous) become elements to strive for. In addition, the ability to succeed in these pursuits becomes a measure of one's worth. Here is the key to the role of the father in the self-esteem and self-image of the child. The child uses the symbols of success in society as tools to overcome the sense of humiliation felt by small children thrust into a world populated and, in large measure, controlled by grownups. The child invokes the parents' big cars, physical strength, large size, athletic ability, clothing in style to demonstrate his competence and shore up his self-esteem vis-a-vis his peers. At times these are private thoughts; sometimes they are loudly espoused, as in the song duels of the Eskimos (see Hoebel 1954).

An example of a "word" duel follows.

> Three children stood on opposite sidewalks. A girl and boy of 8 years stood to the north. A boy of 7 stood alone on the south side of the street; the 8-year-old boy was the target of his abuse. The girl cheered on the 8-year-old boy; her approval was obviously precious to him. "You don't know nothing," screamed the 7-year-old. "I do so," yelled his adversary. "What's more," said he, "my Daddy is taller than your Daddy." Immediately, the 7-year-old rejoined with, "Well, my Daddy is a lot more richer than your Daddy." Humbled, the 8-year-old looked down, mumbled, and then, recovering his composure, brightened as he threw the ultimate barb, "My Daddy is fatter than your Daddy."

I once worked with a youngster whose father beat him. I expected to hear him tell of his latest tragic confrontation with the father the day after a particularly severe altercation. Instead, the child busied himself with reinforcement of his shattered self-esteem through identification with his father, who that very day had acquired a new car. A man of modest means, he had traded in his small car for a station wagon to facilitate the transport of his family. It meant something else to his 6-year-old son, who proclaimed to all who would listen, "My father has the biggest car."

Dostoevski, in *The Brothers Karamozov* (1880), tells the story of 9-year-old Ilusha, who has been exposed to a scene in which his father is humiliated and stripped of dignity. His father had been dragged from a tavern by the beard in the presence of the child and his classmates. The child rushed to his father's side and humiliated himself further by begging the assailant to release his father while kissing the hand of the attacker. The father later says

> ". . . at that moment in the square when he kissed his hand, at that moment my Ilusha had grasped all that justice means. That truth entered into him and crushed him forever, sir . . ."

The following days, the child was teased by the other boys. He engaged in rock throwing. He developed physical illness, depression, and intense fantasies of growing up to be, unlike his father, a competent fighter who would return to take revenge on his father's attacker.

If the father cannot provide tools in the form of valued culture elements identified with the father for use in bolstering self-esteem, lasting elements of lowered self-image are added to the child's character. The father's lacks must be truly severe, for most children use the ego mechanisms, the structure of latency, to set aside their humiliations through the evocation of the fantasied image of the father as someone who could have the accoutrements of manliness and power if only he wished. Many times, while working in a residence for homeless normal children, I was confronted with youngsters who pointed with pride to parents who had failed them completely.

> An 11-year-old boy was taken from the "home" to an impressive mansion near Long Island Sound. The walls of the great room that formed the center of the mansion reached far above his small frame. He looked about as the guide spoke with self-impressed bravado about the cost and effort that the man who first built the house had expended. She fell into shocked silence when he interrupted her to say, "My Daddy could a' had a house like this, but he didn't want it."

In the normal child-care setting we learned to delay visits to parents until the children were 14 years of age. It was then, we found, that the children's impressions of their parents' capacities were sufficiently realistic and sufficiently disengaged from the need to protect themselves from feelings of humiliation for their impressions to be useful in contributing to or responding to realistic future planning.

In early adolescence the child is big enough and physically mature enough to enter the adult world. Sexual expression with partners may become a reality. In addition, intuitive responses to situations are replaced, as the result of cognitive gains, with realistic interpretations of events. At this time, the moment of disenchantment occurs. Fortunately, it is at a time when overvaluation of the father is not needed. At the moment of disenchantment, with the *need* to overvalue the father set aside, overvaluation of the father is torn aside by improved cognition and realistic symbolic elements in symbol usage. The father is then seen in true perspective within the context of the world.

Children need to overvalue the father in order to deal with their own feelings of humiliation. This is an effective manifestation of the structure of latency. At times, events involving the father are so distinct and strong that the defense fails and is followed by rage in reaction to the uncovering of the humiliation defended against. Children exposed to chronic humiliation of this sort (exposure to failure of family function or finances below the community norm) are often left with a permanent depression and a sense of low self-worth.

Summary

In the arena of family interaction, the latency period is a time devoted to the acquisition of culture in areas that are parentally approved, though outside the home. In prelatency, the culture elements that characterize the home are emphasized. In adolescence, the door is opened for influences beyond the boundaries of the home and the inclinations and wishes of the parents. In latency there is a drop in the degree of influence of parent on child. Culture, language, and social attitudes begin to establish nuclei that consist of elements beyond the interests and preferences of the parents. Parental influence continues its dominion in the areas of self-esteem, superego content, and sexual identity. Parents have a special influence on certain areas of development during the latency years. Cognitive styles of perception and understanding and the organization of memory take root in parental preferences, precepts, and examples that are conveyed to the child during the latency years.

Chapter 14

Character Development and Superego Formation

The Concept of Character

In the context of this chapter, the concept *character* refers to a consistent and dependable pattern of behavior that is the product of personality functions. Generally, such a definition holds up best in adult years. During the latency and early adolescent years, the term character must be used with awareness that ego transformations and cognitive growth produce continuous changes in character. Consistency is not the rule. The permutations of personality that accompany maturation and development during latency and early adolescence (6 to about 15 years of age) cause marked variability in behavior patterns. The internal psychic structures of which personality consists do not become dependably consistent until early adolescence, perhaps about 16 years of age. For this reason, characterological diagnoses have little predictive value in the early teen years and before. Prediction is more reliably based on an evaluation of the developing underlying personality structures. In keeping with this, psychotherapy is most effective in the long-range view when targeted on the development of personality structures (e.g., symbolizing functions, structure of latency, self-reflective awareness) than on symptoms, which are their evanescent products of the moment.

Psychotherapy and Character

Personality describes the panoply of available reactions at work coordinating the needs of conscience, drives, and the outside world. *Char-*

acter describes the structure derived when a dependable response resulting in such coordination becomes a property of the individual.
Character means fixity; it implies dependability in a socially positive
context. In working with latency-age children and early adolescents,
not character, but the flexible antecedents from which adult character
is to be drawn hold our attention. Psychotherapy during these years
contributes to the character of the adult the child is to become.

Personality and Character

The distinction between personality and character becomes especially
clear when one turns to the use of these words in generic contexts.
Precede each word with the adjective "weak." Is a weak personality the
same as a weak character? A weak personality is not well fitted to
weather the storms of life. A person of weak character may have a
strong personality, but cannot be depended upon, for he uses his
strength to serve his own needs. The weak character is not bound to
assert strength of personality in the service of a self-discipline that puts
the needs of others or social requirements ahead of his own. Mark this
well, for it is the key to understanding "falling in love." Men of strong
personality can be found amongst felons in prisons. Men of strong
character are rarely there.

The term *character* as used here, then, refers to the behavior that
involves the interface between the personality and the demands of
family, country, and culture. This usage is strongly influenced by
generic contexts and the following from Freud's (1905) thinking on the
matter:

> What we describe as a person's character is built up . . . from
> . . . constructions employed for effectively holding in check per-
> verse impulses which have been recognized as unutilizable.
> [p. 239]

When built up? When constructed? When recognized? These steps
in the development of character do not occur the moment before
character patterns appear during adolescence or adulthood. Rather
they are gradual processes, and occur during the years of latency and
early adolescence. These processes accompany the *superego* while it
accumulates the contents of its "demands."

Our definition of character may be somewhat different in emphasis from those used elsewhere. For one thing, our emphasis permits the
viewing of character as dynamic and variable. This takes into account
the fluid nature of character during latency and early adolescence.

From this perspective, we can postulate, and recognize, character patterns in children. There is an heuristic value to such recasting of definitions: it permits the creation and recognition of new categories.

One might have matched the definition to preexisting conclusions. That approach is hallowed by usage, and it is useful if one wishes to exchange ideas within the context of the established order of adultomorphic conventions. In the area of child therapy, such tight semantic boundaries tend to rigidify and limit the knowledge of childhood character to that which is known of adult patterns.

As a guide to normal development, a knowledge of character patterns appropriate for each stage provides the therapist with an atlas of age-normal organizations of behavior. These patterns can in turn be used to establish appropriate goals by which the course of child therapy may be guided and judged. A latency-age child should derive from therapy the capacity to "enter" latency.

Character in Childhood Versus Adult Character

Character components in childhood have the characteristic of transiency. Childhood character elements consist of two components; the first is the transient character pattern by which a phase is defined (characters en passent), and the second is the set of developing characterological precursors that will produce the permanent form that established character will assume in adult life. Object-ground differentiation fits the latter category. So do awareness of danger, the ability to symbolize, and the capacity for reflective self-awareness. Established character is not present until well into adolescence.

In psychotherapy, one should differentiate the personality elements that compose the characters en passant, typifying the phases of childhood, from the personality elements that are developmentally related to—and are the precursors of—adult character. Characters en passant, for instance latency states, should be encouraged through strengthening the structure of latency as an end in itself. Pursuit of developmental precursor functions in child psychotherapy strengthens character in the future adult, albeit no immediate results may be seen, and the personality trait(s) may be considered only peripherally important for adjustment during the age at which treatment takes place (e.g., reflective self awareness).

Character en Passant

Character en passant refers to any pattern of stable behavior that is as transient as the developmental stage it typifies. The consistent, but soon vanished, character pattern of calm, cooperativeness, pliability, and educability that is found in the child with a healthy latency is an example of such a pattern. One does not expect this pattern to continue into adolescence.

In spite of the above, changes in character that occur in late-latency and early-adolescent psychotherapy patients are not uncommonly attributed to psychotherapeutic interventions. The admonition to beware post hoc ergo propter hoc conclusions is especially appropriate in theorizing about the sources of the character changes that mark the developmental phases of childhood, latency, adolescence, and adulthood. Character change during development is most often the product of maturation of underlying personality skills rather than a reaction to a chance and current event, such as a psychotherapeutic intervention. Psychotherapeutic interventions for which one might seek credit should be the products of strategy and design—or else they are not likely to be meaningful.

The consistent character en passant of typical latency-age children permits education, control of drives, and the expectation that one can take them anywhere and expect good behavior. They appear to be calm, quiet, and cooperative; in fact, they are—dependably so. These character traits may be expected throughout the latency period. Most children of this age can achieve the state of latency.

The State of Latency

The state of latency is the product of a multitude of personality traits. Amongst these are some separate and consecutive personality elements that contribute to the eventual form of adult character, as well as to the latency character. They are the root of character, giving rise anew to traits of character in succeeding developmental periods much in the way that seeds planted in different environments mingle their genetic destinies with the permissions of wind, weather, and soil. They should be differentiated from permutations of character elements. An example of the latter would be the metamorphosis of the structure of latency into the capacity for future planning.

Personality Traits: The Roots of Character

Functions evolved during late latency contribute lasting modifications to the elements that make up the adult superego and adult character. Of the personality traits developed at this time, which contribute to the form of adult character, let us focus on two by way of illustration.

These are the acquisition of superego contents and the capacity for reflective self-awareness.

Superego Formation and Character

The Acquisition of Superego Contents

We now shift emphasis from the cognitive maturational aspects of the life cycle, which influence behavior through making possible the production of sustained patterns of character typical of developmental phases, to a focus on the process of acquiring the ego ideal. The *ego ideal* consists of the superego contents which provide the imagoes by which adult character is defined. In the definition of character that I have been using, the capacity to remember and use internal clues to appropriate behavior is central to successful character development.

The superego comprises three parts. They are (1) the superego demands (the ego ideal), (2) the affects that motivate action (i.e., guilt, shame, depression, and anxiety), and (3) the functions of the ego that implement the demands of the superego.

They may be further studied by breaking their structures into the following elements to be studied:

1. The source of the conceptual contents of the superego
2. The nature of the affects that arise in response to awareness of the degree to which behavior conforms to conceptual contents
3. The dominant affects associated with a particular ontogenetic period of superego development
4. The development of the cognitive skills necessary for the acquisition of conceptual contents
5. The nature of the effectors of the superego (these are defined as functions of the ego concerned with the implementation of superego demands)

If any of these fail, character development will be weak. The following case illustrates intact superego demand contents, but impaired internalization of the affect source.

A child of 7 was poorly behaved at home, but well behaved in school. I asked him the reason for the difference. This youngster, who had defined guilt as "when you want to do something wrong, but you think you'll get caught" in contrast to the healthier answer "when you know something is wrong, so you don't do it," told me that he behaves in school because the teacher is

sharp-eyed, and sure to catch him and report him to his mother
in a note, so he won't be able to lie his way out of it.

This child knew right behavior from wrong; however, he had
insufficiently internalized the affects needed to enforce the expectations of the world through the medium of threat of punishment from
within himself. This failure to develop adequate maturation (internalization of the source) of the superego-motivating affects provides us
with information by which we can predict that in addition to his
current problems in childhood, there will be inadequate character as
an adult. The existence of such a thought illustrates the fact that ego
ideal alone does not create character.

Origins of the Ego Ideal

What is the process by which children acquire internalized culture
imagoes (ego ideal)? Culture imagoes are the social patterns that shape
the unyielding banks through which behavior flows. The obligatory
twists and turns in patterns of flow give us the basis for judging
character in the adult. The sources of these patterns are many. The
time of their acquisition is spread throughout child development. This
concept is at odds with the classical psychoanalytic view that all of the
contents of the superego demands are derived from the introjects of
the parents, acquired at about 6 years of age during the passing of the
Oedipus complex. If the latter were true, it would be no wonder that
there has been little emphasis on character in the child psychiatric
literature. In a sense, the final whistle was blown before the game
began!

Sources of Ego Ideal Found in Art and Narrative

Cassirer (1923), Berkeley, and Hume (see Meisenhelder 1977) have
pointed out that there is a sort of *symbolic moralism* by which our
words shape our ethical expectations of ourselves from the moment we
begin to speak. In latency, the fairy tale and moral story prospectively
dictate the expectations of society. They replace the rites of passage
which for primitive peoples dictate to youngsters sitting on the hinge
between childhood and the adult world, the behavior to be expected in
their adult years.

Awareness of diversity of views and the awareness of motivation in
selecting a course of action introduce the potential for ethical considerations in evaluation of one's own decisions and those of others.

Ethical decisions encountered in the lives of others and in the activities of characters in the histories, myths, folktales, and current events with which the child comes into contact have far-reaching effects in shaping the ethical characteristics added to the ego ideal during latency. A verbal catalog of solutions begins to accumulate. Much more subtle and complex problems can be solved through the use of the virtual library of potential responses acquired during this period.

Curiosity and concept hunger support the educability of those in the latency state. There is a need for stories, legends, myths, and other verbal schemata for use as patterned outlets for the drives, whose outlets previously had been through the evocation of sensations and experiences related to prior gratifications. As these patterned outlets are acquired, associated ethical concepts augment the content of the ego ideal. The influence of society through cautionary tales presented in the media of the culture (Dhondy 1985) skews these contents to match its needs and to ensure conformity and proper fit for the individual in the society of the masses.

Examples of such cautionary tales are any movie or story that tells a tale of a person in a moment of life transition. Luke Skywalker in "Star Wars" is followed as he makes the transition to independent manhood. Ulysses in the *Odyssey* is in transition from war to peace. Predominant are tales that tell of the preambles to marriage. For each problem shown, there is a solution, which the watching child adds to his armamentarium of memories to be called upon when he must choose to do the right thing in a new situation. Examples told by teachers and set by fiction as well as by parents and friends serve for many children the prime function formerly served by myth. For many, if not most, the religious moral tale still serves. Values such as morality, ethics, the importance of marriage, and home are there to channel the life pattern and foster acceptable decisions. These culture elements "supply the symbols" (J. Campbell 1968) that carry the spirit and essence of a society forward and shape character in the next stage of life for children on the "thresholds of transformation" between prior stages of life and adulthood.

As the child begins passively to participate in the myths of his culture and to recognize ethical crises akin to those he is experiencing in the adventures of the protagonists with whom he identifies, he finds within those stories elements that are familiar and comfortable for him, or which provide him with responses that he can use in his own problem solving tasks. When the child expresses his drives through fantasies, identification with characters, internalization, and introjection of certain components related to that character, he becomes himself like the character.

Parental Guides to the Ego Ideal

The early latency child is guided to the character stability of latency by superego contents informed by parental admonitions. The child learns what to do, or not to do, either because the parent says so or as a result of introjection of parental attitudes and behavior. There is no logic at work in the process. The child is guided by an absolute. Piaget has referred to this type of superego guiding content as a morality of constraint. (See Flavell 1963.)

A child in early latency may have internalized such behavioral guides and still not behave properly. There is a further requirement, adequate ability for abstraction, so that the child can comprehend where or when a given behavior is required and where not. (That is, the child must be able to differentiate the situations where rules and guides to behavior apply.) When the internalized concept of right and wrong is coupled with the abstraction-based ability to know when to apply the knowledge, what I have chosen to call *behavioral constancy* has become a part of the child's behavior. Only then can we say that the typical, though deciduous, latency character has been established. Only then are the foundations of adult character and morality set in place.

As the child matures, reaching about 8 years of age, there is a shift in cognition. The capacity to abstract that permits the differentiation of situations undergoes further maturation; and the capacity to recall abstractions about concrete situations is enriched, so that prior experience with abstractions can be applied to new situations. In line with this, the child's attention can be called to the role of his behavior in the world. At least this potential is available, and may be developed if the parent, or the analyst, succeeds in involving the child in discussions that invoke this skill. At that point, the child can use reflective self-awareness to reinforce internalized superego demands from early latency. In the words of Piaget, a "morality of cooperation" can be established. (See Flavell 1963.)

During the latency years, specific cognitive maturational events provide the child with the potential for transforming cultural demands into an organized, relatively immutable set of internally available memory elements to be used by the child in the regulation of drive and impulse and the organization of social behavior. *Behavioral constancy* is developed at this age. It is the moral equivalent of object constancy. The child is capable of retaining complex ethical concepts, and of appreciating and differentiating the situations in which they apply. With the development of object constancy, an image of the departed object is retainable. With the development of behavioral constancy, concepts of behavior with a degree of subtlety not previously possible can be retained in the absence of the object (the source of the admonitions). Maturation of verbal memory and abstract thinking permit the retention and ensuing transmission into the child's future life of subtle shadings of meaning in moral expectations, as found in the *morality of cooperation*, which contains subtleties, considers motivations, and implies that decisions to act require choices on the part of the child. The individual recognizes that he may choose the way he is going to act in relation to the dictates of the superego.

With such resources, the latency-age character pattern can be enhanced by conscious decision. Morality begins to draw from the germ of reason. There are many who do not develop this second means for acquiring the moral strictures required for social adaptation. Those who do not become adults who conform out of a sense of duty rather than as the result of wisdom. Superego contents remain unchanged at this time. They continue to reflect internalized parental wishes and tastes. Changes that take in the influence of peers do not begin to come into force until after age 9, and usually not in full force until the rebelliousness of adolescence.

Sources of Ego Ideal in Projection–Introjection

Important mechanisms for the acquisition of information for inclusion in the superego demands are coupled projection and introjection. This pattern of coupled defenses has its origins in the separation-individuation period of early childhood. At that time, the child learns that there is a difference between himself and the world outside. There is a self, and there is an object world. As the child establishes the difference between himself and the object world he slowly becomes aware of the content and nature of the object world, especially the nature of the mother.

The child introjects, when the mother goes away, certain partial images of the mother. If the mother has been a person onto whom hostility has been projected, she will be incorporated as hostile and punishing. The child may then distort his view of himself into a person who is hostile and overly aggressive. Projection of interpretations onto the world, followed by adjustments and corrections of the interpretation based on the impact of reality, followed in turn by introjections based on the resulting experience, which change one's view of oneself and the pattern of behavior which is expected of one, is the paradigm of the process of coupled projection and introjection that is repeated constantly over the years. As a result of this coupled mechanism, the reciprocal influence of memory and environment shapes the expectations of the superego.

The child approaches the world through his projections, which are partially corrected under the influence of reality. From teachers and other children, and from stories that he hears, little pictures of the world are provided for incorporation in his own world view. His view of himself, notions of what his superego is *expected* to demand of him, and his interpretation of the world are thus altered. At first, the child, in achieving this alteration of the content of the superego (ego ideal), projects an image based upon earlier projections and introjections. Maternal admonitions to behave, which have become self-expectations, are projected onto the school situation. In turn, the teacher's behavior influences the child and contributes to modifications of the child's expectation of himself. The teacher, other children, and other people in the society take on and continue the role that the mother had been serving in conveying superego content to the child.

Elements that modify superego content in this way are multiple: parents, teachers, pastoral guides, and other children are quite important. Also of great importance because of the shift to greater use of verbal psychic contents, both as a means of problem solving and as the object of drives, are the ethical contexts of stories and tales told during latency. The degree to which reality contacts can alter projections and superego expectations is governed by the tenacity with which the child holds prior beliefs with which he has identified. The more intensely a child cathects his introjects with narcissistic libidinal energies, the less easily will misapprehensions contained in projections of them be modified by reality experiences. As a result, apprehensions of self and expectations of reality will be less easily shaken. Such introjects hold the interest of the child and produce pathological patterns. Even in normal children, narcissistic involvement often leads to an overvaluation of new knowledge at the expense of future knowledge.

Parents who had found children compliant during the latency years begin to notice signs of defiance during late latency and early adolescence. As children gain more independence physically, their financial and emotional dependence becomes painful. They object to their passivity in these areas in relation to their parents. The aggressive drive increases, and besides, is augmented by the loss of ludic symbols as a tool for discharge. The aggression is projected onto the parents. This causes feelings of passivity to intensify. The child's cathexes are withdrawn from this painful situation with the parents and, at first defensively and later constructively, are directed toward peers. Contacts with peer groups are established. Narcissistic mortification at a passive position in relation to the parents results in a rejection of internalized imagoes identified with the parents. The shift from parents to peers in the sense of who is important results in the establishment of a new group of objects to be related to through projection–introjection as a source of role models and elements of ego ideal. Evaluations of acceptable behavior are strongly attuned still to the morality of the home. However, the role of arbiter and source of superego motivating affects has been projected onto the new young swain or peers. Much of the aggression continues to be projected onto the parents, and a good deal of it takes the form of defiance of the parents. This intensifies the acquisition of ego ideal elements that come from the peers and are at odds with the parental wishes. In this way the parental role model shapes adolescent behavior inversely. This is an important factor, but not total.

Projection of parental expectations onto the group occurs, if only because there are no other sources of reference save experiences with parents. Modifications of concepts by the peer group reshape this portion of the ego ideal. With introjections in reaction to partings from peers, enforcement through peer pressure, or as reactive implementation of rage at the presence of parental demands within, these concepts become part of the internalized superego. Thus do changes take place in superego expectations (ego ideal).

An important source of superego content is introjection of the characteristics of loved objects. This accompanies repeated separations. Since the child may have been capable of symbolic distortions and the projection of aggression at the time of the original introjection, there is often distortion of information communicated to him. This is retained with modifications in content and in the intensity of affect. Such distorted parental admonitions represent the parent to the child. The child relates to an absent parent through obeying these admonitions. In effect, he obeys the distorted and remembered parent. Right or wrong does not govern what is to be done. "Good" behavior derives from acquiescence to the distortion-enhanced will of the authority. The peer substitutes of early adolescence participate in this process when they become for the moment the primary objects of the child during late latency and early adolescence.

Reorganizations of superego contents take place during late latency and early adolescence. Two sets of superego contents are established: those derived from introjection and parental imagoes and those learned from the influence on projections of contact with the peer group. The child may alternate between them, depending upon circumstances. This mixed late-latency superego organization tends to persist and dominate behavior until about 26 years of age. At that age people begin to divest themselves of the alternatives and begin again to manifest guilt and identifications with the original internalized parental views.

The organization of ego ideal contents derived from the peer group has a more primitive quality than the organization of the original parental introjects. It is formed during a period of disorganization preceding a reorganization. The instinctual energies involved are less neutralized. The group-derived content has an organization similar to the shame-driven primitive superego organization of prelatency. The children are less concerned with right, wrong, and guilt and more with shame feelings, group approval, and what others will think. Such an immature superego organization tends to be fragile and mutable.

Reflective Self-Awareness

Capacity for reflective self-awareness is not an important and valued element in the character pattern that typifies the early-latency child. It comes to be expected in some children in late latency, and should be present in adolescence. In adulthood the ability to stop and reflect on what one has done or wishes to do, and to make adjustments in accordance with the needs of family, country, and culture is considered to be a sign of strong character (see Smith 1811).

Reflective self-awareness is the product of the application of the abstract conceptual memory organization to the observation of self. One's sense of where one belongs in the social milieu, awareness of that which is expected of one by society, choosing the direction to be taken by plans for change are all subsumed under this personality skill.

Not all peoples of the cultures of the world develop an abstract conceptual memory organization. Therefore, not all peoples have a self-directed awareness, stored as memory, which consists of consciousness of the intrinsic characteristics of things observed and understood about the self in society. For countless eons, the frozen cultures of mankind have eschewed and even condemned the development of such skills. They have preferred to have the laws and limits of human potential within the culture locked in place through myth and dictum. As a result, people were not afforded the opportunity to reflect on themselves or see themselves as individuals with a potential for change.

The sense of *history* (with its root admonition that those who do not remember the past are condemned to repeat it) is a culture element that is a late development. It is a multipersonal manifestation of reflective self-awareness. The group reflects on itself through the act of history, somewhat in the way an individual seeks himself through reflective self-awareness.

Reflective self-awareness of one's role in a social system is a recent accretion of culture. (It, too, has a related root admonition: the uninspected life is not worth living). Memory for the abstract enables people to reflect on and understand themselves and guide their actions in adaptation to new, perhaps unique, and differentiated situations, as well as typical ones. A recent and not universally admired character trait, it is the basis for adaptation and survival in a swiftly changing world.

In many parts of Western society, the skills of reflective self-awareness are acquired as a result of normal social intercourse with parents and teachers. Such results evolve seemingly without effort in children exposed to parents who use such thinking themselves. In these families there occurs a confluence of increasing maturational potentials in the child and preexisting parental skills. As the child's cognitive potential matures, the parental mold shapes its promise into an actuality. One is reminded by this natural process of one of Wordsworth's Lucy poems:

And she shall lean her ear in many a
secret place
Where rivulets dance their wayward round,
And beauty born of murmuring sound
Shall pass into her face.

Children who are deaf, isolated from adults, or are stutterers may miss this developmental step. It takes so long for adults to communicate or exchange ideas with such children that the chance to set examples for abstract concept memory and to develop reflective self-awareness is bypassed. Therefore, in therapy with such children, extra attention to reflective self-awareness is necessary.

Reflective self-awareness is often gained, or at the least hurried, during psychotherapy. It is an epigenetic product of the therapeutic interaction. Self-awareness in a form akin to the observations of a third party is achieved through identification with the therapist's confrontations, observations, constructions, and interpretations. This process of identification proceeds smoothly and unintentionally in the child therapy situation. These are the secret dividends of the psychoanalytic process of insight as it is applied in child therapy. Acquisition of the skills involved in reflective self-awareness readies the child for comprehending, remembering, and using interpretations.

Children who emphasize evocative symbols actively during psychotherapy avoid the acquisition of reflective self-awareness. In fact, all forms of repression and psychoanalytic symbol formation that bend toward the evocative pole serve to block this insight-oriented skill.

Recognizing that it is possible to induce this skill, what is to stop the child therapist from maneuvering his resistant or deficient patient in the direction of such growth? It is possible to devise active maneuvers as part of the therapeutic strategies that will enhance or develop this precursor of adult character. This might be done even though the latency character pattern of the child is being carried adequately by more immature personality elements.

Summary

It is useful in doing psychotherapy on a long-term basis to be aware of the expected character transformations that accompany the transitions from one stage of life to the next. In this way, one does not come to explain improvements with one's theories or blame them on one's psychotherapeutic techniques alone. There are character profiles in this regard which are distinct enough to be characterized as expected at different phases. The demarcation between phases may be so sharp that often the age of an individual can be identified from a description of character traits.

The typical latency-age child is capable of periods of educability, during which he is calm, quiet, and compliant. Sexuality is expressed through the symbolizing function. Drives and conflicts are processed in states of latency through such internal mechanisms, leaving the child free to adapt comfortably to society, which in turn expects little in the way of contribution from the child.

With the arrival of the adolescent years, there is a need pendant to biological and cognitive maturation to turn to the world for the resolution of conflict and the gratification of drives. Asceticism, withdrawal, experimentation, or chaotic behavior patterns make up a menu of characters en passant from which the typical characters of adolescence are derived. In early adolescence, cathexes are turned toward peers and society. Parental imagoes are replaced with internalizations of peer pressure. New moralities come into play and contribute essential elements to adult character. Personality strengthenings in the form of ego reorganizations can be expected at the age of 18. In those with chaotic behavior patterns that extend beyond adolescence, a reassertion of introjected parental imagoes in the area of superego demands can be hoped for by the mid twenties.

Chapter 15

Psychotherapy and Personality Change

Evidences of personality change during dynamic psychotherapeutic treatment of a latency-age child must not be measured by the same yardsticks as those used in the evaluation of personality change in adults undergoing similar procedures. This principle applies to therapeutic gains during early childhood and during the period of late latency–early adolescence, as well. The core of this principle lies in the fact that natural developmental changes in personality are manifested during the latency time period. They influence therapeutic outcomes. There are developmental influences and events that are characteristic of the latency period. They are as unique to the latency time as are those that accompany early childhood and adolescence, though not as well known. This chapter will be devoted to a study of these developmental events and the mutual influences that exist between them and therapeutic maneuvers during the latency period.

There is an offshoot of the concept that a progressive march of cognitive, conceptual, and mnemonic developmental events normally accompanies and influences personality changes in the latency period. As patterns of defense are formed to deal with the drives and bring them under sufficient control for states of latency to occur, there are established personality precedents which are echoed in adult behavior. As Freud (1905) observed, it is during the latency period "that are built up the mental forces which are later to impede the course of the sexual instinct . . ." (p. 177). Later, Freud (1926a) spoke of "normal traits of character which develop during the latency period" (p. 157). His emphasis was placed on the roots of adult morality and social conformity in latency. There are other areas of adult personality whose origins are to be sought and found in latency. These are organization of memory, cognitive styles in approaching the interpretation and organization of perception, awareness of danger, capacity for self-reflective awareness, future planning, sublimation, channelization of aggression, and the nature and quality of the symbolizing function. An exploration of these origins during the analysis of an adult personality can contribute to insight and foster change.

Awareness of latency-age sources for certain aspects of adult behavior was found in folk sayings of the pre-Freudian world. We may recall "As the twig is bent, so grows the tree," and "The child is father to the man." The sources of many of the individual features of pathological adult personality dwell not in the first years of life, but in the real world and time of the latency-age child.

In those children who have not yet found their way to the beginnings of the aforementioned elements of adult personality at the time they enter treatment, improvement in personality function is often attributed to the treatment, but it should not be, unless it can be backed up with an evaluation of the relative contributions of normal maturation and therapeutic intervention to the demonstrated progress.

Personality growth and maturation continue whether there is therapy or not. Any personality change during therapy of a latency-age child might be viewed as the product of therapeutic technique set in a context of biologically mandated maturation. Study of individual cases reveals just how much of each factor is involved. Some results are primarily psychotherapeutic. Others are primarily maturational, and many are the product of mixed factors. Typical is the situation in which maturational potential of skills or the debut of new skills takes place as the result of therapeutic intervention.

The last of these circumstances raises a moral issue. Levels of cognition or superego contents that are not derivable from the home environment, or are at odds with that which is available there, can be introduced by the therapist. Essentially the therapist in these situations departs from the professional role and becomes a parenting figure. The right by which a therapist enters this area and the choice of contents or styles of mental function introduced (a good example has to do with the transmission of superego contents) are questions of medical ethics yet to be explored. Implied in this is the power of psychotherapeutic intervention during latency to affect adult patterns of personality. Examples of such traits in addition to superego contents are *self-reflective awareness* and the *capacity for abstract concep-*

tual memory organization. These skills stand out because neither is necessary for a functioning adult, and there are some societies whose value judgments consider these skills to have negative value. Yet both are necessary if insight is to be part of the therapeutic process in child therapy. (In some therapies, insight is not necessary to achieve a clinical result. In these situations, playing out and communicating manifest fantasy are all that is needed to achieve mastery of an internalized fantasy structure that has driven behavior or sensitized the child to react extraordinarily in ordinary situations.)

Self-Reflective Awareness

Where insight born of self-awareness is required, this personality skill must be developed if not yet present, or enhanced if present but insufficient for the needs of the therapy. This process may introduce skills and personality features that differ from those that would have been present if the child's rearing were left to the parents. Often these enhancements of such skills are achieved without conscious choice or effort on the part of the therapist. The acts of interpretation, clarification, and description of the patient's behavior become sources from which identifications with the therapist can be drawn, giving rise to the cognitive skill of self-directed awareness (cf. MacDonald 1980). An example follows.

A 10-year-old boy showed marked aggression toward his parents after his return from summer camp. In the second treatment session following his return, he began regaling the analyst with ribald songs he had learned at the culture- and science-oriented camp to which his parents had sent him. As he sang the songs under great pressure, his excitement mounted. Attempts to discuss the content were made by the analyst. This blunted the child's pleasure in the songs. It was a technique to be preferred to joining the child in the seductive excitement of the songs; however, the technique failed. No insight developed. Instead, his excitement, which had now lost its discharge function, doubled back and roused more excitement, which was in turn countered by a new mechanism: a reversal into the opposite produced manifest hostility. He seized a toy gun that shoots soft pellets and, turning his weapon on the therapist, loudly ordered him to choose a weapon with which to fight. The therapist was aware of the closeness to the surface of the aggression and of the child's hyperaggressive, excited state. He knew that the child was close to totally losing distance from his feelings and was ready to involve himself in a destructive physical interchange with the analyst and/or his equipment. The analyst chose to avoid any participation in the child's plan to involve them in a play fight with weapons that shoot. The child's personality structure was known to him; he knew that the child rejected his own aggression. He disavowed it and only struck out at those he provoked verbally to strike him first. In this way he could justify his anger as self-defense.

The therapist responded to each invitation to an aggressive interaction with a reflection on the child's planned use of an act of aggressive play on the part of the therapist as an excuse to discharge his (the child's) own aggression. He related this to the child's behavior with his parents, who unknowingly responded, as required by the child, to his requests for a parental provocative act that would justify his anger. In addition, he pointed out that which the child had noted previously: when anger was stimulated, either in school or in the analyst's office, his increased anger and excitement fueled attempts to induce provocations at home. This disrupted his comfort. The more he became aware of himself and what he was doing, the more focused became the therapy and his awareness that there was a purpose to the treatment. The session grew to be a place of understanding rather than a place of discharge.

Such self-awareness is a necessary preliminary step in the pursuit of insight. If self-awareness becomes well developed and a part of the personality as a by-product of the analysis, the adult who grows from the child is different in personality from the adult he would have been. He becomes slower to react emotionally; more apt to involve himself in reflection of the role of his actions on his future; he more easily perceives himself as a creature set in a context of time and society where events have causes, and actions give rise to effects in areas remote in time and place from the point of the action. At certain times, during therapies, such awareness can be used as a fulcrum for insight. Even the act of knowing is therapeutic. Thomas Mann (1948) noted that "No one remains quite what he was, when he recognizes himself." (VII).

Without self-reflective awareness, one can only feel what one is doing. For the future this can only lead to the repetition of something practiced. Being able to conceive, hold in memory, and recall in words what one is doing gives the child—and the adult he is to be—an awareness of self that can be worked upon, recognized, corrected, or worked through, as well as repeated.

Abstract Conceptual Memory

The other personality skill that is changed during child therapy, if interpretation and insight are to be the routes the therapeutic process will take, is abstract conceptual memory organization. This is an ego or personality function that goes a step beyond the ability to follow an interpretation. It is the ability to remember the interpretation in terms of its abstract sense. Here is a developmental step that begins to occur in the 8th year, primarily in children in literate societies and industrial societies. It is not mandatory for adult function. In fact, Murphy and Murphy (1974) report that Mundarucu Indian girls in Brazil who were convent-trained were ostracized when they returned to the tribe until they stopped speaking Portuguese and ceased thinking about and remembering things and experiences in terms of their intrinsic nature. Such thinking and remembering is the essence of abstract conceptual memory. It is unnecessary and even counterproductive in a society in which all things are interpreted, remembered, and understood in terms of myths, slogans, and culturally fixed, verbally encoded explanations. Here words are things in and of themselves. In psychotherapy, the ability to perceive similarities and to retain abstract awareness is a key to making insight meaningful for more than a moment:

> An 8-year-old boy who was devoted to a primitive form of memory organization—in which he remembered all he heard by rote, with no concern for the meaning of the words he could recall—was converted to coding of memories through abstractions when his therapist pointed out that the themes of two of his most oft-told tales ("Star Wars" and "The Rescuers") had a multitude of characters and situations that were identical. He began to interchange the characters in the stories. The kidnapped girl in "The Rescuers" became the kidnapped princess of "Star Wars." The hideaway riverboat of "The Rescuers" became the Death Star in "Star Wars." In school there was an improvement in abstraction and mathematical skills.

Behavioral Constancy

When the internalized concept of right and wrong is coupled with the ability to recognize when to apply the knowledge, what I call *behavioral constancy* has become a part of the child's behavior, and we may say that the typical latency character has been established. The child has the capacity to behave as expected as long as the situations are uncomplicated and recognizeable on the basis of external characteristics. The child responds appropriately and by rote.

At 8 years of age, the capacity to abstract that permits the differentiation of situations undergoes further maturation of abstract conceptual memory. Development need not expand the personality to contain these new skills. They may develop as the result of contact with such thinking through a literate parent or a therapist in need of abstract memory to support the retention in memory of abstract insights. With the development of this form of abstract memory, as a by-product of therapy, a more mature form of superego becomes a part of the personality. Prior experiences, understood abstractly, can be applied to new situations. The child's attention can be called to the role of his behavior in the world. At the least, this potential is available and susceptible of development if the parent or analyst can involve the child in discussions that invoke this skill. At this point the child is able to use self-reflective awareness to reinforce the internalized superego demands of early latency. The calm, pliability, and educability of the latency-age character pattern can be maintained by conscious decision.

Therapeutic Result or the Product of Maturation?

So far our focus has been upon personality changes associated with the incidental effects of the technique of therapy on memory, cognition, superego, and abstract thinking. These personality skills undergo marked changes during the latency age period. There are associated marked changes in personality functioning in the child. When it is clear that the child is lagging in the development of these skills, the child therapist can consciously introduce or inadvertently produce moves towards maturity in these functions. These changes are accompanied by improvements in social behavior, which are often attributed to the therapy. It is difficult to know whether therapeutic technique has produced improvement, or if maturation of skills which would have occurred anyway are at the root of the improvement. It is important that the therapist recognize both the limits of his technique and the potentialities of maturation in evaluating outcomes. There are times when internalized conflicts, which are the roots of neurotic illness, although unanalyzed are no longer manifested in behavior. An apparent remission occurs. In actuality, shifts in personality functions have produced a more socially acceptable manifestation. As an example, consider the cessation of latency-age phobias with the onset of adolescence. This coincides with a period of permissible rebelliousness and the shift in cognitive symbol formation from culture elements (animals, monsters) to real people. With reassertion of superego demands and parental imagoes in the mid 20s, the phobias reappear.

In both child and adult therapies, the true therapeutic result is manifested in the mastery and resolution of internalized fantasy structures, and a shift from adjustment through pathological defenses to adjustment through mature defenses, the replacement of primary process thinking with secondary process thinking, and the shift of the attribution of the quality of reality toward things in the object world and away from elements in the inner world of fantasy.

Distinguishing Characteristics of Child Therapy

As these goals are achieved, personality changes must follow. When a capacity for *self observation* and *the ability to retain interpretations* is present, these goals are attainable as they are with adults, through insight. However, this configuration of personality function is not always well developed in a child. Therefore, with children there is less emphasis on transference, free association, and dreams as sources of information about the internalized fantasy structures of the system unconscious. In their stead, there are secondary sources, such as parents' reports, and primary sources, such as reports of fantasies by the child and fantasy play in which leads to insight are derived from the child's manipulation of play symbols. The content of play with these objects is dominated by unconscious fantasy; this is the free association of the child. This is not to say that more adult forms of communication and slips of the tongue do not occur in child analysis. However, the field of action contains more activities through which the child can express the unconscious, and the elements that dominate adult analysis are less apparent.

The following vignette could have come from the analysis of an adult.

A 9-year-old boy came into the office with a manner of aggressive bluster. "Remember," he said, "when I had a make-believe where you were a crook and I put you in jail?" He went on without waiting for an answer. He walked over the wall blackboard in the playroom and wrote as he chanted: "Jale before Bale," "Jale before Bale" (sic). The words were written from above down. I sensed that he was organizing a prison fantasy. This was a sure sign that he felt concerned about his anger and was about to master his feelings with a fantasy about crime and punishment. His excitement was mounting and it would be wise, I felt, to try to get his attention before his defenses emerged and hid his true state of mind in a fantasy that shifted anger and guilt from himself to a masking fantasy. I called out his father's name, which began with I. He stopped short. He thought that I had misrecalled his name. I pointed out that in misspelling Jail (Jale) and Bail (Bale) he had blocked out the first initial of his father's name. "I'm angry at him," he said. "I drop him out. To hurt him I drop out of anything he wants me to do with him like the tennis junior game. I leave like his brother." He went on to tell of the tragic and unexpected death of his uncle. The event frightened and overwhelmed him.

Free association and parapraxes were clearly in evidence here. Such elements, however, do not dominate analyses in children as they do with adults. Instead, the child brings his conflicts into focus through fantasy play and symbols. Children who cannot do this are usually too excited to settle down to therapeutic work. They have poor control in the sessions as well as in the world. They are easily recognized as having failed to enter latency. Therapeutic measures aimed at changing their personalities into that of someone who is capable of entering states of latency revolve around helping the child to develop age-appropriate symbolizing functions.

In children who are capable of entering latency, symbol-laden fantasy play is an outlet for drives. For this reason, fantasy play can be helpful in achieving our goals. It is encouraged in those who fail to enter latency as a means of evoking calm. Fantasy play can be a source of knowledge to be used for insight. The actual act of play is therapeutic. It appears to help the child achieve reparative mastery of the traumas against which the fantasy defends. This tends to lessen the strength of fixations. The contents of the fantasies are used in working toward insight. Most of the fantasies produced by children capable of entering states of latency are products of the structure of latency. This is a fantasy-producing group of functions which produce symbol-laden fantasies of a marked degree of displacement. The displaced symbols help the child to master sexual and aggressive overstimulation and uncomfortable affects and feelings. This strengthening of symbols through displacement results in an improved capacity to maintain the state of latency. The structure of latency serves as a safety valve for the instinctual pressures that clamor to push aside the mechanisms of restraint that hold the drives in check, and it enables to exist a calm personality capable of directing its attentions to reality and learning.

"Future Planning" Evolves

Once more we have described an ego function and its underlying structure, which strengthens as a result of either maturation or unwitting therapeutic actions on the part of the analyst. Encouraging fantasy and symbolic play enhances the structure of latency. Again, it is hard to decide whether changes in personality have been produced by the analyst or by maturation.

The structure of latency uses symbols for the mastery of humiliation. As the child grows into adolescence, the nature of the symbols themselves and their use changes. Play symbols disappear. Dream symbols persist and assume a more important role in the psychic life of the child. The symbols used by the structure of latency become more and more realistic. In adolescence, reparative fantasies manipulate the real world. No longer is the child comforted by thoughts of being a king. Now comfort comes from plans that encompass the sites, partners, and professions offered by the real world. The structure of latency, which produces these fantasies, converts as the symbols are drawn more and more from reality into its adult form and comes to be called *future planning*. Psychotherapeutic strengthening of the structure of latency in the child enhances the maturity of planning capacities in the adult.

Latency and Adult Sublimation

So far we have described symbols actively produced. The structure of latency also adapts the symbols of others (found symbols) as seen or heard in films and stories to the discharge needs and mastery needs of the child. This process continues into adult life. A common example of this is the cathartic role of theater in the lives of adults. Exposure to symbol elements to be used for discharge provides a pathway for acquiring the ethical messages of the stories used. Thus, strengthening of the structure of latency to forward therapeutic goals has the by-product of providing an ample conduit through which culture elements can be transmitted to the armamentarium of potential responses of the personality to life situations in adulthood. The words and messages of the stories used by the structure of latency for passive discharge shape the adult life of the child.

Summary

Psychotherapy in childhood produces personality change through resolution of neurotic conflict and mastery of internalized fantasy structures, and at times of need, through strengthening the personality and ego functions that create states of latency and later become the ego functions underlying adult cognition, superego content, memory organization, and character.

References

Abraham, K. (1924). A short study of the development of the libido in the light of mental disorders. In *Selected Papers of Karl Abraham*. New York: Basic Books, 1954.

Anon (c. 1520). *Lazarillo of Tormes*. Boston: John W. Luce, 1923.

Anthony, E. J. (1959). An experimental approach to the psychopathology of childhood: sleep disturbances. *British J. Med. Psych.* 321:19–37.

Barrie, J. M. (1911). *Peter Pan*. New York: Scribners, 1950.

Bemporad, J. and Kyu, W. L. (1984). Developmental and psychodynamic aspects of childhood depression. *Child Psychiatry and Human Development* 14(3):145–157.

Bender, L. (1947). Childhood schizophrenia. *Journal of the Academy of Orthopsychiatry* 17:40–56.

Berry, J. W. (1971). Ecological and cultural factors in spatial perceptual development. *Canadian Journal of Behavioral Science* 3:324–335.

Bibring, E. (1953). The mechanism of depression. In *Affective Disorders*, ed. P. Greenacre, pp. 13–48. New York: International Universities Press, 1953.

Blanchard, P. (1953). Masturbation fantasies of children and adolescents. *Bulletin of the Philadelphia Association for Psychoanalysis* 3:25–38.

Boorstin, D. J. (1983). *The Discoverers*. New York: Random House.

Bornstein, B. (1951). On latency. *Psychoanalytic Study of the Child* 6:279–285.

Broughton, R. J. (1968). Sleep disorders: disorders of arousal? *Science* 159:1070–1078.

Campbell, J. (1959). The masks of god. *Primitive Mythology*, Vol. 1. 2nd ed. New York: Viking, 1971.

Cassirer, E. (1923). *Language and Myth*. New York: Dover, 1946.

Chalfant, J. C., and Scheffelin, M. A. (1969). *Central Processing Dysfunctions in Children*. NINDS Monograph No. 9. Bethesda, MD: U.S. Department of Health, Education, and Welfare.

Chambers, W. J., Puig-Antich, J., Hirsch et al. (1985). The assessment of affective disorders in children and adolescents by semistructured interview. *Archives of General Psychiatry* 42:696–703.

Chandler, L., and Roe, M. (1977). Behavioral and neurological comparisons of neonates born to mothers of differing social environments. *Child Psychiatry and Human Development* 8:25–30.

Connell, H. (1973). Depression in childhood. *Child Psychiatry and Human Development* 4:71–85.

De Mauss, L. (1975). *The History of Childhood.* New York: Atcom.

De Saussaure, R. (1946). J. B. Felix Descuret. *Psychoanalytic Study of the Child* 2:417–424.

Despert, J. L. (1948). Hallucinations in children. *American Journal of Psychiatry* 104:528–537.

——— (1952). Suicide and depression in children. *Nervous Child.*

Dhondy, F. (1985). Keeping faith: Indian film and its world. *Daedalus* 14(4): 125–140.

Di Leo, J. H. (1970). *Young Children and Their Drawings.* New York: Brunner/Mazel.

——— (1973). *Children's Drawings as Diagnostic Aids.* New York: Brunner/Mazel.

Donnellon, G. J. (1977). Symbolization, fantasy and adaptive regression as developmental tasks of the latency period. Unpublished doctoral thesis, California School of Professional Psychology, San Francisco.

Dostoevski, F. (1880). *The Brothers Karamazov.* New York: The Modern Library.

Erikson, E. H. (1945). Childhood and tradition in two American Indian tribes. *Psychoanalytic Study of the Child* 1:319–350.

Faima, C., and Winter, J. S. D. (1972). Gonadotropins and sex hormone patterns in puberty. In *The Control of the Onset of Puberty.* New York: John Wiley & Sons, 1974.

Fein, S. (1976). *Heidi's Horse.* Pleasant Hill, CA: Exelrod.

Ferenczi, S. (1913a). A little chanticleer. In *The Selected Papers of Sandor Ferenczi.* Vol. 1. New York: Basic Books, 1950.

Fisher, C. et al. (1970). A psychophysiological study of nightmares. *Journal of the American Psychoanalytic Association* 18:747–783.

Flavell, J. H. (1963). *The Developmental Psychology of Jean Piaget.* New York: Van Nostrand.

Foley, J. M. (1977). Beowulf and Anglo-Saxon culture. *American Imago* 34(2).

Freud, A. (1946). *The Psychoanalytic Treatment of Children.* New York: International Universities Press.

——— (1949). Certain types and stages of social maladjustment. In *Searchlights on Delinquency,* ed. K. R. Eissler. *New Psychoanalytic Studies.* New York: International Universities Press.

——— (1965). *Normality and Pathology in Childhood: Assessment of Development.* New York: International Universities Press.

Freud, S. (1905). Three essays on the theory of sexuality. *Standard Edition* 7:123-243.

—— (1908). Character and anal eroticism. *Standard Edition* 9:167-176.

—— (1909). Analysis of a phobia in a five-year-old boy. *Standard Edition* 10:3-149.

—— (1911a). Formulations on the two principles of mental functioning. *Standard Edition* 12:213-226.

—— (1916-1917). Introductory lectures on psychoanalysis. *Standard Edition* 15/16.

—— (1917). Mourning and melancholia. *Standard Edition* 14:237-258.

—— (1921). Group psychology and the analysis of the ego. *Standard Edition* 18:67-144.

—— (1923a). The ego and the id. *Standard Edition* 19:3-68.

—— (1923b). Two encyclopaedia articles. *Standard Edition* 18:235-262.

—— (1924a). The dissolution of the Oedipus complex. *Standard Edition* 19:173-182.

—— (1924b). A short account of psycho-analysis. *Standard Edition* 17:191-212.

—— (1925). An autobiographical study. *Standard Edition* 20:7-76.

—— (1926a). Beyond the pleasure principle. *Standard Edition* 18:419-439.

—— (1926b). Inhibitions, symptoms and anxiety. *Standard Edition* 20:77-178.

—— (1926c). The question of lay analysis. *Standard Edition* 20:179-258.

—— (1950). *The Origins of Psychoanalysis. Letters to Wilhelm Fliess, Drafts and Notes: 1887-1902*, eds. M. Bonaparte, A. Freud, and E. Kris. New York: Basic Books.

Friend, M. R. (1957). In the latency period. Rep. Samuel Kaplan. (Scientific Proceedings—Panel Reports). *Journal of the American Psychoanalytic Association* 5:525-538.

Hampson, J. L., Hampson, J. G., and Money, J. (1959). The syndrome of gonadal agenesis (ovarian agenesis) and male chromosomic patterns in girls and women. *Bulletin of Johns Hopkins Hospital* 97:207-226.

Harris, L. J. (1979). Variances and anomalies. *Science* 206.

Hartmann, H. (1948). Comments on the psychoanalytic theory of instinctual drives. In *Essays on Ego Psychology*, ed. H. Hartmann. New York: International Universities Press, 1964.

—— (1958). *Ego Psychology and the Problem of Adaptation*. New York: International Universities Press.

Hershey, R. (1978). Home delivered policies still give assurance to britons. *New York Times* January 28, p. 27.

Hippler, A. (1977). Latency and cultural evolution. *Journal of Psychohistory* 4:419-439.

Hoebel, E. A. (1954). Song duels amongst the eskimos. In *Law and Warfare*, ed. P. Bohannan, pp. 255–262. Garden City, NY: Natural History Press, 1967.

Huizinga, J. (1950). *Homo Ludens*. Boston: Beacon.

Jones, E. (1931). *On the Nightmare*. New York: Grove, 1959.
—— (1957). *The Life and Works of Sigmund Freud*. Vol. 3. New York: Basic Books.

Kales, A. (1969). *Sleep*. New York: J. B. Lippincott.
Kinsey, A., Pomeroy, W. B., Martin, C. E. (1948). *Sexual Behavior in the Human Male*. Philadelphia: W. B. Saunders.
—— (1953). *Sexual Behavior in the Human Female*. Philadelphia: W. B. Saunders.
Klein, M. (1932). *The Psychoanalysis of Children*. London: Hogarth.
Kramer, S., and Byerly, L. J. (1978). Technique of psychoanalysis of the latency child. In *Child Analysis: Technique, Theory, Applications*, ed. J. Glenn. Northvale, NJ: Jason Aronson.
Krim, M. B. (1962). Psychiatric observations on children with precocious physical development. *Journal of Child Psychiatry* 1:397–413.

Laughlin, H. P. (1967). *The Neuroses*. Washington, D.C.: Butterworth.
Lee, D. (1950). Codifications of reality: lineal and nonlineal. In *The Nature of Human Consciousness*, ed. R. Ornstein, pp. 128–142. San Francisco: W. H. Freeman, 1972.
Lewin, B. (1950). *The Psychoanalysis of Elation*. New York: W. W. Norton.
Lippman, H. S. (1956). Discussion. In panel report: the dream in the practice of psychoanalysis, rep. L. Rangell. *Journal of the American Psychoanalytic Association*. Vol. 4.
Luria, A. R. (1968). *The Mind of a Mnemonist*. New York: Basic Books.

MacDonald, M. (1980). Character in childhood, psychodynamic issues: development and destiny. Tufts University School of Medicine, Boston, MA, November 7, 1980.
Machover, K. (1958). Personal communication.
Mack, J. (1976). *A Prince of Our Disorder*. Boston: Little, Brown.
Macnish (1834). *Philosophy of Sleep* as quoted in Jones (1931).
Mahler, M. (1969). *On Human Symbiosis and the Vicissitudes of Individuation*. New York: International Universities Press.
Mahler, M., and Gosliner, B. J. (1955). On symbiotic child psychosis. *Psychoanalytic Study of the Child* 10:195–214.
Malinowski, B. (1962). *Sex, Culture and Myth*. New York: Harcourt Brace Jovanovich.
Mann, T. (1948). *Joseph and His Brothers*. New York: Alfred Knopf, 1963.
Mead, M. (1958). Culture determinants of behavior. In *Behavior and Evolution*, ed. A. Roe and G. Simpson. New Haven, CT: Yale University Press.

Meisenhelder, T. (1977). Symbolic action, art and social order. *Journal of the History of Behavioral Sciences* 13:267–273.

Money, J. (1972). Comment. In *The Control of the Onset of Puberty*, ed. Grumbach et al. New York: Wiley, 1974.

Murphy, Y., and Murphy, R. F. (1974). *Women of the Forest*. New York: Columbia University Press.

Nielson, J. M. and Thompson, G. N. (1947). *Engrammes of Psychiatry*. Boston: E. B. Thomas.

Nurcombe, B. (1976). *Children of the Dispossessed*. Honolulu: University of Hawaii Press, 1976.

Oates, J. C. (1982). Stories that define me. *New York Times Book Review*, July 11, pp. 1, 16.

Piaget, J. (1945). *Play, Dreams and Imitation of Childhood*. New York: Dutton, 1951.

Proust, M. (1911). *Swann's Way* New York: Random House, 1928.

Radin, N. (1976). The role of the father in cognitive, academic, and intellectual development. In *The Role of the Father in Child Development*, ed. M. E. Lamb. New York: Wiley.

Rapaport, D. (1958). The theory of ego autonomy: a generalization. *Bulletin of the Menninger Clinic* 22:13–25.

Read, K. (1965). *The High Valley*. New York: Scribner's.

Sachs, L. (1962). Emotional acrescentism. *Journal of Child Psychiatry* 1:636–655.

Sarnoff, C. A. (1957). Medical aspects of flying motivation: a fear-of-flying casebook. San Antonio, Tex.: U.S. Air Force, Air University.

—— (1972). The vicissitudes of projection during an analysis encompassing late latency to early adolescence. *International Journal of Psycho-Analysis* 53:515–522.

—— (1974). Sonhos do infancia-aspectos clinicos e electroencephalograficos de fenomenos relaonals ao sono na infancia precoce. Temas Livres of the X Congresso Latino-Americano De Psicoanalise (in Portugese). Rio De Janiero, Brazil, July.

—— (1976). *Latency*. Northvale, NJ: Jason Aronson.

—— (1987). *Psychotherapeutic Strategies in Late Latency through Early Adolescence*. Northvale, NJ: Jason Aronson.

Schachtel, E. (1949). On memory and childhood amnesia. In *Metamorphosis*. New York: Basic Books, 1959.

Shakespeare, W. (1610). "The Tempest."

Shott, S. (1976). Society, self and mind in moral philosophy. *Journal of the History of Behavioral Sciences* 12:39–46.

Smith, A. (1811). *The Theory of Moral Sentiments.* Aalen:Zeller, 1963.

Sorensen, R. C. (1973). *Adolescent Sexuality in Contemporary America.* New York: World.

Sperling, M. (1959). Equivalents of depression in children. In *The Major Neuroses and Behavior Disorders in Children,* ed. O. Sperling, pp. 383–394. Northvale, NJ: Jason Aronson, 1974.

Spitz, R. (1946). Anaclitic depression. *Psychoanalytic Study of the Child* 2:313–342.

Sterba, E. (1955). A child analyst's contribution to the panel on dreams. In panel report: the dream in the practice of psychoanalysis, rep. L. Rangell. *Journal of the American Psychoanalytic Association* 4.

Still, F. (1900). Day terrors. *Lancet* 1:292–294.

Switzer, J. (1963). A genetic approach to the understanding of learning problems. *Journal of Child Psychiatry* 2:653–666.

Voth, H. H. (1978). Dream analysis in the treatment of an eleven-year-old boy. *International Journal of Psychoanalytic Psychotherapy.*

Werner, H. (1940). *The Comparative Psychology of Mental Development.* New York: International Universities Press.

Winnicott, D. W. (1953). Transitional objects and transitional phenomena. *International Journal of Psycho-Analysis* 34:89–93.

Witelson, S. (1975). Age and sex differences in the development of right hemisphere specialization for spatial processing. Paper presented at a meeting of the Society for Research in Child Development, Denver, April.

Wittig, M. A., and Petersen, A. C., ed. (1979). *Sex Related Differences in Cognitive Functioning.* New York: Academic.

Woodward, M. (1965). Piaget's theory. In *Modern Perspectives in Child Psychiatry,* ed. J. G. Howell, pp. 58–85. Springfield, Il: Charles C Thomas.

Wordsworth, W. (1800). "Nature's Gift to Lucy" from "Three Years She Grew in Sun and Shower." In *The Limits of Art,* ed. H. Cairns, p. 1014. New York: Pantheon, 1948.

Yochelson, S., and Samenow, S. (1976). *The Criminal Personality.* Northvale, NJ: Jason Aronson.

INDEX

Abraham, K., 221
and depression, 216
Abstract conceptual memory
organization, 52-54, 98, 121-
122, 281, 282-283, 346-347, 349
competent, treatment of child
with, 290
delayed, treatment of child with,
287-290
Abstract operational thinking, 51
Abstraction, definition of, 92
Acceptable behavior, and normal,
117-123
Action
conversion of, into fantasy, 284
on defensive fantasies of
overstimulated child, 47, 48
repeating in, interpretation of,
144-145
Actualizing, 245
Adolescence
early. See Early adolescence
readiness for, 94-95
sexual drive in, 257-263
work of, 261-263
Adolescent experiences, and
maturation, 69
Adult character, character in
childhood versus, 331-333
Adult schizophrenia, of early onset,
207

Adult sublimation, latency and,
353-354
Affect(s), 60, 61
depressive, diagnosing depression
in absence of, 214-215
as free association, 284-286
Affect-starved child, 219-220
Affectomotor memory organization,
96-97, 120-121, 279-281
Age, in definition, 15
Age-appropriate fantasies, 42
Age period, latency. See Latency age
period
Aggressive drive, 231-248
Ally, of child, 164
American Psychoanalytic
Association, 21
Amorphous images, 75
Amorphous persecutors, fears of, 57,
95-96
Anal phase, and playroom, 133
Anal-sadistic level, regression to,
45-46
Anesthesias, genital, 60
Announcements, making of, 166-
167
Anthony, E. J., 210
Anthropomorphic images, 75, 95-96
Art, and narrative, sources of ego
ideal in, 334-335
Artistic sublimation, 71